Creating cultures *of* thinking

Creating cultures *of* thinking

The **8** Forces We Must Master to Truly Transform Our Schools

RON RITCHHART

JB JOSSEY-BASS™
A Wiley Brand

Cover Design: Ron Ritchhart
Cover Image: © Justin Lewis | Getty
Author photo: Max Woltman

Published by Jossey-Bass
A Wiley Brand
One Montgomery Street, Suite 1000, San Francisco, CA 94104-4594—www.josseybass.com

Library of Congress Cataloging-in-Publication Data is on file.

ISBN 978-1-118-97460-5 (pbk.)
ISBN 978-1-118-97462-9 (ebk.)
ISBN 978-1-118-97506-0 (ebk.)

Printed in the United States of America
FIRST EDITION
PB Printing   10 9 8 7 6 5 4

CONTENTS

LIST OF FIGURES

To the great teachers who are never satisfied,
always expecting more of themselves
and more of their students.

ACKNOWLEDGMENTS

As with creating a culture of thinking, writing a book is very much a collective enterprise. My efforts have not been realized by working alone in isolation but have been elevated by the support and encouragement of those around me. I am lucky to be surrounded by people who have allowed me to develop my ideas. These individuals have listened to my nascent thoughts while asking me questions and offering up challenges to push my thinking. As my ideas developed, these individuals have been willing to give them a go and try them out in the classroom. In doing so, they have made the ideas that much better. Among my cadre of collaborators are those who have invited me into their schools and classrooms to learn from and with them. I am greatly indebted to all those who have encouraged my learning, and thus to this book. At the risk of leaving out some important contributors to my thinking, research, and writing, I want to acknowledge a few organizations, schools, and individuals who have played a particularly significant role.

My exploration of the importance of classroom culture to learning started in 1998 with the generous support of the Spencer Foundation to study six exemplary teachers to understand how they developed students as powerful thinkers and learners. That early research produced the framework of eight cultural forces explored in this book and set the stage for nearly two decades of work with schools around the world. Since then, other funders have supported my research, allowing me to move the ideas forward in the world, most notably the Carpe Vitam foundation in Sweden; Abe and Vera Dorevitch in conjunction with Bialik College in Melbourne, Australia; and the Melville Hankins Family Foundation in Santa Fe, New Mexico. As a researcher, I am indebted to all these entities for their backing and encouragement.

In addition to my major funders, many schools and school districts have been interested in pursuing the ideas that embody "cultures of thinking," and thus they have proven invaluable partners. I could not have produced the rich stories shared here without their willingness to support this work through the substance of their practice, inviting me into their schools and classrooms to learn with them. The list of these schools is extensive. However, I would like to mention specifically the International School of Amsterdam in The Netherlands; Bialik College, Melbourne Grammar School, and Wesley College in Melbourne, Australia; Marblehead School District in Marblehead, Massachusetts; Washington International School in Washington DC; Way Elementary, Bemis Elementary, Clarkston Community Schools, West Middle School, and West Hills in Oakland County, Michigan; and Pymble Ladies College, Shore School, Masada College, and Emanuel School in Sydney, Australia.

These schools and many others have allowed me to spend time in their schools and classrooms taking notes, talking with teachers, and gathering the pictures of practice that breathe life into the ideas explored in this book. Many of these individual teachers' stories are included here. To all of these teachers, I owe a special obligation. They not only took the ideas of a culture of thinking seriously but also put them into practice in truly transformative ways. Through their examples, I have been stretched. In addition to inviting me into the classrooms, they allowed me to interview them, and they read the drafts of their cases to make sure I accurately represented them and their students.

In the actual writing of this book, I am particularly indebted to Julie Landvogt, Connie Weber, Lauren Childs, Jim Reese, and Mark Church. These individuals read, commented on, and offered suggestions on early versions of this book. They also provided careful proofreading and editing skills to help make the writing as clear as possible. Many other teachers read the chapters of this book as they were being written, allowing me insight into how the ideas and stories might be received. Finally, there are my family, friends, and colleagues who supported in the wings providing encouragement to keep writing. Of special note are Kevon Zehner, David Perkins, and Karin Morrison.

At its best, a culture of thinking lifts up the individual to achieve heights that he or she could not reach alone. The worldwide community of educators that surrounds me is my culture of thinking. I owe each and every individual in that community a debt of gratitude for his or her support. It has been my pleasure to learn with and from them all.

ABOUT THE AUTHOR

Ron Ritchhart is a senior research associate at Harvard Project Zero and fellow at the University of Melbourne, Australia. Prior to becoming a researcher, Ron was a classroom teacher working in New Zealand and later in the United States. In 1993, he received the Presidential Award for Excellence in Mathematics Teaching from the National Council of Teachers of Mathematics in the United States. The thread running through all of Ron's work as an educator and researcher has been and continues to be the importance of fostering thinking, understanding, and creativity in all settings of learning. His research is classroom based and often focuses on understanding the complexity of teaching by examining the work of expert teachers.

In 2002, Ron published the book *Intellectual Character*, which put forth the idea that a quality education is about much more than scores on tests; it is about who students become as thinkers and learners as a result of their time in schools. Ron's research into how teachers developed students' thinking dispositions illuminated the important role that classroom culture plays in nurturing the development of students as thinkers. His identification of the forces shaping the culture of groups and organizations resulted in a framework now being used widely to help educators both in and out of the classroom think differently about teaching and learning. This framework has also been the foundation for much of Ron's research and development work in schools around the world.

In 2011, Ron coauthored *Making Thinking Visible* with Mark Church and Karin Morrison. This best-selling book documents one aspect of teachers' development of a culture of thinking: the use of thinking routines as tools to make thinking visible. These simple structures scaffold and support learners' thinking in all kinds of learning situations. *Making Thinking Visible* has done much to popularize the use of thinking routines at schools and museums throughout the world.

These three core ideas—that schools must be about developing students' thinking dispositions, the need to make students' thinking visible, and the crucial role of classroom culture in supporting and shaping learning—are the foundation of Ron's decades-long work to help schools transform themselves into cultures of thinking.

Creating
cultures
*of*thinking

Demystifying Group and Organizational Culture

W hen and where have you been a part of a culture of thinking? That is, when have you been in a place where the group's collective thinking as well as each individual's thinking was valued, visible, and actively promoted as part of the regular day-to-day experience of all group members? It might have been any type of learning group—a book study, committee, graduate course, online community, museum tour, or hobby group—or it might have been a school or classroom. Take a moment to identify a single instance from your life as a learner in which you were a part of such a group. A time when you felt that everyone's thinking in the group was valued, that thinking was expressed in a way that made the thinking itself visible, and you felt pushed to think and to advance your thinking.

Now, with that particular experience in mind, what were some of the practices or ingredients that helped shape, promote, advance, and sustain that group? Try to think beyond general features or qualities to identify specific actions. For instance, you might well identify "leadership" as a key ingredient in such a group. However, most groups have leaders, yet not all would be considered cultures of thinking. Even "having an effective leader" doesn't really help us understand the types of practices we might want to employ in our own quest to create cultures of thinking, considering that one might say that virtually all leaders set out to be effective. In contrast, "The leader kept the group focused on our goal" offers a glimpse of an action that helped promote and sustain a culture of thinking. Try for that level of practical specificity if you can. After you have made your list, you might want to pick a second example from your experience that represents a different type of learning group and see what new action items you can identify.

This set of memories and actions you have just identified is a good place to start our exploration of what it means to be a part of and to create a culture of thinking. A culture of thinking isn't something mysterious or foreign to us, but rather represents some of our best and most productive experiences as learners. Drawing from this experience has been the basis of my research over the past decade and a half.

Over the years, I've asked thousands of people—teachers, administrators, parents, businesspeople, academics, museum educators, doctors, and so on—to reflect on the cultures of thinking they have experienced. The qualities that each of these constituencies identify as being effective "shapers" of cultures of thinking are surprisingly similar. Here is a short list of the most common responses:

- Everyone in the group had a high interest in the topic and brought a sense of passion.
- There was a shared vision and common goal that was both challenging and attainable so that everyone had buy-in.
- Everyone's input was valued, creating a sense of respect.
- We developed a shared language and vocabulary for talking about ideas.
- There was constant questioning and probing of ideas by everyone in the group, not just the leader.
- The chairperson/leader monitored participation and shared the floor so that no one dominated.
- The leader was engaged, interested, and passionate. She was a learner with us.
- There was open communication and active listening going on. You felt heard.
- We had time to think, respond, and develop ideas.
- We felt safe to take risks and make mistakes. It was even expected as part of the process.
- There were stimulating group interactions. We liked each other. We pushed and supported one another.
- Our learning was connected to our lives. It had value and meaning.

How does that list fit with your own reflections? Does your experience of being in a culture of thinking echo the sentiment of these statements if not their exact language and framing?

Looking through this list of practices, it is clear that people's experience in cultures of thinking and their responses to this exercise tend to be clustered around a few important themes. One of the most common responses from groups is that in a culture of thinking, there is a sense of *purpose* to the learning. This not only provides a sense of direction and a goal to pursue but also imbues the group's efforts with personal and collective meaning. Having a well-articulated purpose lays the foundation for the development of *commitment*, both to the task at hand and to the learning of the group as a whole. People often mention that in a culture of thinking, they feel committed to the learning of others and not just to their own. It is this commitment and the recognition of the symbiotic relationship between one's individual learning and that of other group members that help create a sense of community. That feeling of community is further enhanced through a dedication to promoting *equity* within the group. People often mention shared leadership, valuing everyone's contribution, a nonhierarchical structure, and the leader's being a learner as important actions or characteristics that support the development of equity.

It might go without saying that once you have a sense of purpose and a commitment to both the task and the group, you will also have *engagement*. Indeed, the idea of engagement is one that is often mentioned as people talk about the very active nature of cultures of thinking. There is a sense that one can't sit back and that everyone must take part. That might be because of another quality: *challenge*. People often mention that in cultures of thinking, they feel propelled by the leader and the group as a whole to do their best. In addition, they feel that their thinking is constantly being pushed. They aren't sitting back. They are learning.

Together these qualities, and the practices that breathe life into them, create a dynamic group of people who feel that they are learning together and creating something greater than that which any individual might produce. This is not to say that people aren't aware of their own individual growth and development, only that they are uniquely aware of how much their learning is tied to that of the group. In short, we might say that the leitmotif running through cultures of thinking is that of *connection*: connection to the task at hand, to the topic, to the leader, to each other, and to the learning.

When you thought of a group you had been a part of that was a culture of thinking, how did it make you feel? Uplifted? Energized? Eager to step back into that space? In collecting these ideas from groups, I am always struck by the sense of enthusiasm and excitement on people's faces as they recount their involvement in such groups. They become animated as they recount their experiences. It feels good to be a member of a culture of thinking. It produces energy. It builds community. It allows us to reach our potential. This is something we as educators need to remember. A culture of thinking is not about a particular set of practices or a general expectation that people should be involved in thinking. A culture of thinking produces the feelings, energy, and even joy that can propel learning forward and motivate us to do what at times can be hard and challenging mental work.

A NEW STANDARD FOR EDUCATION

This book is about transforming our schools and classrooms into the kinds of learning communities we have just brought to mind. As educators, parents, and citizens, we must settle for nothing less than environments that bring out the best in people, take learning to the next level, allow for great discoveries, and propel both the individual and the group forward into a lifetime of learning. This is something all teachers want and all students deserve.

Admittedly, there are amazing schools all around the world, and many remarkable teachers, too, who regularly accomplish this goal. You'll be inspired by just such teachers in the chapters to come. Nonetheless, such environments aren't the norm for many students. Low-performing schools often lack the energy for learning; high-performing schools may narrow learning to simply preparing for tests. In both cases, and those in between, we as a society should want more for children. Indeed, the twenty-first century will demand that we provide more and that we rethink the purpose and promise of schools, a topic I take up in chapter 1.

I believe that culture is the hidden tool for transforming our schools and offering our students the best learning possible. Traditionally, policymakers have focused on curriculum as the tool for transformation, naively assuming that teachers merely deliver curriculum to their students. Change the deliverable—Common Core, National Curriculum, International Baccalaureate Diploma—and you will have transformed education they assume. In reality, curriculum is something that is *enacted* with students. It plays out within the dynamics of the school and classroom culture. Thus culture is foundational. It will determine how any curriculum comes to life.

THE FORCES THAT SHAPE CULTURE

If culture is the key to transformation, then we must understand how group culture is created, sustained, and enhanced. We must have a framework for understanding and assessing it. Some people look on culture as a mysterious, nebulous ethos that somehow grows up amorphously around a group. Others view group culture as a mere reflection of the leader's or teacher's personality, a view perpetuated in Hollywood movies about great teachers or books on the business genius of the latest CEO guru. Both of these takes on culture are misleading and unhelpful.

Culture does emerge and define a group. However, it needn't be mysterious. Likewise, although it may be true that some people have an intuitive knack for harnessing the forces that shape culture, once we are clear what those forces are, then anyone can begin to work with them to move a group's culture in a more positive direction. I will identify and briefly introduce the eight cultural forces here and then explore them more fully with case studies from various classrooms in the chapters to come.

Expectations

Ask teachers about expectations, and they will often talk about their expectations of students. For instance, expectations of behavior, the amount and type of work, or neatness. Although important in terms of class order, which is a concern for teachers, such expectations do little to motivate the actual process of learning and can, in some cases, represent "defensive teaching" that maintains order while actually decreasing learning (McNeil, 1983). The expectations that help to shape culture are those that outline and define the learning enterprise itself while signaling the kinds of thinking necessary to its success. Not our expectations *of* students, but our expectations *for* students.

This means that we teachers must have expectations that focus our teaching—for instance, the expectation that school will be about learning rather than the mere completion of work and merely accumulating enough points to score a top grade. Likewise, when we hold the expectation that understanding is a chief goal of learning and take students further and demand more of them than solely focusing on the acquisition of knowledge and skills, then our teaching becomes focused on deep rather than surface learning. An expectation for student independence rather than dependence demands a different way of teaching as well, one that empowers rather than controls students. Finally, when both teachers and students have the expectation, or mindset, that one gets smarter through one's efforts, then challenge and mistakes can be embraced as learning opportunities.

Language

Words mediate, shape, inform, and solidify much of our experience. Lev Vygotsky (1978), whose work explored how learning unfolds within social contexts, wrote, "The child begins to perceive the world not only through its eyes but also through its speech. And later it is not just seeing but acting that becomes informed by words" (p. 78). Through language, teachers notice, name, and highlight the activity, thinking, and ideas that are important within any learning context, drawing students' attention to these concepts and practices in the process. To many teachers' surprise, they often find that when they begin to notice and name students' thinking and positive learning moves, their students begin to exhibit more of those behaviors.

Time

Time is one of the scarcest commodities in schools, a constraint that every teacher feels and something we all struggle to manage. This pressure makes it hard for some teachers to allow time for thinking, but giving students time to think actually helps teachers achieve learning goals faster because students are more engaged. Of course, wait time after asking a question is important, and so is providing longer blocks of time for students to gather ideas and thoughts before a discussion. Teachers must be cautious about asking students to jump into complex discussions without providing them with time and structures to gather their thoughts first. This might mean giving a prompt and then a chance to write down a few ideas before beginning the discussion, as well as stopping discussions periodically to take stock of the learning.

Modeling

Teachers are quite familiar with notions of modeling. However, this is often limited to instructional modeling, the "Now watch me and I'll show you" kind of modeling. Instructional modeling certainly has its place, but it isn't really a shaper of culture. The kind of modeling that creates culture is more subtle, ubiquitous, and embedded. It is the modeling of who we as teachers are as thinkers and learners. This kind of modeling can't be "put on" for students' benefit; it must be real. Students know if a teacher is passionate about a topic, interested in ideas, engaged as a learner, reflective, and deliberative.

Teachers can struggle with this kind of authenticity, however, particularly when it comes to modeling risk taking, reflection, and learning from one's mistakes. Some teachers try to derive their authority from their superior content knowledge (Buzzelli & Johnston, 2002) and worry that showing any lack of knowledge will be perceived as ineptitude. This view harkens back to the notion of teaching as transmission. However, when teaching is seen as fostering engagement with ideas, a teacher's fear of inadequacy is reduced. Furthermore, teachers often find that students respond to authenticity better than they do to false bravado.

Opportunities

Typically the language teachers use to talk about teaching is in terms of lessons, activities, tasks, units, assignments, and so on. Sometimes, these words may reinforce a work rather than a learning orientation. By instead thinking about creating opportunities, we focus on what it is that is potentially powerful for learners within a lesson. Even when teachers teach a lesson out of a book, recognizing the opportunities the lesson affords allows teachers to focus on maximizing those opportunities. Does it allow students to challenge misconceptions? Does it push learners to clarify a position? to consider different perspectives?

Powerful learning opportunities invite all students to the learning, having a low threshold for entry and a high ceiling so that learners can take themselves as far as they wish. Such opportunities provide students with the chance to apply their skills and knowledge in novel contexts even as they acquire new understanding. Powerful learning opportunities don't feel merely like doing work for the teacher but have their own worth that students readily perceive.

Routines

Classrooms and groups are dominated by routines, often invisible to outsiders. This is why it is often difficult for new teachers to learn classroom management and organization from experienced teachers. What appears to happen effortlessly in well-managed classrooms is actually the result of established routines. Getting new teachers to think about creating patterns of behavior is important, but this must extend beyond managerial concerns. We must also establish learning and thinking routines in our classrooms that offer students known structures within which to operate and tools that they can take control of and use for their own learning. Ultimately a routine can be thought of as a pattern of behavior, as a manifestation of a group's way of operating. One way of thinking about a routine is simply, "This is how we do things here."

Interactions

Perhaps nothing speaks louder about the culture of a classroom than the interactions that take place within it. This is also where mystery and the power of personality dominate, but this needn't be the case. Listening and questioning are the basis for positive classroom interactions that can in turn shape meaningful collaboration, which can then build a culture of thinking. At the heart of these two practices lies a respect for and interest in students' thinking. Of course, these practices apply equally to student-to-student interaction, and therefore teachers must teach students these skills through their example first.

Environment

Walk into any classroom or learning space, even in the absence of students or teachers, and you can tell something about the learning that happens in that space. The arrangement of furniture will tell you about how the group is expected to interact. What is up on the wall will tell you what the teacher or leader thinks is important to highlight and showcase. What learning needs is the environment set up to facilitate? For instance, does the space facilitate learners' needs to communicate, discuss, share, debate, and engage with other learners—or is it meeting only the students' need to see the board? Thinking about the messages an environment communicates and the needs it facilitates can help us construct environments that better support students' learning.

TOOLS FOR TRANSFORMATION

The eight cultural forces represent the tools or levers we have for transforming school and classroom culture. In the first chapter, "The Purpose and Promise of Schools," I lay out the case for a new vision of schools and schooling and identify ways you can better understand the current culture of your school or classroom. Each of the eight subsequent chapters then addresses one of the aforementioned cultural forces.

Although I have thought carefully about the order of the following chapters, placing the most engrained and foundational forces (expectations, language, time, and modeling) first, followed by those more easily designed and planned for (opportunities, routines, interactions, and environment), the fact is that there is no hierarchy or order to the cultural forces. One is not more important than the other, and all interact simultaneously in a group setting. As Nellie Gibson, whose case is presented in chapter 9, once said to me, "I think of the cultural forces as dominoes. It doesn't really matter where you start; you will soon find yourself knocking up against the others and addressing them at some point in your teaching." Therefore, feel free to start your reading with whichever cultural force you like. However, I do make references to earlier chapters as I go along, so reading sequentially will have its benefits.

In writing about each of the cultural forces, I draw on my work with schools in Australia, Europe, and the United States as part of the Worldwide Cultures of Thinking Project to demonstrate each force within the embedded practice of teachers. Many of these teachers have been involved with these ideas for years and have created robust cultures of thinking that produce powerful learning—often with amazing results. Where I have the information about student performance on standardized tests, I make mention of those data as a way of providing context. However, I am not reporting on the results of experimental research in doing so, merely providing you with additional information. Although we all want students to do well on tests, I hope I have portrayed the real power of each teacher's efforts through the actual example of his or her teaching presented here.

These cases of teaching offer inspiration as well as a contextualized understanding of both what and how each force contributes to the culture of the classroom. From these cases, I then pull out and identify core elements or practices that all teachers can use as they seek to better engage that cultural force to its best effect. In doing so, I have attempted to weave together research with real teaching in a way that illuminates that research and, I hope, makes it more accessible.

Because this book is about transformation and not simply learning about culture, I conclude each of the following chapters with a set of possible actions. These actions should be viewed as first steps teachers can take to better understand and leverage that particular cultural force. In some cases, teams of teachers may want to collaborate to take action together as part of an inquiry-action group. Working through this book in cycles of reading, discussion, action, and reflection can be a powerful mechanism for whole-school change.

To take this charge for transformation further, I conclude this book with a series of case studies in chapter 10 written by a superintendent, a principal, an instructional coach, a head of professional learning, and two educational consultants. All of these individuals provide a unique picture on what it means to grow these ideas to truly transform a classroom, school, district, or county. As these cases demonstrate, there is no single way to go about the process of developing a culture of thinking. You will need to consider your own context to determine what is most appropriate.

Clearly this book has been written with school leaders and classroom teachers in mind; however, the fact is that anyone interested in group learning will find herein the tools needed for unlocking, understanding, and shaping powerful learning environments that get the best out of people. This includes educators in nonschool settings as well as those who manage groups in the business world. Indeed, the eight cultural forces, first identified as part of my analysis of great teachers' teaching, have proven to be a very robust model for understanding all groups, whether they be a museum tour, committee meeting, retreat, or project team.

The creation of any group culture is ongoing and evolving. As educators, we construct classroom culture over time with the active participation and input of those around us. This emergent culture is powerful because it sends messages about what learning is and how it happens. For teachers, understanding this process and how they might more directly influence it, as well as having the language to talk about classroom culture, can go a long way to demystifying teaching. Awareness of the presence of the cultural forces in any group context helps prospective and experienced educators alike take a more active role in shaping culture. In doing so, we move away from the view of teaching as transmission and toward the creation of a culture of thinking and learning in which curriculum comes alive. Let the transformation begin.

CHAPTER 1

The Purpose and Promise of Schools

How do we talk about the value of school? How do we define the meaning of a quality education? The value of school has traditionally been measured in term of results—grades on exams, projects, and essays designed by teachers to match the taught curriculum and dutifully recorded in report cards sent home to parents each term. Over the last two decades, these kinds of results have lost ground to external measures: standardized tests that allow for the easy ranking and comparison of students across disparate settings. Increasingly, these have become the markers of quality, the measures by which we assess progress, and the outcome that teachers are teaching for, that students are working toward, and that parents expect. But is this really why we send our children to school? Is this truly the goal of education to which we collectively aspire?

Commenting on education reform in a back-to-school issue of the *New York Times Magazine,* historian Diane Ravitch stated, "The single biggest problem in education is that no one agrees on why we educate. Faced with this lack of consensus, policy makers define good education as higher test scores" ("How to Remake Education," 2009). Although the definitions of policymakers surely matter, they are not the final arbiters in this debate. Policy is ultimately shaped by societal, organizational, parental, and student-held definitions of "good" or "great" or any adjective we use to define exceptional quality. These definitions establish the broader context in which schools operate. It is these conversations about quality that give rise to the standards that shape the lives of teachers and students and that define the outcome to which all efforts must be aligned. We must change the way we talk about education. As Elliot Eisner (2003) has said, "As long as schools treat test scores as the major proxies for student achievement and educational quality, we will have a hard time refocusing our attention on what really matters in education" (p. 9).

Ultimately, our definition of "a great school" or "quality education" matters because it will define what we give time to and what becomes a priority in the day-to-day life of the classroom. It will shape our expectations of what schools can contribute to our lives and to our society. In short, our definition of what makes a quality education shapes our aspirations as parents, educators, and as a society at large. So, yes, it matters how we talk about schooling and its purpose. It matters how the society talks to its politicians, how policymakers talk to the media, how principals talk to teachers, how teachers talk to students, and how parents talk to their children. It matters because our talk shapes our focus, and our focus directs our energies, which will shape our actions.

THINKING DIFFERENTLY ABOUT OUTCOMES

To help us think about what makes a quality education and about the purpose of schooling in our society, try this simple thought experiment. When I speak with groups around the world, be they made up of parents, teachers, or administrators, I often begin by posing a question: *What do you want the children you teach to be like as adults?* Although I use the word "teach," I mean this in the broadest sense of educating, so that it applies to parents and administrators as well as teachers. When speaking to parents, I emphasize that I want them to think about all the students at the school, not just their own children. This ensures that they consider outcomes as a member of society who has a much broader stake in the outcomes of education. Take a moment now and consider how you would respond to this question. What do you want the children we are teaching in our schools to be like as adults?

Frequently, I have people engage with this question by using the Chalk Talk routine (Ritchhart, Church, & Morrison, 2011). In this routine, individuals share their thoughts silently by recording them on large sheets of chart paper. As individuals share ideas, they read and respond to the written ideas of others by making comments, raising questions, asking for elaboration, making connections between comments, and so on. At the end of ten minutes, we have a very rich image of the kind of student we, the collective members of this particular group, want to graduate from our schools. We are hoping for someone who is curious, engaged, able to persevere, empathetic, willing to take risks and try new things, a go getter, able to problem-solve, creative, passionate about something, a listener, open-minded, healthy, committed to the community, respectful, analytical, inquisitive, a lifelong learner, an avid reader, a critical consumer, helpful, compassionate, able to take a global view, willing to learn from his or her mistakes, collaborative, imaginative, enthusiastic, adaptable, able to ask good questions, able to connect, well rounded, a critical thinker . . . And the list goes on with much elaboration, explanation, and assorted arrows connecting the various qualities.

What is interesting about the lists and charts created by these disparate groups all over the world is how similar they are. It matters little whether the group is from a suburban district of Detroit, an all-boys' school in Melbourne, a gathering of teachers from international schools in Europe, a group of parents in Hong Kong, a consortium of charter schools, or an urban high school in New York City. The same sets of qualities tend to appear over and over again. There is often an emphasis on attributes that drive learning: curiosity, inquisitiveness, questioning. And those that facilitate innovation: creativity, problem solving, risk taking, imagination, and inquisitiveness. There are the skills needed to work and get along with others: collaboration, empathy, good listening, helpfulness. And those that support the ability to deal with complexity: analysis, making connections, critical thinking. And usually there are those that situate us collectively in the world: as a global citizen, a member of a community, someone aware of his or her impact on the environment, able to communicate.

You'll notice that there are few traditional academic skills mentioned. Does that mean they aren't important? Of course not. It's just that they do not adequately define the kind of students we collectively hope to send into the world. Nor do they define the kind of employee whom businesses are looking to hire in the twenty-first century. In a survey of four hundred businesses across the United States conducted by a consortium of human resource, education, and corporate entities (Conference Board, Partnership for 21st Century Skills, Corporate Voices for Working Families, & Society for Human Resource Management, 2006), employers were asked to rank the skills they were looking for in potential applicants, working from a list that included both academic and applied skills. Applied skills such as professionalism, work ethic, collaboration, communication, ethics, social responsibility, critical thinking, and problem solving topped the list over more traditional academic skills. Only when it came to the hiring of recent high school students did a single traditional academic subject, reading comprehension, make the top five (it was ranked fifth) in terms of its importance. This list from employers mirrors the qualities that Tony Wagner (2008) heard mentioned in his interviews with business leaders. Wagner distilled these into what he calls seven survival skills: critical thinking and problem solving, collaboration, agility and adaptability, initiative and entrepreneurialism, communication skills, the ability to analyze information, and curiosity and imagination.

It could be argued that businesses assume a high level of basic skills and knowledge as a given and are thus only identifying these applied skills as the icing on the cake. Perhaps, though in the aforementioned survey, this appears not to be the case. Prospective employers recognized deficiencies in academic skills, yet still ranked applied skills as both being more important and even more lacking in applicants than was academic preparedness. One crossover category topped the list in terms of deficiency. Writing in English was identified as deficient among 72 percent of applicants, and its applied skill corollary, written communication, as deficient among 80.9 percent of applicants. After that, the skills, both applied and academic, listed as most deficient were (in order): leadership, professionalism, critical thinking and problem solving, foreign languages, self-direction, creativity, mathematics, and oral communication. All of these skills were identified as deficient in more than 50 percent of applicants. Perhaps the biggest takeaway is that applied skills are not considered an add-on, but rather an integral part of workplace preparedness.

The goal of cultivating a lifelong skill set that propels innovation and invention is championed internationally as well. In a 2011 study of the educational practices of the top-performing countries as measured by the Programme for International Student Assessment, Marc Tucker (2011) reported that "one cannot help but be struck by the attention that is being given to achieving clarity and consensus on the goals for education in those countries" (p. 5). His group, the National Center on Education and the Economy, found a concern, particularly among Asian countries, with the development of cognitive skills as well as noncognitive skills that facilitated both global competitiveness and personal fulfillment. This sentiment is captured in remarks made in 2002 by Singapore's minister of education, Tharman Shanmugaratnam, in which he described as a top priority the need for Singaporean students to develop "a willingness to keep learning, and an ability to experiment, innovate, and take risks" (Borja, 2004, p. 30). Likewise, China's Central Committee stated that education in the country must begin to "emphasize sowing students' creativity and practical abilities over instilling an ability to achieve certain test scores and recite rote knowledge" (Zhao, 2006).

The qualities I consistently hear as important to teachers and parents, like those emerging from the world of work, are being called for by other sources as well. In 2002, in the book *Intellectual Character,* I reviewed the call for habits of mind, intellectual passions, and thinking dispositions being championed from various circles and found agreement around six broad characteristics: curiosity, open-mindedness, being strategic, having a healthy skepticism, being a truth seeker, and being metacognitive. The learner profile of the International Baccalaureate promotes students as inquirers, thinkers, communicators, and risk takers, and as being open-minded, reflective, well balanced, caring, principled, and knowledgeable. Likewise, the Building Learning Power initiative (Claxton, Chambers, Powell, & Lucas, 2011) seeks to develop a set of some twenty learning capacities around reflectiveness, resourcefulness, reciprocity/collaboration, and resilience that are quite similar to many of those already mentioned. Philosophers recognize these traits as encompassing a set of intellectual virtues. Once again, the more traditional academic skills that make up the standardized tests, define our graduation requirements, and serve as gatekeepers for university entrance don't appear explicitly on these lists.

Thus a new vision of what a quality education is and what it should offer arises from the data. Although a host of different vocabulary is used and the traits parsed slightly differently, what emerges is a rich portrait of *the student as an engaged and active thinker able to communicate, innovate, collaborate, and problem-solve.* What we see as most important to develop is not a discrete collection of knowledge but rather a set of broad characteristics that motivate learning and lead to the generation of useable knowledge. Some might say this is the profile of a twenty-first-century learner (Trilling & Fadel, 2009); others might see it as what it means to be a well-rounded citizen (Arnstine, 1995; Meier, 2003); still others might incorporate this definition as part of global competency (Boix-Mansilla & Jackson, 2011). I choose to see this portrait of a student as the vision of what a quality education affords. This is what we must be teaching for and trying to achieve for every student. The big questions then are: How do we get there—how do we realize this vision? How are our schools doing currently in producing this vision of students as thinkers? What are the forces we must marshal and master to truly transform our schools? These are the questions I take up in this book.

TEACHING AS ENCULTURATION

The qualities found in the various lists I've mentioned—reflective, imaginative, curious, creative, and so on—are often classified as *dispositions.* A disposition is an enduring characteristic or trait of a person that serves to motivate behavior. When we say a person is curious, a particular dispositional attribute, it is because we see a pattern of behavior—such as questioning, exploring, probing, and so on—emanating from that person over time and across circumstances that relates to that particular disposition. Our dispositions define who we are as people, as thinkers, as learners. In previous writings, I've argued that the dispositions that define us as thinkers make up our intellectual character (Ritchhart, 2002).

We might think about these dispositions not only in terms of the outcomes of a quality education but also, to borrow a phrase from Ted Sizer, as the residuals of education—that is to say, what is left over after all the things practiced and memorized for tests are long forgotten. What stays with us long after we have left the classroom? Speaking at the Save Our Schools rally in Washington DC on July 30, 2011, Matt Damon highlighted the importance of these residuals, saying, "As I look at my life today, the things I value most about myself—my imagination, my love of acting, my passion for writing, my love of learning, my curiosity—all come from how I was parented and taught. And none of these qualities that I've just mentioned—none of these qualities that I prize so deeply, that have brought me so much joy, that have brought me so much professional success—none of these qualities that make me who I am . . . can be tested."

The key aspect of these dispositions, even though they are manifest in the exhibition of specific skills and actions, is that they cannot be directly taught or directly tested. Think about it. It would be absurd to teach a unit on curiosity or risk taking or collaboration and then to give a multiple-choice test to assess students' development. Sure, students might learn "about" the disposition, but they would be unlikely to develop the disposition itself. Rather, these qualities, these dispositions, have to be developed over time. They must be nurtured across a variety of circumstances so that they become ingrained and are likely to emerge when the situation calls for them. *Dispositions must be enculturated—that is, learned through immersion in a culture.*

One of Russian psychologist Lev Vygotsky's most famous quotes is, "Children grow into the intellectual life of those around them" (1978, p. 88). This statement beautifully captures what enculturation means. It means surrounding the child with the kind of intellectual life, mental activity, and processes of learning to which we want them to grow accustomed. It suggests that learning to learn is an apprenticeship in which we don't so much learn from others as we learn with others in the midst of authentic activities. If we take Vygotsky's quote to heart, then we must take a hard look at our homes, schools, and classrooms and ask ourselves about the kind of intellectual life with which we are surrounding our children. What kinds of models do they see? What kinds of opportunities do they experience? What kinds of thinking are being valued, privileged, and promoted on a day-to-day basis?

CULTURE AS THE ENACTMENT OF A STORY

Parents play an important role in building character, both intellectual and moral, and enculturating dispositions in their children. Parents are the first and most important models for children. A parent's values and dispositions are regularly on display, and his or her behaviors are the ones a child will first imitate. At the same time, when it comes to the dispositions related to thinking and learning, schools play a privileged role in society. Schools are designed as places of learning and so send important messages about what learning is, how it happens, and what kinds of learning are of value. Each and every day, year in and year out, students are being told a story of learning. Enculturation is a process of gradually internalizing the messages and values, the story being told, that we repeatedly experience through interaction with the external, social environment.

This internalization takes time as we identify the messages and values that are consistent and recurring in our environment.

This notion of culture as a story we tell is a metaphor that I have been employing in my work with schools and organizations for a number of years. It was first presented to me in the book *Ishmael*. In the novel, author Daniel Quinn invites readers to be a part of dialogue between a skilled teacher and a skeptical but willing student around the very nature of the role of humans on the planet. The fact that the teacher, Ishmael, is a gorilla eager to pass on his acquired wisdom about the human race through telepathy adds a bit of a twist to things. Early on, Ishmael lays out some definitions that will be key to the dialogue, in particular that of "culture." He defines culture as "a group of people enacting a story" and says that to enact a story "is to live so as to make the story a reality." For the purposes of the novel, the story being enacted concerns the relationship between man, the world, and the gods. Drawing on this metaphor, I define the culture of schools as a group of people enacting a story. The story concerns the relationship between teachers, students, and the act of learning. Everyone is a player in this story, acting in a way that reinforces the story and makes it reality.

The idea that culture can be transmitted through storytelling has long been recognized. Likewise, the idea that a culture sends messages about what is valued and worthwhile through its use of traditions, behaviors, symbolic conduct, and other means is also generally well understood. Carolyn Taylor (2005), writing for a business audience, takes this idea a step further, saying that "culture management is about message management. If you can find, and change, enough of the sources of these messages, you will change the culture" (p. 7). Clearly, the role of messages in revealing and shaping culture is important. However, it is the self-reinforcing, continual construction of culture through the dynamic enactment of both individual and collective values that I find so powerful. This perspective on the power of the story *in the making* can help us understand the symbiotic role every participant plays in creating culture, as well as the privileged role leaders play.

So to understand the culture of a school or classroom, we need to look at the story about learning each is telling. Beliefs, messages, values, behaviors, traditions, routines, and so on are not the culture itself, but are significant indicators of culture to the extent that they reinforce the core story being told. They are the means by which we identify the story of learning. With this in mind, there are three stories of learning we should examine before we can look at how to transform culture. The first is the old story—that is, the story each of us was told as a student. The second is the current story dominant in schools and classrooms today. The third is the new story we want to be telling.

Uncovering the Old Story

We all have different experiences of schooling. Even within any individual's experience, there are different teachers and classrooms that might be enacting different, even competing, stories. Acknowledging these differences, it is nonetheless useful to individually uncover the story of learning we were told. This is as true for parents as it is for teachers, principals, classroom aides, museum educators, or corporate trainers. The story that we were told as students is most likely to influence, positively or negatively, how we interact with our own children and students.

Michael identifies a recurring theme from his school experience:

> From my first days in school, I was told a story of sorting, classification, and ability. We were put in reading groups, and it wasn't hard to figure out who had the right stuff and who was struggling. At the end of first grade I experienced another kind of sorting, being left back. I didn't make the grade and wouldn't stay with my peers. But for some reason, the next year I was still in that low reading group. And so it went up through middle school and being placed in shop class and then in high school in the vocational track. There was never talk about what I wanted, just imposed sorting and classifying.

Jason recalls his elementary experiences most vividly:

> I remember school as being a silent place, at least for me. We weren't allowed to talk. One time I recall the teacher asking me, "Why are you talking? Your work isn't done." I remember thinking how strange it was to link talking with being done with my work. I was a slow worker. I was never done with my work early. So that meant never talking. Of course, recess was my outlet. That was real for me. The classroom wasn't.

It was a pivotal experience in just one class that left a big mark on Ruth:

> I remember one particular algebra class. Algebra was new and different, and for me exciting. I liked the puzzle aspect of it, and it was much more interesting than just doing sums. One day in class, the teacher was explaining a difficult problem, and I remember being totally engrossed in the problem and trying to figure out why he was doing it the way he was when it seemed like there should be another way. My way. I kept puzzling over it until I was convinced I was right. My way did work. I worked up the courage to raise my hand to ask about it. The teacher said he had already answered that question. Wasn't I listening? From that day on, I never asked another question in that class, and I lost my interest in math, even though I was good at it. I guess the message I got was school was about listening to the teacher, not figuring things out for yourself.

For Nicole, the story of learning she was told is a familiar one:

It was all about the grades and pleasing the teacher. I was good at that, but I don't really feel like I learned all that much. I played the system and got rewarded for it. I used grades to keep score.

A similar theme comes up in Max's account:

It seemed to be all about speed. I remember timed tests and spelling bees, and everything always having a time limit. If you got done early, it meant you were smart. First hand up to answer the teacher's question? Smart. I guess it was like a competition.

Distance and exclusion were themes for Marcella:

My language and culture weren't represented or even acknowledged in my school. We were told we were not to speak Spanish. Of course, among my friends we did, but we had to be careful not to get caught. Even in simple things like asking for help or chatting between classes, we were to speak in English. It sent the message that something was wrong with our home language, that school was a foreign place we were visiting rather than a place in which we were included. We could only get a small bit of the instruction at first and so were always struggling, which sent the message we weren't good learners.

These are just a few accounts of "old stories of learning" that were told. Maybe they resonate with your school experience. The themes of these stories are powerful and pointed: that school is a sorting mechanism, that you either fit or you don't, that there is not a place for dialogue and conversation, that learning requires individualized seat work and practice, that learning is competitive versus cooperative, that being fast means you are smart, that there is no room for questioning, that getting the grade is what learning is all about. These themes shape students' experience, frame how they come to view learning, and in some cases distort what true learning is.

Although the stories presented here aren't particularly positive, I don't mean to suggest that this is always the case. When I ask groups of parents and educators to share the stories of learning they encountered as students, I invariably hear a story like Antonia's:

I remember my fifth-grade teacher. She was passionate about learning and so excited. She was always telling us stories about new things or places she had been. It was contagious. You wanted to learn because you wanted to be a part of her world. Have a conversation with her. That has always stayed with me. She was a big reason I became a teacher.

As parents and educators, we should never forget the power of the individual to make a difference and often to transform negative, unproductive, and demoralizing stories of learning into positive ones. At the same time, as a society, district, or school, we need to examine the dominant story that students and teachers are enacting. What messages about learning and thinking are we imparting over time?

Taking a Hard Look at the Current Story

Although students aren't always the best evaluators of their long-term educational needs, they can be excellent barometers of the focus of instruction and its meaningfulness to them. They know when they are and are not being intellectually engaged, and they are quite adept at recognizing when they are truly learning and developing as human beings. It is in their voices that we will find the current story of learning being told in our schools. Bringing students into the conversation about outcomes and purpose is important for all schools and teachers, as it helps develop a shared mission that all can work toward. The Building Learning Power initiative (Claxton et al., 2011) in Britain includes students in the regular audits of classrooms to help look for the kinds of thinking the school says it values. Masada College in Sydney, Australia, also engages its students in planning part of the Cultures of Thinking initiative there. To better uncover the story of learning in your classroom and at your school, you'll need to elicit students' perceptions of the learning they are encountering. Suggestions for doing so can be found at the end of this chapter.

As never before in history, students around the world are making their voices heard and talking about the story of learning they are experiencing by using social media, blogs, YouTube, and Internet news sites. Nikhil Goyal (2011), a sixteen-year-old student at Syosset High School in New York, wrote an article for the *Huffington Post* about how a focus on test preparation has "hijacked classroom learning." He expressed the need to focus more on "creativity, imagination, discovery, and project-based learning." In his YouTube video titled "Open Letter to Educators," university student Dan Brown (2010) discusses why he decided to drop out of a system dedicated almost solely to imparting information over stoking creativity and innovation because "my schooling was inter-fering with my education." Cultural anthropologist Michael Wesch (2008) has labeled this a "crisis of significance" in which "education has become a relatively meaningless game of grades more than an important and meaningful exploration of the world in which we live and co-create" (p. 5). He captured this disconnect in the 2007 YouTube video "A Vision of Students Today," featuring his own students at Kansas State University.

At Teenink.com, Sophia W. (2011) writes a scathing article about Advanced Place-ment courses in which she renames them as "**A**bsolutely **P**reposterous **W**eapons of **M**ass

Instruction," decrying how these courses only teach students what to think, not how to think, and serve to distance students from their own ideas, opinions, creativity, and reason. Sophia's rant about the disconnect between AP courses and real learning is borne out by a 2006 study by researchers at Harvard University and the University of Virginia which found that AP science courses do not significantly contribute to success in college (Bradt, 2006). Instead, the study found that a focus on the in-depth study of a few topics, rather than the coverage approach of AP, was a better indicator of university success in science. Thus the very thing being promoted as preparing students for college isn't.

The story of learning emerging from these voices is that school can be mind numbing and irrelevant, focusing mostly on memorization. Of course, these voices belong to those speaking out in very public forums to express discontent and frustration. It is reasonable to ask how typical they are of most students. These same themes can be found in the much more representative Gallup Youth Survey (Lyons, 2004). In this survey, middle and high school students were asked to select three words from a list of adjectives to describe how they usually feel in school. Topping the list, the word "bored" was chosen by 50 percent of the students. In second place was "tired," with 42 percent. "Happy" and "challenged" were next with 31 percent, a bit more hopeful and positive to be sure. However, it should be noted that students were more likely to choose positive adjectives if they self-identified as being "above average" or "near the top," indicating that the story of learning that students are encountering may differ by ability.

One can also see this same pattern of experience in the findings of one of the largest longitudinal studies of how students experience elementary schools, conducted by the National Institute of Child Health and Human Development (Pianta, Belsky, Houts, Morrison, & National Institute of Child Health and Human Development Early Child Care Research Network, 2007). The ongoing study involves classroom observations of 1,364 students as they progress through school to assess the type of instruction they experience. The most recent assessment, of students' fifth-grade year, involved 956 students (some students dropped out of the study) enrolled in 737 classrooms distributed across 502 schools (both public and private) in 302 districts (mostly middle class) in thirty-three different states. Taking just the fifth-grade observations as an example, it was found that 58 percent of students' time was spent on basic skills learning and less than 13 percent on higher-level learning involving analysis and inference. Furthermore, less than 5 percent of the instructional time involved collaborative work, and less than 1 percent of the observed class episodes (approximately six hours in each classroom) were classified as instances where students were highly engaged. The image that emerges from these classrooms is similar to that expressed by Daniel Pink

(Starr, 2012): too often the good kids are compliant, the so-called bad kids are defiant, but no one is engaged.

One might expect things to get better as students progress through school, but the evidence says otherwise. The Collegiate Learning Assessment tracked twenty-three hundred students through their university experience at twenty-four schools in the United States and found that just slightly more than half (55 percent) of students showed any significant improvement in key measures of critical thinking, complex reasoning, and writing by the end of their sophomore year (Gorski, 2011). These statistics improved only slightly by the end of four years, with 64 percent demonstrating improvement on these measures. The study found that the overall school experience for students was similar to that reported by Michael Wesch's students in his YouTube video, in which the reading isn't relevant, little writing is done, and lectures dispense information but don't ask students to think (Wesch, 2007). As University of Missouri freshman Julia Rheinecker stated, "Most of what I learned this year I already had in high school . . . I just haven't found myself pushing as much as I expected" (quoted in Gorski, 2011).

It may seem from these reports that there isn't much of a difference between the old story many of us experienced and the current story, with its emphasis on rote learning and grades, and in many cases an irrelevant curriculum. Some are arguing that the current emphasis on testing and accountability is actually leading schools to diminish students' opportunity rather than enhance it (Meier, 2003; Ravitch, 2011; Ritchhart, 2004; Rose, 2009; Wagner, 2008; Zhao, 2009). What is being created is a testing culture rather than a learning culture, in which we see scores on tests going up but learning, understanding, and engagement decreasing (Shepard, 2000).

Although we don't have good historical data to make such a comparison, there is evidence that current educational policies do in fact have an inhibiting role when it comes to opening up learning, promoting creativity, and promoting thinking. In a 2000–2001 survey by the National Educational Association (2003), 61 percent of public school teachers said that testing stifles real teaching and learning. This survey predated the implementation of the No Child Left Behind reform, which mandated much more testing. In their book, *Imagination First,* Eric Liu and Scott Noppe-Brandon (2009) note how the test culture has warped our perspective of what it means to educate: "Too many public schools focus on the measurable to the exclusion of the possible. As a result, too many students end up better prepared for taking tests than for being skillful learners in the world beyond school" (p. 30). In the United Kingdom, the focus on the national curriculum has made it harder for teachers to bring enthusiasm, creativity, thinking, and a responsive curriculum to students as teachers struggle with the increasing standardization, centralization, and vocational focus of education (Claxton et al., 2011; Lipsett, 2008; Maisuria, 2005; Robinson, 1999; Wagner, 2008).

As Australia began its move toward a national curriculum and its associated testing, policymakers looked at the impact similar reform efforts had in the United States and the United Kingdom. One analysis concluded, "Full-cohort [all students system wide] tests encourage methods of teaching that promote shallow and superficial learning rather than deep conceptual understanding and the kinds of complex knowledge and skills needed in modern, information-based societies" (Queensland Studies Authority, 2009, p. 3). Nonetheless, policymakers enamored with notions of accountability, value added, and measurable results seem poised to impose a testing policy that mirrors all the failed aspects of those imposed in the United States and the United Kingdom, ignoring the mounting evidence that such testing warps and distorts the story of learning for both teachers and students.

Nikhil Goyal, mentioned earlier, talked about classrooms as test-prep factories. Indeed, the Center for Educational Policy found that since 2001–2002, most school districts in the United States (84 percent) had made changes to curriculum and the allocation of instructional time to focus on tested content (McMurrer, 2007). Tony Wagner, author of *The Global Achievement Gap,* has visited classrooms in some of the best public and private schools in the United States, assessing the intellectual challenge being offered to students through schoolwide learning walks. In typical learning walks, he finds that little time is spent on activities that require higher-order thinking and that teachers rarely ask questions involving more than recall. He is lucky to visit a single class out of a dozen where all students are actively engaged and thinking. In my own research group's study of teacher questioning in direct-instruction classrooms in the United Kingdom—defined as classrooms where teachers deliver instruction based on meeting specific objectives as delineated in an externally prescribed curriculum—we found that the majority of teachers' questions (58 percent) were either of a procedural nature or focused on reviewing content. Just 10 percent were designed to push, probe, and facilitate students' thinking. In Jo Boaler's study of traditional high school mathematics classes in the United States, she found that virtually all, 97 percent, of questions involved recall and review (Boaler & Brodie, 2004).

Several themes are emerging from these disparate accounts: that learning in schools is often boring, largely entails memorizing and repeating facts, rarely demands that students think, and is generally an isolated exercise. These themes are given much of their traction, life, and longevity by another common story thread: competition. The idea that learning is a competitive rather than collaborative venture is practically baked into our system of education, in which rankings, GPAs, and exam scores are used as measures of accomplishment and criteria for admission to university programs. In the documentary *Race to Nowhere* (Attia, 2010), the effects of this competition on students are explored in terms of the stress, disengagement, alienation, cheating, loss of creativity, and overall mental health issues that competition induces in many of those who choose to buy in, and the high dropout rates that result when students choose not to buy in or find themselves locked out by the testing culture. The documentary gives voice to students, mostly from highly competitive public and private schools, who feel that grades and scores, rather than learning, have become the purpose of school. Inspired by her own daughter's stress-induced illness, documentary director Vicki H. Abeles and writer Miamone Attia have issued a wake-up call for schools to change the story of learning they are enacting.

Another wake-up call was issued by Sir Ken Robinson (2010) in his widely popular TED talk viewed by more than five million people, "Bring on the Learning Revolution!" In his address, Robinson stresses the urgent need for nurturing human potential on an individualized basis as an educational outcome, a theme that emerged from his committee's report to the secretary of state for education and employment in the United Kingdom (Robinson, 1999). To the TED audience, Robinson speaks about this need as a crisis of human resources being brought about by an education that dislocates people from their natural talents rather than helping them identify and develop those talents. He lays the blame for this dislocation and death on the dominant story of learning being told in our schools today. Specifically he identifies two story themes: linearity and conformity. Schools present learning as a track that students are placed on, with the end goal often being attending a good college. However, this linear view of education ignores the organic nature of learning and human development. This linearity also leads us to seeing education as a competition to reach the end goal faster and better (attending a more selective college) than others.

Accompanying, and perhaps even exacerbating, the linearity Robinson identifies is the theme of conformity, the idea that we can have a one-size-fits-all system of education. One sees this playing out in the increasing calls for standardization of curriculum, tests, and teaching. Robinson (2010) says that "we have sold ourselves into a fast food model of education, and it is impoverishing our spirits and our energies as much as fast food is depleting our physical bodies." Instead of accepting the belief that quality comes from conformity, he suggests that we attain the highest quality when we strive for customization over standardization. The focus on conformity kills creativity and imagination, Robinson argues. This is more than a mere belief, however. A review of almost three hundred thousand scores of children and adults on the Torrance Creativity Test reveals a steady and "very significant" decline in scores since the 1990s, with those of American elementary school students showing the "most serious" decline (Bronson & Merryman, 2010).

As with our review of the old story, this examination of the current story has to be considered as only a partial view. Certainly there are schools and classrooms telling a different, more engaging, and more thoughtful story of learning. Having worked with Disney's American Teacher Awards program and coauthored the Creative Classroom series, I know many excellent teachers. I'm sure you also know of some excellent schools and dynamic teachers. That said, we shouldn't be too quick to pat ourselves on the back or become complacent about how our students are experiencing learning in our schools and classrooms on a larger scale and over time.

It takes a degree of nerve, ambition, and fortitude to steadfastly and honestly work to uncover the story of learning one is telling students. Once we have done so, we must then assess how that story stacks up against what we truly want for our students. Are we in fact cultivating the kinds of adults we want our students to be? This alignment isn't easy, precisely because we have allowed low-level outcomes on tests to shape our view of what a quality education is and should offer. The story of learning we are enacting also gets framed through the lens of our own experience as students. We tend to perpetuate and reinforce the status quo because it is the only story we know. In this way, the culture of schools, the story of learning we are enacting, becomes invisible to us. However, as the large-scale studies mentioned earlier have all found, the dominant story is not one that is serving students well or adequately promoting the outcomes we say we value. Therefore, we must think about telling a different story of learning.

Crafting a Different Story for Schools

Creating a new story requires us not only to rethink the purpose and vision of education but also to examine the way schools operate and function as delivery agents of that vision. To change the story and achieve different outcomes, such as those set forth previously, we must send new messages about what learning is and how it happens. Crafting and sending new messages is not an easy task. It requires us to really walk the talk. The old story and its accompanying practices are quite ingrained in us as students, teachers, and parents, making it easy to fall into familiar ways of doing things. In the following chapters, we will focus on how we can marshal and master the forces at work within group culture in a way that will enable us to enact a different story. But first, we must allow ourselves to dream a new vision and articulate its essence.

All too often, we educators find it difficult to dream. There is a tendency to see the barriers, constraints, and structures around us as impenetrable. There's the time table, the external exams, university entrance requirements, fifty-minute instructional periods, government mandates, annual yearly progress measures, outside inspectors, parental expectations, and so on. All these cause us to throw up our hands and say, "Until the system changes, there is nothing we can do." David Jakes (2012), an educational advocate interested in transforming schools through technology, also uses the story metaphor to think about schools and their vision. He suggests that we need to change our language from one of limits to one of possibilities: "Creating a new story requires that the author or authors of that new story cast aside the destructive 'Yah But' mentality, and ask 'What If?'"

Let's consider a few "What ifs" that suggest a new story:

- What if schools were less about preparing students for tests and more about preparing them for a lifetime of learning?
- What if schools measured success not by what individuals did on exams but by what groups were able to accomplish together?
- What if schools took the development of students' intellectual character as their highest calling?
- What if understanding and application of skills and knowledge rather than the mere acquisition of knowledge were the goal?
- What if students were really engaged in their learning rather than merely compliant in the process of school as it is done to them?
- What if students had more control of their learning?

There is an endless array of "What if" questions we might ask to help us rethink our schools and to dream a new vision of education. The ones here might spark fresh thinking and rich dreaming on the part of you and your colleagues as you explore what the implications of these "What ifs" might be for teachers and students. In addition, you might want to identify your own "What if" questions, either individually or as part of a professional group, for exploration.

The "What if" question at the core of this book is: *What if we sought to develop a culture of thinking in our schools, classrooms, museums, meetings, and organizations?* Taking up the question in earnest, in a way that transforms schools and organizations, means enacting a new story by harnessing the power of the forces that shape group culture. These forces will be explored in detail in the coming chapters. However, before we jump into the "how," we need to have a bit more clarity around our story. Just what is it we are trying to accomplish? Only when we are clear about the core messages we wish to send can we hope to capture the essence of this story in a way that we can tell it to ourselves over and over again until it becomes the very heart of our new vision.

In this story, our schools, classrooms, and organizations become *places in which a group's collective as well as individuals' thinking is valued, visible, and actively promoted as part of the regular, day-to-day experience of all group members.* This is the beating heart of our story. We must strive to constantly make thinking valued, visible, and actively promoted in all our interactions with learners; as part of the lessons we design, central in the assessment process, and part and parcel of our instruction; and in ways that are generally integrated in all we do. Each of these core actions—making thinking valued, visible, and actively promoted—needs a bit more unpacking so that we understand our mission and have a better idea of what it entails.

We must begin by sending a robust message about the value of thinking. Of course, what educator is going to say he or she doesn't value thinking? But in fact, schools send students very mixed messages about the value and importance of thinking, and often may be clear about the task at hand but not always about the thinking needed to accomplish it. Too often students are sent the message that memorization is the only tool necessary for learning and that there isn't a place to bring in complications, questions, or connections from outside the classroom that might make learning more real. If we truly value thinking, then we must be able to articulate what kinds of thinking we are after, why they are important, and how they might help one's learning or accomplishment of the task at hand. We must communicate that learning is a consequence of thinking, not something extra that we tack on but something in which we must actively engage to promote our own and others' learning.

So what kinds of thinking are of value? What are we after? Naturally, this depends on the learning context, but broadly speaking we want students to become proficient with the kinds of thinking they can use to develop their own understanding of things. For example:

- Asking *questions,* identifying puzzles, and wondering about the mysteries and implications of the objects and ideas of study
- Making *connections,* comparisons, and contrasts between and among things—including connections within and across the discipline as well as with one's own prior knowledge
- Building ongoing and evolving *explanations,* interpretations, and theories based on one's ever-developing knowledge and understanding

- Examining things from different *perspectives* and alternative points of view to discern bias and develop a more balanced take on issues, ideas, and events
- Noticing, observing, and *looking closely* to fully perceive details, nuances, and hidden aspects and to observe what is really going on as the foundational evidence for one's interpretations and theories
- Identifying, gathering, and *reasoning with evidence* to justify and support one's interpretations, predictions, theories, arguments, and explanations
- Delving deeply to *uncover the complexities* and challenges of a topic and look below the surface of things, recognizing when one has only a surface understanding
- Being able to *capture the core* or essence of a thing to discern what it is really all about

This is by no means an exhaustive list of types of thinking. My colleagues and I have written elsewhere in more detail about what might constitute effective thinking (Ritchhart et al., 2011), but this list is a good place to start. In addition, one could take some of the goals identified earlier and begin to unpack them for the types of thinking they require. What kinds of thinking are important in problem solving? What kinds of thinking encourage innovation and creativity? What kinds of thinking are needed to be an effective communicator or advocate? What kinds of thinking support the development of global competence? You'll likely find some overlap with the list here, but some new types of thinking are likely to emerge as well.

Once we are clear on the kinds of thinking we are trying to encourage, we must strive to make this very elusive entity, thinking, as visible as possible so that it, too, can become an object of development as much as the concepts, knowledge, and skills that are more typical parts of the curriculum. When we make thinking visible, we are provided a window into not only what students understand but also how they are understanding it. Uncovering students' thinking provides evidence of students' insights as well as their misconceptions. We need to make thinking visible because it provides us with the information necessary to plan the opportunities that can take students' learning to the next level and enable continued engagement with the ideas of study. It is only when we understand what our students are thinking that we have the information we as teachers need to further engage and support our students in the process of building understanding. Making students' thinking visible thus must become an ongoing component of our teaching.

Teachers are used to asking questions that uncover students' knowledge and test their memories. Individually and collectively, we also must get better at asking questions that probe, push, and help to uncover students' thinking (Ritchhart, 2012). Then we need to listen to our students so that we can truly hear what they have to say. Listening means taking a vigorous and genuine interest in the other. When we do that, we send students the message that their thinking and ideas matter, that they are part of the conversation and integral to the learning. We then can take our listening to the next step and document students' thinking so that we have a record of our collective thinking and our community's progress toward understanding. This record becomes one way to examine and talk about our thinking and its development. It is a vehicle for both capturing and advancing learning. What is more, the very act of documenting students' thinking sends an important message about its value and importance.

But we can't stop at visibility. We must also seek to actively advance and promote students' thinking if we are to produce students who are engaged learners and active thinkers able to communicate, innovate, collaborate, and problem-solve. This means that a chief goal of instruction, right alongside the development of content understanding, is the advancement of thinking. This dual focus, what Claxton et al. (2011) call split-screen teaching, depends on and builds on our efforts to value thinking and make it visible. It is the completion of our triadic goal.

Taking the promotion of thinking seriously moves most teachers into new and somewhat less charted territory. On the one hand, one advances any skill through the opportunities one has to engage it. Therefore, teachers must create opportunities for thinking and provide time for it—not always an easy thing amid the press for coverage, but a necessity nonetheless. On the other hand, practice alone does not ensure progress and meaningful development. One also needs feedback and coaching on one's practice. This kind of coaching calls for a nuanced, situated, and embedded assessment of students' efforts in the moment. It is an assessment that feeds and spurs the learner's efforts, being purely formative in nature.

I hesitate to use the word "assessment" in this context because it carries so much baggage for educators. Some cannot get the red pen or grade book out of their minds as soon as they hear the word. Others cringe at the deadening effect so many forms of school-based assessments have on the learning and teaching process, turning even the most enjoyable exploration into mere "work" for the teacher to grade. But these are most assuredly not the forms of assessment that are helpful in advancing students' thinking. We are after the kind of assessment employed by a coach on the playing field, able to identify where a player is in his or her development and what is needed to take performance to the next level. This is the skill of a coach. It is also the skill of an effective teacher. Practically anyone and, increasingly, anything can dispense information. Real learning is advanced through the creation of powerful opportunities for mental engagement accompanied by the discerning eye and targeted feedback of someone more expert than oneself.

ENACTING OUR NEW STORY, REALIZING OUR VISION

In this chapter, I articulated a new outcome defining a quality education: the promotion of the dispositions needed for students to become active learners and effective thinkers eager and able to create, innovate, and solve problems. It is this outcome that is most needed for success in the world today. Although not wholly new, it is an outcome that has enjoyed only peripheral attention, seldom capturing our attention, too often pushed to the side by a focus on exam scores alone. However, it's an outcome that encapsulates a higher vision for us as educators, representing what we are able to achieve when we allow ourselves to dream outside the well-worn constraints of the school bureaucracy. It is the stuff of passion, energy, and drive—for both our students and us.

I then identified the vehicle needed to get us there: enculturation. We must surround our students with an intellectual life into which they might grow. To do this, we need first to identify and evaluate the story of learning we are currently telling our students through the messages we send them. Some ideas for doing that follow at the end of this chapter. Then we must work to shift those messages in order to enculturate students into a new story of learning where thinking is valued, visible, and actively promoted as part of the ongoing, day-to-day experience of all group members. We must become shapers of culture and message managers to realize our vision and transform our schools.

But how do we shift the messages within an already established culture? How do we enact a new story of learning for both our students and ourselves? How can we understand the ins and outs of group culture so that we may harness its power and shape it to tell our new story? These are the questions we take up in the coming chapters as we delve into an exploration of the eight forces shaping group culture.

UNCOVERING THE STORY OF
YOUR SCHOOL OR CLASSROOM

- Using the method of the Gallup Youth Survey, create a list of twenty-five adjectives: ten positive (engaged, interested, curious . . .), five neutral (coasting, comfortable, fine . . .), and ten negative (tired, bored, frustrated . . .). Ask students to select three words from the list to describe how they usually feel in school in general or in your class in particular. Include a question asking students to identify how they see themselves academically: near the top, above average, average. What does the pattern of response tell you?

- Use the "My Reflections on the Learning Activities in This Class" survey (appendix A) to assess students' views about the types of thinking that are most present in a particular class lesson. How do students' views match with your own?

- Uncover the messages the school sends teachers about what it means to teach at your school. Have the faculty respond in writing to the prompt, "For a first-year teacher beginning his or her career at our school, what messages would he or she pick up about what it means to be a teacher here? What kinds of professional conversations would he or she recognize as dominating our time? What would he or she notice about how one develops as a teacher over the course of his or her career if one stays at this school?" Share and discuss people's responses in small groups to identify themes, and then share them with the larger group.

- Go on a "learning message walk." Visit as many classes at your school as you can on a given day, stopping in each class for just five to ten minutes. The purpose is not to evaluate teacher performance but to get a general feel for students' experience in classes. Pay attention to engagement and participation. Are all students participating or just a few? Note the level of intellectual challenge and the teacher's press for thinking. Is this just more of the same, or do students really have to dig in and think? Get a feel for the discourse in the classroom. Are students engaging and responding to one another, or is it only a Ping-Pong dialogue with the teacher? Take note of how students are working: whole class, small groups, in pairs, or individually.

CHAPTER 2

Expectations
Recognizing How Our Beliefs Shape Our Behavior

ex•pec•ta•tions |ˌekspekˈtāSHəns| noun: A set of strong beliefs surrounding future outcomes and anticipated results. • A demand we place on others. • What we regard as likely to happen given certain actions. As a culture shaper, expectations operate as "belief sets" or "action theories" that influence our own efforts in relation to the achievement of desired goals and outcomes. In this way, expectations not only set our course but also act as an internal compass that keeps us moving toward our goal. It is important to note that this departs from the way teachers more typically think of "expectations"—that is, as explicit expressions *of* standards used to direct and inform the behavior of others. It is our expectations *for* students, ourselves, and the learning process itself that form the foundation for the culture of the group.

S itting in the back of Karen White's algebra classroom in suburban Colorado, I found myself growing increasingly uncomfortable. When I had interviewed Karen the year before about the possibility of observing in her classroom, she shared with me how important thinking was to her in her teaching. She had been through several professional development seminars about promoting "habits of mind" and enthusiastically rattled off the lingo associated with that program as she talked about her goals for students. She stressed the importance of metacognition to learning and discussed how she integrated writing and problem solving in mathematics. On the basis of these conversations, I was excited to see how these elements would play out in her classroom. However, observing in her class that first morning, I had a hard time finding moments when students actually were engaged in any thinking. Karen was extremely well organized, greeting each student at the door and getting the class started quickly and efficiently. She was firm but pleasant to all students, and managed the classroom with the efficiency of a seasoned teacher. But for all this order and efficiency, there was something missing. Why didn't this feel like a thoughtful place? Like a culture of thinking?

As I observed class period after class period that first day, Karen communicated very clear guidelines and standards to every set of students. Each homework question was worth a point if it was attempted. You could still get some points for homework even if it were late, so you should always do it. Scores were collected each day and point accumulations were publicly posted at the end of each week so that every student would know exactly where he or she stood in terms of a final grade. If you didn't understand a concept, ask. Karen assured the class that she was "the best explainer in the West" and would be happy to supply a second or third explanation until a procedure was clear. In the end, doing the work and trying would guarantee that a student would pass the course—and not have to repeat it next year—even if one wasn't any good at mathematics. Thinking was mentioned, but not in a way directly connected to the learning at hand. For instance, there were reflection journals to encourage "metacognition," but these were used to record how students were feeling about their performance on tests and assignments rather than a careful analysis of their learning. There were "problems of the week" that students would do independently outside of class, but these problems were opportunities to gain more points rather than a well-integrated part of students' learning.

Throughout that first week of school and on into the school year, Karen was reliably consistent with her students. Still, the thinking remained largely elusive, and the culture seemed never to approach a true culture of thinking. Classes started promptly with a review of homework. New procedures were cheerfully explained, questions answered, and new practice sets given for homework. True to her word, scores were posted on the bulletin board beside the door each week, and students were informed at the beginning of class if any assignments were missing or late. At times it seemed like each student in the class had made an internal calculation regarding how much attention needed to be paid to complete the homework successfully or prepare for the looming test. Each student operated just slightly below this threshold and rarely stretched beyond it, creating an atmosphere of compliance and passivity.

"Order." "Clarity." "Predictability." These were the words students and colleagues used to describe Karen's classroom and teaching style. The other word that kept coming up was "expectations." Karen had clear expectations of students. Students knew what to expect in her class. Indeed, these evaluations seemed to hold with my own observations. Karen did have very clear expectations, communicated effectively and upheld relentlessly in an admirable fashion. But somehow these expectations, the clearest manifestation of what Karen's classroom was like, seemed to be standing in the way of creating a culture of thinking. How could that be? Why would having such clear expectations for students' behavior and performance inhibit their development as thinkers?

To understand how this could happen and to understand better how expectations operate as a cultural force in learning groups, we have to make a distinction between two types of expectations: directives and beliefs. In schools and classrooms, we often talk of expectations in terms of the behavioral actions and performance outcomes adults want from students. Our expectations *of* students. Such standards, expressed to anyone in a subordinate position, have the nature of a strong request or even an order. Think about these as top-down directives whose aim is to clearly define what the person in charge desires with respect to another's performance. To be clear, there is nothing inherently wrong with communicating such behavioral standards or criteria for assignments to students or subordinates. Effective teachers and leaders do this all the time and with consistency, as did Karen.

The second kind of expectations operates on a deeper, more systemic, and ultimately more powerful level. These are the expectations that are rooted in our beliefs about the nature of things and how the world operates. In the context of a learning group, they are working theories about the nature of teaching, learning, thinking, schools, or the organization itself. Our expectations *for* students. These beliefs focus our attention, direct our action, and define our understanding of how things work. These beliefs form the basis for what my colleague David Perkins calls "action theories"—that is, theories about how our actions relate to obtaining desired results. Perkins (1999, p. 19) explains the utility of such theories: "We try to cope with the complexity and uncertainty of the mission of life through such action theories," and explains that their power comes from their compactness, simplicity, and efficiency. They are the "rules of thumb" and the "internal compass" with which we operate. This second layer of expectations is a constant influence on the actions of a teacher or leader, providing the underpinning for the more explicit, surface-level directives he or she might express.

After decades of research into how to create a theoretical model that would explain teaching behavior, Alan Schoenfeld and his colleagues at the Teacher Model Group in Berkeley developed a goal-oriented decision-making model of teaching (Schoenfeld, 2010). In this model, knowledge of a teacher's goals and beliefs provides the basis for understanding much, if not all, of a teacher's behavior. Indeed, Schoenfeld claims that "if enough is known, in detail, about a person's orientations, goals, and resources, that person's actions can be explained at both macro and micro levels. That is, they can be explained not only in broad terms, but also on a moment-by-moment basis" (p. iv).

Schoenfeld's model suggests that teachers do not so much work from a set of practices, either prescribed or ingrained, as they are guided profoundly and implicitly by their belief sets (what he calls "orientations") about teaching, learning, and the meaning and purpose of school. The power of these expectational belief sets helps explain why changing teaching is much more than giving teachers a new set of practices to deploy. In fact, teachers may employ a new method of instruction, only to find that it falls flat and doesn't achieve the kind of lift its proponents had promised. They then discount the method, ignoring completely how their expectational beliefs may have undermined the new instructional practices.

Back to Karen White's classroom: Why were her directives inhibiting the creation of a culture of thinking? Why should her clarity regarding behavioral standards and outcomes impede her efforts to create a culture of thinking, given that thinking was something she expressly valued? It wasn't that her directives were necessarily "bad" or "wrong"; it was that the action theories and beliefs that gave rise to them tended to be more inhibiting than facilitating of an agenda of thinking. Consequently, the deeper-level expectations, her action theories, on which she based her directives were not supportive of an agenda of thinking. Peeling back Karen's surface directives to uncover the beliefs and action theories that lie beneath them, we can see why this is the case.

In Karen's very clear standards for students about points, grades, and keeping score, one sees a belief that school is about work and that students must be coerced or bribed into learning through the use of grades. You may recall that this was a recurring theme emerging from many people's stories of learning shared in chapter 1. In the way Karen planned and focused her classes, one sees the belief that learning algebra is primarily about acquiring knowledge of procedures rather than developing understanding, and that memorization and practice are the most effective tools for that job. This theory of action, "One learns through memorization and practice," made it hard for Karen to bring out and facilitate students' thinking. Instead, thinking existed as an add-on to the regular rhythm of the class, something she did as an "extra" to the regular work of the class. Through her strong focus on grades and passing the course, even if one is "no good at mathematics," Karen sent the message that our abilities are largely fixed and that "getting by" was all that some could hope to accomplish. One might not understand algebra, but with effort one could at least pass the course. Finally, in her efforts to promote order and control, certainly worthwhile and important goals in any classroom, Karen tilted the balance toward students' becoming passive learners who were dependent on her.

In this chapter, I'll explore five belief sets that act as action theories and lay a foundation *for* our expectations in learning groups. They can either facilitate a culture of thinking, though they can never fully ensure it, or act as an inhibiting challenge to that development. The five belief sets are as follows:

- Focusing students on the learning vs. the work
- Teaching for understanding vs. knowledge
- Encouraging deep vs. surface learning strategies
- Promoting independence vs. dependence
- Developing a growth vs. a fixed mindset

By way of introducing these, we've taken a brief look at how each of these sets of beliefs played out in Karen White's teaching. We'll now explore them more fully to understand how these specific expectations for students (as opposed to *of* students), which operate as our guiding action theories, are important to establishing a culture of thinking. You'll notice that I've framed each of these belief sets as a natural tension. I've done this because forming a powerful theory of action for oneself is not a simple matter of merely adopting a nice-sounding platitude some author spouts off. Rather, the creation of a real-world action theory demands that we acknowledge and try to reconcile for ourselves the pushes and pulls that exist in a given context. Only then can we know why we are coming down on one side or other. Furthermore, before any given belief is to fully exist as an action theory, we have to make the connection between actions and outcomes. Thus it is important to explore how a belief gives rise to a set of actions that then results in certain outcomes. Finally, we must recognize that there are other possible goals, beliefs, and expectations out there competing as possible action theories. Having clear expectations— that is, the kind of expectational beliefs that guide our own and students' actions— requires a conviction on our part. We must first set and then calibrate our internal compass if we want it to act as a reliable guide.

FOCUSING STUDENTS ON THE LEARNING VS. THE WORK

The metaphor of work—learning as work, students as workers, and classrooms as workplaces—is well entrenched in our notions of schooling and education. This shouldn't be surprising given that public education began to take hold around the world at the same time that child labor laws were beginning to be instituted. The writings of Charles Dickens, most notably *Oliver Twist*, served to publicize the issue of child labor, and Great Britain subsequently led the way in passing a series of reforms to curb child labor during the nineteenth century. In 1821, the first public high school was opened in Boston. Just a decade later, the New England Association of Farmers, Mechanics and Other Workingmen passed a resolution stating, "Children should not be allowed to labor in the factories from morning till night, without any time for healthy recreation and mental culture" (timetoast, 2011). Four years later, the first US law governing compulsory attendance in school was passed in Massachusetts. Still, it took over a century before the first US federal law regulating children's work was instituted in 1936. We see a similar progression of laws occurring throughout Europe, Australia, and Canada. Thus children's work moved out of the factory and farmyard and into the school, with teachers becoming the new managers, bosses, and overseers.

As Hermine Marshall (1988) points out, the work metaphor has been firing on all fronts in education ever since these early days. It guides the research that has been done in education, influences the design of teaching methods, impacts the way in which we organize schools, and shapes the form of interventions. Just take a look at the language used in schools; we are swimming in a sea of work-related metaphors. Principals get called "chief academic officers." Researchers assess "time on task" and look for "value added" in terms of student output. Prospective teachers are trained in "classroom management" and held "accountable for results." Students are taught "work habits" and receive "rewards" for their performance. Students are issued workbooks, given work time or work periods, and are assigned seat work and homework. In a London school, a group of teacher researchers (Claxton, Chambers, Powell, & Lucas, 2011) sat in on classrooms to listen for just how prevalent teachers' use of the words "work" and "learning" were. To their astonishment, "work" was used forty-nine times more often than was "learning." The ubiquity of the work metaphor for schooling serves to ingrain it not only in our language but in our psyche as well, causing few to question it.

But why should this matter? What's wrong with work or being a good worker? Doesn't one have to work to learn? Why vilify the notion of work? Isn't work noble and worthwhile? Can't we do good and meaningful work? And isn't this focus on language just splitting hairs anyway? What difference does it make if a teacher asks, "Is your work done?" or "Where are you in your learning?" To address these questions, we must first understand that what is at issue here isn't merely a selection of words and phrases but a more fundamental choice we are making in terms of how our energies and those of our students get channeled.

In their seminal book, *Metaphors We Live By*, George Lakoff and Mark Johnson (1980) make the case that the metaphors we use do not merely pepper and enliven our speech; they help us organize our experience and create our realities. Although metaphors may initially grow out of our perceptions or derive from the apt and fitting connections we make, eventually their use over time by individuals and groups comes to shape the way we perceive the world. Lakoff and Johnson take this a step further, asserting that metaphors actually "structure our actions and thoughts. They are alive in the most fundamental sense: they are metaphors we live by" (p. 55). Thus, when educators employ a work metaphor, they are framing and shaping the experience of the classroom, focusing students' attention on the completion of work rather than helping them focus on the learning that might be achieved. As Marshall (1990) explains, "Metaphors 'set' or structure both the way classroom problems are perceived and the solutions that are proposed. . . . If classrooms are seen as workplaces, many people believe that their 'productivity' can be improved by rewarding greater efficiency and better products, that is, higher test scores. The solution suggested by this metaphor, however, disregards whether what is produced is meaningful learning. For some teachers, meaningful learning seems to be secondary to maintaining the work system" (p. 96).

In work-oriented classrooms (Marshall, 1987), teachers and students are focused on work completion. We hear students asking questions about the work: "How long does this have to be?" "Will this be on the test?" These aren't questions about the ideas or about the learning; they are about the work. Teachers then monitor students' work and hold them accountable for it, as we witnessed in Karen White's classroom. Of course, the underlying assumption is that the work will result in the learning. However, the way one frames a task often determines how one goes about accomplishing that task and what one is likely to get out of it. Try this quick thought experiment: Recall something you were asked to do by someone who was a higher-up or in a supervisory role, something that you just didn't see the point in doing. Now think about how you went about doing that task. That is what work feels like. It is done for someone else, not yourself, and the focus becomes completing the work, getting it done and over with, and possibly pleasing the superior. Now identify the flip-side example: Think of a time when someone did what you asked, but not what you intended. Why didn't that person do what you intended? It was most likely because he or she focused on the work rather than its purpose.

In contrast, in a learning-oriented classroom, teachers and students focus their attention on the learning as the priority, letting the work exist in context and serve the learning. The work is a means to an end, not an end in itself. What does this look like in practice? To begin, it means that teachers normally introduce a task or assignment by highlighting the learning that can potentially arise from it. Contrast this with the more common delineation of the assignment and all its requirements, which serves to focus students more on the task than on the learning. Next, teachers sustain and support the learning through their interactions with groups and individuals. When the purpose of the task is on the learning, teachers are also more likely to provide choice and options in completion of assignments as long as the learning is being achieved. In contrast, when the focus is on the work, students are often given less choice as teachers exert a greater degree of control.

In work-oriented classrooms, teachers "monitor the work," making sure everyone is on task and getting things done: "Are you finished?" "What number are you on?" "Are you ready to move on to question 4?" In contrast, when teachers are focused on learning, they spend their time with students "listening for the learning": "Tell me what you have done so far." "What questions are surfacing for you?" "What does that tell you?" Finally, we see a learning orientation in the way that teachers respond to and treat mistakes and errors. In learning-oriented classrooms, mistakes are seen as opportunities to learn, to grow, to rethink. In work-oriented classrooms, errors and mistakes are to be avoided because they indicate incompetence. Thus learning-oriented teachers often provide more descriptive feedback that informs learning, whereas work-oriented teachers tend to give more evaluative feedback as a judgment on performance.

Of course there is more nuance to developing a learning orientation and keeping students focused on learning than just these few tweaks. Teaching is a complex task, after all. However, making a clear distinction between work and learning helps us as teachers to keep our focus and that of our students on the learning. It allows us to reject the naive theory that "if I just keep students busy and on task, then they will learn" in favor of the more complex, "If I keep students focused on the learning, then I will be better able to monitor and assist their development of understanding."

To get a sense of how our big-picture goals, beliefs, expectations, and action theories influence and shape teaching behavior, consider an experiment conducted by researchers in Colorado (Flink, Boggiano, & Barrett, 1990). The researchers wanted to test the effects of teaching done with a focus on learning versus a focus on performance/work. They predicted that when teachers felt pressured to perform by an outside authority, then these teachers would be more likely to employ controlling teaching strategies as an instructor, thus impairing student performance. The researchers randomly assigned fifteen fourth-grade teachers to one of two teaching conditions. One group was given the instruction, "Your role will be to facilitate the children's learning how to solve the anagrams and sequencing problems. Your job is simply to help the students learn how to solve the problems." We can equate this with a learning orientation. The other set of teachers was told, "Your role will be to ensure that the children perform well on the anagrams and sequencing problems. It is a teacher's responsibility to make sure that students perform up to standards." We can equate this with a work orientation. These teachers then taught small groups of students, four to seven students per group, across a total of 267 students. All sessions were videotaped and evaluated for the presence of "controlling teaching strategies," such as hints, pressure, tenseness, and the use of evaluative criticism and praise.

The researchers were correct in their hypothesis. Under the pressure conditions, the teachers were more likely to use more controlling teaching practices, and this coupling of pressure on teachers with controlling practices led to impaired student performance. Keep in mind that none of the teachers were told how to teach. They were not told to be directive or controlling; they were only given a set of expectations by the researchers in the form of a simple statement. The story not to be missed here is that teachers' actions were shaped by the way the task of teaching was framed. The metaphor, the action theory in play gave rise to certain behaviors in teachers and subsequently in students. A work orientation didn't always lead to poor student performance, however. Nor did a teacher's use of controlling teaching strategies. It was the combination of the two that caused student performance to dip. Thus we see the power of facilitative expectations coupled with effective teaching practices. We must have both operating in tandem.

TEACHING FOR UNDERSTANDING VS. KNOWLEDGE

The words "understanding" and "knowledge" are ubiquitous when it comes to talk about learning, education, and schooling. However, the terms are somewhat ambiguous and can lead to confusion among people who think that the two are one and the same, or cause some to wonder what all the fuss and debate is about. For instance, the term "knowledge" can, on one hand, refer to the accumulation and storage of facts, procedures, and skills: *Do you know how to make a pie crust?* On the other hand, it can also be used in the broader sense of wisdom and more broad-based "modes of relating to the world" (Maleuvre, 2005): *He really knows his way around the kitchen.*

Likewise, the word "understanding" can be used in very different ways. Some thirty years ago when Madeline Hunter (1982) talked about "checking for understanding," she meant assessing students' basic comprehension or grasp of knowledge: *Do you understand the explanation I just gave on how to diagram a sentence?* However, the term "understanding" also can be used to express a much deeper and more complex level of learning, describing a state of enablement beautifully expressed by Jerome Bruner (1996): "Being able to 'go beyond the information' given to 'figure things out' is one of the few untarnishable joys of life. One of the great triumphs of learning (and of teaching) is to get things organized in your head in a way that permits you to know more than you 'ought' to. And this takes reflection, brooding about what it is that you know. The enemy of reflection is the breakneck pace—the thousand pictures" (p. 129).

None of these various meanings is in any way wrong or incorrect, and people are certainly entitled to define terms as they see fit. However, because ambiguity exists, before we go further we must define what we mean by understanding and how understanding is different from knowledge. Understanding requires knowledge, but goes beyond it. Understanding depends on richly integrated and connected knowledge. This means that understanding goes beyond merely possessing a set of skills or a collection of facts in isolation; rather, understanding requires that our knowledge be woven together in a way that connects one idea to another. This web of connections and relations becomes the vehicle for our putting ideas to work and seeing the applicability of our skills in novel circumstances and in the creation of new ideas.

David Perkins often speaks of understanding in terms of "knowing one's way around" a particular topic. This suggests that there are multiple sides of a topic to be navigated, and that we need always to be on the lookout for new perspectives and opportunities to explore. Understanding a particular topic then leads not just to familiarity but also to a state of enablement. In contrast, knowledge and skills can be possessed in isolation and without the accompanying understanding that would permit us to use them flexibly and adaptively in new situations. Thus the metaphors for knowledge focus on possession, storage, and retrieval. Knowledge is seen as a commodity; it is something you have. This often leads to a binary notion of knowledge as something one either has or doesn't. In contrast, the metaphors for understanding focus on action: applying, performing, adapting, and so on. Understanding is viewed as a performance; it is something you do. Understanding often varies in degrees and context. It is decidedly nonbinary in nature, and in fact some might argue that understanding can never be fully complete and absolute.

In many classrooms, to reach for this kind of understanding—that is, an understanding that stresses exploring a topic from many angles, building connections, challenging long-held assumptions, looking for applications, and producing what is for the learner a novel outcome—represents a new, different, and sometimes even radical agenda. Teaching for understanding is not school as usual. In the 1990s, when the Spencer Foundation funded one of the largest-ever nongovernmental research projects in education, they recognized that teaching for understanding represented a new direction for both students and teachers. The aim of the research, carried out at Harvard Graduate School of Education, was to explicate a specific pedagogy of understanding. The rationale was that much of the previous research in education had focused on helping students acquire information and learn skills rather than develop understanding. Although a wealth of prior research had focused on how to structure, sequence, deliver, and assess gains in knowledge and skills, it was believed that to really develop understanding required new curriculum, new methods, and a different set of approaches—and this required a new line of research to uncover. As technology was advancing, globalization increasing, and whole new industries and new career trajectories forming, it was becoming increasingly clear that an educational focus on knowledge and skills alone wasn't going to take students very far in life.

The model that eventually emerged from the research analyzing and distilling what effective teachers did when they were trying to promote understanding came to be known as the Teaching for Understanding (TfU) framework. It delineates four essential elements to which teachers need to attend:

1. **Generative topics:** focusing the curriculum around big, generative ideas worth understanding

2. **Understanding goals:** identifying a small set of specific goals for understanding (as opposed to a list of things they want students merely to know)

3. **Performances of understanding:** designing a sequence of ever more complex performance tasks that require students to use their skills and knowledge in novel contexts

4. **Ongoing feedback:** providing a steady stream of ongoing feedback and assessment information that students can use to improve their performance

Sounds easy, right? Of course the reality of putting this in place in real classrooms requires a lot of new thinking and effort by teachers. But it also requires students to assume a new role as well. When teachers attempted to teach a TfU unit for the first time, many ran into problems because they didn't address the new set of expectations for learning with their students. The new goal, the new agenda, and the new expectations about what it would mean to be a learner in that class were an important subtext that was hidden. Students knew the game of acquiring knowledge and skills (some better than others), and they kept trying to apply those methods in this new context. Students were frustrated. Teachers were frustrated. All because the central expectations, the beliefs and action theories shaping the classroom, were not shared, discussed, and explored at the outset.

The definitions, goals, and teaching methods related to teaching for understanding may all make sense to you, yet you still might be uneasy with why this belief set is framed as a tension: teaching for understanding vs. teaching for knowledge. As we have seen, knowledge, skills, and information play an important role in understanding and are a necessary component of it. So knowledge is presented while teaching for understanding with an expectation that that knowledge will be used, applied, discussed, analyzed, transformed, and so on. The tension arises when the teaching of knowledge becomes the primary goal, which is often the norm in many classrooms. When this is the case, such an approach can, at worst, actually impede students' understanding or, at minimum, may lead us to gloss over the gaps in students' understanding.

Mathematics offers a classic example of how this plays out. Numerous studies of students' performance on basic mathematical tasks have linked errors to an over-application of rule-determined behavior (Brown & Burton, 1978; Young & O'Shea, 1981). Although such overapplication and generalization is not uncommon in the learning process, it may be exacerbated by instruction that overemphasizes "learning the rules." However, the problem becomes even more extreme when students are asked to apply what they know to problem-solving situations. In the United States, a consistent finding from the National Assessment of Educational Progress is that students at all levels of testing (ages nine, thirteen, and seventeen) are generally able to show mastery of the procedures taught, but struggle to apply their knowledge to problem-solving situations that are not clear-cut matters of applying a rule (Carpenter, Corbitt, Kepner, Lindquist, & Reys, 1980).

A long line of research in science education also has shown that merely imparting information to students does little to affect their understanding. In fact, students may be able to produce results on tests when simply asked to recall facts, but can't apply that knowledge to problem-solving situations or give explanations for common events. As Nickerson (1985) notes, "a superficial knowledge of how to manipulate formulas and solve textbook problems may suffice to carry one through standard course requirements" (p. 215).

Examples of these failures of "teaching for knowledge" achieved infamy in two Harvard-Smithsonian Center for Astrophysics series of videos, A Private Universe (1987) and Minds of Our Own (1997), in which Harvard University and Massachusetts Institute of Technology graduates showed that they didn't understand basic concepts related to the seasons, electricity, light, and plants. Others have documented how students' prior conceptions and real-world experience often stand in the way of their understanding of force (Minstrell, 1984), rates of change (Trowbridge & McDermott, 1981), projectile motion (McCloskey, 1983), and causality (Perkins & Grotzer, 2005).

In his book *The Unschooled Mind*, Howard Gardner (1991) showed how this problem of "teaching for knowledge," which has as an underlying metaphor of "teaching as transmission," leads to very superficial learning in all the disciplines, even among our best students. The point made by Gardner, and exemplified in the flesh by the Harvard-Smithsonian video interviews of Harvard and MIT graduates, is that students' lack of understanding is not a shortcoming of the students. These are the best and the brightest. It is a shortcoming of the teaching, specifically of a belief set and expectation that teaching for knowledge is our goal as educators.

ENCOURAGING DEEP VS. SURFACE LEARNING STRATEGIES

The preceding two expectations, that our classrooms will be about learning and that our collective goal will be the development of understanding, are certainly synergistic and share a natural affinity. However, it is important to keep in mind that they are still distinct goals to work toward. It is possible for a teacher to focus on the learning over the work yet still emphasize the acquisition of knowledge as the primary goal of that learning. Thus, although they are complementary, the goals of learning and understanding should be viewed as separate. Likewise, this third belief set is also a natural extension of the previous two. And, similarly, it cannot merely be assumed as naturally occurring as a result of taking on the previous two expectations.

Assuming that one has embraced the expectation that school is about learning and that the focus of that learning is on the development of understanding, it would be natural to then ask oneself, "So how will I get students there? What do I need to do differently to promote the development of understanding?" In the previous section, I briefly explained the Teaching for Understanding (TfU) framework, which serves as a partial answer to these questions. At the instructional heart of that framework lies the idea that the way one develops understanding is through an ever more challenging and demanding set of "performances"—that is, through activities that allow for both the development and demonstration of understanding. The central idea of the concept of understanding, that of action and going beyond, comes into play in designing such performances. Consequently, a major task for teachers who embrace teaching for understanding, whether they are using the TfU framework itself or not, is answering the question: What will I actually ask students to do with the skills and knowledge they are acquiring that will develop their understanding and push it forward?

Working with many teachers in applying the TfU framework to their teaching, I've noticed that people often get hung up on the idea of "performances," and wind up creating elaborate and complicated tasks. Frequently this gets associated with "performance assessments," and the focus shifts from developing understanding to demonstrating mastery of the content taught. The key to designing successful "understanding performances" is to step back a bit from both of these positions. Although a performance can be elaborate and complex, it need not be so. Understanding is built up of many small performances of ever-increasing complexity stitched together. Even though an understanding performance always provides a window into students' understanding, such assessments need not always be formalized and summative in nature. The key to designing performances that build understanding is asking oneself: What will learners do with the information and knowledge? How will I ask them to process it—that is, to interact, use, manipulate, or change it? It is the level of processing that is key to developing understanding.

Within the completion of any learning task, assignment, or activity, there exists a wide range of potential strategies any individual learner might employ, either independently or with support, in completing that task. Although many possibilities exist for how such strategies might be classified, identifying strategies by their *level of processing* has a long history within the field of cognitive science. Craik and Lockhart (1972) suggest that depth of processing affects recall, and propose a continuum ranging from the shallow to the deep to classify students' processing. Marton and Saljo (1976) use this same notion to classify the approach students use in processing text as either deep or surface. Biggs (1987) builds on this work in proposing a framework for understanding students' motives and strategies for learning. Biggs proposes three levels: surface, deep, and achieving, with achieving being characterized as focusing on the behavior consistent with being a good student. Van Rossum and Schenk (1984) use different language to refer to similar constructs, calling surface-level strategies "reproductive" and referring to those that build understanding and require greater depth in processing as "constructive." In my work with teachers, I have found the simple language of "surface" and "deep" thinking to be intuitively useful. These words provide an easy metaphor for us to hold on to and work with as an action theory. Surface strategies focus on memory and knowledge gathering, whereas deep strategies are those that help students develop understanding.

In designing any episode of learning, effective instructors tend to prompt their students to employ certain modes of processing. This prompting can be done either explicitly as part of the assignment itself, as with the use of thinking routines (Ritchhart, Church, & Morrison, 2011), or implicitly by signaling the use of what have become commonly expected modes of processing within that learning group for completing such tasks. Strategies for creating these kinds of episodes will be discussed more in the chapters focusing on the cultural forces of routines and opportunities.

It is important to note that two less effective alternatives to this explicitness exist, and unfortunately these tend to dominate. Perhaps most common is that no processing is signaled or required at all. Here instructors are operating on the naive assumption that presenting information is all that is required of them, assuming that students themselves must do whatever processing is needed. Such individuals should label themselves as presenters or lecturers, as a true teacher must assume responsibility for fostering learning. If students merely sit through lectures or presentations, or do the reading without actively processing it, they are unlikely to learn much.

Another common classroom scenario exists in which the general need for processing may be indicated by the task, but there is an absence of explicit directions and supports to use specific modes of processing. When this occurs, which is all too often, students are likely to employ whatever processing strategies they have readily at their disposal or are most comfortable with using, and that have yielded some success for them in the past. This accounts for why "strong" students are often successful even with "poor" teachers, but "weaker" students will flounder in such situations.

It perhaps seems obvious that teaching for understanding would require deep process-ing. However, this expectation for deep processing isn't automatic. An excellent example of this gap can be found in a study of portfolios submitted by US teachers seeking certification as highly accomplished teachers from the National Board for Professional Teaching Standards (NBPTS) in the area of Early Adolescence/Mathematics (Silver, Mesa, Morris, Star, & Benken, 2009).

The NBPTS certification process, run by a nongovernmental professional group, is multifaceted and comprises video evidence, a test of teacher's content knowledge, and a portfolio consisting of artifacts (tasks, student work, and teacher reflections) that highlight "Developing Mathematical Understanding" and "Assessing Mathematical Understanding." Hence, these samples highlight the best work (chosen by the teachers) of teachers who believe they deserve special recognition as highly accomplished teachers. Furthermore, the requested samples clearly indicate that understanding is to be the focus of the work submitted. Therefore, one might expect that such a highly selective sample of classroom tasks from a highly selective group would contain clear evidence of "deep processing," right?

In an assessment of the tasks submitted by teachers applying for NBPTS certification, researchers found that less than 30 percent of the Developing Mathematical Understanding tasks submitted by teachers were rated as "high cognitive demand" tasks involving deep processing. When it came to tasks dealing with "numbers and operations," the major topic of emphasis in most math classrooms, only 10 percent of submitted tasks were judged high demand. High-demand tasks were those that require students to explain, describe, justify, compare, assess, make choices, plan, formulate questions, or work with more than one representation. In contrast, low-demand tasks ask students to make routine applications of known procedures or present what could be a demanding task in a highly structured or constrained way (breaking it into nondemanding subtasks) so that students were no longer asked to think.

When researchers analyzed the "Assessing Understanding of Mathematics" tasks, they did tend to be a bit more challenging, with 38 percent being rated as high-demand tasks. However, the majority were still low demand, and within the category of numbers and operations, only 20 percent were rated as high demand. The researchers note, "The fact that about half of the teachers in our sample failed to include in their portfolio entries even a single task that was judged to be cognitively demanding can be viewed as disappointing because teachers were showcasing their best practice" (p. 520).

Although it can certainly be argued that this is only a single study from the United States and only within the area of mathematics and therefore should not be overgeneralized, other researchers have found similar patterns in the teaching of mathematics and other subject areas (Hiebert et al., 2005; Newmann, Bryk, & Nagaoka, 2001; Wagner,

2008). The more important point is that one cannot assume that a teacher's expectation for understanding will automatically indicate that that teacher will have a classroom dominated by deep-level processing strategies. The expectations are complementary but distinct. Furthermore, as the goal of understanding becomes more widely accepted, it is likely to receive only lip service by many. Its true realization will depend on the rigorous adoption of deep learning strategies as the norm rather than the exception in classrooms.

ENCOURAGING INDEPENDENCE VS. DEPENDENCE

We have seen that there is a clear link between expectations for learning, understanding, and use of deep learning strategies. Although each is distinctive and must become an explicit part of one's belief set, the action theories that evolve from their adoption are synergistic. If one truly embraces understanding in a full and complete sense, then learning will be the focus, and deep-level learning strategies will be important in achieving that goal. At the same time, we have seen that one can seek to foster learning without being focused on understanding. Likewise, one can embrace understanding and not necessarily be employing the deep learning strategies needed to foster it. The encouragement of student independence rather than dependence on us doesn't cleave as closely to the preceding expectations, however. Although in no way in conflict with the previous set of beliefs, fostering independence is most clearly a discrete goal.

Recall the study done by Colorado researchers (Flink et al., 1990) examining the effects of teaching done with a focus on learning versus a focus on performance/work. They found that it was the combination of a work orientation with controlling teaching behaviors—thus a promotion of dependence—that was connected with a decline in students' performance. However, controlling teaching—that is, teaching that is more directive and evaluative in nature—combined with a learning orientation didn't result in any such decline, but instead resulted in a very slight increase. Furthermore, the teachers in the pressured-to-perform group were rated as being more enthusiastic, interested, and competent by outside coders analyzing the videotapes. One explanation for this rating is that there exists a widely held societal belief that pressuring students to achieve, providing highly structured support and evaluations of work, is a generally effective teaching technique and serves to enhance students' motivation and learning. This perception has received pop culture cred in Amy Chua's (2011) international best seller, *Battle Hymn of the Tiger Mother.*

So if being directive and controlling may not impede learning and might even enhance it, at least when coupled with a learning orientation, why then shouldn't we embrace that as our action theory? The answer is twofold. First, there are potential downsides to instruction that is controlling and that fosters student dependence. Second, I will argue that the idea of fostering student independence exists as an important, worthwhile goal in its own right.

Some potential downsides to student dependence are

- Deterioration of problem-solving strategies (Dweck & Leggett, 1988)
- A focus on extrinsic motivation
- Diminished enjoyment of learning
- Lack of resilience when faced with difficulties and challenges
- Decreased creativity and motivation (Koestner, Ryan, Bernieri, & Holt, 1984)

When we talk about student independence as a goal of education, it is useful to define what we mean. Rose-Duckworth and Ramer (2008) offer the following definition: "Independent learners are internally motivated to be reflective, resourceful, and effective as they strive to accomplish worthwhile endeavors when working in isolation or with others—even when challenges arise, they persevere" (p. 2). Certainly that definition embodies many qualities that parents and teachers alike wish to see students exhibit. Some additional benefits of independence as a goal include

- Resilience in the face of difficultly
- Openness and willingness to accept challenges
- Greater motivation, engagement, ownership, and "drive" (Pink, 2009)
- Intrinsic motivation
- Interdependence and independence
- Development of a learning or mastery orientation in oneself
- Enhanced self-esteem and sense of efficacy (Kostelnik, Whiren, Soderman, Stein, & Gregory, 2002)
- Development of lifelong learners

DEVELOPING A GROWTH VS. A FIXED MINDSET

The final belief set that exerts a profound impact on the culture of a classroom, organization, or group concerns how individuals view intelligence, ability, and talent. Specifically, it concerns what psychologist Carol Dweck refers to as one's "mindset" and how that view shapes the way one approaches learning opportunities. Let's examine just what this mindset is, how it is developed, and how it ultimately shapes learning.

As a freshly minted researcher some thirty years ago, Dweck (2006) set out to try to understand how people cope with failure. In administering to subjects a series of increasingly challenging puzzle tasks that would ensure failure, Dweck thought she was investigating resilience in the face of adversity and how individuals cope with it. However, and to her amazement, she found that some of the individuals in the experiment didn't experience failure at all. It was not that they were successful in completing all of her puzzles—she had ensured that that would not happen—rather, it was that some people looked at the task as an opportunity to stretch their minds and learn to get better at solving puzzles. These individuals were energized by the challenge being presented and didn't register their incompletion of the task as a failure at all. What was going on?

Dweck has spent a career investigating just what was going on with these learners. In the process, she uncovered the power of one's beliefs about the nature of talent, ability, and intelligence to shape how one approaches challenges, deals with setbacks, and looks at opportunities. In study after study, Dweck has found that individuals who see talent, ability, and intelligence as fixed—that is, as something you either have or you don't—are much more likely to give up when they encounter difficulty and to judge their performance harshly. What is more, these same individuals actually shy away from opportunities to learn new things and develop their talents out of a fear that failure will expose them as not being as smart or talented as others might think they are. In contrast, her research has revealed that "in a growth mindset students understand that their talents and abilities can be developed through effort, good teaching and persistence. They don't necessarily think that everyone's the same or anyone can be Einstein, but they believe everyone can get smarter if they work at it" (Morehead, 2012).

In the summary of her research presented in the book *Mindset* (2006), Dweck shares how having a growth mindset allows athletes to bounce back from defeat and continue to develop their skills, CEOs to remain open to ideas and challenges from others, people in relationships to work through difficulties, artists to develop their talents, and so on. Regardless of the context, the thread running throughout these cases is a focus on ongoing growth and development through the situation and a lack of feeling threatened, beaten down, or counted out by difficulties and challenges. This facilitative approach to learning is markedly different from that of people who have a fixed mindset, who, by comparison, tend to gravitate toward situations that validate their perceptions of themselves and avoid those that will threaten it. But don't confuse a growth mindset with an overly optimistic view of the world or just telling yourself you can accomplish great things. Recent research on the brain demonstrates that the brain does in fact grow as a result of learning and that people really do get smarter and more skilled, and improve their natural talents as a result of their efforts. The growth mindset reflects the reality of learning.

Dweck has found in her surveys that roughly 80 percent of people can be classified as primarily one mindset or the other, with the numbers evenly split between the two mindsets. The remaining 20 percent cluster in the middle. A person's mindset can vary by context as well; for example, someone might see his artistic abilities as fixed but see his leadership abilities as continuously developing.

Mindsets are powerful shapers of our experience, but people aren't born with them. They develop through one's interactions with others, particularly in learning situations and in the feedback and input one receives in those situations. Our mindset develops through the subtle messages we encounter in classrooms and from teachers, mentors, and parents. To see how a belief in either a growth mindset or a fixed mindset can be shaped in a classroom, one need not look further than Dweck's personal experience growing up: "My 6th grade teacher seated us around the room in I.Q. order . . . , and although I did well in that metric it created this fear of falling from grace, of making the mistake of not being as perfect as I needed to be" (Morehead, 2012). Although the idea of seating by IQ might seem extreme, many schools today track or stream students by level or arrange seating clusters based on students' ability.

Teachers and parents also deliver implicit messages to learners about the nature of abilities through praise and feedback (Dweck, 2007). Comments like "You're so smart," "You're a really good reader," and "You're very talented," though intended to praise and motivate, send a message that one's abilities, such as they are, define you and that these are inherent in who you are as a person. If one accepts that one just is "a good reader," then one opens the door to also accepting that one "is just no good at math." In contrast, comments that focus on a person's efforts, something that is controllable, tend to aid in fostering a growth mindset: "You really worked hard at this, and it shows!" "That was really difficult, but you stuck to it and accomplished something." "I'm noticing that as you push yourself, your reading just keeps getting better and better."

It doesn't take much effort to envision how mindsets play out in the classroom, but what we may miss is the subtle ripple effects a mindset can have over the course of a student's education. Students with a fixed mindset may be more likely to shy away from challenges or may even refuse to have a go at new things. They may give up when they encounter difficulties, constantly ask for directions and reassurance to make sure they won't make a mistake, or even blame the assignment (or the teacher) for being unfair and unreasonable when they get a bad grade. In longitudinal studies, Dweck discovered that students with a fixed mindset were more likely to fall apart, experience stress, and have difficulty when transitioning to more demanding environments, such as when moving from elementary to middle school.

When fixed-mindset students get back an assignment with a bad grade, they are likely to wad it up or stash it away in an effort to hide the evidence of failure. But the ramifications may go even further than that. In a large sample of middle school students, Dweck and her colleagues found that after receiving a poor score on a test, "students with a fixed mindset say yes, they would seriously consider cheating." Dweck provides evidence that the effects are not just cultural or generational: "A TV show in Korea recreated our praise studies and they showed that children and adults who were told they were brilliant before a task cheated substantially more than those praised for their process, for their effort" (Morehead, 2012). In some instances, the ripples of failure can extend further. After repeated failure and frustrations, some students with a fixed mindset will simply accept defeat and label themselves: "I'm just no good at math." "I can't draw." "I've never been able to do sports."

In contrast, those with a growth mindset, while not necessarily relishing bad news or bad grades on assignments, are unlikely to be defeated by them. These students will ask for clarification, suggestions, and feedback for the next time, seeing learning as a continuous process. In this way, growth-mindset students are more likely to focus on the learning over the work, framing challenges and questions as opportunities to learn and develop their understanding. In these behaviors, one can see that such students embody all the sets of expectations we have discussed: a learning orientation, a focus on understanding, depth of processing, and independence as a learner. Taken together, these five sets of beliefs lay a foundation for teachers' expectations in the classroom and form the basis for the action theories that will guide their instructional practice.

EXPLORING AND DEVELOPING EXPECTATIONS

- Evaluate the five belief sets. Each belief set exists as a natural tension for educators, meaning that although we might intellectually embrace the more facilitative end of each continuum, we might sometimes find an individual expectation hard to implement. Where are the tensions in each belief set for you? What conditions give rise to that tension? How do you resolve or lessen those tensions?

- Collect data on students' questions. Pay attention to the questions your students ask over the next week. Are they about learning or about the work? At the end of each class period, make a quick estimate of how many were work related and how many were about the learning and ideas being studied. What does this information reveal about how your students are approaching the lessons and class activities you have designed? How might you push students to be more focused on the learning?

- Focus on the learning. Talk with your students about the distinction between work and learning. Tell them that because your goal is always to focus on the learning, they should let you know if they aren't clear where the learning is in a given assignment. Make sure you introduce new assignments and tasks by highlighting their purpose and what you want students to learn. Pay attention to your own language and the use of the words "work" and "learning."

- Identify key understandings. Developing true understanding of anything is a complex, ongoing endeavor. If you could pick only three things that you want your students to understand after their year with you, what would they be? Why are those three things worth understanding? What future learning does understanding these three things enable?

- Analyze understanding experiences. Identify the one unit you teach that you feel does the best job of developing students' understanding. Analyze that unit to pinpoint the elements that helped build students' understanding. Look at that unit through the four elements of the Teaching for Understanding framework. Do those elements easily map on to your plans? How can you take "what works" from this unit and apply it to other units you teach?

- Look for deep vs. surface learning in the classroom. Take a quick tour of classes at your school to understand the expectations students face in their classes. The goal is not to evaluate the teaching but to get a read on the expectations for students with regard to the depth of processing. Visit classrooms briefly to look for the level of processing students are being asked to do. You could shadow a student, visit a cross section of classes at your grade level, or look within a department.

- Look for deep vs. surface learning in assignments. Working either on your own or with colleagues, collect all the assignments given to students over the course of a week. Look through the assignments to determine the level of processing each requires of students. It is likely that an assignment might require both surface and deep levels of processing, but try to determine where the greater emphasis is in the assignment.

- Define independence and its supporting and inhibiting conditions. Identify the most independent students in your class. What actions do they exhibit that made you identify them as independent? Divide a sheet of paper into three columns and make a list of these actions in the center column. In the left-hand column, identify things that make it hard for other students to engage in these behaviors. What stands in the way? In the right-hand column, identify things you do or could do that would provide opportunities for or facilitate the behaviors you identified in the center column.

- Explore students' mindsets. Ask students to write their responses to the simple prompt: "When do you feel smart?" Answers that focus on appearing accomplished and the demonstration of prowess ("When I get an A+ on a test"; "When I'm the first one done with problem") tend to suggest a fixed mindset, whereas responses that focus on process and development over time ("When I've accomplished something I've set my mind to doing"; "When I solve a really difficult problem") tend to suggest a growth mindset.

- Develop students' growth mindsets. Numerous resources exist for exposing students to the idea of a growth mindset. For example, see "The Brain Is Like a Muscle" lesson plan (Ferlazzo, 2011). Typically such instruction focuses on how the brain literally grows as a result of learning. You might use a short article or video clip that describes this growth. Search YouTube for "how neurons work" to find such a clip. More elaborate teaching resources can be accessed at Carol Dweck's own Brainology program (http://www.mindsetworks.com).

CHAPTER 3

Language
Appreciating Its Subtle Yet Profound Power

lan•guage |ˈlaNGgwij| noun: The system of communication used by a community to negotiate shared meaning and build group coherence and understanding around ideas, behaviors, and actions. As a culture shaper, language helps us to direct attention and action. However, the words and structures that make up language not only convey an explicit surface meaning but also impart a set of deeper associations and connections that implicitly shape thought and influence behavior. This is the hidden power of language: its ability to subtly convey messages that shape our thinking, sense of self, and group affinity.

A few years ago, I was in Lisa Verkerk's fifth-grade classroom to shoot a video about the use of the thinking routine See-Think-Wonder. Lisa had used the routine throughout the year as part of a Visible Thinking pilot project and had volunteered to demonstrate the routine in action so that others could see how it worked. My focus at the time was squarely on the activity itself and making sure we were capturing the various aspects of the routine that would help other teachers learn how to use it.

Using a photograph of children in a school hall taken at the end of the nineteenth century in America, Lisa modeled and set up the routine easily and effectively for her students. After her quick whole-group introduction, students began using the routine to structure their conversations in pairs as they examined different sets of photographs taken of children from around the world. Each set highlighted some type of hardship or inequity a child might experience, forming a connection to the United Nations Convention on the Rights of the Child. As I moved around the room with the cameraman, I was pleased that we were capturing good footage of students talking and sharing their thinking at each step of the routine. We also got ample footage of Lisa as she interacted with the student pairs and discussed their thinking with them. It was a very smooth and productive class. I knew we would be able to use her lesson to showcase the See-Think-Wonder routine effectively, and I left Lisa's classroom pleased that we had captured on tape a well-executed lesson. It wasn't until we began the process of turning the raw footage of that hourlong lesson into a six-minute video that the true power of Lisa's teaching began to emerge, however.

Yes, the lesson was well planned. Lisa chose good content, prepared materials in advance, and had a clear sense of where the lesson was headed and how it connected to the development of larger understandings. However, a whole other layer of instruction emerged as we transcribed the lesson to make the edits. With the ability to watch and review each aspect of the lesson, I became more and more engrossed, not in the lesson itself, but in how Lisa's language served to effectively guide and direct the students' learning and thinking. Although I knew I was impressed with how easily Lisa managed her classroom and how involved her students were, it was only by carefully attending to Lisa's language that I was able to begin to understand how all these aspects of expert teaching took shape.

And that is the thing about language. It is at once ubiquitous, surrounding us constantly, yet we hardly take notice of its subtleties and power. Due to its constant presence, it is shaping our behavior, interactions, thinking, attention, and feelings in ways that we might not be consciously aware of. We can see this in reviewing how Lisa introduced the lesson. To model for her students, she holds up the photograph of schoolchildren from the late 1800s and asks, "What do we see?" Students identify several concrete things they notice in the picture, such as children, flags, desks, people standing, chalkboards, and so on. Lisa then asks the class, "What do you think might be going on with those children?" Students immediately begin to offer possibilities and alternatives: "They're singing," "Maybe they are in an assembly," "Maybe they are singing the national anthem because of the flag." Students put forth possibilities, add on to one another's ideas, and connect to things that had been seen. Good responses. Good engagement. Good collective sense making. But what did language have to do with this?

When Lisa asks, "What do *we* see?" her choice of the pronoun "we" sends a subtle signal to students that the group is working on this together and that the activity is a cooperative endeavor rather than a competitive one. Students respond accordingly and find it easy to build on others' ideas. When Lisa asks, "What do you think *might be* going on with those children?" her choice to use the words "might be" rather than "is" cues students that they are seeking alternatives, possibilities, and options rather than trying to definitely name the activity of the picture. Consequently, we notice students responding in this open manner. Furthermore, students build on one another's ideas without anyone complaining, "That was my idea!" Thus the spirit of cooperation and collective sense making continues.

Now, to be sure, these subtle language moves aren't working some instant magic, turning a group of unruly students into a cadre of engaged learners. Lisa's students were familiar with the See-Think-Wonder routine prior to this experience, so they knew what to expect. Furthermore, they are used to working cooperatively. However, I expect that in those previous instances, Lisa was making the same language moves. In fact, I'm sure of it. Having spent time in Lisa's classroom on other occasions, I know that these language moves were consistently deployed across any number of instructional occasions. What we see here is not a miraculous transformation occurring as the result of some small tweaks in the choice of words, but rather a very clear alignment between intention and word choice that over time has shown a powerful effect in nurturing a culture of thinking. Lisa desired to engage students in collective meaning making and wanted to encourage building on others' ideas; therefore, the choice of the pronoun "we" aligned with this intention. Likewise, Lisa sought to avoid early closure when students looked at the photographs and wanted to promote divergent ideas; her choice of the verb "might be" reinforced this goal. Thus our intentions, beliefs, and philosophy as teachers and leaders all give rise to our language (Baker, 2007). At the same time, our language helps to shape our intention and that of our students, making it worthwhile to examine our language and strive to harness its power.

Word choice isn't the only way in which language operates. Language is the medium of conversation and thus interactional. Therefore, we need to pay attention to these instances of language use as well. As students work in pairs, Lisa goes around the room, not to check that they are on task and doing their jobs but to join in conversation with the students in ways that will push the collective understanding forward. In the following transcript, Lisa joins with Hung-Joon and Alex, who are looking at photographs of children working at various menial and physical jobs:

HUNG-JOON: *(pointing)* I think he's also making carpet.

ALEX: Yeah. I'm pretty sure he is too. I think he's rolling something, like, paint, maybe.

LISA: There seem to be some threads?

ALEX: Yeah, threads. I've seen in a TV show that they had these wood things, and they put them on the carpet and they hit them down, and it had a pattern on the carpet.

LISA: Pushing the threads down into place?

ALEX: Yeah.

LISA: OK, you've said here *(pointing to sheet)*, "You see kids working." "Most kids making something." "The kids look like they're under the age of fifteen." Oh, that was a good observation. I would agree with you. They all look about your age or younger. *(reading from sheet)* "The kids look unhappy."

ALEX: Well, some of the kids look unhappy.

Notice how Lisa's interactional language conveys interest in the students' thinking and signals authentic engagement with the task at hand. Lisa engages with the students around what they are noticing in the picture and joins with them in the interpretations they are making. Feeding their own words back to them, she gives them a chance to elaborate on their initial thinking and modify it if necessary, as Alex does when he adds, "Well, *some* of the kids look unhappy." Although Lisa interjects and adds to the conversation, she is careful not to dominate it. She effortlessly weaves in feedback in a nonevaluative way by pointing out the good thinking they have done: "Oh, that was a good observation." Lisa continues the conversation by again returning to the students' own observations and interpretations that they have written down on the recording sheet:

LISA: *(reading from the sheet)* "I wonder if the kids are working for their families." If they weren't working for their families, who might they be working for? I should ask you probably, what did you mean? What did you mean when you were saying . . . ?

ALEX: Like, maybe their family was poor. And they needed money, and he was the strongest, the oldest out of the kids, so maybe he's going to work.

LISA: So to help his family.

ALEX: Yeah.

LISA: OK. Or were you thinking that maybe his father owned that business? And he was working *for* the family. Shall we maybe make that two different parts, then? So, "I wonder if the kids were working for their families, or to help their families?" Because I think that's what you're also saying there, too. *(Hung-Joon writes.)*

LISA: This is great. You've got lots out of these pictures.

In the preceding interaction, Lisa once again conveys the interest of a good listener by taking on what the students have written and asking clarifying questions about it: "What did you mean when you were saying . . . ?" It may seem strange to think of a "language of listening," but it is through our responsive language that we convey to others what we have heard and what questions, connections, or possibilities others have raised in us. Lisa's language makes it clear to Hung-Joon and Alex that she isn't checking their responses for correctness but engaging with them in coming to a deeper understanding. This process deepens in the next interchange:

LISA: Now the next one's really interesting; you've said, "I wonder if they're orphans." What made you say that?

ALEX: It looks like they don't have a home, and also him *(points)*. It kind of looks like he lives there maybe. But, I don't really know. But we just thought some of them looked a bit like they didn't have a place to go, to live. I mean, like these ones *(pointing)*—these five—they looked like they had somewhere to go. But these three people, they looked a bit . . .

LISA: And what do you think you were basing that idea on? When you're looking at them, what is it that you can see about them that made you think they have a home to go to?

ALEX AND HUNG-JOON: They have clothes.

LISA: Yeah, they've got nice clothes on, haven't they? They look fresh. They look clean. And are you thinking that it's something to do with the way these children look that makes you think that . . . ?

HUNG-JOON: They have dirty clothes on.

LISA: Yes, they look a little less well kept, maybe? OK, well that's an interesting idea. Do you think that if their parents were still alive, would they let them do this kind of work?

ALEX: If they were very poor, then probably, yes. But, if they had enough money, then probably, no.

In each interchange with Hung-Joon and Alex, Lisa asks a question that takes the students' thinking deeper, pushing them for the evidence and reasoning behind their responses. In doing so, she encourages the students' sense of agency as directors of their own understanding. In the first exchange, Alex says, "I don't really know." However, rather than shutting down because he doesn't know, Alex continues to think and to generate possibilities and eventually pieces together an explanation of how the clothing of a child might reflect the presence or absence of an economically stable home. Throughout, Lisa doesn't tell the students anything or directly give them new information. Instead she gently directs their attention and pushes them forward in their thinking. Note, as well, how Alex uses the pronoun "we" when talking, showing that he recognizes that the ideas on their recording sheet are jointly owned.

Clearly, there is much to attend to as we pour over the words, language, and discourse of the classroom. Whole fields of research exist in discourse analysis, conversational analysis, cognitive linguistics, linguistic anthropology, rhetorical criticism, conceptual metaphor theory, Whorfian theory, and so on. Each of these fields offers unique frameworks, perspectives, and tools for researchers seeking to understand how language operates. Drawing on this wealth of analytic frameworks at our disposal, while not cleaving too tightly to any one of them, we can distill a number of key "language moves" that can facilitate the creation of a culture of thinking in schools, classrooms, and organizations. These consist of

- The language of thinking
- The language of community
- The language of identity
- The language of initiative
- The language of mindfulness
- The language of praise and feedback
- The language of listening

We've already seen how a few of these language moves showed up in Lisa Verkerk's teaching. We'll now explore each in more depth, along with some of the underlying theory and relevant research, to better understand how each operates in context, what it might look and sound like, and how it can shape the learning of individuals and the group. When appropriate, I'll draw a contrast between a particular language move and its opposing manifestation in order to help us become aware of not only what language we should be using but also the types of language that can be counterproductive.

One aspect of language that I will be leaving out of our exploration for the time being is the role of classroom talk, discourse, and questioning. At first glance, it would seem that these are a natural fit for a discussion of language as a cultural force, and to a large extent that is true. However, after spending time analyzing classroom videos, audios, and transcripts to better understand how teacher questioning, student talk, and classroom discourse shape culture, I've come to see these components as better fitting under the cultural force of interactions and to some extent as being connected to time as well. Consequently, I'll save our exploration of these classroom features for later and link back to our discussions of language and time when I do so.

THE LANGUAGE OF THINKING

When I first began my study of classroom culture, I was sensitive to the fact that language played an important role in promoting students' thinking and that there was, in fact, a language of thinking. Art Costa (1991) had written an article titled "Do You Speak Cogitare?" in which he talked about the importance of teachers' having and using a rich vocabulary of thinking words. There certainly isn't any shortage of thinking words—that is to say, the words that describe what we do when we are thinking or the results of that thought. I'm sure that with just a little bit of effort, you can identify many words that describe the action of thinking in much more specific terms: inquire, generate, question, puzzle, theorize, imagine, explore, and so on. My colleagues Shari Tishman and David Perkins (1997) took my understanding of the vocabulary of thinking a step further in suggesting that the language of thinking could be sorted by those words defining processes (for example, justifying, examining, reasoning), products (for example, a hypothesis, a question, a judgment), and epistemic stances that reflect one's attitude toward a bit of knowledge or an idea (for example, agreement, doubt, confirmation). In my analysis of classroom language undertaken as part of my study of classroom culture, I used these three categories and added one more: states (for example, confusion, awe, wonderment) that describe one's mental status or state.

As you can see, if we take into account all these various categories of words, there is a very rich vocabulary of thinking at our disposal. But what does it matter? What does it buy our students or us? Of course we need a language of thinking to communicate with others—that is, to talk about our mental states and actions as well as the products. Perhaps more important for the classroom, the language of thinking helps to cue action and provide a means to regulate our activity. We don't just want students to "think" about the text they just read. We want them to consider alternative actions for the characters, make predictions about what might happen next, raise questions about the characters' motives, and so on. Being more specific in our use of language directs students to specific cognitive acts. This is particularly helpful to students who are struggling to engage mentally. Peter Johnston and colleagues (2011) point out that when we draw students' attention to causal processes, we create a "strategic narrative" that becomes available to the student and to others. That is a very powerful notion: using our language to cue, promote, and make visible the various strategic narratives of learning.

In addition, the language of thinking assists metacognition in both its reflective component as well as its planning aspects. When we think about our thinking, we are not only reviewing what we have done or the products of thinking we generated but also examining the processes we used or didn't use. Having a language of thinking helps us identify these processes for examination. Metacognition isn't merely backward looking, however. Metacognition involves ongoing monitoring and directing of one's thinking. This is easily seen in the process of reading. As we read, we monitor our comprehension, and when we notice it flagging, we slow down and direct ourselves to do something about it. For instance, we may reread and come to the conclusion that our problem is a lack of vocabulary, and choose to look up a particularly problematic word. Other times, we may stop and try to make a connection between what we are reading and other things we have learned in order to work through a tension or point of confusion. This kind of direction of mental processes is enabled by what is called our metastrategic knowledge—that is, our knowledge of the strategies for thinking at our disposal (Ritchhart, Hadar, & Turner, 2009; Zohar & David, 2008). Having a language to identify thinking processes is a requirement for us to call them into play. If we cannot name the processes, then we can't easily and effectively activate them.

So how do students develop a language of thinking? The main way is by being in situations where others are using the language. This is the way learners acquire any new language, whether it be a mother tongue, another indigenous language, the language associated with a particular discipline, or the highly specific language of a technical field such as medicine, law, or computer science. But we can be more proactive and targeted than just trying to use thinking language and provide an immersive experience for learners over time. Noticing when and where students are thinking and specifically naming the thinking being demonstrated is a key move that teachers, parents, and mentors can use to develop awareness, direct attention, and reinforce processes. Peter Johnston (2004) refers to this as "noticing and naming," a practice I often share with parents as a key way they can make their child's thinking visible. In the classroom, this practice makes the thinking visible to both the child demonstrating the thinking as well as to others. Paula Denton (2007) refers to this practice as using "reinforcing language" to draw students' attention to that which we want to highlight and acknowledge.

How does this work? It starts with us as teachers, or leaders of a group, being aware of what it is we want to highlight and reinforce. For instance, in Lisa Verkerk's class, the routine See-Think-Wonder asked students to look closely, notice details, observe carefully, make interpretations, build explanations, reason, generate alternatives, provide evidence, make connections, and raise questions. Getting students to do all of that is the key to making See-Think-Wonder a powerful learning opportunity. As students worked in their pairs, Lisa joined each group and looked to catch students engaged in any of these activities. In her interaction with Hung-Joon and Alex, Lisa commented, "OK, you've said here [pointing to sheet], 'You see kids working.' 'Most kids making something.' 'The kids look like they're under the age of fifteen.' Oh, that was a good observation." Rather than just telling the students they had done a good job, she used language to notice and name something specific that they had done well: observing.

Noticing and naming is a much more specific way of employing the language of thinking than just trying to use more thinking language. It is also likely to be more effective and productive in building a culture of thinking as well. Why? Because to notice something, it has to first be on our radar. Thus we need to identify what kinds of thinking we are looking for in a particular lesson. What kinds of thinking are needed to be successful? What do I want to reinforce? To what do I want to call students' attention? Becoming more aware of thinking ourselves and identifying what is needed to facilitate learning help us to be more responsive teachers. Then, having activated our instructional radar, we are more attuned and more likely to notice what we are looking for, as well as noticing when and where it might be missing. When it is missing, we can step in and scaffold the learning productively. When it is present, we can catch students in the act of thinking and make it visible to them. These interactions build a strategic narrative throughout the classroom or group, reinforce an expectation for thinking, and develop a sense of individual competence that can be empowering.

Of course we can use language to notice, name, and reinforce things other than thinking, and this is certainly appropriate. A teacher might be working on getting students to work cooperatively with others, to listen to directions, to take pride in their work. All of these behaviors can be noticed, named, and reinforced. The important thing is to be aware that whatever we are noticing and naming, we are reinforcing as well. Our actions are sending messages about what we value. If all that students hear us noticing is such behaviors as being quiet, paying attention, completing their work, not talking, or not making mistakes, they will learn that these are the behaviors that matter most. Instead, we want to make sure we are drawing students' attention to the behaviors and practices associated with a community of learners and a culture of thinking. In general, this will be tied to the processes that we want students to master and gain control over. Think of students as apprentices trying to develop a set of skills that allow for more and more independence. We want to draw attention to those skills and processes that are authentic to the learning task at hand and not just the completion of work.

THE LANGUAGE OF COMMUNITY

If you were to walk into Lisa Verkerk's classroom, you would have a clear sense of a learning community—a group of people dedicated to learning with and from each other in a cooperative rather than competitive manner. Listen closely to the talk of both students and the teacher, and you will find it is peppered with the use of words like "we," "our," and "us." Take the following example, when Lisa calls students back together after looking at their sets of pictures:

LISA: Folks, thank you very much for sitting so quietly. What we're going to do is: you're going to come with your table and your photograph, your recording sheet, and the "Rights of the Child" [handout]. Come with all three pieces of paper. Come and sit up at the board. And we're going to see what conclusions we can draw about the pictures, and you'll get a chance to look at each other's pictures as well.

At the outset, Lisa uses the pronoun "you" to praise students and then to indicate exactly what they are going to do. This allows students to recognize that there are directions for them to attend to individually. Next, she switches to the pronoun "we." This shift places the next endeavor as a collaborative one and signals to the students that Lisa is now a part of the new endeavor as well. Notice that she also makes explicit the thinking that students will be doing: "we're going to see what *conclusions* we can draw about the pictures."

In his research on the subtleties of language, James Pennebaker (2011a, 2011b) points out that our use of pronouns and other function words reveals a personal style and is psychologically very revealing of our motives, intent, connection with others, and even mental state. Pennebaker asserts that "warmer," more personal language tends to include fewer articles (*a, an, the*) and more pronouns. In addition, a speaker's use of pronouns tells listeners where the speaker is focusing his or her attention. In the previous transcript, we could see that Lisa placed her attention on the activity of the individual children in order to help direct and move them. She then switched to the pronoun "we," indicating that her attention was shifting to the group as a collective and to cue students to do the same. An important note here: almost all teachers find themselves using "we" on occasion to include themselves in the group's activity. However, there is a difference between "We're going to start chapter 6 tomorrow," indicating a shift in everyone's general activity, and "We're going to be identifying connections," which indicates that the teacher is thinking and learning with the group. In terms of creating a community of learners, the "we" must include the teacher not only as the director of activity but also as a participant in the learning processes of that activity.

Although we tend to think that our verbal and written communication is dominated by content words—the nouns, verbs, adjectives, and adverbs that help us express ideas—Pennebaker points out that function words are in fact used at a much higher rate (around 30 percent of our speech and writing). Significantly, they are even processed differently in the brain than are content words. Research on brain injuries has shown that Broca's area in the frontal lobe, the same area that controls our social skills, is tied to processing function words. This makes sense, as these words rely on social connections and shared understandings, while being indicators of our relationships and relatedness. When a speaker refers to "this" or "that," "he" or "she," the listener has to have a shared frame of reference or connection in order to make sense of what the speaker is saying.

In his book *The Secret Life of Pronouns*, Pennebaker (2011a) identifies many ways that pronouns reveal our connectedness to others. For instance, he has found that in reviewing email exchanges, the person with less power is apt to use the pronoun "I" with greater frequency than the more powerful individual in the relationship. In speed dating, he found that when two people were attracted to one another, they tended to mirror one another's use of pronouns. All fascinating stuff, the kind of stuff that has made Pennebaker quite popular in the media, but the question arises: Does our language merely reveal what already exists—that is, power dynamics or affinity—or is it shaping and transforming situations?

My answer to this question is that pronoun usage is a two-way street, as are all of the language moves we are discussing in this chapter. Our use of language does reveal our priorities, beliefs, intentions, and so on. Therefore, we should examine it to see if it is revealing what we want. To the extent that it isn't, we can make shifts in our usage. Will students notice that we are using more inclusive and community-oriented language? Pennebaker states that use of function words is almost impossible to grasp in listening to everyday speech. Consequently his work involves analyzing transcripts. He asserts that it is the patterns over time that are revealing. I would assert that group culture is also revealed by the patterns that emerge over time.

One last issue with pronouns before we leave the topic: we also use pronouns to refer to those outside the classroom. How often have you found yourself asking students, "What do you think *they* are getting at in question number 7?" or "What kind of answer are *they* looking for in this problem?" The potentially problematic aspect of this use of pronouns is that it brings an anonymous outsider into the classroom community in a way that disconnects students from their learning. It places control of learning outside the classroom, the teacher, and the student. I think it would be more productive to place the focus back on the learner: "What do you think is the main idea behind this question?" "What kind of answer do you think fits this problem?"

Nick Fiori (2007) sees this as a particular problem in mathematics classrooms because it situates authority outside the classroom. Fiori protests, "It can't be healthy for a subject to be controlled by a bunch of nameless cronies" (p. 696). Without giving students a reference for who the people are to whom we are referring, there is no possibility for connection. It is harder to build an affinity with the discipline of study if one sits outside it and doesn't even know the major figures who have contributed to it. Here we can build community, not by using pronouns without a proper reference, but by making connections to real people and their contributions.

THE LANGUAGE OF IDENTITY

In his book *Making Learning Whole*, David Perkins (2009) identifies a chief problem in much of school learning: our tendency to teach a subject in terms of its elements, pieces, topics, and so on rather than engaging students in authentic activities such that we let them "play the whole game" of history, math, science, or whatever subject we might be teaching. Perkins calls this tendency "aboutitis." We teach *about* the subject rather than engaging students as members of it. Think back to your own education. How much aboutitis did you encounter in the classes you took? Probably a fair amount. Unfortunately, the situation isn't much better today (see chapter 1). As standardized tests become the de facto measure of learning, we see an increasingly fractured curriculum focused on the bits of the subject that get tested. Even when better standards and curriculum guidelines are put forth, it seems inevitable that some bureaucrat somewhere will chop them up into test-sized bites that will make them fit into discrete lessons and formal assessments.

Despite these obstacles, I have found expert teachers around the world who valiantly work against the disease of aboutitis. These teachers help their students come to see themselves not as outsiders looking in on a subject but as members of it. They help their students not only to see the whole game, as Perkins describes it, but also to play the game. This means that rather than learning about history, they become historians; rather than learning about science, they become scientists; rather than learning about literary criticism, they become literary critics; and so on. These culture-of-thinking classrooms have an authentic feel to them, and the learning is palpable.

The language of identity is one tool for avoiding aboutitis and helping students come to see themselves as members of a field. For decades, those involved in literacy education have embraced the language of identity and have come to refer easily to students as readers, writers, authors, poets, and so on as a matter of course. This language helps students assume these roles, which goes well beyond merely having a certain knowledge base at one's disposal to actually engaging in the thinking and key processes that are important in these areas. Students are playing the whole game, even if at times it is a junior version. In this way, using the language of identity in the classroom signals to students that they need to activate certain applicable ways of thinking.

Consider these two alternative ways of framing an identical, hands-on, practical lesson in science: (1) "Today we are going to learn about chemical reactions" and (2) "Today as scientists we are going to be investigating how chemicals react under various circumstances." Does one framing feel more passive to you as a prospective learner? Does one of the framings prompt a more active response and engage a different set of mental processes? Does one framing feel more exciting than the other to you? What roles do you imagine for both the teacher and student under each framing? If we assume that framing and setting up a lesson are important aspects of effective teaching, I would suggest that the second framing does a better job.

Once again, the use of language, in this case the language of identity, doesn't work magic. Students won't suddenly become mathematicians merely because we call them that one day. However, our language both conveys intention and cues behavior. When we recognize that true understanding of a discipline involves learning its processes and ways of thinking as well as its content knowledge, then we naturally create opportunities for developing those abilities. Likewise, we naturally want to see our students assume these roles, and our language follows suit. Students then come to expect that a large part of their learning in the subject area involves acquiring the thinking abilities and processes of the discipline, not just learning about it for the test.

In using the language of identity, we are not only placing students in a specific role with an attendant set of behaviors and ways of operating but also tacitly rejecting other roles. Specifically, we are rejecting the role of teacher as deliverer of information and student as passive receiver. Breaking this paradigm can be a challenge, and many students may want to rebel and demand that teachers "teach correctly" or spoon-feed them the information for exams. However, a necessary part of breaking the paradigm is helping students envision and take on a new role. This includes not only discipline-based roles (scientists, artists, historians, and so on) but also process-based roles (thinkers, researchers, data collectors, analysts, commentators, advocates, inventors, and the like).

THE LANGUAGE OF INITIATIVE

In chapter 1, we explored the changing economic, social, and political landscape of our society and how those changes are having an impact on what is needed and expected from schools. In contemplating the skills and dispositions required for success in the twenty-first century, we saw that the need for flexible, independent learners able to demonstrate initiative and innovation emerged as a common demand across multiple constituencies. Reed Larson (2000), an expert in adolescent development, has expressed this need for initiative succinctly: "Individuals will need the capacity to exert cumulative effort over time to reinvent themselves, reshape their environments, and engage in other planful undertakings. A generation of bored and challenge-avoidant young adults is not going to be prepared to deal with the mounting complexity of life and take on the emerging challenges of the 21st century" (p. 171).

If we accept that initiative is indeed an important goal for education in the twenty-first century, then we need to know what actually develops when we foster initiative. A key aspect of initiative, or what researchers in sociology and psychology sometimes refer to as "agency," is the ability to make choices and direct activity based on one's own resourcefulness and enterprise. This entails thinking about the world not as something that unfolds separate and apart from us but as a field of action that we can potentially direct and influence. As a person develops initiative, she comes to see the world as responsive to her actions. This direction and influence involves identifying possible actions, weighing their potential, directing attention, understanding causal relationships, and setting goals, among other things. In short, it demands learning to be strategic and planful. As Peter Johnston (2004) elaborates when discussing the importance of students' having a strong sense of personal agency, "If nothing else, children should leave school with a sense that if they act, and act strategically, they can accomplish their goals" (p. 29).

How does language relate to the development of initiative? In our interactions and questioning of learners, adults—whether leaders, teachers, or mentors—can use language to direct a learner's attention. In this way, teachers help students identify, weigh, and plan potential courses of action. Our language can draw students' attention to the strategies being deployed and their consequences, whether students are immediately aware of them or not. Simple queries, such as "Tell me what you just did," "What's your plan for tackling this?" and "Where will you go next?" ask learners to identify strategies and be explicit about them. Lisa Verkerk's question, "What do you think you were basing that idea on?" or the frequently used "What makes you say that?" asks students to identify their reasoning and make their thinking visible. In doing so, students come to see that ideas don't merely pop into one's head but are under one's control and influence and act to shape one's reasoning. Likewise, adults can use language to frame situations and make explicit causal relationships and possible contingencies. Lisa did this when she asked Alex and Hung-Joon, "Do you think that if their parents were still alive, would they let them do this kind of work?" By framing this question as a hypothetical, Lisa shows the students how to examine a set of conditions that might influence outcomes.

In their study of adolescents' participation in community organizations, linguists McLaughlin, Irby, and Langman (1994) looked at how the language of the adolescents changed over the course of their involvement in such groups. Research in this context was particularly instructive regarding the development of initiative because these community organizations were groups that the youth themselves identified as being attractive and effective for them personally. These groups, such as art or drama groups, Boys and Girls Clubs, and sports teams, provided an environment in which the motivation, direction, activities, and goals came primarily from the participating adolescents and not the adult mentors. These real-world contexts, in which participation was voluntary and activity was self-directed, created venues in which one might expect to see initiative develop, and indeed it did. The research showed that within three to four weeks of participation, students' language shifted dramatically. It moved from being largely unfocused, passive, defensive, and sometimes defeatist to being more planful, strategic, and initiative based. For Heath (1999), these shifts in language are a reflection of what students learned from their participation and picked up from their adult mentors. Let's examine these changes in more depth.

First, students began to use hypotheticals, statements such as "If we do it this way, then . . ." or "Well, let's imagine that is true . . . what will happen then?" or "If we spend money on food, how much will that leave us for buying the supplies we need?" This language does two things: it clearly situates the individuals and the group as active agents, and it deals with likely outcomes that might occur as a result of their actions. Both of these are keys to initiative. A second language shift that Heath (1999) identified was an increased use of modals—that is, "would," "could," or "should" statements: "Could we do this?" "Would this work?" "Should we be thinking about it another way?" These modals link to identifying options for consideration as well as weighing those options. This modal language reflects the development of contingency thinking.

The other two language shifts identified relate to students' awareness of being participants both in a group and within the larger world. Specifically, students began to question other members to get clarity from them. This clarification allowed them to fully understand consequences of actions and to weigh those consequences. "OK, so you mean if we do this, we then . . . ?" Finally, students' language use began to reflect the perspectives and language of others, such as board members, business leaders, government officials, reporters, or other influential entities. "If we rent the hall, will the city require us to get a permit?"

Of course, the opportunities for student initiative were strong in these groups, and that context can account for students' shift in language. However, one would have to ask from whom the students learned such language. Heath (1999) noticed that both leaders and older members of the group regularly used the language of initiative, thus providing new members the opportunity to internalize it. Larson (2000) highlights the importance of students' ongoing, dynamic development of language: "Participants did not merely acquire a language, they learned to adapt and use it generatively . . . New participants appeared to undergo a paradigm shift in their way of thinking, reflecting qualitative developmental change" (p. 178). He sums up this process appropriately by stating, "They [students] ingested a new mode of action" (p. 178).

One way to know that we are using the language of initiative and independence, rather than rescuing students and furthering their dependence on us, is to ask ourselves, "Who is doing the thinking?" Reviewing the snippets of language from Lisa's class, we see that in each instance, Lisa frames her contributions to ensure that students are doing the thinking. Our goal as educators, parents, and mentors is to encourage those whom we are trying to nurture to be the thinkers and to see themselves as thinkers, planners, and doers.

THE LANGUAGE OF MINDFULNESS

Can language cause us to be more aware, mindful, and flexible? A long line of research suggests that it can. The amazing thing is that this language is subtle in its presence but powerful in its impact on our thinking. Specifically, language that allows for the possibility of interpretation and that opens the door to even a small bit of ambiguity has the power to keep the mind in an open state, avoiding early closure, pursuing possibilities, and listening to information presented by others. When Lisa Verkerk was setting up her lesson, she asked simply, "What might be going on in this picture?" The use of the word "might," what is called conditional language, sends the mind a subtle clue that definitive answers aren't warranted, but speculation is. As a result, Lisa's students offered multiple interpretations of the picture rather than coming to an early closure. Alternatively, Lisa could have asked, "What is going on in this picture?" The use of the word "is," what is called absolute language, sends a different message about what is expected. Now one must find the correct interpretation.

Understanding of this power of conditional words to keep the mind open and flexible emerged more than two decades ago in the groundbreaking research of Ellen Langer (1989) on mindfulness. Mindfulness is defined as an open, flexible state in which new categories and possibilities can more easily be created. In her early research, Langer sought to identify what types of environmental cues might cause someone to remain more open and mindful versus those that might produce more rote, fixed, and mindless kinds of behavior. In an early study (Langer & Piper, 1987), she set up an experiment in which subjects casually encounter a rubber object in a room where they are working with an experimenter. The experimenter comments to some subjects that the object before them *could* be a dog's chew toy (conditional language) and to others that this *is* a dog's chew toy (absolute language). The experimenter then sets the object aside and begins to interview the subjects, writing down their responses with a pencil. At some point, the experimenter claims that she has made a mistake and needs to erase what she has written. When this happened, subjects who heard the conditional language (this might be a dog's chew toy) were much more likely than their counterparts to consider using the rubber object as an eraser. By hearing that the object could be a dog's chew toy, the participants were able to remain mentally open and consider using the object in a new way once the conditions changed. In contrast, labeling the object definitively tended to produce cognitive closure.

Nice experiment, but do these effects of conditional and absolute language play out in other contexts? In my own work with Langer (Ritchhart & Langer, 1997), we designed an experiment to teach an invented mathematical concept and procedure called "pairwise" to university students. The procedure didn't involve more than the use of basic operations with integers. Some of the students were introduced to the new procedure by hearing the statement, "One way to solve a pairwise equation is . . ." (conditional language) and then shown the designed method. Another group was told, "This is how you solve a pairwise equation" (absolute language), and the same method was shown. In a posttest, students who received the conditional instruction were more accurate in solving pairwise problems, used more workable methods likely to yield accurate results, were more able to produce accurate workable alternative methods for solving the problems, and were less likely to misapply the pairwise procedure in circumstances where it didn't apply. In this scenario of learning a new bit of mathematics, we theorized that participants receiving instruction using absolute language were more likely to turn off their prior knowledge and frame their task as trying to memorize a procedure that might not have made sense. They became passive recipients of information. In contrast, the conditional language allowed students to integrate their prior knowledge and seek to understand the mathematics rather than simply try to learn a procedure.

Another finding from research with implications for the classroom comes from my colleague Daniel Wilson's study of team learning in the context of adventure racing (2007). Wilson studied how teams negotiated meaning and dealt with uncertainty as they navigated their way through an unfamiliar course spanning some four hundred miles. These teams, consisting of both men and women athletes skilled in orienteering, frequently found themselves lost and had to quickly get themselves "unlost" in order to progress. Reviewing the teams' language in these situations, Wilson found that the most successful teams, the top finishers, were twice as likely to use conditional language when they were lost than were those teams finishing in the bottom of the pack.

What does this language sound like? A winning team member might say something like, "I think maybe we have been here before," whereas a member of a lower-performing team might express that same sentiment in absolute language: "We've been here before." Imagine someone speaking these two sets of words to you. The conditional language almost invites others into the conversation to offer their opinion, and thus the group begins to pool information and make sense of the situation. In contrast, the absolute language sounds defensive, aggressive, and dogmatic. Offering your opinion now feels more like calling the speaker out and inviting a confrontation. Now imagine that you are tired from lack of sleep and physically weary from exertion. It is easy to see that by using absolute language, these teams were also depriving themselves of the opportunity to pool information and make the best choices.

Now visualize yourself in a classroom, and a fellow student makes an absolute statement with which you disagree. His or her words might have the effect of shutting down conversation. In contrast, when someone expresses an idea in conditional language, it can be much easier to add your thoughts to the conversation. In fact, in the Worldwide Cultures of Thinking Project, we see this shift naturally happening in students' language as teachers begin to focus on developing students as thinkers and make their thinking visible. Students quickly pick up on the fact that teachers don't want them trying to guess correct answers but want them instead to make meaning of complex issues collectively and to build on others' ideas. As teachers model the use of conditional language, students begin to adopt the use of conditional language as well.

At this point, you might be thinking to yourself, "Yes, but some things are absolute. There are right and wrongs." This is true, though perhaps not as true as we sometimes suppose. There usually are many ways to solve problems rather than just one way, for instance. In the case of the adventure racers, some paths were right and some were wrong. Sometimes the team had in fact been to that place before. The important point here is that the teams using conditional language were actually better at finding those right answers and getting themselves unlost because they did a better job of pooling information and weighing it appropriately to determine a response. Conditional language is not about forgoing answers; it is about forgoing early closure to the process of finding answers. Researchers have found that the use of conditional language encourages people to think more critically rather than just accept what they are being told (Herrenkohl & Guerra, 1998; Ironside, 2006).

THE LANGUAGE OF PRAISE AND FEEDBACK

Step into almost any classroom, and you are likely to hear words of praise regularly peppering the speech of teachers: "good job," "well done," "brilliant," "exactly right," "you got it," "perfect," "excellent." However, such words may not be accomplishing what we think. As researchers Harris and Rosenthal (1985) point out, "This kind of feedback is not informative to the student; consequently, it may have no impact on the child beyond the realization that he or she got the answer right or wrong" (p. 377). Others go much further, saying that such words can have a detrimental effect on learning. Barbara Larrivee (2002) asserts, "Teacher praise discourages freedom of expression, creates dependency on the teacher, and promotes conformity by conditioning students to measure their worth by their ability to please others" (p. 77). Of course, those who expect that classrooms should be well managed and orderly see praise as an effective control mechanism for just these reasons (Lampi, Fenty, & Beaunae, 2005).

Carol Dweck (2007) suggests that "praise is intricately connected to how students view their intelligence" (p. 34), and therefore praise of one's abilities may produce a burst of pride but ultimately be detrimental to learning. In numerous studies, she has found that when praise is targeted toward the person, as in "You're so clever" or "You're good at this," it may actually encourage a fixed view of intelligence rather than a growth mindset (see chapter 2). Dweck suggests that praise which draws attention to a person's efforts and actions, as in "You worked really hard" or "I can see you have pushed yourself," is more likely to encourage ongoing learning, risk taking, and the embracing of challenge. Consequently, educators need to carefully consider what they are praising and their reasons for praising.

Praise is not feedback, as Harris and Rosenthal note. This is in part due to the lack of information praise typically conveys. "Good job" hardly gives one much to go on. To truly be considered feedback, our words have to take on an instructional role, providing the learner with information related directly to the learning task at hand (Hattie & Timperley, 2007). Furthermore, this information has to be received and actionable, guiding future learning. This suggests that our comments should identify what has been done well as much as what still needs improvement and then give guidance in helping the student achieve that improvement. If our words don't achieve this, then our comments are probably best understood as evaluation rather than feedback.

Certainly, good feedback is situational and highly dependent on both the learner and the task at hand. Nonetheless, some general strategies in terms of shaping a language of feedback can be distilled from the research (Black & Wiliam, 2002; Dangel & Durden,

2010; Hattie, 2009; Hattie & Timperley, 2007). For instance, it is important for the language to be specific, descriptive, and informative so that it tells learners about what they did correctly and should continue to do in the future as much as indicating what they might do differently. Lisa's words to students Andrea and Miran after they had conducted their See-Think-Wonder routine convey these qualities as she comments, "You've done a really good job of looking at those pictures. I can see you've really tried to find an explanation for what's going on. And I really like the way that you used what you already know, things that you've already seen, maybe on television or news reports."

Lisa then directs their attention to the next task, again highlighting the thinking to be done: "So, now you can turn over to the other side, and you can find out what's going on with these pictures. And then, when you know that, you can carry on down here [points to the lower half of the recording sheet] and look at the rights, yes? And see what rights might be being respected and which ones might be being neglected. And what makes you say that?"

Notice that Lisa begins with global praise to assure the students, "You've done a really good job," but then quickly moves to specifics. She notices and names the thinking they did ("tried to find an explanation") and then goes on to name several other specific actions they undertook ("[using] what you already know"). Lisa then connects what the students have done already to the next learning task: "So, now you can turn over to the other side . . ." All of this is offered in a sincere tone and demonstrates that Lisa has really attended to what the students have been doing and where they need to go next in their learning.

THE LANGUAGE OF LISTENING

I recently gave a talk sponsored by a group of graduate students at a university in Australia. The leader of this group was a very energetic young woman completely invested in promoting greater thoughtfulness in schools. Her dedication and hard work culminated in a very rich conference experience for local educators and teachers in training. After my talk, which was very interactive in nature, she approached me with a somewhat quizzical smile on her face and asked, "I loved what you had to say, but what really struck me was how you listened to people. I find that so hard to do when I am teaching. How do you do it?"

I think lots of new teachers, and perhaps even some experienced ones, struggle with learning to listen, yet listening is one of the powerful ways we show respect for and interest in our people's thinking. As Sue Patton Thoele has said, "Deep listening is miraculous for both listener and speaker. When someone receives us with open-hearted, non-judging, intensely interested listening, our spirits expand" (quoted in Rao, 2010, p. 24). Of course, listening starts with genuine interest in the other. This means we have to pause our own talk and give students time and space to air their thoughts. At the same time, there are specific skills and actions we can learn. There is, in fact, a language of listening we can use to demonstrate our interest.

Stephen Covey made famous the expression "Seek first to understand, then to be understood" in his articulation of important habits for us all to cultivate in ourselves. This sentiment captures a common linguistic move made by listeners: clarification. We witnessed this when Lisa probed Alex and Hung-Joon about their statement, "I wonder if the kids are working for their families." Good listeners ask authentic questions to clarify points, unearth any assumptions they may be bringing to the situation, and be sure of the speaker's intent. To verify their understanding, good listeners may paraphrase what speakers have said and ask speakers to verify that they have correctly represented their ideas.

Once clarity is achieved, a whole host of moves are possible depending on the context and goals. For instance, a teacher or leader may want to connect what was said to other points people have made or to other ideas being discussed. These connections help to thread various ideas together and to facilitate a conversation rather than just a collection of disconnected statements from various speakers. Threading is important for anyone in the role of facilitating learning in groups, as it helps build coherence and move the agenda of learning forward. This threading requires us to listen for the expression of key ideas, questions, or issues that might not yet be well formed in the speaker's mind. We highlight these ideas for the group by noticing and naming them, thus bringing them forward for further discussion.

Consequently, it is through our listening that we facilitate conversation. We'll be exploring classroom conversation and discourse more when we explore the cultural force of interactions, but for now it is useful to highlight a couple more language moves associated with listening that help bring about discussion. One of those moves is to challenge ideas being presented, not in terms of correctness or accuracy, but in the exploratory sense, as in a Socratic dialogue: "How do you think that idea would play out in another context?" "Let's follow that line of thinking; what's the action that might follow from it?" In addition, we can advance the discussion further by inviting others in: "Joaquin, what do you think about what Marcy just said?" "Kate, how does Clinton's idea connect with yours?" Questions such as these don't come from some preplanned lesson; they emerge from our careful listening to students.

LEVERAGING LANGUAGE

In this chapter, we have looked at many of the languages that operate to support learning and build a culture of thinking. Understanding how to leverage and utilize these languages is useful for teachers in the classroom, principals leading a school, leaders of an organization, or adults working with others in groups. However, the seven languages we have looked at are by no means the only ones operating in classrooms and organizations. There is also the language of trust (Maslansky, West, DeMoss, & Saylor, 2010), which focuses on how one builds rapport and connection with others to assist in working toward shared goals. There is the language of direction, with which we direct students' activity (Chilcoat & Stahl, 1986; Denton, 2007). This language focuses on being precise, clear, and succinct so that we are understood. There is the language of responsibility, which, like the language of initiative, places us at the center of our actions and locates us as agents rather than victims (Kegan & Lahey, 2001). There is the language of framing, which deals with the way teachers or leaders frame a task, thus affecting the way recipients are likely to approach it (Lemov, 2010). There is the language of metaphors, which both reveals and shapes our thinking about issues, events, concepts, and problems (Lakoff & Johnson, 1980). And we haven't even touched on body language, much less the more interactive use of language in creating discourse and talk in the classroom. This is something we will take up in chapter 8.

This collection of possible language moves could certainly be expanded. It is a fascinating area of study precisely because language is so ubiquitous, shaping virtually all our interactions with others. We must examine our use of language to see if we are conveying the sentiments and intentions we truly desire. Sometimes simple adjustments to our language are easy to make, such as beginning to notice and name thinking. Other times it can be harder, as in learning to limit or avoid global praise statements that don't offer students much, or learning to use a language of listening when we are focused on getting through a lesson and covering specific content. In addition, monitoring our language can be difficult to do in real time. Many of our patterns of speech are so ingrained in us that we hardly notice them. Becoming more aware of our language and striving to align it with our intentions is the first step.

BECOMING PROFICIENT USERS OF THE LANGUAGES OF THE CLASSROOM

- Become more aware of the language moves you are currently making. You might do this by audiotaping a lesson or two and then listening to it for specific language moves. What kinds of pronouns do you use? Are you using a language of thinking? Do you use conditional language to facilitate discussion? And so on. Alternatively, invite a trusted colleague or colleagues into your classroom to act as scribes. Select no more than two language moves on which to have them focus to avoid overwhelming them.

- Listen to your students. Do they make contributions using conditional or absolute language? If they do use absolute language, reframe those contributions in conditional terms. For instance, if a student says, "I think the answer is X," you might reframe it by saying, "Jacqui thinks the answer might be X. What other possibilities do we want to consider?"

- When planning a lesson, list the key thinking moves you want students to make. (See chapter 1 for a description of some different types of thinking). Read over this list just before the start of the lesson to prime your naming and noticing of these types of thinking.

- Practice the language of praise and feedback in writing. Begin your written comments by naming specific things the student has done well. Mention no more than two things that the student might work on as next steps in the process. End your comments with another positive statement on the growth, progress, or effort you have noticed or are looking forward to seeing.

- To become a better listener, try to avoid making assumptions about what others are saying or presuming you understand their intent. Work on asking at least one clarifying question before commenting or moving the discussion further. If nothing else comes to mind, the question "What makes you say that?" is a good way to learn more about the speaker's ideas and their formation.

- To check if you are nurturing initiative versus developing dependence, ask yourself, "Who is doing the thinking here?" as you interact with students. If you find yourself doing much of the thinking, acknowledge it by saying something like, "I'm sorry. It feels to me that I am doing most of the thinking here, and that means I'm the one learning. I want you to be learning. Let me step back and give you a chance to tell me what you are thinking/planning/feeling."

- Make a list of the various roles you want students to step into in your classroom. Your list might begin with discipline-related roles, such as scientist, writer, historian, or artist. From there, identify the subroles students might undertake, such as editor, data collector, analyst, critic, and so on. Post this list in the room to remind you to use the language of identity as you are framing lessons and activities.

CHAPTER 4

Time
Learning to Be Its Master Rather Than Its Victim

time |tīm| noun: The "containers," consisting of measurable periods, that we allocate, assign, or use to accomplish tasks of our choosing. • An entity through which we recall, sequence, and make sense of our experience. • A qualitative dimension through which our experiences flow, allowing us to speak of good times, time dragging by, losing track of time, and so on in order to mark its value. As a culture shaper, all of these conceptions of time are in play. Our allocations of periods of time reflect our values. Our sequencing of events, construction of moments, and reflections on actions allow us to scaffold and draw a connecting thread through learning occasions to create a unity. Finally, our ability to generate, sustain, and capitalize on periods of total engagement allows us to create the energy needed for learning and thinking.

It's the third week of school, just past those hectic first days of everyone adapting to a new schedule, new teachers, new students, and a new school year. There is still some settling in to do as students learn the routines of a different set of teachers and tackle the demands of fresh assignments. Despite all the novelty, Nathan Armstrong's grade 12 class is buzzing with a sense of direction and collective involvement. Although all good teachers work hard to establish an atmosphere conducive to learning from the first days (Ritchhart, 2002), I am struck by how Nathan has directly confronted some of the unique obstacles that stand in his way as a year 12 teacher through his and his students' use of time.

For Nathan's students, as for grade 12 students throughout Australia, the senior year is all about preparation for the high-stakes tests they will take at the end of the school year (Brundrett, 2010). In this year, the pressure is on for students and teachers alike. There is no coasting, hanging back, or taking it easy for anybody. Students know that their ability to enroll in a specific course of study at a university will be determined by their scores on these tests. At the same time, teachers know that students, parents, and administrators will judge their effectiveness as teachers by the kinds of scores their students garner. And yet this pressure to perform, to score better than one's peers on these highly competitive exams, to cram for the tests, and to fill students up with all they need to know seems to have been replaced by a relaxed yet focused atmosphere in Nathan Armstrong's classroom. How did Nathan accomplish this? How did he think about time differently to relieve the pressure on both himself and his students? Observing him for a day, I get some answers.

Before the start of third period, Nathan has cued up a YouTube video of the artist Pink singing "Glitter in the Air" at the 2010 Grammy Awards. It is playing softly in the background from the interactive whiteboard as students enter. Nathan circulates around the room passing out materials for the lesson, simultaneously greeting students as they trickle into the room. I notice that he follows up each greeting with a question: with one student he inquires about her weekend, with another his new music discoveries, and with yet another her sports activities. When students notice the Pink video playing, Nathan asks, "Did you watch it?" Nathan informed me previously that every Friday he sends a link to a video for students to watch in preparation for Monday's class. I'm wondering how Nathan will make the connection between "Glitter in the Air" and *Cosi*, an

Australian play by Louis Nowra about a bunch of patients at a mental hospital putting on Mozart's *Cosi fan tutti* that the class has read independently and is now analyzing.

Nathan's interactions with students are not separate from his preparation for class; they are part of it, laying the groundwork for the participatory, empathetic community he is working to create. This is more than just making good use of time and being efficient, however. It is putting first things first. Attending to the building of relationships with students is fundamental to good teaching, and it is important to do this at the start. Teachers can't wait till later to build those connections; they may have lost students by then. Nathan is also creating a qualitative experience of time for his students that allows them to transition from their other classes, connect to him and to each other, and to focus on the new class that is about to start. Through his seemingly simple actions, Nathan signals that he is fully present. Students see the preparation and are acknowledged as individuals. He is there. They are there. Learning is expected.

The classroom itself is already adorned with the students' efforts from previous classes. The windows are covered with quotes from the book clustered around images of the characters from the play. On one wall is a poster of Maya Angelou with her words, "I've learned that people will forget what you said, people will forget what you did, but people will never forget how you made them feel." The desks are arranged in clusters of six to accommodate the learning teams that Nathan created the first week. As students enter, they quickly find a seat with their team and settle in. The team seating arrangement is just one indicator of the collaborative approach to learning that will unfold in Nathan's class throughout the year. It is also a time-saving device, as students know where to sit when they enter and are aware of how they will be working, as teams, without need for added direction from Nathan. The teams also provide a vehicle for communicating to students who might be absent. Students can check in with teammates, and teammates take on the responsibility of collecting handouts and information for absent team members. As the last student enters the room, Nathan calls out, "Isaac, do you mind closing the door?" And with that Nathan begins the class with a quick review, not of *Cosi*, but of the role of the teacher and the student. He flashes an assortment of images on the screen. First up is an image of a teacher standing at the front of the room before a large class. "What's this an example of?" Nathan asks as he moves among the students. "Lecturing," a student responds. Nathan quickly interjects, "Our class time isn't about me lecturing. If I do need to lecture, to give you information, I'll give it to you in writing or through video or through notes." Next up is an image of a spoon to which students quickly answer in unison, "spoon-feeding." Nathan asks, "Is it my job to do this?" As students answer with a chorus of noes, Nathan nods and adds, "That's not how you're going to learn."

Although this isn't the first time Nathan has told students he won't be lecturing or spoon-feeding them material for the test, it is worth noting that this stance not only reflects Nathan's teaching style but also represents a radical rethinking of time. Traditionally the classroom has been the venue for dispensing information and content to students. Nathan hasn't said that content isn't important or unnecessary; he has only signaled that he won't use class time for its distribution and will accomplish delivery through other means, thus freeing up class time for other activities. The other images Nathan shares with the class reveal what learning in his class will in fact look like.

"What about this?" Nathan asks as an image of a skydiver flashes on the screen. "What's this got to do with learning? Is this me?" A student replies, "It's us; we have to take risks to be adventurous." "To try new things even if they are scary sometimes," another adds. "And that holds true for me as well," Nathan throws in. "I can't always play it safe as a teacher. I need to take risks too." The last image up is of Glinda from the movie version of *The Wizard of Oz*. "Why would I put this up?" Nathan asks. "Uhmm, because you're a fairy godmother?"

Nathan chuckles and adds a query, "Who has watched *The Wizard of Oz*?" Only a few hands go up. "Well, your homework is that you have to watch it if you haven't. For those of you who have seen it, why would Glinda be an example of good teaching?" "Because you have to do the learning yourself," one student adds. "Because she let Dorothy make mistakes." Before moving on, Nathan looks around the room and asks the class if they want to watch the film. There is a general nodding of heads, and Nathan says, "We'll try to find a time after school or at lunch one day."

This brief review of modes of teaching and discussion of what it means to learn have taken just a few minutes, but it is time well spent, an investment of sorts. Nathan wants students to understand his actions as well as the active role he expects of them in his classes. He knows that in the past, students have experienced other styles of teaching, even some spoon-feeding, and he wants to shift those expectations among this new cohort of students. By prioritizing learning and being overt about what learning will look like and how it will unfold, Nathan heads off potential anxiety about the looming test. He assures them that by focusing on the learning, they will be well prepared.

Pulling back up the YouTube video of Pink with a click of the remote, Nathan launches into directions: "At your tables there are copies of the lyrics to 'Glitter in the Air.' You've watched that this weekend, this amazing performance by Pink at the Grammys, and now I want you to think: How does this connect to *Cosi*?" He then concludes by explaining the format of the activity: "I'll play the video again—it takes exactly five minutes—and when it is done, you'll discuss with your teams what each member came up with."

That's it. Just one paragraph, only three sentences, a mere sixty-six words that take about a minute to deliver, and students are set to their learning: analyzing, making connections, building explanations, and looking for metaphoric representations of concrete actions and activity. The brevity is made possible by the way Nathan has used time. Through his email to students, which they were alerted to expect from the first week of school, Nathan primed his students' thinking and provided them the stimulus they would be exploring. These brief directions then were nothing more than a reiteration of information they already had. The written lyrics weren't new information, just a hard copy from which to work.

As students start to work individually, Nathan circulates and listens in on conversations. Students aren't afraid to raise questions or share their emergent ideas. A girl at the front table says she is thinking about the "La-la-la's" in the bridge of the song and wondering if something so simple could have a deeper meaning. "How is she singing it?" Nathan inquires. "Sad," the girl replies. "Ah, so maybe the message is in the tone," Nathan offers. "It's kind of like a lost love," the girl continues. "So what is in her mind?" Nathan probes. "Memory," the girl says, brightening, and begins to write down her thoughts. The video ends, and Nathan signals to students to share their thoughts with their teams and to try to connect every line of the song to *Cosi* if they can.

"Let's come together as a group and discuss this," Nathan announces. Once he has their attention, he explains, "Rather than me telling you what I know and how it relates to *Cosi*, you are going to listen to each other. At the end, you are going to think about how these ideas connect to what you already knew, how they extended what you know, and how our discussion is challenging you or may require further study in order to know more about *Cosi* and its characters and themes." He continues, "I am most interested in your challenges because if you already know everything, then we might as well sit the SAC [school assessed coursework]." Here again, Nathan gives simple directions for what will happen next, keeping the focus on the learning rather than the work, on developing understanding over the acquisition of knowledge.

The class works through each line of the song, offering possible connections and raising questions as they do. "Have you ever fed a lover with just your hands? Closed your eyes and trust it, just trust it?" Nathan reads the first two lines of the song. Jenny offers, "Lewis is taking a leap of faith." Nathan pauses and comments, "I love that phrasing." Max raises his hand to add, "When they are in the dark in the theatre, they trust each other, and they can kind of reveal themselves to each other." "Good observation," Nathan comments before reading the next line: "Have you ever thrown a fistful of glitter in the air?"

"Lewis is the hand holder, and the glitter is the patients. He's allowing them to be free," Sam offers. To which Megan adds, "It's like doing something just because. Just because you can, and the opportunity is there. Lewis is very serious, but he's kind of letting himself go with the play." As the discussion continues, it's clear there are no right answers, and students focus on building meaningful connections that provide insight into the text, not simply answers to comprehension questions.

After a very rich twenty minutes spent discussing each line, Nathan draws students' attention to one of the other sheets at their tables. "I've passed out a sheet that says Connect-Extend-Challenge at the top," Nathan announces. "I want you to think about the discussion we've just had using Pink's 'Glitter in the Air.'" He then explains the purpose of the recording sheet: "On the sheet, jot down what immediate *connections* came to mind for you between *Cosi* and the lyrics. We've talked a lot about those already. Then turn your attention to how our discussion has *extended* your thinking about the play or about the characters. Finally," Nathan sums up, "record any questions or *challenges* that are coming up for you as you try to understand this text."

As the class comes to a close, I notice that once again the individual conversations between Nathan and his students resume. They check in with him, tell him stories, share experiences, and alert him to upcoming events he might want to attend.

For almost the entire period, Nathan's students have spent their time actively engaged in learning. And, because students were working in teams and building off one another's ideas, all students—not just a small portion of the class—were engaged. It wasn't possible to sit back. The first five minutes reviewing the role of teacher and students wouldn't fall into the category of "engaged learning," but because it helped lay the groundwork and expectations for students' actions as learners, it was, nonetheless, a prudent investment of time in order to lay the groundwork for future learning.

As exciting as it has been to be an observer in Nathan's class, I'm particularly intrigued to sit in on the next portion of Nathan's day, an Individual Feedback Session or IFS (Armstrong, 2012). During his second year of teaching, Nathan began a process of meeting with each of his grade 12 students weekly to give feedback on his or her writing. During the first weeks of school, Nathan creates a meeting schedule for each student, finding a time that works for both him and the student either before school, during lunch, free periods, or after school. This regularly scheduled meeting time then becomes the date when work will be due for that student. Students bring their written work, and Nathan writes grades and comments on the writing at the IFS. Students take notes or record the session on their phones, and the next assignment is given with very specific target goals.

When I initially heard about Nathan's IFS structure, my first thought was, *How does he find the time?* True, Nathan has made some modifications to the original structure, as the number of grade 12 classes he teaches has increased. For instance, he now does the sessions once every two weeks and often with two students together rather than one-on-one. Still, the time commitment is not insignificant. In devising the system, Nathan thought carefully about how he was currently allocating his time. He considered the effectiveness of his current efforts in terms of the time given for the gains received. He also thought in terms of his energy rather than only his time. Taking a stack of papers home to read through and mark is rarely an energizing task for any teacher. By comparison, Nathan genuinely likes spending time getting to know his students. Furthermore, there is something naturally energizing about feeling that one's efforts are appreciated and making a difference.

Nathan explains, "One of the problems that I had encountered with offering feedback through written comments was that I was not sure if students actually read them, understood my comments, or even if they knew how to put my suggestions into action. By creating the IFS system, I wanted to offer a more authentic and beneficial way of offering feedback." He acknowledges the trade-off he is making in the reallocation of time: "While many staff members have commented that the IFS is 'time consuming' and that I have no time during the day, ultimately it saves time. I take no year 12 work home!" Finally, he identifies the messages about learning he is sending students: "By taking my time to meet with the students, they understand that I believe in the task that has been set and that it deserves time and attention. By making my time available to students, they see that I am willing to put time into their learning, but only if they are also."

When I sit down with Nathan and Siobhan for their first IFS of the school year, the attention to building relationships, supporting individual goals, and having students take ownership is clearly on display. Nathan begins by asking Siobhan about the classes she is taking and her future goals. When she indicates that her interest is in arts and photography, Nathan comments, "Well, bring some of your work with you to our IFS. I'd like to see your work." He then asks her about how she finds English generally, to which she responds, "It's interesting but also quite challenging. I think I struggle with structure and putting my ideas into writing."

Nathan probes, "What do you mean by that?"

Siobhan elaborates, "Putting what is in my head down."

To which Nathan replies, "Come along on the journey. You're going to have the knowledge of how to talk about Ruth [from *Cosi*] by week 7. You will have that." Siobhan then talks about the difficulty she has with integrating quotes, to which Nathan interjects, "We'll work on that."

Next, Nathan explains the format of the IFS to Siobhan: "Each time we meet, I will bring your file and put your writing and things in it. So if you bring a printout, we both will have copies. At the end of the IFS, I'll give you an assignment. In terms of due dates, your work is always due when we meet next, so that is easy to remember. If you don't have your work, then there won't be anything for us to go over." And with that, the conversation moves into the first writing assignment, analyzing the character Ruth from *Cosi*.

Marking pencil in hand, Nathan begins reading Siobhan's essay silently, and stops to make a verbal comment about word choice as he writes notes on the paper. "Word choice is important in an essay. Don't repeat words. What could you say here instead?" Siobhan comes up with a few alternatives, and Nathan continues reading. "I notice you often begin your sentences with names, and in a long essay that gets tiresome. So we will look at complex sentences. Did you do complex sentences last year?" Siobhan shakes her head. "No?" Nathan confirms, adding, "No worries. We are going to go over that. You will know how to do that in your sleep. If you watch the news, newsreaders always begin with a complex sentence."

Reading on, Nathan comments, "This use of the quote is very smooth. It is like jazz. Nice use of evidence. Nice use of irony." Further along in the essay, he comments, "Oh, look here, you wrote 'Ruth is a dogged realist.' What does that mean?" To which Siobhan meekly answers, "I don't really know." A knowing smile comes over Nathan's face as he responds, "I know you don't. That's why I asked. The takeaway here is, don't steal other people's language. Let's unpack this together. It is just fancy language." And together the two talk about the character Ruth's fixation on facts, the truth, and the here and now.

Working through the rest of the essay, Nathan makes comments, always both verbally and in writing, and the two of them discuss points. Oftentimes, Nathan flags issues, such as complex sentences and word choice, for future attention, but doesn't deal with them directly at the time. Because this is Siobhan's first IFS of the year, the dialogic session goes for a full class period. As the year progresses, the meeting times will vary depending on the work and the need, but at this first session, Nathan wants to get to know Siobhan (a student new to the school), set goals, and establish a structure.

As the session closes, both Nathan and Siobhan seem energized. There is a feeling of trust and almost relief emerging from Siobhan already. Despite her reticence as a writer, there is a sense that she now knows she will have the support to improve. Reflecting on the process and the relationship that is being built, Nathan goes to the heart of why he thinks the IFS system works in his own writing about the process: "Most humans want to feel secure, supported, validated, and to be given opportunities to reach their full potential. I have found that the IFS supports such aims and, throughout the course of an academic year, students feel that they can test the limits of their thinking and take risks in their learning and work, all while feeling supported and encouraged" (Armstrong, 2012).

Spending a day with Nathan and talking with him about his teaching, I am struck by his attention to developing relationships with his students through his interactions and by his creation of powerful learning opportunities. These are important aspects of good teaching and will be taken up in future chapters. However, what I keep coming back to, and what I find most radical about Nathan's teaching, is how he has thought about time differently. From this brief look at Nathan's practice, we can distill a number of key approaches and perspectives on time that can facilitate the creation of a culture of thinking in schools, classrooms, and organizations:

- Recognizing time as a statement of your values
- Learning to prioritize and always prioritizing learning
- Giving thinking time
- Investing in time to make time
- Managing energy, not time

We've already seen how some of these responses to time underpin Nathan's teaching and shape the learning of both individuals and the group. We'll now explore each of these responses in more depth, along with some of the relevant research, to better understand how each of these actions can transform our response to time and help move us from being its victim to being its master. Throughout this exploration, I'll try to address the natural tensions and conflicts that may arise in the constant struggle over time. However, I present no magic bullets that will suddenly resolve all of the pressures our modern age places on us as individuals or on schools as institutions. Instead, what you will find in this discussion are approaches to and ways of thinking about time that may help you feel more in control and proactive as you seek to leverage time as a cultural force.

RECOGNIZING TIME AS A STATEMENT OF YOUR VALUES

It has been said that if you want to figure out what any organization, group, family, or individual values, you only have to look at two things: how they spend their money and how they spend their time (Taylor, 2005). Credit cards and calendars, as it were. It can be easily argued that time is the more valuable as well as the more telling resource, as it is limited, no one gets to create more of it, and it is equitably distributed to us all. What does your allocation of time say about what you value in the classroom? How about the way time is spent and allocated across your school? If someone were to follow you throughout the day as I did with Nathan, what would your allocation of time say about your priorities and values?

Spending a day with Nathan, it was easy to see that he valued building relationship with students and building a community in his classroom. He gave time to these things, particularly at the beginning of the year. When it came to instruction, the most time was given over to discussion, in contrast to the presentation of information. However, the discussion was not just a working through of the lyrics of Pink's song "Glitter in the Air." At the heart of this discussion was the idea of building a deeper understanding of the text, *Cosi*, through looking closely, making connections, and reasoning with evidence.

It is worth noting that Nathan did not merely "provide time to talk"; there were specific components of creating an effective discussion to which Nathan gave time, threading each component together to create the desired outcome. These elements reflect a deep understanding of what exactly goes into creating a good class discussion. For Nathan, getting everyone involved and contributing was one of these elements. Consequently, he first gave time at the outset for individuals to prepare. Because some students just aren't able to respond on demand, this time increases the likelihood that everyone will have something to contribute. In addition, giving time to prepare helped ensure better-quality responses. Second, Nathan gave time to small-group discussion. This provided an opportunity for more students to talk and share as well as a chance for the teams to build community. This instructional move also allowed Nathan to call on shy or less able students by asking, "What was one of the ideas that was shared in your team?" Finally, there was the actual group discussion itself, during which Nathan made sure he heard from all groups and that they interacted with one another's ideas.

To be sure, Nathan did not sit down and plan out every second. However, he did work from his values in allocating his time. His time allotments flowed from how he sees teaching and learning, its purposes and its mechanisms. His perception of what counts in teaching and learning reflects his deeply held priorities and values. These in turn shape his actions. As Stephen Covey stated in *First Things First*, his classic book about taking control of time, "The way we see (our paradigm) leads to what we do (or attitudes and behaviors); and what we do leads to the results we get in our lives" (1994, p. 28). If we want different results, we don't begin by changing our behaviors, Covey argues; we begin by changing our perceptions, our paradigms, and the way we are looking at the world before us. To the extent that Covey's advice is true, it may explain why merely training teachers in new techniques has so often failed as a strategy for improving teaching. We need to first change how they look at the process of teaching and learning.

In addition to planned or anticipated allotments of time, teachers make constant, on-the-spot decisions about time: Do I allow this discussion to continue? Do I move on because I have three more points to make? Do I take time to review the material that students were supposed to have read? Do I allow students to experiment, raise questions, and get confused, or do I just give them the information? Do I entertain that interesting question that is just a bit off topic? How much time do I allot for the group to discuss before I bring them back together? Each and every one of these decisions about time sends a message about what we value and think is most important.

"But wait," you say. "I have the curriculum to get through. I have to prepare students for the tests they will take. I have thirty-five students in my class. My class periods aren't nearly as long as I would like them to be. I want to give time to discussion and questions and exploration and developing relationships, but, well, there is no time!" These pressures are real. Furthermore, it is certainly reasonable that an individual might not be happy with the way he or she is allocating time. The key takeaway here is that our choices, even if we aren't happy with them, are sending messages to our students about what is deemed important and worthwhile in the classroom. That allocation, even if it isn't what we want, is nonetheless shaping the culture of the classroom.

Breaking through this contradiction between what we would like to be doing and what we are in fact doing takes us back to values, while pushing us a step further to identify priorities. To do so, we need to explore our deeply held perceptions of teaching and learning, its mechanisms and purposes, to see what is truly guiding us. If we believe that teaching is presenting information and that learning is largely memorizing information, we will give time to these things. If we believe that getting through the curriculum or keeping the class quiet are high priorities, then we will put more time and energy toward such things.

LEARNING TO PRIORITIZE AND ALWAYS PRIORITIZING LEARNING

One of the qualities that stands out for me in Nathan's class is how much class time is devoted to what is sometimes referred to as "academic engaged time" (Gettinger & Walter, 2012), "academic learning time" (Karweit & Slavin, 1981), or "interactive instructional time" (Saphier, Haley-Speca, & Gower, 2008). Whatever the moniker, these terms refer to the time students are actively engaged in learning as opposed to sitting back waiting for learning to happen or disengaged from the learning process. This can be contrasted with the "allocated time," the time that is actually scheduled for school, and "instructional time," the time devoted to teaching, which may include time when the teacher is talking as well as time when students are disengaged. Not surprisingly, the amount of interactive, engaged time that students experience is most strongly correlated with learning outcomes (Silva, 2007). However, studies of secondary students have shown that students are more likely to spend their class time in noninteractive activities—listening to lectures, taking notes, doing seat work, and so on—than in interactive activities (Shernoff, Csikszentmihalyi, Schneider, & Shernoff, 2003). Similarly, elementary reading lessons are likely to be dominated by nonreading activities, such as completing worksheets (Ford & Opitz, 2002).

Paul Cripps, a middle school science teacher in Montana, had an aha moment when he realized that his tendency to talk, give directions, and generally pontificate about science was reducing the amount of interactive instructional time his students experienced. As a result, he now sets an eight-minute timer at the beginning of each class and never allows himself to go beyond that limit in pure teacher talk. This is but one strategy to ensure more engaged learning time. You may be familiar with others, since such strategies generally connect with notions of good teaching. Some include minimizing disruptions, reducing transition time, establishing routines for common tasks, facilitating active student responding, focusing on explicit goals, providing feedback, matching instruction to students' needs and abilities (responsive teaching), encouraging independence, and teaching students metacognitive strategies, among others (Gettinger & Walter, 2012).

These strategies can increase interactive instructional learning time. Yet the most effective method of ensuring more engagement is not through any particular strategy, but through a more radical rethinking of time. When we think in terms of students' engagement, the question of allocating time shifts from "How do I as a teacher choose to use my allotted class time to accomplish my goals?" to "How will I enable my students to use their time in class to maximize their learning?" This shift in perspective, first, moves our focus from ourselves to our students. Second, it recalibrates our thinking about time, forcing us to move away from *prioritizing one's schedule* to accomplish all that needs to be done—giving our attention to urgency, demands, and pressures—toward *scheduling one's priorities,* which for us as teachers should always be student learning.

Making this change in perspective is certainly not easy. Schools live in a world of to-do lists, bullet points to cover, objectives to address, test deadlines, and so on. The call of the urgent is certainly with us at almost every moment. How often have you found yourself starting a class by saying, "Today we really have to . . ." to express the need to attend to an unmet, urgent item? To break through the tyranny of the urgent, we first need to identify a few core principles that can serve as guides in our allocation of time. By exploring your deeply held perceptions of teaching and learning, its mechanisms and its purposes, your own principles will begin to emerge. The following questions might be useful in jump-starting this process:

- What "residuals" do you want students to take away from their year with you?
- If you had your students for only six weeks, what would be the single most important thing you would want them to understand?
- Recall a time from your past teaching in which you knew your entire class was fully engaged in and excited about learning. What were the feelings and energy like in that moment?
- If you could wave a magic wand and equip all students with one learning tool that would assist them in being more effective learners, what would you choose?
- Recall a time when you were really dedicated to understanding something new. What did you do to develop that understanding?
- Recall a class you were in as a student in which the learning didn't stop for you just because the bell rang. What happened in that class that kept you thinking well beyond the class period?
- Thinking about students' learning in your class last year, what are the one or two things you wish you had spent more time developing?
- Drawing on your own teaching experience, what have you learned are keys to motivating learning, creating engagement around ideas, and propelling deep, thoughtful discussions?

Your responses to these questions may give you insights into some personal core principles about teaching and learning. You want to make time for these principles in your teaching—not as a backdrop to your teaching or as something nice to fit in, but as the centerpiece.

One of the timeless metaphorical stories about scheduling priorities is that of "The Big Rocks." The story goes that a philosophy professor, wanting his students to take control of their lives in a way that reflected what was truly most important, began his class one day with a demonstration. As students entered the lecture hall, he placed an empty, clear one-gallon glass cookie jar on the desk in front of him. He then silently began to fill the jar up with rocks about the size of his fist, carefully placing each one to fit in as many rocks as he could. He then asked the class whether the jar was now full, to which the class replied yes.

Reaching under the desk, the professor then brought out a container of pebbles and began to pour the pebbles into the jar. He shook the jar slightly as he worked to get as many pebbles in as possible. Once again, the professor asked the class whether the jar was now full. Once again, the class responded yes, though some with a bit less assurance in their voices than they had the first time. The professor again reached under the desk and produced a container of sand. After pouring the sand in, the professor once again asked the class whether the container was full. Many, catching on to his game, began to chuckle, even as they were unsure about what he would produce next. Reaching under the desk one last time, the professor produced a container of water that he proceeded to pour into the jar.

The professor then explained the meaning of the demonstration. It is not, as some students initially suggested, that you can always fit more into your life. Rather, the jar signifies our life, and the big rocks are the things we value and feel are truly important. If we place our big rocks in first, there is space to fit in the other things we have to do. These things will fit in the margins and cracks. However, if we were to begin by filling our jar with water, sand, or pebbles, we would find that they quickly take up all the space and squeeze out any room for the big rocks. (You can see one demonstration of "the big rocks" on YouTube at http://www.youtube.com/watch?v=6_N_uvq41Pg.)

In building a culture of thinking, there are a few key principles—our big rocks—that we want to be sure we are giving time to in every school and classroom:

- Learning is a consequence of thinking.
- Coaching and providing feedback propel learning and create momentum.
- We learn when we are being challenged, stretched, and pushed in novel ways, performing just beyond what we are able to do already on our own.

This is certainly not an exhaustive list of all the potentially important things around teaching and learning. Instead, it is a list of a very few high priorities taken from our own work in the Cultures of Thinking project as well as that of others (Dweck, 2006; Hattie, 2009; Hattie & Timperley, 2007; Perkins, 1992; Vygotsky, 1978). The point is to establish for yourself a short list, preferably short enough that you can keep it in your head, that you can use as your own big rocks. These should become your priorities, the things you want to make room for in each class period.

At the whole-school level, one of the priorities must be building the professional culture for the adults in the building. In the Cultures of Thinking research group, one of our mantras is that *for classrooms to be cultures of thinking for the students, schools must be cultures of thinking for the adults*. It is easy for adult time in schools to be taken up with the business of schooling: scheduling, field trips, report writing, policies, due dates, and so on. School leaders must make professional learning time a priority, a big rock that they put in first. If they don't, then the creeping sands of minutia will quickly fill the time available for professional learning and conversation. Likewise, at team, departmental, and division meetings, put in the big rocks first.

GIVING THINKING TIME

Although a close examination of all of one's big rocks is worthwhile in order to fully vet each of them and understand its role in supporting students' learning, I want to take the space here to examine one extremely big rock when it comes to establishing a culture of thinking: learning is a consequence of thinking. I first raised this in chapter 1 as a key message in the story of learning we want to be telling our students. Now we will look at how our allocation of time sends the message to our students that learning is a product of thinking.

Quick impressions, opinions, and the recall of known answers can be offered on the spot in very little time; in contrast, time is a necessary ingredient when it comes to thinking. Complex cognitive processing or more thoughtful, contemplative, or creative responses require time to construct. Even though studies have shown that it is indeed possible for people to be creative under pressure if they are focused and there is a sense of meaningful urgency—think of the NASA team dreaming up a primitive but effective fix for the failing air filtration system aboard *Apollo 13* within a few short hours because lives literally depended on it—under most circumstances, time pressure diminishes creative responses (Amabile, Hadley, & Kramer, 2002). One of the issues at work is that original ideas do not tend to cluster near the surface of our thoughts but tend to be remote, located away from the original problem or situation (Mednick, 1962). Thus it takes time to move away from one's initial ideas and toward those that are more original. When we give thinking time, we are signaling that we are after such responses and not just a known answer.

The classic research on the relationship between time and thinking comes from Mary Budd Rowe's study (1986) on teacher's wait time that began in the late 1960s. One of the biggest challenges Rowe faced in her research was that the typical time teachers waited for a response was so short that it was hard to measure. Stopwatches were useless. The audiotapes had to be fed through a computer to detect and measure the pauses. What she found as a baseline was that when teachers question students, they typically wait less than one second before calling on someone for a response. Rowe called this Wait Time 1. After the student has stopped speaking, the teacher typically reacts, comments, or asks another question in less than one second. This is known as Wait Time 2. Other researchers have found this short time frame to be true across subject and grade levels as well as cultures (Cheprecha, Gardner, & Sapianchai, 1980). It doesn't take much imagination to infer that such short wait time doesn't give students a chance to prepare a thoughtful elaborated response or provide an explanation for their answers. Instead students in such classrooms learn to play "guess what's in the teacher's head," compete for teacher time and attention, and see learning as predominantly an act of memory.

Rowe's real breakthrough came when she noticed that the pacing in some of the elementary and secondary science classes she was studying differed from the norm. In these classes, both Wait Time 1 and Wait Time 2 increased to between three and five seconds, as opposed to the more typical fraction of a second. She reasoned that even this small increase in time would begin to change the dynamics of the conversation by providing time to think: "To grow a complex thought system requires a great deal of shared experience and conversation. It is in talking about what we have done and observed, and in arguing about what we make of our experiences, that ideas multiply, become refined, and finally produce new questions and further explorations" (1986 p. 43).

Over a twenty-year period of research, Rowe (1986) studied the effects of increased wait time, both 1 and 2, on students. She found that wait time above three seconds was associated with

- An increase in the length of student responses, ranging from 300 to 700 percent more than under the typical conditions. Increase in Wait Time 2 was particularly effective in increasing students' elaboration.

- Greater use of evidence and reasoning. In fact, this became the norm with increased wait time rather than the exception.

- An increase in speculative thinking to explore possibilities.

- An increase in both the number and types of questions students asked. Under typical conditions, the few questions students asked tended to be procedural in nature. With increased wait time, more questions were asked, and they grew more substantive.

- An increase in attending to what other students have said and a greater tendency to build on and connect to the contributions of others. This was particularly influenced by Wait Time 2.

- Greater participation and confidence, as demonstrated by students giving fewer "I don't know" responses as well as a reduction in students giving tentative responses that sought validation from the teacher.

- Greater achievement on written tasks that were cognitively complex and required thinking in order to produce a response.

It is impossible to adequately capture the feel of wait time in a transcript, to represent the extra second or two given over to silence in a way that will provide a reader who was not actually present in the classroom that moment the sense of engagement and thoughtfulness it creates. However, in Nathan's class, we can in fact witness and make note of most of the outcomes of those extra seconds of wait time listed previously. Most notably, students' contributions are full and rich rather than truncated. Students present their ideas with conviction and confidence rather than with tentativeness. Participation is distributed widely, and students add on to others' ideas, changing the pattern of discourse. As a result, one notices a clear departure from the typical Ping-Pong model of questioning that goes back and forth between teacher and students. Instead, in Nathan's class, there is a sense of a real discussion with lots of participation and students talking to one another, building and extending others' ideas. It begins to feel more like a basketball game in which we have lots of players taking turns with the ball, rather than a simple back-and-forth with the teacher (McIntosh, 2012). In addition to the effects listed earlier, providing that extra bit of time also changes the student-teacher interactions and the types of questions that teachers ask (Gambrell, 1980), something we will explore further in chapter 8.

Building on Rowe's research, Stahl (1994) proposed the idea of "think time" as a way of both highlighting the primary task to be done, which is thinking, and broadening the concept to include time other than the time after questioning. For instance, think time would include any "distinct period of uninterrupted silence by the teacher and all students so that they both can complete appropriate information processing tasks, feelings, oral responses, and actions" (p. 2). As opposed to wait time, for which effects have been found when time is increased somewhere between three and five seconds, think time is not necessarily measured in so short a time span. The time given for thinking should be "the period of time that will most effectively assist nearly every student to complete the cognitive tasks needed in the particular situation" (p. 2). Think time comprises wait time, but also "pause time" to allow students to take in information or consider what has just happened before responding, time to complete tasks, and post-response wait time to allow others to jump into the conversation.

Think time can also include the time given to consider ideas and prepare for discussion. Before Nathan engaged his students in a discussion of the connection between "Glitter in the Air" and *Cosi*, he gave them five minutes. This allowed his students to gather their thoughts and generate new ideas before commencing their small-group discussions. Note that Nathan told his students exactly how much time they had, and then timed them by playing the five-minute video. In my research, I have often observed teachers telling students that they will have a certain amount of time to work or prepare, and then the actual time is quite different. A teacher's being inconsistent about time trains students to use time poorly or to stop working early because they really aren't sure how much time they have.

INVESTING TIME TO MAKE TIME

When we feel short of time, we often seek out ways of being more efficient, of maximizing our activity and production within the constraints of time. However, this quest for efficiency doesn't always yield the results we are after. Providing think time is a good example of why the quest for efficiency may actually shortchange learning. We need to call into question the underlying assumption present in schools, organizations, and society at large that doing more and doing it faster are always better. Increasingly, research is tackling this assumption as it relates to one area in particular: multitasking, the attempt to attend fully to more than one thing at once.

Although the brain can carry on two unrelated activities without much conflict—say running and listening to music or ironing and watching television—when it comes to engaging in slightly more complex mental functions, such as processing information or just paying attention, it must switch back and forth between the activities. This switching causes mental fatigue, as the brain must once again pick up the thread of the previous activity in making the switch back. In this back-and-forth, information is lost and errors are made. In fact, studies show that a person who is interrupted takes up to 50 percent longer to accomplish the task at hand and makes up to 50 percent more errors (R. D. Rogers & Monsell, 1995).

The allure of multitasking—studies show that a third of eight- to eighteen-year-olds multitask while doing homework, and that up to 80 percent of university students use social media while in class—coupled with its effects on performance have obvious implications for schools (Paul, 2013). As bad as the noted effects on task completion are, the effects on learning appear to be even more worrying. Studies have shown that attempted multitasking, what we should really call "divided attention," has a severe effect on memory. It is the moment of encoding, or taking in of new information, that matters most for our retention. When our attention is divided during this encoding process, we remember that information less well or not at all (Fernandes & Moscovitch, 2000).

Even more distressing is the research by Russell Poldrack (Paul, 2013) showing that our brains actually process and store information differently in distracted situations. Under such conditions, individuals tend to believe they are being just as effective in their learning. This might be attributed to the fact that it is often difficult to effectively monitor and evaluate how well our mental processes are functioning in the moment. In one study, Poldrack asked an experimental group to do a secondary task while engaged in a learning activity. A control group just focused on the learning task. Poldrack found that "subjects who did both tasks at once appeared to learn just as well as subjects who did the first task by itself. But upon further probing, the former group proved much less adept at extending and extrapolating their new knowledge to novel contexts—a key capacity that psychologists call transfer" (Paul, 2013). And, of course, transfer is the holy grail of learning. We want students who can actually use and apply their skills and knowledge in novel situations, not just give us back information on a test.

Although efficiency does not always equal effectiveness, aiming for effectiveness will almost always bring us more efficiency in the long term. We see this in Nathan's actions at the beginning of the school year. Through his establishment of routines, setting of expectations for learning, leveraging of learning teams, and advance preparation, Nathan was able to maximize students' actual engaged learning time as a portion of his instructional time. Rather than seeing his early attention to building community and enculturating students into the learning of his class as taking time away from learning, Nathan saw them as an investment that would yield big dividends as the year progressed. This expenditure of time within the first few days of school to establish routines, build community, create patterns of discourse, focus on big ideas, and set an agenda of understanding is a common characteristic of schools and classrooms that are cultures of thinking (Ritchhart, 2002). Indeed, these actions can't wait. Teachers must invest time early on to creating a culture where thinking is valued, visible, and actively promoted if they are going to cultivate long-term success.

This early outlay of time to yield greater efficiency later can also be seen in Nathan's design of the Individual Feedback Session (IFS). Early in his teaching career, Nathan looked at how he was giving feedback, by writing comments and putting grades on students' essays as most English teachers do, and saw a largely ineffective practice. He was spending a lot of time and depleting his energy without feeling that his comments were even being read, let alone making a difference to future performance. By investing time in the IFS system, particularly early in the year, Nathan creates long-term efficiency by helping students set goals, become more independent, push themselves in their writing, take greater risks, and eventually learn to self-assess. Over the years, Nathan has received dramatic evidence that his efforts have paid off. Prior to initiating the IFS system, the percentage of Nathan's students achieving in the top tier of outcomes—that is, a "study score" above 40 on the Victoria Certificate of Education, which places one in the top 10 percent of students in the state—was on par with the other English teachers at his school, at around 20 percent. However, during the first year of the IFS system and every year since, Nathan has had over 50 percent of his students scoring in the top tier. This is at an open entry, nonselective private school where students are randomly assigned in their class placements.

MANAGING ENERGY, NOT TIME

Have you ever walked into a school, classroom, or organization and had the immediate sensation that the people there were stressed? Sometimes group members themselves will even acknowledge it: "We're so stressed at the moment." "I've got so much going on." "We just can't take this on at the moment; people are too stressed." At times, it seems that some people may even wear their stress as a badge of honor, as an acknowledgment of their importance, their work ethic, or their commitment. Although there are many potential causes of stress, it is often inextricably linked to the issue of time—that is, feeling pressed for time amid all that has to be done. Consequently, we often think about managing stress through our management of time.

However, managing stress through management of time is rarely effective. It could be argued that feelings of being stressed are actually just an indication of the depletion of one's resources: physical, mental, emotional, or spiritual. Thus what one really needs to do to combat stress is to manage one's energy. Although the hours and minutes in a day are fixed, energy is a renewable resource.

Before discussing ways to manage energy, to recharge, and to tap into natural rhythms, I want to point out that stress, particularly wide-scale group stress, is decidedly not a feature of a culture of thinking and might in fact be seen as a sign that a true culture of thinking hasn't been achieved. In the introduction to this book, I asked you to consider a time when you were in a group that you felt was a culture of thinking—that is, *a place where the group's collective thinking as well as each individual's thinking was valued, visible, and actively promoted as part of the regular, day-to-day experience of all group members.* I asked you to identify some of the practices that helped create and sustain that group. Then I asked you to identify how you felt while in that group. If you think back over your mental lists, I doubt very much that "stressed" would be one of the words you used to describe a culture of thinking of which you were a part. On the contrary, feelings of energy, enthusiasm, being uplifted, and engagement are more likely. Although you might also have felt challenged, pushed, or stretched, you mostly likely also felt supported and able to take on those demands. Therefore, stress is actually a counterindicator of a culture of thinking, reflecting that one's purpose and direction are being swamped by the urgency of "to dos." The questions before us then become: What are people doing differently in a culture of thinking to avoid that stressed-out feeling? How are they thinking about and using their time in a way that feeds rather than diminishes a culture of thinking?

Stephen Covey (1994) created a time management matrix to identify four distinct categories of human activity. On the horizontal axis, he placed "urgency," ranging from high on the left to low on the right. Bisecting this horizontal line is the vertical axis of "importance," ranging from high on the top to low on the bottom. The resulting intersecting axes create four quadrants: (1) Urgent and Important, (2) Not Urgent and Important, (3) Urgent and Not Important, and (4) Not Urgent and Not Important. Covey labels quadrant 2 as the *quadrant of quality*. This is where we plan, invest in others and ourselves, anticipate problems, learn new things, take risks, and create. He states, "Increasing time spent in this quadrant increases our ability to do. Ignoring this quadrant feeds and enlarges quadrant 1, creating stress, burnout, and deeper crises for the person consumed by it" (p. 38). Consider what we saw of Nathan Armstrong's teaching. Almost all of his actions were in the quadrant of quality. This is where the big rocks reside. This is where we invest time to make time. This is also the quadrant where we are most likely to feel a gain in energy rather than energy depletion.

Thinking in terms of energy expenditure, energy gains, and energy renewal can help us think differently about our daily schedules, and indeed our lives. In their book *The Power of Full Engagement*, Jim Loehr and Tony Schwartz (2003) encourage readers to reflect on two key questions: "How am I spending my energy now? How should I be spending my energy so that it is consistent with my deepest held values?" (p. 15). These are useful, big-picture questions. They relate to our values and priorities. To get a better sense of energy as opposed to time, the following exercise can be helpful. Over the course of the next week, reflect at the end of each day on your energy expenditure. Begin by making a list of all the major activities you engaged in over the course of a day. You don't need to use your schedule to do this or to worry about being 100 percent accurate in capturing everything. Recalling events will help you review the day. With that list in front of you, mark each item in one of three ways:

Green = "I came out of that activity feeling energized. For the energy I put into it, I feel I got a net gain. This was time well spent."

Yellow = "This was neutral for me. I didn't feel that it depleted me, but I also didn't feel I gained energy from it."

Red = "This was an energy vampire. I had to summon energy resources to keep going and get through it. If I could have fast-forwarded through this, I would have."

After a week of daily review and rating of your activities, examine your color codes. What color dominates? Does the dominant color correspond to your energy level at the end of each day? at the end of the week? The long-term goal for each of us should be to create days in which our activities are more energizing than depleting. Several studies have shown how important such experiences are to our lives. Howard Gardner's research team found that "time well spent" is universally valued and held at a premium in terms of eliciting personal satisfaction (Gardner, 2013). Although his studies didn't directly link the notion of "time well spent" to energy, it isn't hard to see the connection. Likewise, Matthew Killingsworth's research on happiness (2012), in which he found that people would choose to fast-forward through roughly 40 percent of their day, indicates that as a whole we are close to a tipping point of dissatisfaction with how we are spending our time. Changing this allocation has rewards for us personally in terms of our life satisfaction and happiness, but also for our students. Energy begets energy, whereas stress and negativity can create a downward spiral.

When Nathan looked at the time he was spending marking essays, he saw that this was largely an energy drain for him. Dragging papers home every night was something he didn't look forward to doing. Although his marking was not at odds with his deep conviction that learning is personal and derives from a relationship with students, he felt it wasn't doing much to build a relationship with students or to personalize learning. It wasn't an effective practice. Whereas other teachers might look at the IFS system and see it only through the lens of time, Nathan saw it through the lens of energy. He genuinely enjoyed spending time with his students. This built energy. Like all of us, he found that knowing he is being effective and making a difference, which the IFS does, is another source of energy. Finally, through its rollout over the years, Nathan was also able to see that the IFS built energy for his students. As the year progressed, they became more willing to engage and take ownership of the process.

Of course, one isn't always able to turn every energy-draining activity into an energy-gaining one. Therefore, it is important that we build in recovery routines, occasions to recharge, downtime, and opportunities for renewal. This is true for us as well as for our students. Our bodies naturally begin to crave periods of rest and recovery after about 90 to 120 minutes (Loehr & Schwartz, 2003). Consequently, it is important to build in moments to recharge and refresh even in the best times. This might take the form of a movement break, conversation with a friend, or deep breathing. In addition, downtime, daydreaming, and periods of silence can also be rejuvenating.

IT'S TIME TO RETHINK TIME

Over fifty years ago, psychologist John Carroll (1963) argued for a radical rethinking of time in schools. His call to think about instructional time as the key to learning was later picked up by Benjamin Bloom (1974). However, not much has changed in schools in the intervening years. Mike Schmoker (2009) argues that the poor performance of students is due to the fact that schools are dominated by time-consuming activities that only masquerade as instruction.

Rethinking time is difficult. We too often find ourselves prisoners of the sacrosanct timetable. We are told by the powers that be that one small change will result in a cascade of catastrophe. Yet, as noted educator Lee Shulman (2008) states, "Once you break the shackles of time, you will find yourself imagining ways to improve teaching, learning, student motivation and course design that can make a real difference."

When we consider time not as periods of the day that we fill but as a cultural force sending messages about what we value and shaping students' learning, we take a step toward thinking about time differently, toward changing our paradigm with regard to time. It then becomes crucial that we marshal and allocate the resource of time in a way that supports thinking, both our own and that of our students. This means getting clear about our priorities so that we can look beyond the schedule and the coverage of material to focus on the learning and thinking that needs to happen in classrooms. From this understanding of the nature of time, we become more confident and effective in our efforts to provide time for thinking; create as much active, engaged learning time in our class periods as possible; invest time on high-leverage practices early in the school year to build the culture; and nurture and renew the energy needed for learning.

This shift in thinking about time grounds many emerging educational practices today—for example, flipping (Pink, 2010); blended learning (Akyol & Garrison, 2011); banking time (US Department of Education, 1998); block scheduling (Anderson, 2011); massive open online courses, or MOOCs (Friedman, 2013); FedEx days (Pink, 2009); Genius Hour or 20% Time (20-Time in Education, 2013); and slow learning (Quinn, 2006)—as well as more radical moves to rethink the school day, such as those being done in Expanded-Time Schools sponsored by the National Center on Time and Learning (Kaplan & Chan, 2012) and at schools in Ewan McIntosh's network of Design Thinking Schools (http://www.designthinkingnetwork.com/). All of these approaches, methods, and techniques are worth exploring, and I encourage you to do so. We need to shake up the orthodoxy of the school day in a way that will reach more students and produce the kind of engaged, thoughtful, and creative learners we seek. However, bear in mind what Stephen Covey (1994) has observed in his work with thousands of organizations around the world: "If we want to create significant change in the results, we can't just change attitudes and behaviors, methods or techniques; we have to change the basic paradigm out of which they grow. When we try to change the behavior or the method without changing the paradigm, the paradigm eventually overpowers the change" (p. 29). That is why top-down efforts to institute new practices, such as block scheduling, so often fail to thrive. In Covey's words, such practices "can't be installed; they have to be grown. They emerge naturally out of the paradigms that create them" (p. 30).

GETTING A BETTER PERSPECTIVE ON TIME

- Explore your deeply held perceptions of teaching and learning, its mechanisms and its purposes, using the questions posed in the section "Learning to Prioritize and Always Prioritizing Learning."

- Conduct a general time audit of your class. Videotape yourself or enlist a colleague to observe how instructional time is spent in your class. The observer records the time spent on various activities, such as instructions/directions, transitions, discussion, lecture, independent work, group work, and so on. Gathering data over a week would be ideal to get a good picture of how you are spending time. Remember, you're looking to maximize students' interactive instructional time.

- Conduct an "engaged time" audit of the students in your classroom. Enlist an observer to capture data on each student. Working from a class roster and seating chart, every five minutes the observer records how engaged each student is. You can use a simple ranking: F = focused; N = neutral or can't determine; and D = distracted. Using 5-minute intervals (I) in a 60-minute class of 25 students (S), for example, will yield 300 data points (I × S). Divide the number of focused observations (F) plus half the neutral observations (N) by the total number of data points to obtain a *percentage of engaged time* (PET). As a formula, this is: $(F + \frac{1}{2}N) \div (I \times S) = PET$. A total PET score of < 50% is low, 51–60% is average, 61–70% is good, 71–80% is high, above 80% is outstanding.

- Practice increasing your wait time. The best way to do this is to silently count to yourself after you have asked a question before calling on a student. Do the same after a student has answered before you respond, to give the student time to elaborate or for other students to jump in. Take note of any effects you observe. Did more students raise their hands? Are students' responses longer? Are students connecting to others' ideas more often? Do students' elaborate their own initial responses with Wait Time 2?

- Make a list of the various ways that you think you spend time in your class. This should be a personalized list reflecting your own thinking about how you are spending class time. For instance, one teacher might list demonstrating new procedures, answering students' questions about homework, getting started on homework, and discussing possibilities. Another teacher might write getting the class settled, examining different perspectives, exploring possibilities, working through problems in small groups, and analyzing texts. Allocate a percentage for each of the items on the list. This percentage should reflect the total class time over all of your days together, not just a single day. Percentages should add up to 100 percent. Are you spending time on the things that matter the most to you?

- Gather students' perceptions of how you spend time. Type up the list you generated for the previous exercise. Add the category "Other" to the list before making a copy for each student. Have students allocate a percentage for each of the items on the list. This percentage should reflect the total class time over all of your days together, not just a single day. Percentages should add up to 100 percent. Compare your result with your students' ratings. At the bottom of the students' sheet, you might want to add the reflective prompt "To help my learning, I wish our class would spend more time . . ."

- Conduct a time reflection on a unit, course, or year. Write your response to the following prompts: "Based on what I know now, I wish I had spent more time in this unit/course/year on _____. To further my students' learning, I wish I had spent more time doing _____." Now explain and justify your responses to yourself. What makes you say that?

- Identify your "big rocks." What are your top priorities? When it comes to teaching and learning, what are the key practices that for you are "first things" that must receive the highest attention? This is a list of values, principles, and priorities. It is fine to do this in brainstorm mode and generate quite a long list. Working from that list, try to narrow it down to a few key ideas, a list small enough that you could rattle it off to someone who asked.

- Identify your investments. What are you investing time in now so that you will save time later? Are there any things you are doing now that appear efficient on the surface but aren't proving to be very effective in the long run? Share your ideas with other teachers as a way of expanding the group's repertoire of effective strategies and helping hone those that aren't.

- Examine your energy. Over the course of a week, reflect on your energy expenditure each day using the technique described in the section "Managing Energy, Not Time."

- Have students at your school do their own energy assessment using the same method. Examine the schoolwide data for trends. Where are students energized? What kinds of activities are leaving them depleted? What might be done about that?
- Create energy renewal rituals. Look through your schedule to predict where and when you might be running low on energy. Create a ten-minute ritual (walking around the building, deep breathing, having coffee with a friend) to renew your energy in your day.
- Turn an energy drain into an energy gain. What important things are you currently doing that don't feel as effective as they could be and that are causing a drain rather than a gain in energy? How might you go about accomplishing that task in a way that would be more energizing?
- Try out something radical and new (for you). Read more about genius hour, 20% time, flipping, or the IFS, and trial your own mini version of it. Reflect on your experience. Was it time well spent for you and your students?

CHAPTER 5

Modeling
Seeing Ourselves through Our Students' Eyes

mod•el•ing |ˈmädl-iNG| (Brit. modelling) verb: To display, demonstrate, or draw attention to as an example for others to follow or imitate. • To teach by example as in a role model, mentor, or expert-apprentice situation. Noun: A system or thing used as an example to follow or imitate. As a culture shaper, modeling operates on both an explicit and an implicit level. Explicitly, we may demonstrate techniques, processes, and strategies in a way that makes our own thinking visible for students to learn from and appropriate. Implicitly, our actions are constantly on display for our students. They see our passions, our interests, our caring, and our authenticity as thinkers, learners, community members, and leaders. Adult models surround students and make real a world that they may choose to enter or reject.

T here is always a sense of ongoing, extended inquiry present whenever I visit Natalie Belli's classroom, and today is no exception. Currently the room is busting at the seams with half-completed student projects related to the Triangle Trade, the trade route that existed between New England, Africa, and the West Indies during the colonial era. This is just one of the many long-term or ongoing projects Natalie manages as a teacher of humanities. When her fifth graders are not preparing for a mock town hall meeting, redesigning the city's recycling program, building their own shelters, collaborating with the New England Aquarium, or writing books to go into the library at the Mukwashi Trust School in Zambia, they can be found curled up with a book on the large sofa in the back of the room, conversing with peers in a book club, or getting feedback on their writing from a friend.

While remaining faithful to the curriculum she needs to address, Natalie doesn't expressly worry about preparing her students for the state's standardized test. As a group, her students consistently exceed expectations for their performance on the state test, this even with a sometimes significant special needs population. Rather than focusing on the test, Natalie sees her main goals as empowering students as readers and writers, building a strong connection with both the local community and the world, and igniting the sparks of creativity, passion, and imagination that propel lifelong learning. Achieving these goals is a matter not only of providing powerful learning opportunities but also of modeling. In reflecting on her teaching, Natalie comments, "I want them to know that I am authentic, that I am true, and that I value them. If they leave me a book [that they wish to share with me], they know I will read and comment on it, and those comments have to be authentic. They have to be genuine."

The snow has melted in Marblehead, Massachusetts, and there is a hint of spring in the air as Natalie's fifth graders enter the room fresh from their recess outside in the newly minted warmth. Students chat, and Natalie holds brief side conversations with individual students as the class settles into their seats. As soon as Natalie begins to speak to the whole class, it is clear that she is presenting herself to her students as a thinker and learner, not merely as someone who will direct their actions and monitor their time. "You know how sometimes I get to thinking about something at night and it wakes me up and then I can't stop thinking about it?" Natalie inquires.

"Yeah," a number of students respond, nodding their heads.

"Well," Natalie continues, "last night, I woke up thinking about something that happened yesterday." With this brief introduction, I'm alerted to the fact that such personal stories of Natalie's thinking are not new to her students. The class seems well aware of Natalie's preoccupation with ideas as well as her proclivity for late-night ruminations. Her remarks also provide a powerful backdrop for the learning of the class in that her comments reveal for her students how her instructional plans come together.

Natalie explains the thought that kept her awake. "Yesterday, Josh said he was done with his book and he needed a new book. That planted a seed in the back of my mind that started me thinking, 'Oh no, there is so much to do. I need to start new book clubs.' And I started to think, 'Oh no, we are behind. I need to keep up.'" With these words, Natalie demonstrates to her students just how much their words and actions play into her thinking. She lets her students know that she is not marching through a presequenced set of activities but that everything that happens in their classroom is a responsive act based on their learning needs.

In sharing the angst that woke her up, Natalie has captured students' attention and revealed herself authentically to them. Slowing the cadence of her voice and projecting a more even, less anxious tone, Natalie signals to the students that something different is about to happen as she continues her story of late-night thinking:

> Then I thought of a time I was in camp, and we were hiking up a mountain. I was following our guide, and I got worried I wasn't keeping up, so I started walking faster and faster. When we got done with our hike, the guide said how tired he was. How he had never done that hike in that short a time before. And I said, "Really?" He said, "Yeah, I kept trying to keep up with you." And I said, "I thought I was trying to keep up with you!" Then he told me he didn't ever set a pace, that he always just tried to walk at the pace of the fastest hiker.

Natalie pauses to let the meaning of the story sink in for her students before making the transition back to her concern about keeping up with the needs of the class. "And so I let Fletcher [her dog] out, and then I started to jot down my own thinking about our pace, about where we were at in our hike."

Natalie's recounting of a long-ago experience is much more than demonstrating an activation of prior knowledge. On the surface, her story of hiking has no connection to a student needing a new book to read or her general concern for shepherding the learning of the class. What the story represents is both a moral and a metaphor. In recalling it, Natalie is demonstrating that the things we learn from our life experience often transcend the experience itself. Natalie didn't just learn to walk slower; she learned something about pacing, unspoken expectations, and how the pressures we feel may come from ourselves and not others. She is demonstrating that in recalling events, one can also recall larger lessons that might apply to new situations. Interestingly, Natalie doesn't spell out these lessons for her students, but she does allow time for their meaning to sink in before picking up the hiking story as a metaphor that guided her next actions in thinking not about "pressure" and "needs" but about "pace" and "our hike."

Sarah, clearly captivated by the tale of night awakening, recollections, and a dog, raises her hand to ask, "What time was it?" "It was 2 a.m.," Natalie replies as she reaches for her journal. Opening her journal to last night's entry, she slides the book under the document camera and flicks it on, illuminating the whiteboard with her late-night jottings:

- Writing a library
- Making cultural connection through poetry
- Mukwashi Trust & learning together
- *Hatchet.* Crocs, snow, otters and tribes
- Pen pals and learning about culture
- Found out that they [Mukwashi Trust School] want to build a library
- We decided we could write them one
- The birth of our snow poems
- Reflections
- What we needed to know about Mukwashi students
- What we wanted Mukwashi students to know about us
- Photographs, illustrations, Ron Berger and Austin's butterfly. Revisions
- Thinking routines: 321, CSI, STW, Ladder [of Feedback] Protocol
- Collaborating w 4th graders and 2nd graders

No doubt Natalie's students were already familiar with the fact that she kept a journal. Furthermore, the idea that she would share her thoughts with them seemed not to be unusual. Yet I am struck by the power of this simple act and what it communicates. First, in keeping her own journal, as she asks her students to do, and using it authentically as a means of capturing her thinking, Natalie serves as a model for students to emulate.

She is not merely showing students how to write in a journal; she is modeling its actual utility. Her story of waking, worrying, thinking, and then writing in her journal highlights for her students how to integrate a journal into one's life. Second, in displaying the journal page in its informality with side notes, highlighting, and use of red pen, she makes her thinking visible in all its messiness. Third, there is a transparency, authenticity, and vulnerability to this sharing that forges a bond between teacher and student. This is enhanced because Natalie has made it so clear to her students, through the modeling of her thinking, how she plans for learning in their classroom by constantly taking stock of where the class is, their needs, and a puzzling-through together of where to go next.

Deciphering her notes for the class, Natalie explains, "I started jotting and thinking about all the things we have been doing, what we have done this year, and accomplished. Not about being behind, but about where we are and what we have learned. I started thinking about Mukwashi [the school in Zambia where Natalie volunteers and for whom the students are creating a library] and where we started. I started just writing down some words that came to mind." Natalie reads through the list, expanding and clarifying some of the things she has written. When she has finished, she raises her arms toward the ceiling in a gesture that says, "Look at how much we have accomplished."

Leaning against the table where the document camera resides, Natalie lets out a sigh of contentment. "You know sometimes when it is going so fast and life is moving forward, it takes slowing down and taking time to notice where you are," she reflects. Looking around the room, she adds, "So I am going to pause and let you do some thinking about this process. So let's just think about what all of this meant to you." She pauses to give students time to think and then adds, "Talk to me about your reflections. Use your language of thinking. What do you value about where we are and what we have done?"

As students ponder Natalie's request, she moves around the room and finds an empty seat among the students. Ava raises her hand and, with a nod from Natalie, begins to speak. "I really value how we are helping them [the students at Mukwashi Trust School] learn about snow. I think it is nice that we can put some images from our lives into theirs through writing. And then maybe they will write [us] back something about what we don't know . . . We've never been [to Zambia]. Maybe they will write us about the mud seasons." Following on, Sean adds, "Sort of like Ava's [comment]. I value. I realize how much different one thing we might think is common and doesn't really matter might be so different to someone else." Natalie elaborates on Sean's remarks: "Something that we take for granted perhaps. Isn't that interesting. That is how I felt as well when I was over there. What we take for granted or just assume someone else might know."

In these students' comments we see the effects of Natalie's previous modeling. Early in the year, Natalie introduced the Ladder of Feedback (Perkins, 2003) as a structure for both giving feedback and responding to others (see appendix B). Using the ladder, respondents begin by asking any clarifying questions they might have; they then state what they value about the work or the object of reflection before moving on to concerns, wonderings, and suggestions. Natalie took time to explicitly model use of the Ladder of Feedback using a fishbowl technique (Miller & Benz, 2008) with a small group while the rest of the class observed. Natalie also uses the Ladder of Feedback in her own conferencing with students. This demonstrates to students the authenticity of the steps—this isn't just something students do but is also a technique that adults use in giving feedback—as well as Natalie's commitment to the process. In students' comments about the class's activities, we see how they have picked up the language of valuing as both positive and useful.

As the sharing continues, more students offer their ideas about what they have learned through the class's work with the Mukwashi Trust School: the value of sharing with others, learning about new cultures, and being surprised along the way. Ben, a highly able and mature student, then takes the conversation in a slightly different direction, reflecting on the actual writing of poems about snow to share with the students in Zambia: "I thought it was hard. I do value that we were teaching them stuff about snow. But I thought it was really hard to write poems. You know how you said it just flows. I tried to do that," Ben explains ("Me too" another voice in the room echoes), "but it ended up looking just really weird. I just wrote down everything that came to my mind, and it didn't look right."

Natalie rises from her seat and begins a dialogue with Ben:

NATALIE: This is my question: Did you feel safe in knowing that you had opportunities for revision and to talk to your friends?

BEN: Yes, Anna helped and so did Sean, and AJ did one day. I did have a lot of contribution from . . . from (another student whispers the word "peers") . . . peers.

NATALIE: Can I ask specifically how did they help? Did they just say, "Oh good job," or how did they help?

BEN: They told me some words could be changed and also on the drawing. I got a lot of help from Sean especially. There is a very different way of drawing things like buildings. The way I draw is I mostly just draw people. No buildings. Just mostly focused on people. So I'm not used to drawing buildings, and that was harder for me.

NATALIE: So I am wondering then, with that observation, if this were a second project if you would be taking a photograph of something that would be more your style. I think it very interesting that you said it was difficult because for me I was thinking, oh I'm going to have them writing about snow and that might seem easy or simple.

BEN: No. It was difficult.

In this exchange, Natalie doesn't try to minimize Ben's discomfort or that of others. Instead she directs the discussion to what strategies and supports existed to move beyond the initial discomfort. In doing so, Ben's reflections become a model for others of how to deal with difficulty and challenge. The fact that he is a highly able student demonstrates that all learners face challenges. His use of his peers to facilitate his learning, a process constantly encouraged by Natalie, reinforces the message that learning is as much a collaborative endeavor as it is an individual enterprise.

Natalie directs the class's attention to their current study of the Triangle Trade, making the connection between their past and current efforts in writing poetry. "As we get ready for our simulation of the Triangle Trade, you will be writing a poem that captures the essence of the commodity you chose and its role in the trade. To help you generate some ideas, you might want to use one of the thinking routines to really help you understand it and to gather some ideas." Natalie then reviews some of the thinking routines students might find helpful, such as See-Think-Wonder; 3—2—1 Bridge; and Step Inside (see Ritchhart et al., 2011).

To give students a better feel for the creative process she is offering, Natalie shows them, by thinking aloud for them, how these processes might look. "I tried this out. I tried this out with one of Tom Feelings's pieces of art [from his book *The Middle Passage*] to look at and stare at for a while to just think." Natalie slides a page from the book under the document camera, and a dramatic pen-and-ink drawing of a ship is revealed on the screen. Feelings's drawings combine realistic scenes overlaid with evocative spiritual imagery as if the ghosts of the past inhabit the scene. "So, if my cargo was 'the enslaved,'" Natalie offers. "If that is who I am. I wanted to really start thinking and step inside that person or persons and think about what was it like on that ship?" She then extends her questioning: "What was it like crossing that Middle Passage? What was it even like before that in my own village I left?"

Keeping in mind the goal of understanding what it might be like to be the cargo in the Triangle Trade, even if that cargo might be inanimate, Natalie begins to think aloud for her students using the routine See-Think-Wonder as a loose framework. "Looking at this picture, I'm looking at these two people with their mouths open," Natalie offers as she points to two figures in the drawing. "I'm wondering what they are saying. I wonder what is coming out of their mouths. I'm looking at their eyes, and they look really, really frightened. They look like they are coming right out of the ship, but at the same time they look like they are in the water." Directing students' attention to another part of the drawing, she adds, "And it also looks like there is an image of the moon, the moon and sun almost eclipsing. Then I looked at the ship, and the ship itself looks like a musket or rifle, and this makes me think that there is so much death in this picture." Because her focus is on capturing feelings and mood to provide a basis for students' poetry, Natalie's quick think-aloud focuses on these elements. A careful analysis of the artwork isn't needed, as students have already read the book together and are familiar with the Middle Passage.

Using her See-Think-Wonder as a starting point, Natalie continues her think-aloud to demonstrate how she turned those initial thoughts into words that might form the basis for a poem: "So what I said to myself was, all right, I am going to start my thinking with a 3, 2, 1 [3 words, 2 questions, 1 metaphor]. This was just the start of my thinking about ideas for my poem." Replacing Tom Feelings's image under the document camera with that of her journal, Natalie reads the 3, 2, 1 that she has recorded:

Bondage. Property. Inhuman.

Will I survive? Do I want to survive?

I'm a submissive animal that shivers in the bowels of the ship.

"And that was my start of thinking about this. You might want to use other routines or combine routines to help you get started with your thinking," Natalie concludes. Before sending off students to work independently, Natalie shares one last model, a trite bit of rhyming poetry on the Triangle Trade taken from an old textbook. As Natalie reads the poem, her students' eyes widen at the poem's banality. I notice many students' backs stiffening as they listen. "I know," Natalie empathizes. "That's not really what we've come to expect from good poetry, is it? You'll be able to do much better."

Students get to work on their ideas, some thinking aloud with peers. Just as Natalie had modeled, students use various strategies to generate words, phrases, and ideas for their poems as a starting point rather than jumping into writing a poem. Natalie moves around the room talking with students about their ideas. As students begin the actual writing of their poems, Natalie conferences with them using the Ladder of Feedback.

Marcus has chosen molasses as his commodity and is eager to share his poem with Natalie. After he has read the poem aloud, Natalie works her way up the Ladder of Feedback, beginning with clarifying questions. "Could you clarify for me how you started?" she asks. Marcus responds that he created a concept map to get his initial ideas out. Natalie reads a bit of the poem aloud: "I am the running engine of the huge Triangle Trade . . . I am crammed into a tiny cask, on a tiny boat, going on a not so tiny journey." Moving up the ladder, she responds, "I value the figurative language you have used and the sensory images. I like the repetition, the alliteration." Moving to concerns, Natalie points out a few lines in the poem that she feels could be made stronger. "Maybe you need to play around with some different language here," she suggests as she reaches the top of the Ladder of Feedback. It's a brief interchange, but yet another authentic model of a process she wants her students to own.

As the end of the school day rapidly approaches, Natalie stops to confer with one last student, a particularly shy boy who doesn't often speak out in class. As she reads the draft of his poem about the commodity of guns, she gasps. "Can I share this? This one line?" she asks. Ryan nods his head yes, and Natalie calls out, "Class, listen to this." She pauses for emphasis and then slowly reads, "'I am the spine of war.'" "That is such a powerful metaphor and image," she says to Ryan as she stands, once again modeling her love of language and delight in what her students produce.

One certainly wouldn't be alone in asking, How can you possibly get fifth graders excited about writing poetry connected to the Triangle Trade? Yet Natalie accomplishes this with ease, making the task feel new, meaningful, and important. As students begin to pack up, Natalie gives some parting feedback to the group: "Great efforts, everyone. I can't wait to see how these poems develop. So many good ideas, and your use of metaphors and language is just blowing me away, guys. You've really stepped inside the cargo you are representing."

It is easy to be captivated by the learning going on in Natalie's classroom. There is a level of engagement with ideas, curiosity about the world, support for the learning of others, desire to challenge oneself at the highest level, and genuine pride of accomplishment that permeates the class. It is a learning community in the best sense, dedicated to raising the individual up with the group. While energy abounds, it is also a calm space. To understand how Natalie accomplishes this, it is instructive to look at how she teaches both implicitly and explicitly through her modeling. Teachers often think of modeling as demonstrating, standing up before the class to show them a process or procedure that they want students to take on. This is explicit modeling. But there is also the modeling of who we are as thinkers and learners, our implicit modeling. We see in Natalie's teaching a range of modeling practices that span this continuum from implicit to explicit. In formal terms, these can be identified as

- Dispositional apprenticeship: being a role model of learning and thinking
- Cognitive apprenticeship: making our thinking visible
- Gradual release of responsibility: modeling for independence
- Interactive modeling: learning from examples, practice, and reflection

Because modeling is almost a hidden dimension of teaching, understanding each of these practices more fully can be useful as we seek to create a culture of thinking in our schools, classrooms, and organizations. In addition, understanding teaching through modeling helps us better understand the power, nuance, and complexity of incidental learning while shattering the paradigm that the practice of teaching consists largely of the delivery of information.

DISPOSITIONAL APPRENTICESHIP: BEING A ROLE MODEL OF LEARNING AND THINKING

In the 1970s, Dr. Daniel C. Tosteson, dean of the Harvard Medical School, was already thinking about how computers would revolutionize medicine. In addition, he was concerned with the focus of medical schools on transmitting vast amounts of information for students to ingest and spit back on exams. He knew that this kind of training didn't make for good doctors, and he wanted to shift the focus of medical education from the acquisition of knowledge alone to the ability to use that knowledge to solve problems. Largely through Tosteson's efforts, the "case study method" became the norm for learning not only at Harvard but also at medical schools around the world (Weber, 2009). Speaking at a meeting of medical school deans, Tosteson (1979) told the audience, "We must acknowledge again that the most important, indeed, the only, thing we have to offer our students is ourselves. Everything else they can read in a book or discover independently, usually with a better understanding than our efforts can convey" (p. 693). He went on to say, "I believe that the modern jargon [for this] is 'role models.'"

If speaking today, Tosteson might have changed "read in a book" to "get online." However, his words, spoken nearly four decades ago, are no less prescient. Teachers are indeed role models. We inspire. We teach by example. And we manifest for our students what it means to be a thinker and a learner. Working with our colleagues, we provide an intellectual life into which our students may grow. However, it would be a mistake to equate "role model" with "exemplar." No one is perfect, and although we might have personal heroes or mentors whom we aspire to be like, seldom do they embody every quality to perfection. Indeed, research has shown that people in new learning situations don't seek out total role models, but use partial models that embody specific qualities, practices, or behaviors, and learn from what those models have to offer (Filstad, 2004). In thinking about being role models for our students, we need to think about what we have to offer through being the best of who we are.

Another reason why we must avoid the notion of being an exemplar is that it actually goes against the grain of what it means to be a thinker and a learner. Learning is messy. Thinking can run into dead ends. We get stuck in solving problems and have to get ourselves unstuck. Our decisions often try to balance competing needs, but those decisions may seem less balanced in hindsight. Thinking and learning don't require perfection as much as they require constant monitoring, assessment, revision, and reflection. Indeed, it could be argued that little is learned when things go perfectly. Our mistakes offer some of the best avenues for learning. What we want to show our students is this reality. How we handle mistakes. How we learn from experience. How we plan but also how we adjust midstream. How we reflect. All this, as well as the questions that burn inside us and drive our curiosity.

Writing about passionate teachers, Robert Fried (1995) says that they "are always taking risks, and they make at least as many mistakes as anybody else (probably more than most). What's different is how they react to their mistakes: they choose to acknowledge and learn from them, rather than to ignore or deny them." Fried explains the effect these actions have on classroom culture: "they help make the classroom a safer place for students to make their own mistakes and learn from them" (p. 27).

Of course, sometimes vulnerability can be hard for teachers to model. Our authority, ego, and identity can get wrapped up in the expertise we possess, and this kind of exposure can feel to us as though we are losing our hold on that identity. The important thing to remember is that in modeling your learning, you are not giving up any of your expertise. In fact, what you are modeling is the desire to develop even more expertise. If students seem shocked that we "don't know" something or that we made a mistake, we need to quickly disabuse them of the notion that being learned means not making mistakes or covering up for a lack of knowledge. We, as well as our students, need to lay claim to the power of "not knowing" yet "still seeking."

We can think of this kind of role modeling as providing students with a dispositional apprenticeship. In any apprenticeship, an individual learns from someone who is more skilled in a particular target area. Apprentices are newcomers to a community of practice who have the opportunity to advance their skills through their organized participation within that community (Rogoff, 1990). In a dispositional apprenticeship, our students have the opportunity to learn from us the traits, characteristics, and values of a mature and dedicated learner and thinker. Through our modeling, we have the opportunity to nurture the very attitudes, values, and behaviors we want to see in our students.

While a learner's observation and reflection on what is observed is a useful part of any apprenticeship (Cruess, Cruess, & Steinert, 2008), our learning may occur on a more subliminal level as well. Recent neurological research has shown that human beings are hardwired to experience events and feelings through observation alone, due to what are called mirror neurons (Hari & Kujala, 2009; Winerman, 2005). This neural mechanism is both automatic and involuntary. Merely watching someone engage in an activity can cause our neurons to fire as if we were engaging in it ourselves. Think of your automatic response when you witness someone bumping his head. Interestingly, studies have shown that we are even able to distinguish the intent of actions as well. In studies, subjects responded differently to a person picking up a teacup to drink than they did to a person picking up a teacup to clear the table.

Mirror neurons fire most strongly for people with whom we identify (Immordino-Yang, 2008), which may also explain why modeling is such a powerful teaching tool, as Tosteson and others have recognized. They also may help explain why we recognize that curiosity is often contagious and why being treated with respect causes us to return the sentiment. We are literally programmed to pay attention to and learn from others.

Because apprentices learn largely through their informal, ongoing, and perhaps even involuntary observation of experts rather than through direct teaching, it is important to acknowledge that as teachers we are always modeling. We are always on. Our students will take note of the dispositions we display whether we would like them to or not. Ted and Nancy Sizer (2000) captured this sentiment nicely in the title of their book *The Students Are Watching*.

In Natalie's classroom, we see the modeling of dispositions in her telling the story of her late-night waking. Looking at the metanarrative being communicated through her story, we can identify a host of messages about thinking and learning. Her story revealed to students that thinkers worry and get concerned sometimes. At the same time, she demonstrated how not to get caught up in such worries or to let them control you. By using her journal to make notes of all that the class had accomplished, Natalie showed students how to step back and get perspective on a problem rather than jumping in to solve it too quickly. She also exhibited how to question assumptions, in this case about pacing. Furthermore, she modeled for them what it means to be part of a learning group by working to identify the right pace for the group rather than trying to set a pace that others might not be able to match. Later in the lesson, Natalie modeled her passion for language. Throughout this lesson and in others I have observed, I have seen her exhibit a dedication to understanding, respect for others, and a desire to learn. I witnessed these dispositions becoming a part of students' repertoire in the class I visited.

By putting herself on display in all her authenticity, Natalie gave her students a chance to learn from her. She didn't need to plan for this or devise a lesson for her students. She just needed to "be" it. In fact, at the end of the day, Natalie apologized to me for the lesson, saying that this wasn't what she had originally planned, but that it was just where she and they were at this point in time, and she had to be true to that. This is perhaps the hardest part of a dispositional apprenticeship: others can only learn from what we have to offer. We can't fake this kind of modeling, but we can, and must, open ourselves up to it. We must allow ourselves to be genuine. This genuineness lies at the heart of Parker Palmer's work and his book *The Courage to Teach* (1998). The courage he speaks of is allowing ourselves to be genuine in the classroom and to bring ourselves to our teaching. This means we must bring our vulnerabilities as well as our strengths.

In a community of learners, teachers are not the only models, of course. Students are influenced by their peers and by seeing their attitudes and dispositions on display. In Natalie's class, Ben's reflections on his struggle writing and illustrating his snow poem provided a model for others. Natalie very astutely moved Ben's reflections from a focus on his frustrations and negative feelings about the process to how he dealt with those difficulties and challenges. By directing his attention to those aspects, Natalie was able to provide students with a model of how even a strong student faces challenges and must persevere through them.

Ted and Nancy Sizer (2000) argue that it is not just teachers who model values and dispositions; it is also the institutions themselves.

All high schools teach. Their rules and routines are lessons of substance and value. Thoughtfully or unthinkingly, students and teachers ingest these values, thereby learning to live by them. These lessons may promote optimism or cynicism, hard work or shortcuts . . . To find the core of a school, don't look at its rulebook or even its mission statement. Look at the way the people in it spend their time—how they relate to each other, how they grapple with ideas. Look for the contradictions between words and practice, with the fewer the better. Try to estimate the frequency and the honesty of its deliberations. (Kindle locations 243, 374)

In short, for institutions to be effective models of the values they espouse for their students, those same values and expectations must hold for the adults. Because institutions can never adequately garner respect, courage, discipline, curiosity, honesty, integrity, and so on through enforcement alone, their best hope is to model these dispositions and to make the school a home for their values. Of course, to do this requires first identifying the values, dispositions, and behaviors we want to see in our students and then turning the mirror on ourselves to see if we are displaying those same virtues.

COGNITIVE APPRENTICESHIP: MAKING OUR THINKING VISIBLE

In the training metaphor of learning that dominates much of what happens in the world of education, novices are seen to be lacking in skills that they must first acquire before meaningful participation can occur. While in training, individuals may be kept separate from experts or more advanced members and given smaller, atomized tasks to do in preparation for "later"—but in some instances, that later never comes. Furthermore, the tasks assigned may bear little resemblance to the authentic tasks engaged in by experts. This is markedly different from an apprenticeship, in which newcomers are regularly given opportunities for meaningful guided participation in an authentic task within a support community. In a true apprenticeship, complex and important skills are learned contextually and often informally through observation, coaching, and successive approximation (Brown, Collins, & Duguid, 1989). The apprenticeship model has long been championed for the authentic learning opportunities it provides (Brown et al., 1989; Dewey, 1916; Lave & Wenger, 1991; Perkins, 2009; Rogoff, 1990; Vygotsky, 1978; Wertsch, 1995). We will discuss the idea of authentic learning more in the next chapter, on the cultural force of opportunities. Here I want to draw a distinction between the cognitive apprenticeship model we are about to explore and both traditional apprenticeship learning and the dispositional apprenticeship discussed in the previous section.

In the dispositional apprenticeship, we extend the traditional apprenticeship model to suggest that the object of learning need not always be a particular skill set, such as cabinetmaking, but can also include the habits, traits, qualities, and dispositions of the expert. Such dispositions are constantly being modeled, thus providing ample opportunity for the novice to take them on. The dispositional apprenticeship is quite informal, always occurring, and often understood in the sense of the expert/teacher acting as a role model. This means that at times neither the apprentice nor the expert may even be fully aware of what is truly being passed on.

In defining a cognitive apprenticeship, we broaden the concept of apprenticeship even further, suggesting that mastery and becoming more expert is more than a matter of acquiring skills but must also include an understanding of how experts think: how they work through difficulties, how they make judgments about quality, how they identify problems, the decision-making processes they employ, and so on. However, these things are not as easily observable as the explicit behaviors and actions in a traditional or even a dispositional apprenticeship. In fact, the very thing to be learned in a cognitive apprenticeship is too often hidden from observation. Consequently, a cognitive apprenticeship requires the expert/teacher to assume a more overt role in modeling as Collins, Brown, and Holum (1991) explain, "In cognitive apprenticeship, one needs to deliberately bring the thinking to the surface, to make it visible, whether it's in reading, writing, or problem solving. The teacher's thinking must be made visible to the students and the student's thinking must be made visible to the teacher" (p. 3).

As Collins et al. (1991) note, making thinking visible lies at the heart of a cognitive apprenticeship. Furthermore, a robust apprenticeship is a two-way street between the teacher and the student. The more expert practitioner must open himself or herself up to illuminate and demystify the thinking process for the learner. This overtness allows the learner to observe, take on, and begin to practice these thinking moves. The student, in turn, must make his or her thinking visible so that the teacher can coach, correct, offer feedback, and provide support as the student gradually takes on these moves.

Without an understanding of the thinking that lies behind an expert's actions, it is all too easy for learners to focus on the wrong things, develop rigid procedures, or engage in mindless mimicry. I'm reminded of a story an acquaintance once told me, and that I've since heard repeated elsewhere, that beautifully captures the ease with which these kinds of errors can occur. My colleague was invited to an Easter dinner with friends. Sitting down to the exquisitely laid table, the guests all expressed their approval as the hostess placed an amazing glazed ham in the center of the table. The hostess remarked how she had baked it using her grandmother's recipe faithfully. During the meal, everyone commented on how tasty the ham was, and my colleague inquired about the recipe.

The hostess went into vivid detail of the process: cutting off the ends of the ham, carefully scoring it and studding it with cloves, roasting it slowly, and of course the basting it every fifteen minutes with the prepared glaze of apricot jam, bourbon, lemon juice, brown sugar, and butter. Acknowledging that the recipe was indeed a success, my colleague then asked, "So why do you cut off the ends of the ham?" The hostess's brow knotted into a quizzical expression as she slowly replied, "I'm not quite sure; I got the recipe from my mother." Her mother, who was also at the Easter table, then chimed in, "I'm not sure either. I just remember watching my mother fix this every Easter and on special occasions. I watched her carefully and wrote down everything exactly as she did it, since she didn't work from a recipe."

Their curiosity now piqued, the hostess's mother got up from the table and called her mother, the grandmother, on the phone to resolve the mystery. Once holiday greetings and pleasantries had been exchanged, the grandmother quickly resolved the group's quandary: "Oh, I always cut off the ends of the ham because the pan I had at the time was never big enough to fit the whole ham."

Because the grandmother hadn't made her thinking visible to her daughter, her daughter picked up on a meaningless action and incorporated it into her schema of how to prepare the ham. This mindless repetition was then handed down to the daughter as it became formalized in a written recipe. Of course, learners can question experts about their thinking, provided there exists a relationship where this is possible and given that the learner recognizes the importance of understanding the thoughts behind actions and not just the actions themselves.

We saw Natalie providing students with a window into her thinking as she thought aloud about the process of writing poetry. The class's topic, the cargo of the Triangle Trade, might have resulted in superficial, uninspired writing if Natalie had framed the assignment with a bunch of constraints about how long the poems must be, what must be included, and so on. Instead, Natalie focused on the authenticity of writing poetry and provided her students with an apprenticeship into this process. Therefore, her efforts began not with requirements but by modeling to demonstrate how to get inspiration in advance of writing and how to gather potentially evocative language that might be useful in writing. Natalie used a drawing by Tom Feelings from his book *The Middle Passage* for this demonstration. She thought aloud for her students while looking at this picture, using the See-Think-Wonder routine loosely as a scaffold. This, too, was a model of how thinking routines are not mere activities for students but tools that all learners can make use of when appropriate. Finally, Natalie segued into using the 3—2—1 Bridge routine (minus the bridging component). It is important to note that students were already familiar with both of these routines. Thus Natalie wasn't demonstrating the routines. She was demonstrating how to gather inspiration and language prior to writing.

What Natalie did is sometimes referred to as a "think-aloud" (Davey, 1983) or "real-time modeling" (Barell, 1991). It is a strategy often used by teachers of reading to model reading comprehension, and may also be referred to as "interactive comprehension instruction" (Lapp, Fisher, & Grant, 2008). Although quite commonly used in elementary schools, it is a less common teaching practice in middle and high schools, despite its effectiveness for helping learners deal with complex discipline-specific texts (Lapp & Fisher, 2007). The strategy is not limited to reading, either. Its use extends to math (Collins, Brown, & Newman, 1989), behavior management (Camp, Blom, Heber, & Doorninck, 1977), the development of the executive function of the brain (Willis, 2011)—and even the baking of holiday hams! In short, it is the strategy of choice when learners need to learn how to think like experts.

Fisher and Frey (2008) point out that such "modeling does not mean providing explanations or questioning students; it means demonstrating the way experts think as they approach problems" (p. 34). Modeling differs from traditional didactic teaching in its embeddedness and authenticity. As Bandura (1986) states, "Learning cognitive skills can be facilitated simply by having models verbalize their thought strategies aloud as they engage in problem solving activities" (p. 74). He goes on to state the importance this has for struggling learners: "Children and adults who suffer deficiencies in problem solving learn effective strategies by observing how successful models go about gaining information for evaluating alternatives" (p. 103).

Using this premise of making thinking visible so that others might learn from its example, several well-researched and effective programs have been designed. One is the Making Thinking Visible approach (Ritchhart, Church, & Morrison, 2011) developed by my colleagues and me at Project Zero at the Harvard Graduate School of Education. Another example is the Paired Problem Solving technique developed by Arthur Whimbey and Jack Lochhead (1999) to facilitate the development of mathematical problem solving. Using this technique, a problem solver verbalizes his or her thought process with the encouragement of a listener. The listener solves the problem with the problem solver, relying only on the processes the problem solver has articulated. If errors emerge, then the listener alerts the problem solver but does not provide a solution. This constant verbalization of one's thinking in the presence of another externalizes a process so that it can become the object of attention and refinement. Over time, the external verbalization becomes internalized in the form of self-coaching and monitoring.

GRADUAL RELEASE OF RESPONSIBILITY: MODELING FOR INDEPENDENCE

In the apprenticeship model, the goal is for the apprentice to gradually take on the performance of the expert/teacher—in other words, to achieve independence. This is as true of the cognitive apprenticeship as it is for a more traditional, skills-based apprenticeship. But this control doesn't happen by chance; it must be carefully nurtured. First, teachers must identify the specific cognitive processes related to the task at hand and make those visible to students, often identifying them by name. Teachers move from this initial modeling of the cognitive strategies to coaching and scaffolding students as they try out these strategies. Finally, teachers strategically fade away and reduce their supports as students gain independence, encouraging reflection at the end of the process (Collins et al., 1991).

Reciprocal teaching, developed by Palinscar and Brown (1984), is a good example of this process. In deconstructing the mechanisms of effective reading comprehension, they identified four key processes: formulating questions based on the text, summarizing the text, making predictions about what will come next, and clarifying difficulties with the text. (The steps are not always done in this order.) These processes are explicitly taught to students with the teacher modeling the processes initially, then coaching and scaffolding students as they use the strategies. As students become more competent with the processes, the teacher's support fades, allowing students to take increasing control. Eventually, students are expected to use this process in small groups to collectively read through text, and later as an independent strategy.

A crucial component that underlies the power of this method is that the cognitive processes students are learning are both authentic to the task (they are in fact what good readers do naturally when reading challenging texts) and that the processes are highly transferable across a variety of contexts. Thus students are learning a skill they can take with them beyond the classroom. Contrast this with teaching students how to construct a trifold display for the results of their science project. Such a task, though important in the moment, is highly specialized, and may be more about meeting grading requirements than about learning an important cognitive skill.

The design and use of thinking routines, something we take up in chapter 7, fits this model of a cognitive apprenticeship that moves learners toward independence. The routines identify key cognitive processes effective learners use in certain situations, and then make those thinking moves explicit for learners (Ritchhart et al., 2011). Teachers may use the routines to help students explore content or work with ideas, but the ultimate goal is that students will take these on as tools for their independent use. Having frameworks, structures, or routines for thinking on which to draw facilitates learner independence. As Fisher and Frey (2008) point out, "we must give students supports that they can hold on to as they take the lead—not just push them onto the path and hope they find their way. These supports include models of the kind of thinking they will need to do" (p. 33). Therefore, it is our cognitive modeling that is more likely to help our students grow into productive thinkers than the mere modeling of tasks and procedures.

We see this happening beautifully in Natalie's classroom, on several fronts. The Ladder of Feedback is an explicit cognitive tool that identifies key moves in the process of structuring feedback. Early in the year, Natalie overtly modeled using the Ladder of Feedback with students through the use of a fishbowl technique. This technique involves gathering students in a circle around a group or a pair to watch a process unfold in real time. The individuals in the fishbowl are engaging in the process authentically so that others may observe and learn from it. Observers are specifically asked to pay attention to the steps, transitions, and language of the process. Once Natalie had modeled a writing conference with a student in the fishbowl, students were given the opportunity to practice with a partner. Their practice and modeling for each other occurred on an ongoing basis. Natalie consistently uses the Ladder of Feedback when conferencing with students, giving them a constant opportunity to learn. In addition, the ladder is used by the class as a structure for commenting. This gives Natalie an ongoing opportunity to coach students in its use. By the time I observed in Natalie's classroom in the spring, her students were working quite independently with this structure.

Natalie's use of thinking routines follows a similar trajectory. Having already introduced and used the routines numerous times, Natalie was able to turn responsibility over for their independent and flexible use during the poetry-writing process. To judge if our modeling of a cognitive process is successful, it is this level of independence that we want to look for in our students. If students are not making use of the cognitive tools we have modeled, perhaps they don't see their utility, or perhaps we haven't given them the opportunity to acquire independence.

This sequence of moving students toward independence is also referred to as the "gradual release of responsibility," or GRR (Pearson & Gallagher, 1983). Although this model is often used for developing independence in classroom procedures and work processes (Fisher & Frey, 2011), it is certainly useful for promoting independence in thinking as well. Its steps are quite similar to that of a cognitive apprenticeship: (1) focused lesson providing purpose and modeling, (2) guided instruction in which the learner is supported, (3) productive group work in which skills are transferred, and (4) independent tasks allowing students to demonstrate their skill. Coaching, though not specifically identified as a step, occurs with the guided instruction and group work phases. A key aspect of the GRR model is that teachers must create opportunities for the gradual release over time and not expect it to occur right away. This means that the GRR model has to be a deliberate goal of instruction and a conscious piece of the teacher's planning.

INTERACTIVE MODELING: LEARNING FROM EXAMPLES, PRACTICE, AND REFLECTION

The three preceding types of modeling discussed have focused primarily on the development of students as thinkers. By modeling for our students the dispositions and cognitive processes that are important for increased autonomy and independence, we help to build individual competence as well as a collective culture of thinking. However, these three ways of modeling are not the only ones in which teachers engage. As teachers, we often want to model things other than cognitive processes—for instance, how to do a particular activity or practice a social skill. In fact, this kind of modeling of "how to do it" is what often comes to mind when teachers first hear the word "modeling."

Although this kind of modeling takes place frequently in classrooms and is well known to teachers—in fact, some may even suggest that it is a hallmark of teaching—it is not without its difficulties. Too much modeling of skills, procedures, or actions can lead to rote learning and imitation, and can inhibit creativity and original thinking (Haston, 2007). What elementary teacher has not had the experience of modeling an art activity and having a large number of students imitate her example?

It is interesting to note how Natalie avoided this trap in her own modeling with regard to the Triangle Trade poems. First, Natalie focused her modeling on the creative process and not the product. She showed students how she got her thinking started and generated potentially useful language, but she didn't turn that into a poem. Although she did share a model of a poem about the Triangle Trade, it wasn't actually a very good one in that it lacked emotional depth, resonance, or the use of powerful language and imagery. Natalie was, however, able to pull out some positive features of the poem, such as its inclusion of historical information and description of the trade route. By combining the model poem with the process, Natalie was able to articulate for her students what their poems should include.

Another strategy teachers use to avoid students' tendency to imitate is to provide multiple models. Rather than all being exemplars, sometimes these models will have different strengths. By analyzing such models, students are able to discern elements of quality and different approaches to achieving that quality that they may combine in creating original work. Of course, in some instances imitation is desired, as in handwriting, learning a movement in sport or how to throw a ceramic pot, and so on. It is when we desire original or creative expressions from students that we have to guard against imitation.

Another challenge with demonstration modeling of the "This is how you do it" variety is that it often flounders if the "it" being demonstrated has any degree of nuance or complexity. An alternative to this "show and tell" type of modeling is the "interactive modeling" technique developed as part of the Responsive Classroom approach, a social and emotional development program for schools (Wilson, 2012). Interactive modeling involves seven steps: (1) stating the purpose, (2) modeling the behavior, (3) explicit discussion of what students noticed as the teacher modeled, (4) a student (or small group) modeling of what the teacher modeled, (5) discussion of what was noticed in that model, (6) practicing by all students, and (7) feedback to the group.

It is not hard to see why this more deliberate type of modeling might be effective. It incorporates many aspects of good teaching, such as setting a purpose and context for learning, analysis of and attention to key criteria, guided practice, the gradual release of responsibility, and providing feedback. The two rounds of "noticing" are particularly noteworthy because this analysis is developing students' capacity to learn from models in the future by identifying key elements and features that must be present in replicating the model. This is similar to the fishbowl technique used by Natalie in introducing the Ladder of Feedback. Of course, such modeling takes more time than a simple demonstration. Teachers will need to think about what they are modeling and determine whether this is a case where it is important to invest time to make time. For instance, it may well be worth the investment to model effective listening, how to disagree with someone's point respectfully, how to lead a team without dominating it, and so on, for the long-term benefits that are likely to accrue.

LEARNING FROM MODELS

In observing models, whether informally or formally, learners have the opportunity to "take on the other," try out new roles and behaviors, and apprentice into new ways of acting and thinking. But what will they choose to take on? Social cognitive theory suggests that we are more likely to take on behaviors that we see as meeting a need we might have, or the behaviors of those we see as similar to us or whom we respect (Bandura, 1986). This has clear implications for us as teachers. First, if we recognize that a primary need for learners is to feel accomplished and in control, then our modeling of how we control, manage, and direct our learning and thinking is likely to have appeal. Second, in establishing a learning community in which we model a respect for and interest in our students, we lay the context for them to see us as models they wish to imitate. Third, we have to look for what gets recognized and rewarded in our schools, classrooms, and organizations. Students are most likely to take on the behaviors that lead to these rewards.

As we worked our way through different types of modeling in this chapter, our progression has been from the informal, ongoing, and embedded to the increasingly explicit, focused, and directed. All these types of modeling have their place in the classroom. However, as a force shaping the culture of a classroom, school, or organization, it is the informal modeling that has the most power. It is this kind of model that tells students who we really are and what we really value. As the Sizers said, "The students are watching." They see us in our glory and our ignobility. However, rather than seeking to hide our weaknesses, struggles, and shortcomings—which students will inevitably see and notice anyway—we can open ourselves up authentically to our students and show them what it means to be an ongoing learner.

MODELING FOR THE DEVELOPMENT OF THINKING, LEARNING, AND INDEPENDENCE

- Allow yourself to be authentic. Bringing ourselves to our teaching means sharing what we do well as well as where we struggle. Look for opportunities to share your struggles as a thinker and learner with your students.
- Clarify your values. If what you have to offer your students is yourself, what do you want them to take away from their time with you? This isn't about being perfect, but it is about imagining your best self and then constantly striving to put that best self forward.
- Identify your thinking role models. Whom do you know who thinks through problems, reflects on learning, or analyzes situations in a way that you admire? Who is a good model of thinking and ongoing learning in your discipline? Who thinks about their teaching in a way that inspires you? This could be a single person, or, more likely, you will identify partial role models. Reflecting on the actions of these models, make a list of traits, attitudes, thinking moves, and behaviors that you would most like to take on and incorporate in your behavior.
- Ask your students. Discuss with your class the difference between knowing a lot and being a good thinker. Then ask students to identify someone in their lives who they think is a good thinker. As a class, identify some of the traits of a good thinker.
- Observe and analyze. Using a video or pairing with a trusted colleague, observe a lesson and look for the apprenticeship subtext. What dispositions was the teacher displaying that his or her students might be picking up on? When, where, and how did the teacher make his or her thinking visible to students? Were there moments when you had a glimpse of the teacher as a thinker and learner? What were these?
- Share curiosity moments. Curiosity is a highly valued disposition as a driver of new learning. Drawing on the power of our mirror neurons to develop empathetic responses in others, create opportunities for you and your students to share curiosity moments. A curiosity moment is a time when you experience, read, see, or hear about something that prompts questions or wondering in you that stays with you beyond the moment. It keeps you thinking, in other words.

Share your own curiosity moments with your students regularly. Have your students reflect on their term break and identify their own curiosity moments.

- Backwards-design a process. Think of a process that you want your students to get better at doing independently. Reflect on how you go about the process and identify the key thinking moves in which you engage. Model and name these steps explicitly for your students.

- Practice a think-aloud with something difficult. A key part of being an effective learner is knowing what to do when you don't know what to do. Next time you engage in something difficult, model your thinking by doing a think-aloud for your students. This might be when reading a challenging text, trying to synthesize a big topic, planning a project, or engaging in any other activity where you don't already have a clear process in place.

- Plan for the gradual release of responsibility. Identify a process with which you want your students to become independent. Identify those moments when you will model that process, give opportunities for guided practice, provide opportunities for more independent group work, and expect independence.

- Give students practice in noticing. Use the fishbowl technique or the steps of interactive modeling to help students learn to focus on the behaviors you want them to take on.

- Learn to apologize. It takes courage and practice to learn to apologize with grace. Start by identifying an instance from your past in which you know your behavior in class was not what you wanted your students to see of you. The instance could be long past or recent. Now write an apology in which you (1) identify the incident and what was wrong or mistaken about it, (2) share your reflection on your own behavior and why it fell short of your personal standards, and (3) identify how you wish you had responded at the time. Keep up the exercise of writing out your apology until you feel comfortable speaking an apology out loud to your students.

CHAPTER 6

Opportunities
Crafting the Vehicles for Learning

op•por•tu•ni•ties |äpər't(y)ōōnitēs | noun: A set of conditions or circumstances that make it possible to do or achieve something. • An occasion or set of occasions in which certain actions are afforded or become possible. As a culture shaper, the opportunities present will serve either to constrain or enhance the activity of both individuals and the group as a whole. Although it is possible for opportunities to lie hidden, remain untapped, or languish, in strong cultures rich opportunities for growth, advancement, and creativity are prominent. In a culture of thinking, these types of opportunities dominate the landscape, guiding and shaping the activity of the group and engaging all individuals.

G enerally the language that we use to talk about what we do as teachers is one of planning units, writing lessons, preparing activities, generating assignments, and assigning work. However, such language simplifies, obfuscates, and generally misses the point of what great teachers actually do. They create opportunities: opportunities for engagement, to challenge misconceptions, to delve deeply, to explore, to create meaning, to think—in short, opportunities to learn. Although a focus on opportunities to learn takes into account what students are asked to produce, the spotlight is better placed on the process of that production. Does it challenge? Does it require them to think? What resources will be marshaled and how? How will information, content, and knowledge be processed to produce something new and original?

Although many researchers do use the language of "opportunities to learn" (Pianta et al., 2007; Thompson, Senk, & Johnson, 2012), others use a different language to focus our attention on what students are actually doing. For instance, Richard Elmore and colleagues (City, Elmore, Fiarman, & Teitel, 2009) use the term "tasks"; Walter Doyle (1983), "academic work"; and Fred Newmann (Newmann, Bryk, & Nagaoka, 2001), "authentic intellectual work." Doyle argued, "Students will learn what a task leads them to do, that is, they will acquire information and operations that are necessary to accomplish the tasks they encounter" (p. 162). Elmore distills Doyle's statement further into one of the core principles of Instructional Rounds by stating simply, "The task predicts performance" (City et al., 2009). Agreeing with these sentiments, Newmann concludes that we need to focus on the "actual intellectual demands" placed on students. What Doyle, Elmore, and Newmann say about tasks is illuminating, and I will delve into this more deeply later in the chapter. However, I will use the term "opportunities" to describe this cultural force rather than "work" or "tasks" because

1. It directs our attention to what is actually present in any activity in terms of the required and afforded actions, rather than to the product that students will produce.

2. It keeps us focused on building learning-oriented rather than work-oriented schools.

3. Opportunities come in many shapes and sizes, and a "task" is only an opportunity of a particular size and duration.

To be fair, I want to acknowledge that Doyle's (1983) use of the word "work" precedes the research done on work- and learning-oriented classrooms (Marshall, 1987). And in fact, he acknowledges that students' focus on completion of work for grades actually makes it harder for teachers to create work that has meaning. I'll say more about that later, but for now I want to emphasize the larger idea I share with Doyle, Newmann, and Elmore: to understand learning, we have to look beyond what students are asked to produce and to what they are required to do and how they are asked to marshal the resources around them in order to get to that product. It is what students *are actually doing mentally* that matters. Tasks are not equal in this regard. They are distinguished by the opportunities embedded within them.

The opportunities that teachers create are the prime vehicles for propelling learning in classrooms. Without the right vehicles, learning slows down, loses momentum, and in some cases comes to a standstill, producing parking lots rather than speedways. If we are to understand the learning that is happening in any group, it makes sense to examine the opportunities with which the group is engaged—that is, to look at what learners are actually doing and how they are doing it. The three cases that follow provide a context for this examination, allowing us to look at opportunities embedded in regular classroom instruction. These cases vary across grade level and subject area, as well as in their scope and duration, thus enabling us to identify core characteristics that make learning opportunities powerful.

CONSTRUCTING CHARACTER: USING MATHEMATICS TO UNDERSTAND *OTHELLO*'S IAGO

"Who wants to be Iago today?" Tom Heilman inquires of the room full of twelfth graders seated before him at Washington International School in Washington DC. After a long pause, a girl in the front row raises her hand, and Tom presses on, "Who will read Othello?" A boy seated next to the door volunteers, and the two readers pick up where the class left off in act 3, scene 3 of *Othello*. It is a pivotal scene in which the scheming Iago convinces Othello, using nothing more than innuendo and vivid imagery, that Othello's new wife, Desdemona, is cheating on him with his trusted lieutenant, Cassio.

As the two students read their parts, Tom frequently asks them to pause as he queries the class: "What's worth commenting on in that passage? What do you notice? What do you see in the language?" The responses to these questions don't always come easily, but Tom doesn't step in to supply the answers. He lets the questions hang in the air. It is clear that it is the students' job to unpack the play and understand its characters, not Tom's to spoon-feed them his interpretation. The point isn't to learn Shakespeare's play, but to learn how to understand Shakespeare's plays. Slowly students venture forward with their tentative ideas. "He's using animal imagery" one student offers, but then adds "but I don't know what Iago is trying to do with that." Another student chimes in, "He can't really prove they are sleeping together, so he's trying to plant an image in his head." Yet another student picks up on this idea, adding, "He's trying to make Othello see this. He can't, so he is trying to give him some juicy bits to visualize."

As the scene comes to a close, Iago has so managed to convince Othello of Desdemona and Cassio's betrayal that Othello seeks vengeance on them both, urging Iago, "Within these three days let me hear thee say . . . That Cassio's not alive." Placidly, Iago accepts the very request he has sought to provoke from Othello but offers a caveat, "My friend is dead; 'tis done at your request: But let her live." With the scene concluded, Tom turns the class's attention to an exploration of the character Othello: "I'm interested in what you think about Othello from the beginning of the play to now."

Those words roll off Tom's tongue effortlessly, but they are worth closer examination to fully understand what they convey. Rather than ask a question here, Tom chooses to make a statement, an expression of his interest in his students' thinking. Although the question, "How has Othello changed from the beginning of the play to now?" is certainly not a bad question, it can come across as a bit of a test and being closed ended. Students may assume there is a specific answer that the teacher is looking to obtain. By expressing interest in his students' thinking, Tom connects with his students and opens up greater possibilities for discussion, sharing, and dialogue. It is what might be called a "low threshold" invitation (Papert, 1980) that aims to pull more learners into the conversation.

It is worth taking another step back to examine Tom's statement a little further. Where did his statement come from? Like most teachers, Tom didn't specifically sit down and plan out this statement, nor did he weigh the benefits of his expression of interest in his students' thinking against asking the more traditional question about how Othello had changed. Rather, Tom's words emerge from his expectations about teaching and learning—that understanding, learning, and independence are primary goals—as well as from his genuine interest in students' thinking. Because Tom has been working to build a culture of thinking over the last five years and has been using various ideas from Project Zero to do so, these words now emerge naturally for him.

Responding to Tom, Nicco quickly offers up his thoughts to get the conversation moving: "At the beginning, he seemed like a normal kind of good guy. But now, he seems weak and not as respected. He seems insecure." Drawing on the scene that the class has just read, Samantha observes, "It took just one person to convince him that Desdemona was cheating." From the back row a student interjects, "It took just five minutes!" As the conversation continues, students' thoughts turn to Iago. "I would place much more weight on Iago's skills and being very skilled at manipulation, but Othello is definitely insecure," Max offers.

Tom picks up on this observation and presses, "That is the second comment on insecurity. Where can you find support for that in the play from earlier on?" With this simple press for evidence, Tom ratchets up the task from one about opinion to one of reasoned argument. Students fire out evidence in rapid succession: "Othello is constantly saying he doesn't speak well." "He uses Desdemona as the main person who could defend his word." "He had Cassio come with him all the time." "Yeah, a third wheel," another student offers. Charlotte returns to the recent scene: "He doesn't doubt it [Desdemona's infidelity] very directly. He doesn't even question Iago very directly." Jason picks up on the comment and adds, "I think what Charlotte said is more an example of Iago being able to completely overwhelm Othello. Othello wouldn't get himself into this mess without Iago warping his mind. He had to lead him. So I think it is a greater example of Iago leading than Othello feeling that way."

Students have now become entangled in the issue of who these characters are, a point that Tom wants to drive home as particularly important in a play that has been performed over and over again through the ages. "This is a big thing as a director or actor. These things have to be resolved before you can stage the play," Tom comments, leaving the issue to dangle in students' minds. Here we see Tom allowing a big, complex, perplexing issue to hang in the air to serve as an ongoing motivation for understanding. Tom has transported students over the threshold and into the problem space he wants to explore further.

Tom now directs the class's attention to one of Shakespeare's most complex villains. "I want to focus on Iago a bit now." Tom explains his motives: "One of the things I noticed in your orals was that a lot of you were referring to Iago as 'evil.' 'His "evil" deeds . . . ' But you weren't really breaking that down. You were too comfortable with that word." In providing this context, Tom is signalling to his students that he is not merely marching them through a prescribed teaching sequence of a familiar play to prepare them for an exam. His desire is to push them to think more deeply, to grapple with the text, and to come to their own understanding. He states this clearly to them: "I want you to break it down, to dig more deeply."

Tom then lays out the next task for the class: "What I want you to do right now is to take a few minutes and write down five or six character traits of Iago. Jot them down, and I will get you to yell them out, and we will write them down." Pressing students to think more broadly, he adds, "Keep in mind that evil is not a character trait." Once again there is a low threshold of entry to the task, allowing all to participate. At the same time, the task involves the beginnings of analysis. Students must review Iago's words and actions, analyzing them for motive and intent.

As students begin to write down their ideas, one student pushes back: "If we say he is evil and we can back that up, we can use that, right?"

Tom reiterates his stance, "No," and then adds, "What is your definition of evil?"

"Someone who harms others deliberately," the student responds.

"Find a new adjective that captures that," Tom tells him. Another student calls out to the class, "What's the opposite of passionate?" Tom interrupts before anyone has a chance to respond. "You're an intelligent young woman. You can come up with something." In both of these exchanges, Tom signals to students that he wants them to push beyond the easy answers and to think more deeply, at the same time showing that he has confidence in their ability to do so.

After two minutes, Tom asks the class to begin shouting out adjectives. Having given students a few minutes to write their initial ideas rather than jumping immediately into gathering responses, Tom ensures that all students have done some thinking on the topic and have something to contribute. After writing down the first dozen responses, Tom enlists the cooperation of the class. "You guys will have to help me if it seems like things are beginning to repeat." In less than five minutes, the class has generated over fifty words:

Clever	Deceitful	Self-respecting
Sociopath	Resilient	Cynical
Manipulative	Honest	Charming
Persuasive	Cunning	Mysterious
Two-faced	Quick thinker	Immoral
Opportunistic	Brazen	Condescending
Conniving	Resilient	Jealous
Spiteful	Shameless	Arrogant
Exploitive	Guilt free	Pretentious
Dangerous	Seductive	Sadistic
Dishonest	Selfish	Careful
Vengeful	Loveless	Personable

Seductive	Creative	Consistent
Sinister	Malicious	Perceptive
Precocious	Vindictive	Narcissistic
Unethical	Unflinching	Meticulous
True	Plotting	Hypocritical
Poised	Façade-y	Calculating

Putting down the white marker and turning to face the class, Tom exclaims, wide-eyed, "This class is on fire." By pooling ideas, the class was able to generate much more than they could individually, while pushing everyone's grasp of the character beyond his or her individual understanding. Tom then adds, "I want to point this out. When I listened to your orals, how many of these do you think I heard?" One student offers, "I used 'manipulative.'" Tom nods and continues, "But most of these were not there. You need to start delving into the complexity of Iago."

Once again, it is interesting to note what Tom has said and what he has not said. In his comments, Tom frames the larger enterprise, "delving into the complexity of Iago," and places his students' focus squarely on that endeavor. Notice that Tom didn't say, "In your final essay, I'll be looking for . . ." or "To get a top mark from the examiner, you will need to use a more diverse vocabulary." Although such comments are not out of place in a system dominated by test scores, we must recognize that such words actually serve to misdirect rather than direct learning by putting the emphasis both outside the learner and away from the goal of understanding. This is not to say that Tom's students lack in any way for preparedness when it comes to sitting for the International Baccalaureate Diploma. His students do extremely well on these exams, and he and his colleagues have seen performance increase as they have worked to create cultures of thinking in their respective classrooms.

To nudge students further into the complexity of Iago, Tom has carefully crafted a unique opportunity to push their thinking. Having provided the low threshold to entry and created engagement by presenting the need to figure out this complex character, Tom wants his students to use mathematics to literally construct the character of Iago. With just ten minutes left in the period, Tom explains the task: "Look at these [pointing to the whiteboard list of adjectives]. If you had to build Iago, which would you pick? Pick five to ten that you think would go into who you think Iago is." As an aside he adds, "This is not a long exercise, so don't be afraid to add as many terms as you like to your list. Don't think that the more terms means more work."

As students finish their selections, Tom continues: "OK, let's go to the next level. Look at your terms. I want you to rate each as a 1, a 2, or a 3 in terms of how much you think that trait plays into the character of Iago." Tom clarifies: "Rate it as 3, major; 2, worth noting but not as much; and then 1. They can be all 3s, all 2s, or all 1s. Think it through."

Notice that the task has now become self-differentiating. Students have been able to draw on adjectives put forward by others, but are making their own choices regarding those adjectives and evaluating each against the character Iago. Their straightforward analysis task has now become more challenging as they seek to determine exactly which adjectives best capture Iago for them. Tom's next move pushes their thinking even further.

"This isn't a huge task, but it is a thoughtful one," Tom announces as he passes out a sheet with the task explained. "The short version of this is that I want you to express Iago's character as a mathematical formula." Tom explains further, "You guys know order of operations?" The class laughs at being asked about a topic the mathematics teachers have drilled into them. "Stick to the mathematical rankings you have given your traits and, using order of operations, create an equation that you think represents Iago. I've made up an example to show what I mean:

$$\frac{(\text{Loving3} + \text{Gentle2}) - (\text{Jealous2} + \text{Insecure2})}{\text{Foolish1} + \text{Vulgar1}} = \frac{5-4}{2} = \frac{1}{2}$$

"Note that I want an explanation of how you put things together to get your equation," Tom adds. Although Tom's example doesn't require much in the way of higher-level mathematics, several boys in the front of the room make the leap into the mathematics they are currently studying, joking about using logarithmic functions and derivatives. Raphael doesn't see it as a joke, however: "I have such a cool idea," he exclaims. "You take those ten adjectives and see how they change throughout the play. You plot the rate of change and the area underneath would be the amount of 'him,' how much of the true self is being shown," Raphael explains to his classmate. "So find the rate of change and the point of inflection when you see his true self coming through!"

Tom, who has been listening in on the conversation, asks, "You want to do it?" Raphael, still ruminating on the idea, comments, "I might. I'm psyched." "Do it," Tom says. "That would be cool." Raphael returns to scribbling notes on his paper as he mumbles to himself, "Mine is going to be like a four-page report." The student seated beside him presses, "Are you going to do it?" "Yeah," Raphael says with more conviction. "It would give me a deeper understanding."

What teacher wouldn't be thrilled at that kind of response to an assignment? Clearly Raphael is able to think about mathematics as a tool for understanding all kinds of phenomena. However, his response doesn't come out of thin air. Tom laid the groundwork in the creation of an opportunity to think deeply about the character Iago. As I've mentioned, Tom established a low threshold initially for students to enter into this area of exploration. He created a perplexing situation—trying to understand the motives of a character in order to assume or direct that character in a play—and then gradually guided students into that problem space. In the equation task, Tom creates opportunities for students to go below the surface of a character's actions and words to examine who Iago is, to analyze the character, evaluate the presence and dominance of various traits, consider those characteristics in relation to one another, and ultimately capture the essence of Iago, not in a traditional essay but in an equation that can be justified. The task is thoughtful, but not time intensive. In fact, it will be due the next class.

Note that the task itself has a high ceiling (Papert, 1980)—that is, there aren't a lot of constraints that limit what students can do. This makes the task an open-ended opportunity to explore. We see this in students jumping to more complex mathematics to capture the essence of Iago, and in Raphael extending the task to think about how a character changes over time rather than the character as a static entity. Tasks with high ceilings are self-differentiating and very useful with heterogeneous groups of students. These tasks also create a natural sense of ownership, as students are able to shape the task through their choices. However, such tasks work best in classrooms that are learning oriented rather than work oriented and where the focus is on developing understanding rather than on mere knowledge acquisition. If students are happy just to cross the threshold and not to reach for the ceiling, then such tasks tend not to succeed as well. That is why engagement is key. Students in Tom's class accepted that the equation task was an opportunity to build their own understanding, rather than work to turn in for a grade (it was in fact ungraded), and responded accordingly. Raphael's comment, "It would give me a deeper understanding," makes this clear.

VoiceThread: USING STORYTELLING TO UNDERSTAND MIGRATION

David Riehl has invited me to his ninth-grade geography class at Washington International School to see what his students are doing around their current topic of study, migration. David hasn't yet arrived, and I have the chance to look around his classroom before it fills with students. It's a small classroom occupying space in one of the original buildings at the school. Outside, workmen clamber up scaffolding to do some repairs on the old building, and their hammers echo through the currently empty classroom. It's clear that the class has been busy with their exploration, as the white walls are covered with chart paper containing hand-drawn flow charts, diagrams, and models. Some student-made graphs about their family's migration history cover one wall. In the front, on a corner shelf, I spot a stack of geography textbooks and open one up.

I find the chapter on migration, fewer than ten pages in length, and leaf through it. Lots of color, maps, clip art pictures, photos, text, and diagrams. At the end of the chapter is a page labeled "Checklist." It lists the key words, terms, and ideas students should have gleaned from the chapter. The list does all the note taking and summarizing for students—in other words, most of the thinking. Once savvy to this resource, I could imagine that enterprising students wouldn't see much sense in reading the bland, emotionless text. The next page is labeled "Questions." Although the answers aren't given, page numbers for looking up the information do appear after each question. The questions—for example, "Name a state that attracts Mexican workers"—strike me as simplistic, narrow, and not overly meaningful. I assume these questions are meant to serve as study material before the test.

At the very bottom of the page is a small section labeled "Skills, Theories, and Models." Rather than providing information, this section appears to identify things students should be able to do: "interpret and use graphs," "interpret choropleth maps" (I had to look that one up: choropleth maps use colors and symbols to display quantitative information according to geographic location), and finally "understand migration issues." Now here is something interesting, meaty, and topical. However, leafing through the textbook in my hand, it isn't clear exactly how such understanding is to be gleaned from the few pages dedicated to migration in the text. Knowing that David only uses these textbooks as a resource, I'll be interested to see how he and his class are tackling "understanding migration issues."

Although the textbook is not the curriculum in David's class, this is the case in too many schools. Despite a long-held recognition that commercially produced textbooks and workbooks fail to engage students in cognitively demanding tasks, little has been done to alleviate this shortcoming (Doyle, 1983; Schmoker, 2009; Shernoff, 2013). I attribute this to the fact that this geography textbook, and others like it, embody a widely held misconception: that teaching is primarily the delivery of information and that learning is memorizing that information. In fact, if you look up the word "teach" in the dictionary, you are likely to see just such a definition: "to give information." Look a little further down the list of alternative meanings, and you might find something like "to cause someone to learn." Although this is truer to the nature of good teaching, one has to admit that such a definition is more than a bit enigmatic. Exactly how does one "cause someone to learn"? Certainly not by delivering them information alone. We have to reach higher than that.

To be clear, I am not disparaging information. It is both valuable and necessary to learning. But being presented with it or being told where to find it (on page 22 in the geography textbook) doesn't cause learning. We have to *do* something with that information. We must think with it and through it. We must process it. That is exactly what David Riehl has invited me in to witness.

As the class enters, it is clear that they're ready to dig into the opportunity David and his student teacher Kyle Cannon have developed for them to facilitate their exploration of migration. Students have their iPads and notebooks out and are already beginning to work even before David has a chance to address them. Two questions posted on the bulletin board at the side of the room serve as guides for both students and teachers in this unit: "Why do people migrate?" and "What are the impacts of migration?" To explore these questions, David and Kyle are asking students to create a three- to five-minute migration story using VoiceThread, an iPad app. VoiceThread allows users to make a voice recording over documents and pictures of their choosing while including animation and highlighting to draw attention to features of those images as needed. Think of it as an animated podcast or tutorial video.

The class has already investigated the migratory patterns represented by the families of students in the class, producing graphs, maps, and tables to display this information. David and Kyle used these data to delve into the question of why people migrate and to introduce the various pushes and pulls, some voluntary and some involuntary, affecting migration both now and throughout history. The three-day migration story project asks students to contextualize what they have learned more broadly about migration to illuminate a single story. Some students have chosen to focus on the story of an individual family member; others have decided to use their family's ethnic background to talk about larger patterns of migration exhibited by a group. David doesn't want students just to do a report; he wants them to think as geographers to analyze and understand an event.

The class is eager to continue their research. However, David takes the first minutes of the period to focus attention on the thinking that they need to be doing to produce their migration story. On a sheet of chart paper, David writes "Integrating Analysis into Your Story." "Remember," David begins, "you are a geographer. You need to think as a geographer." Returning to the chart paper, he writes: *Knowledge → How do geographers measure challenges/benefits of migration? What language do they use?* David underlines the words "measure" and "challenges/benefits" in red. "Keep in mind what we have learned broadly about the factors that influence migration."

On the chart paper, David next writes "Analysis" directly under the word "Knowledge." He explains, "Starting with that background will be crucial to your analysis. You are going to apply that to your specific story selection." He writes on the chart paper as he speaks: *Where, when and how were there benefits and challenges, positive and negative impacts?* David elaborates, "Your analysis will involve you in identifying and distinguishing those impacts and making judgments about them. Which were the most significant, observable, or felt?" David records the words "identify," "distinguish" and "judgment" on the chart paper and then underlines them in red. "Keep this in mind as you are doing research today," he says, pointing to the underlined words. "I know some of you geographers are about ready to write down your narration for your VoiceThread, and you will need to think about these. Keep in mind: How will your story demonstrate the challenges and benefits of migration?" With that, David and Kyle divide the class in half and move some of the students to the empty room next door so that they can spread out and have more room for books, iPads, and notes.

In David's short instructional sequence, we see him focusing students' attention on the core thinking he wants them to do: analysis. However, David is well aware that to a ninth grader, "analysis" can be a pretty ambiguous term, so he breaks it down for them. He reiterates the framework they will be using in their analysis—that is, the way geographers measure challenges and benefits and classify different types of migration. He then lets students know that their task is to apply this framework to their chosen story to help them identify, distinguish, and judge impacts.

In thinking about the opportunities we create for students, we must make sure that both we and they stay focused on the processes that will lead to learning and not let the product dominate. David's students are engaged with their stories, they are enamored of their iPads, and they are enjoying finding pictures for their VoiceThread stories. These are important elements that allow for choice, ownership, and creativity. However, if we let these activities dominate, the result is most likely to be shallow learning. Exploiting an opportunity to learn means keeping students focused on the thinking they are to do and not leaving it to chance. David does this by not only unpacking what analysis entails but also situating the task contextually and allowing the authentic practices of the discipline of geography to carry the day.

Throughout this brief mini-lesson and in his one-on-one interactions with students, David refers to students as "geographers," using the language of identity to help them assume that role. The migration story task itself engages students not just in learning about geography and being able to identify some geographic terms but also in doing the authentic work of geographers to explain phenomena. This is one of the advantages of being authentic. When we engage students in the authentic work of the discipline, the processes and thinking of the discipline take center stage while simultaneously integrating the knowledge, skills, and terminology of the subject area.

In witnessing David's mini-lesson on analysis, I'm reminded of an interesting educational initiative of the Singapore Ministry of Education called Teach Less, Learn More (Yng & Spreedharan, 2012), aimed at reducing the amount of teacher talk and delivery of information so that students have more opportunities to actually engage with content and to learn, rather than prepare for tests. It's unclear how successful the initiative has been, mostly because the test pressures and demands on students haven't changed, but one has to applaud the recognition that teaching as telling and education as test prep are both weak imitations of the real thing. Although I can't vouch for the Singaporean implementation, the essence of "teach less, learn more" is being put to good use in David Riehl's classroom. He recognizes that he needs to get his students engaged with the content, not just have them reading about it. He also recognizes that it is students' actions, not his, that will produce the learning. "Teaching less" as a philosophy can be useful in that it helps focus teachers on creating powerful learning opportunities that encourage teachers to step back so as to allow students to step forward.

MUSIC 2 SAVE MUSIC

Michael Medvinsky wants to break down the wall between "school" music and "real" music. With a new position at West and East Hills Middle Schools in Bloomfield Hills, Michigan, he has the opportunity to build a music program that does just that. Although his students' previous experience of music class has consisted largely of choral singing, Michael believes in creating opportunities for students to compose as well as perform music. Consequently, he has thought carefully about how to make this happen, given that he sees his students for only thirty-five minutes twice a week.

A tech-savvy musician, Michael has a mobile recording studio he can quickly set up in his classroom for just this purpose. With a microphone to record vocals, a digital piano, an input device for recording guitars and mixing sound all linked together with the Logic Pro X recording studio on his MacBook, Michael has the ability to capture students' musical efforts during each class period and play the results back for them the next. Add to this a set of iPad Minis equipped with GarageBand and other digital instruments, and tools are there for both making and recording original music. These tools will help him capture, document, and thread together students' efforts even with the minimal amount of time he sees them each week.

A key component of Michael's thinking about his teaching this year has centered on the power of music to connect, transform, and change lives. He knows he can craft opportunities for the creation of music using his digital tools, but to what end? Michael wants to establish a purpose behind these efforts with which his students can connect. Concerned about the constant defunding of the arts and the resulting struggle of musical programs in many public schools in the United States, Michael thought that his students' efforts to create music could be used as a means to support those programs. Thus the Music 2 Save Music project was born. His fourth- and fifth-grade students will create and record original songs that they will perform in concert but also upload to iTunes for purchase, the proceeds going to fund the purchase of instruments and tools for struggling music programs the students themselves identify and later connect with via Skype.

It's the second month of school when I have a chance to observe one of Michael's classes at West Hills Middle School. It is still early days, and Michael has seen his students only a few times, but the Music 2 Save Music project is well under way. On a whiteboard at the side of the room, the initial preparation and planning process for the songwriting have been laid out:

- Inspiration
- Pick one thing (Big Idea)
- Lyrics
    ◦ Same beat for each verse
    ◦ Different beat for chorus
- Chorus
    ◦ Words repeat
- Verse
    ◦ Change the words
- Keep the same genre

This outline provides the structure for Michael to integrate the basic skills and knowledge that students will need to employ as they create. Michael tells me that one of his fourth-grade classes is starting their composing efforts in the way outlined on the board, beginning with lyrics and then adding the music, but the other is working in reverse. He knows that different approaches work for different people and at different times, so he wants to give his classes a range of creative formats rather than limiting them to just one.

As students enter the room, Michael turns off the lights so that the projection can be seen more easily. His mobile studio is connected, and his computer screen appears on the whiteboard. Clearly visible to the class are the different layers of instruments and voices they have recorded thus far, each stacked atop the other in its own glowing green band. As students sit on the carpet before the screen, Michael comments, "Who will be our engineer today?" Rather than ask for volunteers, he uses a random-number generator to select a student. When he calls the number twenty-three, a student comes up and collects an iPad, carrying it like a treasure back to her seat on the rug.

Michael told me that he uses the application GarageBand almost daily. "Usually, I am the one behind the computer pushing all of the buttons and making the technology a transparent piece of the music making," he explains. "I need to be the one 'driving' so the musicians can focus on the scenery more than the car controls." However, with his new Logic Pro X setup, Michael has been able to put students in the driver's seat by using an iPad interface that allows them to manipulate the controls remotely while the rest of the class watches what is happening on the screen.

Michael feels that allowing students greater control of the process is changing his classes. "This has had quite an impact on the class culture. They have always taken ownership of their songs, but there has been a shift in the ownership of the craftsman-ship." He offers an example: "The other day we stopped and discussed the harmonic progression. The class decided that the chords needed to change at a different point in the melody." Michael explains that he then asked the "engineer" to erase the track and take it back to the beginning. The student responded, "Mr. M, I'm one step ahead of you."

At this point in the Music 2 Save Music project, Michael's students are in what Peter Woods (1993) refers to as the "divergence" stage of an empowering educational event. Woods defines such events as "integrated and focused programmes of educational activities which may last from a number of weeks to over a year" (p. 357). For Woods, these events are creative enterprises in which the outcome is not fully known or knowable in advance, but which contain within them the "seeds for growth" that can promote transformational learning and the development of the person (p. 357). I'll discuss the rest of Woods's stages later in this chapter, but for now it is important to note that the divergence stage is the period in which students are encouraged to be creative, to explore, to stretch, and to experiment. In this stage, anything can happen, and it is important to allow for serendipity to shape the future outcome.

Michael asks the student engineer (note the language of identity) to play back the recording of the group's composing efforts thus far. As a green line moves across the layers of instruments that have been previously recorded, students listen intently. Michael tells the engineer to bring it back to the beginning and instructs the rest of the class to sing the words they have written thus far. To assist with this, he switches the whiteboard screen to a word processing document containing the class's lyrics.

As the music starts, the fourth graders' voices emerge timidly, barely audible, and without much clarity over the track. The song has been crafted around the big idea that there are different ways of being rich. The first verse deals with being rich monetarily, and the second with other kinds of richness. Because of the contrast in the verses, the students felt that the song should shift in its genre between verses one and two as well. At this juncture, the words to the song are still in flux and quite new. As the students sing along, it is clear that some are unfamiliar with the words, while others are struggling to find the melody. Nonetheless, you can see students moving their bodies as they work to stay with the beat and sing along.

Upon the recording's end, Michael instructs the class, "Please turn to a neighbor and talk about what you just heard." After a few minutes he interjects, "Please bring your conversations to a close. What are your thoughts?" An eager girl sitting in the front offers the first idea: "Can we keep the clapping going longer?"

"Why would we want to do that?" Michael questions.

"Because it keeps the beat stronger," the student explains. Michael nods in acknowledgment of the suggestion, but lets it hang in the air as one possibility as he calls on another student.

"Can we also do the viola?" another student asks. Again Michael acknowledges the suggestion and moves to collect more ideas. A boy in the back raises his hand and asks, "What about our singing? Is that in there?"

"Did you hear it in there?" says Michael tossing it back to the student.

"No," the boy says, shaking his head.

"So what do you think we might want to do today?" Michael asks, smiling.

"Record our singing," the boy states as he grins back. The confusion over the singing and the general discomfort with what was just heard sparks more comments from the class. "Can we bring the clapping down so that we can hear our voices better?" one student offers.

Michael recognizes that there is a problem with the singing and what the students just heard, but at this early stage he wants to encourage students to think more holistically about their song. "Let's talk about that," Michael offers. "Who thinks we should bring down the clapping?" Most hands go up. "OK," Michael adds, "let's talk about options here. What might we do?" At this point several alternatives are offered, such as reducing the amount of clapping or singing louder. One student offers a surprise suggestion: "Add the flute so it makes the clapping not seem so loud." Michael picks up on this: "So you are thinking now about the audience member and their listening and what they might be paying attention to." It is a subtle moment, but notice how with his comment Michael moves his students' thinking beyond the generation of possibilities and into the realm of thinking like a musician by considering the audience and what sound might grab their attention.

Moving the class along, Michael offers, "There are many people talking about bringing things down. Let me make this suggestion. Let's record our voices so we can play it back and have more information to base our decisions on." As the preceding interchange showed, there were lots of ideas being thrown out, discussed, and examined without much closure. Part of Michael's skill as a teacher is his understanding of and comfort with the creative process, allowing it to unfold while providing just enough input and structure to move it along productively without stifling the process or taking away his students' ownership.

Michael knows he and his students need to work through this messy and uncomfortable process before things will coalesce. However, this is not merely a stage to "get through"; it is a process crucial to the learning and to the development of a culture of thinking that Michael is after. As he notes, "The way the students are talking about their songs and the purpose behind their musical decision making is shifting the culture of my new classroom." Writing on his blog about the learning in one of his other classes, Michael captures the moment when this transformation first becomes apparent to him:

> There was some apprehension about using voice to create an original melody and taking a risk to share any musical thoughts with the class. . . . The apprehension quickly disappeared when a melody was heard from one of the musicians in the class. Everyone really liked it. I quickly realized the vocal melody on the piano and the class sang through the words a few times. As they became more comfortable with the melody, revisions began emerging. The melody was revised a few times including ending the melody with an ascending pattern to transition to the next line.
>
> When this came together, the energy of the room changed. The musicians were sitting on the edge of their chairs asking to sing the verse over and over. They asked to share their musical idea with their classroom teacher as soon as he came to the door. They were excited. These are magical moments for them. Since this class period earlier

today, there have been many musicians from that class that have come to my room between classes and sought me out during lunch to share new ideas they had. These are magical moments for me.

Michael Medvinsky, http://mmedvinsky.edublogs.org/2013/09/16

As the Music 2 Save Music project develops, it takes on more dimensions to build enthusiasm and extend its reach. The project has its own Facebook page and Twitter account created by Michael to allow parents and the community to follow the project and receive updates on the students' creative process. An eighth-grade student at the school creates an original logo to be used to advertise the concert and on T-shirts to be sold online. Links are made to outside organizations, such as the Arts Empowerment Project in Charlotte, North Carolina, that connects children affected by violence to existing arts programs in the community. Finally, as the date for the live concert nears, a poster advertising the event is created. However, in keeping with Michael's use of technology, this isn't just any poster. Using the app Aurasma, the posters contain an "aura" or augmented reality that becomes visible when the poster is viewed through the Aurasma app viewfinder on one's smartphone. On the Music 2 Save Music poster, one is treated to a video of each class of students telling about their song and inviting you to the concert.

Through this project, Michael has indeed broken down the barriers between school music and real music. He has created opportunities for his students to engage in the creative process of making music in a way that allowed them to learn the dimensions, forms, and language of music while nurturing ownership and independence. He has not neglected the idea of performance, but embedded it within a larger context that gives students' efforts purpose. At the same time, at two new schools with students new to him, he has been able to lay the foundation for a culture of thinking in music that will extend throughout the year.

CATEGORIZING, RECOGNIZING, AND REALIZING LEARNING OPPORTUNITIES

The cases presented in this chapter provide rich and diverse examples of powerful learning opportunities, and in each case I have mentioned some of the qualities that made them engaging and rich learning experiences for students. In this section, I move to a more thorough examination of the three cases collectively to help categorize opportunities on the basis of some of their more basic dimensions. I then sharpen our focus to help us recognize and design for the specific qualities needed to ensure that the opportunities we create foster learning. Finally, I conclude this section by looking at what it takes to actually realize such opportunities in the classroom. How do we make them happen amid what seem like competing demands of time, testing, and students' desires?

Categorizing: What Are the Key Dimensions on Which Opportunities Differ?

The opportunities we create as teachers differ on three distinct dimensions: duration, format, and complexity. The duration or scope of the opportunities teachers create has to do with the dimension of time, varying from brief moments that represent instructional interactions or exchanges to long-term events that may extend over the course of a term, semester, or even a year. In between are opportunities of shorter duration, including tasks that might represent a single assignment done in class or as homework and projects that extend over several class periods.

In the cases just presented, Tom Heilman's students were accomplishing a *task* that was started in class and then finished as homework before the next class's meeting. In guiding students' efforts, Tom created shorter moments of learning, such as identifying and then ranking adjectives describing Iago, that took only a few minutes. David Riehl's migration stories using VoiceThread engaged his students in a longer *project* extending over several days and consisting of several subtasks, such as gathering data on a migration story, analyzing and synthesizing the data, drafting a script, identifying appropriate supporting images, and then recording with VoiceThread. Michael Medvinsky's Music 2 Save Music represents an *event* extending over several months. As such, the event had smaller projects, tasks, and moments associated with it.

One might think of opportunities of different duration as existing not in isolation but within an embedded, nested context. This can be visualized as a pyramid (figure 6.1) in

Figure 6.1   Duration and Scope of Opportunities

which the bottom layer of moments supports work in tasks resting above it. In turn, these tasks support students' efforts in completing projects, and such project work can support larger-scale events. Thus, one cannot create an event without having the projects, tasks, and moments that will support it. This configuration also makes clear that teaching and learning are largely made up of the creation of moments that get aimed at and directed toward larger-scale endeavors.

Because of their scale and duration, events are quite rare in occurrence and therefore occupy the top rung of the pyramid. However, events are unique in their power to engage, motivate, and propel learning. This power can be attributed to the holistic and creative aspects of events, in which learning often extends beyond the academic and promotes personal and social development as well (Sikes, Measor, & Woods, 1985; Woods, 1993, 1995). Events provide a purposeful context for learning and often connect learners to the larger community. We see this in Michael Medvinsky's Music 2 Save Music, which provides students with a purpose for the musical endeavors and an audience both locally and at a distance.

Woods (1993) identifies six stages that events progress through, each of which might be thought of as constituting a project with its own purpose, direction, and outcome. First there is the *conceptualization* of the event. Although the initial spark of an idea may come from the teacher, the teacher must still build buy-in and interest, and engage students in thinking about possibilities if they are to feel a sense of ownership of the event. Second is the *preparation* and planning stage. This is where basic knowledge and skills are imparted. In Michael's class, this meant teaching about the various dimensions and qualities of music so that students would have the tools to create their own music. This phase is often carefully scaffolded, giving students just enough information and skill to move forward in a purposeful way and then layering the next bit that is needed. Third is the *divergence* stage, which I observed in Michael's class. This is the period of innovation and exploration of possibility before entering the fourth stage of *convergence*, in which ideas are integrated and paired down. Fifth is *consolidation*, the final coming together of parts into a whole, and refinement. Finally, there is *celebration*, when the event culminates in some kind of sharing with an audience.

Of course, events take time and energy to pull off. However, Woods (1993) reported that teachers found events particularly fulfilling at a professional level, providing them an opportunity to reconnect with the ideals that propelled them into teaching in the first place.

Opportunities also vary in terms of their format. Teachers make use of a variety of formats for instruction: whole-class discussion, small-group work, pair work, lectures, watching videos, read-aloud, independent work, worksheets, technology-guided activities, and so on. This is by no means an exhaustive list, and within a given class period, the format often changes from one moment to the next. Although some formats—such as lecture, watching videos, or doing worksheets—tend not to engage students in active learning, the format itself is not the determining factor in assessing whether or not something is a rich and engaging learning opportunity. Rather, it is how that format is implemented (Shernoff, 2013). Are students being challenged to think and develop understanding? Are these efforts being supported in such a way that students feel as though they are developing greater competence and autonomy? What level of participation are students required to sustain over time?

All teachers create opportunities of varying duration and format. However, the key dimension that will determine the level of engagement and learning of any of these opportunities is their complexity. A good way of thinking about the complexity dimension is as a continuum ranging from tasks that are, at the low end, largely reproductive in nature to those that, at the high end, are challenging and require an original response. Whereas reproductive tasks make use of largely surface learning strategies such as memory, original and challenging tasks require deep learning strategies that can build understanding (see chapter 2). It is in original and challenging tasks that one will find the demand for thinking.

In his research in the 1980s, Doyle (1983) found that low-level reproductive tasks requiring mostly memory work and the replication of procedures accounted for 60–70 percent of students' class time, whereas tasks focused on understanding, transfer, inference, and novel responses made up only 10 percent. The remaining 20–30 percent was unfocused or transition time. It would be nice if we could say that things have changed over the intervening three decades, but Doyle's pattern regarding the complexity (or lack thereof) of student work in classrooms continues to dominate. In his longitudinal study of over a thousand American middle-class students in more than four hundred school districts, Robert Pianta and colleagues (Pianta, Belsky, Houts, Morrison, & National Institute of Child Health and Human Development, 2007) found that fifth graders received five times as much instruction devoted to basic skills as they did to instruction focused on problem solving, reasoning, and analysis. These findings mirrored what they observed two years earlier when these same students were third graders. Others have found this pattern of reproductive work dominating across all grade levels and subject areas (City et al., 2009; Newmann et al., 2001; Schmoker, 2009; Shernoff, 2013; Silver, Mesa, Morris, Star, & Benken, 2009; Wagner, 2008).

Although reproductive tasks dominate, it is precisely the complexity of the learning opportunity and the challenge it presents that are likely to engage students (Newmann, Wehlage, & Lamborn, 1992; Shernoff, Csikszentmihalyi, Schneider, & Shernoff, 2003). Dan Meyer (2012), one of the leading voices calling for more challenge in mathematics classrooms, lists "perplexity" as an initial goal of instruction and a key to engagement. Likewise, in their studies of student engagement, David Shernoff and Mihaly Csikszentmihalyi found that sustained student engagement and perceived learning are most commonly present in learning environments that combine challenge with support (Shernoff et al., 2003). As Shernoff (2013) puts it, the teacher's role "is to design, create, and invent authentic and intellectually challenging work for students so compelling that they persist and feel satisfaction and delight when they successfully accomplish the challenge" (p. 132). In the absence of such challenge, students find little reason to engage, as Ted Sizer (1984) noted in his seminal work on American high schools, *Horace's Compromise*.

Recognizing: What Are the Specific Characteristics of Challenging Opportunities That Promote Learning?

In the three case studies presented, we witnessed opportunities of differing duration and format, but when it came to the dimension of complexity, all the opportunities challenged students to think and pushed them to original responses. More specifically, all these opportunities share four characteristics that can serve as design principles for teachers wishing to create powerful learning opportunities: novel application, meaningful inquiry, effective communication, and perceived worth. These principles come from a variety of sources, including work on Teaching for Understanding (Wiske, 1997), Authentic Intellectual Work (Newmann et al., 2001), flow theory and student engagement (Shernoff et al., 2003), and Visible Thinking (Ritchhart, Church, & Morrison, 2011).

Novel Application. Understanding entails being able to apply one's skills and knowledge in novel situations. Such applications require students to analyze problem-solving situations, spot occasions for application, and then transfer their skills and knowledge. Transfer is the holy grail when it comes to teaching skills and knowledge, so opportunities that push for transfer rather than just replication are likely to serve students well in the long term and in testing situations. In addition, organizing, interpreting, evaluating, or synthesizing one's knowledge to create something new and original allows knowledge to be sharpened, deepened, and enhanced. Such originality is motivating, as we saw in David Riehl's migration story project.

Meaningful Inquiry. In the Teaching for Understanding (TfU) framework, the use of "understanding performances" are the key vehicles for building understanding. One aspect of an understanding performance is that it allows students to demonstrate understanding, but it must also facilitate in developing understanding. We look for both of these sides in powerful learning opportunities as well. Therefore, it is not enough only to engage in application; also build new understanding and developing personal insights. This is a recurring problem in schools, where high-performing students are able to get good grades, but aren't actually learning anything new. If students feel as though there isn't an opportunity to learn something new in an assignment, they may be reluctant to go beyond what is required. We saw this characteristic being highlighted in Tom Heilman's Iago assignment. Tom pitched the assignment to students as an opportunity to understand Iago in a new and deeper way. In Raphael's response to the assignment, we saw how one student really capitalized on the opportunity.

Effective Communication. Understanding requires and is facilitated by the ability to use the language of the discipline to express, represent, justify, and communicate one's thinking and ideas (Nystrand & Graff, 2001; Schmoker, 2009; Silver et al., 2009). However, this often isn't emphasized in assignments students encounter; when it is, it may not go beyond explaining the choices, steps, or procedures used (Silver et al., 2009). One of the powerful things we have noticed in the use of thinking routines to make thinking visible in classrooms is that it pushes students to give evidence, explain their thoughts, and make explicit connections. This emphasis on communication in the classroom gives students skills that they can transfer into testing situations, particularly those that require writing. Michael Medvinsky's students working together to create original music were put into a situation where communication using the language of the discipline of music was essential. Although students lacked this vocabulary coming into Michael's class, they had ongoing opportunities to develop it within a community of practice.

Perceived Worth. In all three cases, students produced something: an equation, a VoiceThread, a song. Production is common in classrooms, but what is not so common is that what is produced is perceived by students to be of value and worth their time and investment. In their study of students' engagement, Shernoff et al. (2003) found that "not only was perception of importance by far the strongest predictor of engagement of a great variety of perceptions we examined, but it was also the most robust predictor of perceived learning and attention" (p. 141), noting that "the strength of perceived importance as a predictor of engagement should not be underestimated" (p. 138).

It can be argued that perceived worth is a characteristic of the individual student, which is true to some extent. Nonetheless, teachers increase the likelihood that students will view tasks and assignments as worthwhile when students are able to see the purpose behind them. This is not a simple matter of stating one's objectives and goals as many schools require, however. In fact, Shernoff found that a teacher stating his or her purpose behind the lesson had little impact on students' perception of worth. Teacher worth does not necessarily equate to student worth. Instead, it was the ability of the teacher *to place the activity within the context of a larger goal or enterprise* that mattered.

Events, such as Music 2 Save Music, clearly situate learning within a larger context and provide a reason for all the projects and tasks related to it. This is one of the powers of events. David Riehl allowed students choice in creating their migration story, and this enabled students to make meaningful personal connections with family history, adding to the perceived worth of the project. In Tom's case, he situated the Iago equation task as an opportunity to develop one's understanding of Iago and allowed students to take risks and push themselves in a task with a high ceiling.

Realizing: How Do We Make Challenging Opportunities Work for Teachers and Students?

Opportunities are the bread and butter of teaching. The tasks we create set the stage for students' performance, either by inspiring, engaging, and opening up possibilities and originality or by reducing and limiting their efforts to superficial reproductions. Mike Schmoker (2009) identifies the replacement of low-level tasks with purposeful opportunities that engage students in thinking as one of the single most productive and low-cost things that schools can do to improve performance. This means reducing reliance on worksheets, prepackaged curricula, study guides, and scripted teaching—none of which are actually targeted at the collection of individual students you teach. I can almost hear a series of "Yeah, buts" being uttered in response to this suggestion to create more powerful learning opportunities and perhaps in reaction to the three cases. Let me try to address a few of those.

"Yeah, but it takes more time to create opportunities like this." I won't lie or try to sugarcoat this one. It does. But creating opportunities for learning is what teaching is all about. It is part of its joy and challenge. Why should we hand it over to someone else? In all three cases presented here, the teachers were doing something they had never done before. However, it didn't take them long to come up with the tasks, projects, and events they planned. They are used to thinking in terms of pushing students, engaging students, and promoting learning, so they are always looking out for such opportunities. Also,

these teachers are used to taking risks, and know it is no big deal if every once in a while a new idea needs to be adjusted or modified. Most important, these teachers all get their energy from engaging students and trying new things. Recall that it is more important to manage one's energy than one's time (chapter 4).

At the same time, not every opportunity we create is out of whole cloth. Michael was experienced in teaching students to create their own music, so placing that in a new context didn't take much time initially. It is also possible to take existing opportunities, even prepackaged lessons, and do what my colleague Mark Church calls "bumping them up." This involves examining a task one has used before or found elsewhere and asking a few simple questions: How can I involve students in more thinking in this situation? Can the task be opened up so that there is a higher ceiling? Can I extend this task or set it in a more engaging context? Is there too much scaffolding and structure in the task that I should remove? What's the core question or issue I really want to engage students with, and how do I get them there with this task? Meyer (2012) is a master at bumping up tasks in mathematics and making routine problems more thoughtful. If this thought process doesn't come naturally to you, consider engaging colleagues to collaboratively examine the opportunities you are creating.

"Yeah, but the test my students take is reproductive and not thinking based." The assumption here is that the best way to prepare students for standardized tests of basic skills is to drill them on the basic skills. In fact, this is not the case. In Fred Newmann's study (Newmann et al., 2001) of the tasks with which over five thousand students in grades 3, 6, and 8 in the Chicago Public Schools were engaged, he found that students who were in classrooms where they regularly encountered tasks that demanded complex thinking and elaborated communication performed better on tests of basic skills than their peers who encountered more reproductive tasks. This finding held true for students at all ability levels. However, lower-performing students are particularly disadvantaged by a lack of opportunity. In short, students need to spend less time filling in the bubbles on tests and more time connecting the dots.

Emerging from a large-scale study as they do, Newmann's findings are persuasive. Even more persuasive is the fact that they sit beside a long line of research that has shown that developing students' understanding, attending to transfer and application, and teaching them to think with and through content constitute good preparation not only for standardized tests but also for twenty-first-century citizenship (City et al., 2009; Cobb et al., 1991; Knapp, Shields, & Turnbull, 1992; Shernoff, 2013). These findings shouldn't surprise us. Keeping students engaged in learning is the key to achievement as Robert Fried (1995) points out: "Engaging students in content requires teachers to change their pedagogy by limiting the amount of stuff they teach, so that their students learn the important things well and dig deeply into the subject; by posing interesting questions, setting up a framework for inquiry; and then by getting out of the way to let the students do the work" (p. 57).

"Yeah, but the students won't cooperate with this thinking stuff. They want to be spoon-fed." In *Horace's Compromise*, Ted Sizer (1984) identified this as a key dilemma in secondary teaching. In exchange for not being asked to do too much, students agree to be nondisruptive and compliant. School moves on as usual, but the learning crawls at a snail's pace. Likewise, Doyle (1983) found that there was enormous pressure from students to maintain stability in the preexisting task structure, for teachers to deliver content with only an expectation of memorization. Doyle observed, "The type of tasks which cognitive psychology suggests will have the greatest long term consequence for improving the quality of academic work are precisely those which are the most difficult to install in classrooms" (p. 189).

Doyle saw this conflict arising from students' desire to reduce the ambiguity of tasks (the extent to which a precise answer is required) while simultaneously minimizing the risk of failure by not meeting the evaluation criteria. Simple memory tasks are clear and carry a low risk, whereas understanding is much more ambiguous, and one can more easily be wrong and fail. We can see attempts to manage risk and ambiguity in students' reactions to a new assignment. Their questions attempt to clearly define the task, to reduce its ambiguity, and then to pin down the expectations for grading. Other times, students engage in "piloting" (Lundgren, 1977), in which they test out partial responses on the teacher over and over again until the teacher has essentially defined exactly what is expected. It sometimes takes a strong will not to get pulled into students' piloting efforts.

A limitation of Doyle's findings, however, is that the classrooms he studied were primarily work oriented. Doyle didn't question this, nor did he question the notion that grades and assessment are the primary way of motivating students. There is a strongly held notion that students will do only what "counts" in the grade book. To some extent this is true. If you assess for knowledge, students are unlikely to perceive efforts at understanding as worthwhile. Assessment must be aligned with the behaviors, processes, and products we are trying to cultivate. If students don't feel that putting forth effort has any payoff, they won't engage. But this doesn't mean that everything has to be graded. Tom Heilman's Iago equation assignment wasn't graded, but he drew a thread of accountability for students. They knew they would be asked to write about Iago and that efforts to understand him would help their writing. Therefore, there was perceived worth in the assignment. In David Riehl's class, he managed the ambiguity of the task by explicitly teaching the process of analysis that was needed. This kind of explicit teaching scaffolds students' cognitive development while fostering independence (Schmoker, 2009).

Ultimately, students' shift in attitude comes from being immersed in a culture of thinking, and seeing the development of understanding and independence as chief goals of learning. This entails movement away from a work orientation and toward a learning orientation as we align our expectations with the opportunities we create. Setting tasks within a larger purpose while allowing choice, creativity, and challenge in the context of collaborative engagement with others is a key aspect of this process.

ANALYZING AND CREATING OPPORTUNITIES FOR LEARNING

- Analyze a task/project from the perspective of the students' "doing." Read through the task/project and make a list of the verbs that best describe what students will be required to do as they complete the task. Next, rank those verbs in order according to the amount of time students are likely to spend on each. What does this reveal about the task/project in terms of its learning potential?

- Raise or eliminate the ceiling of a task/project. Read through your directions and the description you have written for students. Does it limit what they are likely to produce? How can you word it to increase possibilities? Ask yourself: Are there students in this class who could have done this on day one? If so, then the task definitely needs to be opened up and made more challenging.

- Create "perplexity." What is the reason for learning this? Where does it come into play? How can I create a situation in which we need to learn this material to solve or understand something? That something is your perplexity situation!

- Review and rate the tasks/projects in a unit using the four criteria: novel application, meaningful inquiry, effective communication, and perceived worth. Where is it strongest? Where does it need to be enhanced?

- Bump it up. Take a task that you think provides a good starting point, and think, possibly together with a colleague, about how you can bump it up or extend it so that students are asked to really think and delve more deeply. For example, instead of asking students to "solve this equation for x," ask, "Where might you expect students to typically go wrong in solving this equation for x?" The first asks for application of a known procedure. The second for analysis, identification of misconceptions, and perspective taking.

- Use the "My Reflections on the Learning Activities in This Class" sheet (see appendix A). The sheet asks students to identify the types of activities with which they were most engaged over the preceding class period. It's a good idea to complete the sheet yourself before looking at students' responses to see if your perceptions match theirs. Of course, there is nothing wrong with activities like "gathering information" or "practicing skills," but these shouldn't be the only or even the major opportunities students experience.

- Analyze success. With a group of colleagues, use the Success Analysis Protocol (see appendix C) to identify, write about, share, and analyze your most effective teaching and learning opportunities. Your analysis may identify additional criteria that make learning opportunities powerful.
- Teach less. Look for ways you can step back from center stage so that your students are doing more of the work, thinking, and learning. You may want to videotape yourself to see just how much of class time you are talking.
- Use the Experience Sampling Method to determine how engaged your students are. This method has been used by Mihaly Csikszentmihalyi to gather data on how people experience events. In its pure form, participants are alerted at random intervals to record brief notes or ratings about their experience. Responding should take no more than two minutes. In the classroom, you might stop randomly once or twice to have students respond on a 5-point scale (strongly disagree to strongly agree) to a few statements:

> What the class is doing right now is interesting to me.
>
> I'm enjoying doing this.
>
> I'm learning a lot right now.
>
> I'm having a hard time concentrating on the task at hand right now.
>
> I was thinking about the work/subject matter of the class right now.
>
> I'm really being pushed to think right now.
>
> I already understand most of the stuff we are doing right now.

(*N.B.:* A few of these items are reversed so that students actually have to read the statements to respond rather than just rating everything highly.)

CHAPTER 7

Routines
Supporting and Scaffolding Learning and Thinking

rou•tine |ro͞o'tēn| noun: A sequence of actions designed to achieve a specific outcome in an efficient and productive manner. • The accepted or established code of action within any group for managing and dealing with particular problems, events, or situations that may repeat themselves. As a culture shaper, routines represent a set of shared practices that constitute a group's way of doing things. They are the classroom infrastructure, guiding much of the activity that happens there. Routines—whether they are for management, participation, discourse, instruction, learning, or thinking—help minimize confusion, reduce uncertainty, and direct activity along known paths. Ultimately, routines become patterns of behavior for both individuals and the group. Of particular importance in learning groups is the presence of thinking and learning routines that help direct, guide, and scaffold learning and thinking.

Walking through the doors of the kindergarten classroom, I am more than a little nervous. It has been years since I taught a class full of five-year-olds, and I am feeling rusty. Furthermore, the lesson I have planned was a bit of a gamble. It is something I have never tried before and requires deep faith that this group of students whom I have never met would find the opportunity I have created engaging enough to run with for a full thirty minutes. I hope I am right. I have just started working on mathematical problem solving with the teachers at the school, and the teachers are struggling to go beyond simple story problems involving the application of recently taught arithmetic procedures. The principal suggested that it might be helpful if I were to teach a model lesson so that the teachers could witness an alternative approach.

My goal is not to put on a show of one good lesson but to introduce teachers to some general principles and structures they could use to engage students in authentic mathematics. Specifically, I want to provide teachers with a clear example of mathematical problem solving to demonstrate that even young students are capable of rich mathematical thinking, and to offer a routine for supporting such thinking that can be used beyond a single lesson: enter Claim-Support-Question (CSQ) and the Biggest Smile.

As I enter the classroom, Teacher Kathy informs the students that it is time to come to the mat. I find my place in the chair in the front corner as students arrange themselves in a circle. Kathy introduces me and then finds a seat amid the six other teachers gathered to watch the lesson. The movement of the class from one activity to the next and into place with a simple "Please, come to the mat" is evidence of a well-learned management routine (Leinhardt, Weidman, & Hammond, 1987). Students know how to put away their things and how to find a seat in a circle. The circle itself, with students seated around the outside of the mat and the teacher at the front beside a flipchart, is also a familiar instructional routine to students (Yinger, 1979). Coming to the mat, students have a well-developed schema of how instruction is likely to proceed. In classrooms there are many events that recur frequently as well as instructional formats that get used over and over again, so having routines for managing such activities saves enormous amounts of transition time, and they also make it easier for visitors like myself to function more effectively.

I launch into my problem, crossing my fingers that it will captivate. "I'm excited to do some thinking with you this morning," I begin. "Your teacher has told me that you are a group of really good problem solvers, and I have a problem I need your help with. The other day was school picture day; do your remember?" Dodging the eagerness of five-year-olds to tell stories, I continue. "Well, when I was walking by the gym yesterday, I heard the photographer say, 'You've got the biggest smile.'" Empathetically, a wave of smiles spread across the faces before me.

"Who was it?" one eager student let out.

"Well, that's the thing," I respond. "I couldn't see who it was. I just heard the photographer say, 'You've got the biggest smile.' And that got me thinking." Having set the stage for the problem, I introduce the vocabulary we will be using to discuss it: "When a person says something that might be true or it might not be true, we sometimes call that a *claim*. The person is claiming that something is true." I offer an accessible example: "Like I might say, 'It's going to rain tomorrow.' That is a claim I am making. We don't know if it is true, but we might be able to find some evidence that would support that claim. But we could also come up with some things that might make us question the claim." More vocabulary gets introduced. "Can you think of a reason that would support my claim of 'It's going to rain tomorrow'"?

Up on her knees with arm raised, Mikah offers, "Well, it could rain because it is springtime, and it rains a lot in springtime." Another student adds, "I think on TV they said it was going to rain."

"Ah, so those are two supports for my claim," I offer, reinforcing the language we will use. "What about questions? What would make you question my claim of 'It's going to rain tomorrow'"?

"Well, even if the weatherman says it, he isn't always right," Jacob responds.

"Interesting; so you have to think about where your information comes from and if that person is always right," I add.

Confident that the class seems to understand the language of claims and evidence, I transition the class back to our problem, "So let's get back to the claim of the photographer: 'You've got the biggest smile.' What might support that claim, make us think it is true?"

"But we don't know who he was talking to," offers Jasmine, leaning on my knee.

"You're right. We don't," I respond. "So that sounds like that makes you question the claim, makes you think maybe it isn't true or that it would be hard to tell if it is or isn't." Across the room, Gabriel suggests a support: "But the photograph man sees everyone, so maybe he knows because he saw a lot of smiles." Jamaal, sitting next to him, raises up,

"If it was me, it would definitely be true because I have a really big smile," and with that he puts on his biggest, cheesiest smile for the class. Making eye contact with the group, I ask, "Would it be easier to investigate this claim if we knew who the photographer was talking about?" A chorus of "yes" meets me.

"Well, let's take Jamaal's claim that he has the biggest smile. How could we find support for that claim? What might we do?" A flurry of hands goes up, and at the same time mouths open and out comes "We can measure" as a refrain arising from several students. I'm not surprised that this idea has emerged. Kathy mentioned that the class has just started some work with measurement. Getting young students to think about why, when, and how we measure is at the heart of the thinking we want them to do on this topic and is an important precursor to teaching about standard measures. Questions like Which is more? How much more? How do we find out? How do we know we can trust our measurement? all need a context, not a worksheet, to propel them. Smiles provide such a context. It's not easy to directly compare your smile with someone else's.

With the idea of measurement, an action has been expressed, but the evidence that that action might yield has yet to be clarified. I try to move students' thinking into that space. "What would we measure?"

"Our smiles," the class comes back.

"How would that help us to know if Jamaal's claim is true?" I query. The class seems a little stumped as they think about how this might work. Finally one student offers, "Well, if someone has a bigger smile, then it isn't true."

"You mean if someone has a bigger smile than Jamaal?" I ask by way of clarification.

"Yeah," she states, nodding her head vigorously. Fair enough. You can prove something false sometimes easier than proving it true.

To get at a piece of supporting evidence, I flip the scenario around: "What if we compare Jamaal's smile with Natalie's and find out his smile *is* bigger. Would that be support?" The class seems a bit puzzled. This is captured by Jonathan: "But that wouldn't prove he has the biggest smile in the whole class."

"You're right," I acknowledge. "So a piece of support doesn't always prove that something is true, but it does give us some evidence and reasons to think it *might* be true." I ask, "If Jamaal's smile is bigger than Natalie's, would that be support that his claim *might* be true?" Most of the class seems on the verge of getting this notion of evidence, but it is hard to move five-year-olds out of binary, true-or-false thinking sometimes, so I know it will take additional work with evidence to solidify this idea. It's OK if we don't get all the way there today.

"I want you to take some silent think time. No talking. No hands. Just think to yourself, how might we go about measuring our smiles?" I've given pretty explicit directions here because I don't know the class. However, with more time in this class, the idea of "take some silent think time" could easily become another instructional routine, an expected way of responding to a teacher's question rather than through raising hands. In kindergarten, students are just learning the instructional routines of school. However, older students carry them forward from previous experience. If teachers want to change these routines or stamp out the formation of dysfunctional ones such as calling out, they need to spend time early in the school year cultivating new ways of doing things.

After about thirty seconds, I interrupt. "Please turn to your neighbor and share your idea with them. What were you thinking we might do to measure our smiles?" I can tell that Kathy has used the Think-Pair-Share routine, as it seems natural for the class to find a partner and begin conversation about their ideas. When students just seem to know what to do, it is often a sign that a routine is established. Indeed, that is what routines are: known ways of doing things. Think-Pair-Share is a multifaceted routine: it is an instructional move that also facilitates thinking by providing explicit time for thinking; it is also a discourse routine, as it provides a structure for conversation among students.

As students share with one another, I write "Who has the biggest smile?" on the chart paper. In doing so, I'm aware that as a class we will be moving slightly away from the investigation of a specific claim to the exploration of a more general question: How do we measure a smile? I wanted to introduce the CSQ routine so that teachers could see how it might be used as a structure to investigate a premise or a claim. This is a different way of thinking about problem solving—not translating words into symbols, but investigating the truth or veracity of an idea. CSQ also introduces students to the ideas of evidence and proof, very important concepts at the heart of mathematics.

Whole-class lessons with five-year-olds can be challenging, and I want to make sure that we aren't just talking but are all actively working to solve a problem, trying different measurement techniques, and making comparisons between measurements, and that we are engaging everyone in that process. After several failed attempts at measuring that involved using our fingers and rulers, Katie, a small girl who has been frustrated by these techniques, raises her hand and suggests that we use "the plastic film" to measure. I'm unclear what she means, but she clarifies that she is referring to the plasticized bits cut off from posters and papers the teacher has laminated. Teacher Kathy saves these in a bin for art projects. I ask how we might use the film, and Katie explains that we can put a bit of plastic on our partner's face and then mark the ends of the smile so that the points won't move as our fingers moved. If we do this for both partners, then we can compare. We just get into this technique, which is showing promise, when we run out of time, as the class must now go to music.

Debriefing with the teachers afterward, Kathy admits how hard it was for her not to pull out the yarn so that students could use that to measure. We talk about the challenge of giving students time to think, to work through strategies that might not work, and to go through a process of gradual revision of techniques. This process in itself is a new instructional routine for teachers and students alike: a shift away from "Follow the directions of the teacher to get it done" to "As a group, let's problem-solve strategies for moving forward." Our talk moves away from the particulars of the lesson itself and to the Claim-Support-Question routine.

A ROUTINE IS MORE THAN AN ACTIVITY

Since the publication of *Making Thinking Visible* (Ritchhart, Church, & Morrison, 2011), thousands of teachers around the world have been introduced to thinking routines. Teachers tend to find that these routines "play well" in their classrooms and that they provide for active, engaged learning while helping reveal students' thinking. However, for many teachers there is still the struggle to move beyond routines as good one-off activities to real routines that both teachers and students can activate. Whereas management and instructional routines often become ingrained actions that proceed almost effortlessly, thinking routines provide structures and scaffolds that must be deliberately activated, by the teacher at first and over time by the learner, and then consciously deployed to achieve a goal.

I'm reminded of the cautionary tale presented by David Cohen (1990) in his seminal article, "A Revolution in One Classroom: The Case of Mrs. Oublier." Cohen documents the teaching of Mrs. O, a teacher who has become enthralled with the idea of teaching mathematics with manipulatives. Although Mrs. O feels as though her teaching has been radically transformed, Cohen finds that mindless worksheets have merely been replaced with mindless work with manipulatives. The goal in Mrs. O's classroom is still to follow the teacher and give back to her what she is asking. I worry that in some classrooms, thinking routines might be falling into the same trap of representing only a cosmetic change rather than a fundamental reordering of the teaching and learning. To avoid this, teachers need to use thinking routines as tools and structures to get students to do real thinking for themselves, thinking that will enhance their understanding.

The idea of thinking routines first emerged from my study of expert teachers of thinking (Ritchhart, 2000, 2002). Over the course of a year's observation, I never once saw those teachers teaching a thinking skills lesson. Instead, they had structures that they regularly used to scaffold and support their students' thinking. I decided that the word "routine" was more fitting than "strategy" because of the way I saw these structures playing out in the classrooms observed. The thinking scaffolds I saw were part instructional routines and part thinking strategies; as such, they became part of the infrastructure of the classroom and a known way of doing things. It was this quality, the quality that made them a culture shaper, that is best captured through the use of the label "routines." However, because thinking routines operate in this hybrid space between explicit strategy coaching (Askell-Williams, Lawson, & Skrzypiec, 2012; Beyer, 1998; Harvey & Goudvis, 2000; Rosenshine, 1997) and the instructional routines of teachers, it is not surprising that thinking routines sometimes get stuck more on one side than the other.

The practice of teachers at Bialik College offers a good example of how a thinking routine can move from just a one-off activity or only an instructional routine to becoming a tool that supports students' deeper learning and thinking and eventually becoming a pattern of behavior. A private school serving students age three to eighteen in Melbourne, Australia, Bialik has been the major research site for the Cultures of Thinking project over the past decade. The Bialik story serves as a good model of how to think about routines not as ends in themselves but as just one of the cultural forces that must be employed in building a strong classroom and school culture.

In our work to cultivate a culture of thinking in schools, my colleagues and I often, though not exclusively, begin with thinking routines as an entry point. We do this *not* because routines are the most important cultural force but because they

- Help direct teachers' attention straight to the issue of thinking.
- Provide specific practices that teachers can employ and see results from almost immediately.
- Make students' thinking visible and thus provide teachers with a vivid example of the good thinking their students are capable of doing.
- Encourage action and discussion around thinking.
- Help build the infrastructure for thinking and learning in the classroom.
- Connect easily to the other cultural forces. As teachers work with routines, they often notice changes in their language, in the creation of opportunities, in their interactions, and so on.

There are many individual stories to be told about the use of routines at Bialik. We have written about and presented many of these in various contexts (Ritchhart et al.,

2011; Ritchhart, Palmer, Church, & Tishman, 2006; Ritchhart, Palmer, Perkins, & Tishman, 2004; Ritchhart & Perkins, 2008). The story that I want to tell here is a collective story centered on the use of Claim-Support-Question to promote students' thinking in mathematics across the school. It is an important story because it goes to the heart of just how and why thinking routines can be powerful learning tools in any subject area.

The Bialik story is also important because it demonstrates that the proper focus of teachers is on supporting thinking, not on the number of routines they use. Using one powerful routine well is preferable to using many of them as mere activities. The story begins with the efforts of Caitlin Faiman trying out thinking routines in her extension mathematics classes. The story then moves into the teaching of maths (as it is referred to throughout most of the world) within the regular classrooms of the primary school, particularly in Janis Kinda's second-grade classroom. Finally, when new teacher Jennifer Kain arrives at the school to teach secondary mathematics, she finds that the routine is well established among the students as a method of learning mathematics, and she finds it easy to incorporate in her tenth-grade classroom to guide and structure students' thinking. As you read through these cases, ask yourself how the routine is fundamentally reshaping the teaching and learning in these classrooms. How does the routine go beyond a one-off activity to providing students with a tool for developing understanding?

USING CLAIM-SUPPORT-QUESTION TO DELVE INTO NUMBER THEORY IN FIFTH GRADE

"Claim-Support-Question has now evolved into the very fabric of our classroom, the underlying structure and culture of our learning," Caitlin Faiman explains as she discusses the mathematics enrichment classes she teaches. Having worked with students in grades 2–7 over the past decade and currently working as the school's primary maths coordinator, Caitlin feels that students now "have great experience in generating answers [data] to problems, creating theories or claims around them, supporting these with evidence, and then following an extension or new path in the form of a new question posed by either myself or peers."

This is certainly noticeable as I walk into Caitlin's "classroom" to observe her fifth-grade extension class. There's very little space to maneuver in the all-purpose room in which Caitlin holds class. Although the twelve-by-twenty-foot room serves as a teacher meeting area, computer workstation, professional development space, room for tutoring, and extra storage facility all in one, Caitlin has nonetheless managed to make it into a space that exudes mathematics. With no whiteboard, she relies on chart paper and student notebooks to document, display, and make visible the learning of the group.

On the walls are comments from students, such as "You can talk about one dimension, but you can't draw it," and chart paper of various hues documenting the class's recent work around square numbers, perimeter, and area. On the top of another sheet is a question written in black marker: "The sum of two fractions is $11\frac{2}{3}$. What might the fractions be?" On the surface, this seems to be a pretty straightforward arithmetic problem. However, Caitlin has approached it as an investigation in which there is more to find out than just an answer. Under the question is written "Beginning Claims . . ." and then a set of conjectures notated with students' names:

- Need to use mixed numbers or improper fractions.
- A whole number cannot be made using . . . 11 wholes cannot be made using two common fractions.
- At least one number needs to be a mixed number or improper fraction. $11\frac{1}{3}$ plus $\frac{2}{6}$
- Your two fractions are $11\frac{2}{3}$ divided by 2, which is $5\frac{5}{6}$. Now fiddle around . . . $4\frac{5}{6} + 6\frac{5}{6}$.
- $11\frac{5}{6} + -\frac{1}{6}$
- When using two mixed numbers, one number has to be odd. $5\frac{1}{3} + 6\frac{1}{3}$
- What about $6\frac{5}{6}$ and $4\frac{5}{6}$.

Beside this sheet are two more posters providing evidence for and against various claims, as well as an extension: "What if . . . I said the sum of two mixed numbers with unlike denominators was $11\frac{2}{3}$ (P.S. Denominators can't be multiples of each other)."

As the class begins, Caitlin directs her twelve extension students to gather around one of the two tables. There's not enough room for everyone to sit, so half the class stands around the perimeter. Sitting at one end of the table, Caitlin begins, "We started looking at triangular numbers last session." Looking up, she catches a student's eye and remembers an issue he brought up to her during the last class. "Ethan, you wanted to start with something. You mentioned you had a claim." As Ethan starts to speak, the class gives him their attention: "1 can't be a triangular number because 1 doesn't form a triangle. I think 3 is the first triangular number because you can put those [dots] into the shape of a triangle. And also 1 is a square number."

Almost instantly a flurry of hands go up, eager to dispute Ethan's claim. Caitlin has to ask students to put their hands down while she probes Ethan's reasoning further. "OK, so you said that 1 can't be a triangular number, and your support was that it can't be placed into the shape of a triangle, and your evidence was what we had down here," she summarizes as she directs the class's attention to the chart paper before her. Reading from the chart, she states, "A triangular number is like a square number but in a triangle." Now that the claim has been clarified, Caitlin presses further: "You said that 1 doesn't form a triangle, but how does 1 form a square?" Ethan has a hard time articulating what he means by this statement, but with the help of the class, he manages to clarify that he doesn't so much mean "shape" as dimension. You can have squares that are 3×3 and 2×2, so you can have a square that is 1×1 or one row by one column, as that is how you make squares. "OK," Caitlin affirms without passing judgment on the claim's validity, "I can understand the point you are making."

The claim that Ethan has put on the table and that Caitlin has left unresolved will ripple throughout the class's conversations as students continue to investigate triangular numbers over the next two days. Allowing for ideas to develop over time as well as permitting questions, issues, and uncertainties to hang in the air is not always natural for teachers, and Caitlin acknowledges that it has been an evolution for her. "The thing about using CSQ is that you have to be willing to hand it over to the students. You have to give over some control if you are really teaching the discipline and encouraging thinking mathematically and not just doing a specific piece of content," she explains. "It can be quite frightening. What if they go on a tangent? What if they depart from the skills and outcomes I am trying to teach? You have to see the big picture. That takes practice. That takes confidence. Most of all, it takes respecting students' ideas."

With Ethan's claim setting the stage, Caitlin wants to give students more time to collect and analyze data, look for patterns, and make generalizations or claims. Caitlin quickly recaps the class's thoughts from the last class session as a starting point. These are pretty basic claims about what triangular numbers are and how to make them—for example:

- A triangular number is like a square number but in a triangle shape.
- To start, you need to put a dot at the top and then two below and then three below and so on.
- You have to have the same number of dots on each side.

Turning to the class, Caitlin asks, "Who has a new claim?" Most hands go up. "Step one is to record your claim on a sheet of paper. Step two, if you don't have a claim to write or once you have written it, we need to do something like we did for square numbers. Ethan said we had a formula for square numbers, two rows of two, four rows of four, seven rows of seven, and so on. We need to work out a formula for triangular numbers finding the third triangular number, the seventh, the ninth, and so on. Step three is we will look at these claims and see if we can find evidence for or against them. You've got three minutes absolutely quiet to write your claim and begin further investigating around a formula."

Students return to their seats and begin to work and write. After three minutes, Caitlin asks students to gather around the front table again and to bring their claims. She collects these and reads them aloud:

- Starting with the second or third triangular number, depending on your perspective, you have three equal sides plus a triangle in the middle.
- Another way of drawing a triangular number is drawing some on the bottom, some on the side, and some on the other side and then filling in the middle.
- The number gets bigger in 1, 2, 3, 4, 5, 6 because you add on to the bottom new row by one more.
- 1 is a triangular number because it has one on the bottom and one on both diagonals.
- The first triangular number is 3 not 1 because it is the first lot of numbers that actually form a triangle.
- Any number that is a triangular number cannot be a square number.
- If you want to find the seventh triangular number, you put seven on the bottom and work up.
- A triangle number starts at 1 because you can make it a triangle shaped one.

A few of the students have asked questions rather than made claims. While the Question aspect of CSQ can be used to raise questions or air skepticism about a particular claim, it can also be used to raise more general questions about the topic being explored. Students' questions include

- How do you write triangular numbers in an equation because you have a "2" [exponent] when you want to write square, and you have "3" [exponent] when you want to write cubed. So what do you write for triangles?
- How many numbers are square and triangle numbers?
- Why is a triangular number different than an array?

As Caitlin is reading the claims and questions, it is hard to keep the students from commenting. Many have evidence ready to share to either support or refute the claims.

The issue concerning what exactly is the first triangular number still looms large, and the question of notation has captured the attention of many. However, there is no more time today. As Caitlin dismisses the class, I can hear many side conversations about the number-one issue of the day: Is 1 a triangular number?

It is still early days working with triangular numbers, and Caitlin knows that resolving the issue of what the first triangular number is will be important in helping students dig deeper into patterns and relationships. The next day, Caitlin gets help with this from Jemma, who begins the class by sharing a drawing she has made (figure 7.1).

Figure 7.1 Jemma's Triangles

Jemma explains her drawing to the class: "So maybe the triangular numbers you need to . . . Well, we drew them as circles [dots], but you can also draw them as triangles. So the first triangular number is one triangle. And the second is like this," she says pointing to the drawing. "Jemma brings up a great point," Caitlin remarks. "We've chosen to draw the triangular numbers using dots. But we could draw them however we like." Ethan, who just the day before was insistent that 1 was not a triangular number, has had an epiphany. "Oh, it [the dot] *is* the shape that it *is* [type of number]," he exclaims. "So use a square for a square number and a triangle for triangle!"

"So tell me what you notice about the base of each of these," Caitlin inquires of the class as she points to Jemma's drawing. Jacob quickly jumps in: "The base is always the same as the number. So the second triangle has two and third has three, so that means the first has one," he says excitedly. At this point one of the boys standing on the side turns to the other and exclaims, "See, I was right." Caitlin jumps on the comment as an opportunity: "It's not about being right or wrong. It is about finding evidence. We need evidence that we are comfortable with so that we can move forward," she explains. Caitlin then clarifies why this issue is important: "We can still disagree here, but we do need to have a resolution for us about what is the first triangular number going forward. So for the purpose of this investigation, we are saying 1 is the first triangular number."

Over these two days, I'm struck by how engaged the students are with the mathematics and how the language of claims, evidence, and support has really become routine. It all seems so effortless, and indeed that is the beauty of having routines. They can make complicated tasks and thinking appear effortless and natural. However, this seamlessness wasn't always the case for Caitlin and her students. Furthermore, although Caitlin appreciated how thinking routines supported students' thinking, making them routine initially eluded her.

As a member of an initial Cultures of Thinking learning group at Bialik College, Caitlin worked alongside her colleagues to try out thinking routines and study how they helped shape students' thinking and learning. Although she could find a place for such routines as See-Think-Wonder or Zoom In (see Caitlin's example in Ritchhart et al., 2011), it wasn't easy to make those real patterns of behavior in her classes. When Claim-Support-Question was introduced, there began a real shift in Caitlin's teaching. Although CSQ had been designed initially as a way to investigate issues of truth and opinion in speech and print, Caitlin immediately saw the application of the routine to mathematics: the process of identifying claims, what mathematicians might call a conjecture or theory, and then investigating them to see if they held up went to the very heart of mathematical thinking, bringing together the processes of analysis, speculation, generalization, and proof (Silver, Kilpatrick, & Schlesinger, 1995). Here was the opportunity to develop a real thinking routine that could operate as a guiding structure for virtually all of her students' learning in mathematics.

Caitlin explains how the process started for her: "I would provide them with a question and then give them time to generate some data. We'd record that in some way, and I'd ask, 'What do you notice? Are there patterns?' This would become the initial claims that I would model and shape into statements." In terms of documenting the conversation, Caitlin says, "I started off with columns: Claim, Support, Question. And we would work right through that."

Commenting on the evolution of the routine, Caitlin observes, "You have to learn the rhythm of it. Then the columns fade away, and the students start asking the questions. You give it over to the kids. It changes the way you teach maths, from covering dot points to looking at big understandings."

MORE THAN A GAME: DIFFERENTIATING MATHEMATICS IN SECOND GRADE

It is one thing to expect a group of high-performing students to be engaged in thinking mathematically around a special topic like number theory, but will a regular heterogeneous mix of students respond the same way to Claim-Support-Question? Caitlin thought so, and had the opportunity to find out. Together with the second-grade team of Janis Kinda, Victoria Knight, and Kim Haddix, Caitlin and the group devised a simple game called the King and Queen of Evens to help reinforce students' understanding of odd and even numbers and place value. In the game, a player rolls three decahedrons with sides labeled 0–9, scoring a point for every three-digit even number made.

The game isn't complicated, but using CSQ as an overlay, students have the opportunity to look for patterns and relationships and do more mathematical thinking than they might have if simply asked to play the game. Students with more mathematical understanding have a chance to delve more deeply into the mathematical structure of the game, while those struggling with more basic understandings can focus on reinforcing their knowledge of place value and odds and evens. Janis Kinda identifies this as one of the strengths of CSQ, commenting that it "allows opportunities for peer-to-peer learning. Small focus groups can learn together and explore more basic or concrete claims, and other groups can learn together exploring ideas that are more abstract."

Sitting on the mat in front of the interactive whiteboard, Janis begins her explanation of the game by flashing the directions on the screen:

The King and Queen of Evens

- Play the game with a partner or group of three players.
- Roll three dice and record the digits in ascending order.
- Using these digits, make as many three-digit even numbers as possible.
- Score one point for every even number.

The class reviews terminology: ascending order, odds, evens, and digits, and then begins to work through an example to see how many combinations can be made and thus how many points scored. In the class's practice roll, the numbers 5, 0, and 5 have turned up. Janis asks the class for a three-digit number that can be made from the roll. "505," responds one student. "550," adds another. "Any other numbers I can record?" Janis asks. The space before her fills with hands before she adds, "Three-digit numbers. We're looking at three-digit numbers." All the hands go down amid defeated sighs. "Why did the hands just go down?" Janis questions. Jesse offers an explanation: "You could put down fifty-five, but then the zero would go in the hundreds. But then that is really just fifty-five and not three digits." Janis affirms, "So Jesse's claim is that a zero in the hundreds place still makes it a two-digit number because even though we could say zero hundreds and fifty-five, that's not really how we would say it. We would just say fifty-five."

What's interesting here is that Janis has taken Jesse's idea and reframed it as a claim. You might question that, feeling that Jesse has really just stated a fact. It is true that the convention is not to count lead digits of zero. However, in framing this as a claim, Janis is not suggesting that it isn't true. Rather, she is signaling that in mathematics, our facts come from ideas that must be tested to see how they hold up. That is a radically different way of learning mathematics. Students don't merely memorize blindly; they build a foundation of fully vetted ideas that they understand in relationship to other ideas. In this case, it is not mathematics that tells us we can't have zero as a lead digit but our convention of referring only to the place in which the first counting number appears.

After working through another example, Janis is about to send the students to investigate the game when Angela raises her hand. "What if you both get three even numbers?" she asks. "I'm going to leave that as a question," Janis suggests as she records it on the board. "Let's play the game now. Maybe someone will come up with a claim that will help us answer that question," she adds. Janis likes beginning with students' questions before an investigation. "The initial claims allow me to see who knows something about the topic and the direction we can take the learning," she explains. "It's a perfect opportunity for the more talented mathematicians to use this platform to ask more open-ended questions that they can then investigate." She admits, however, that at the beginning of the year it was mostly she asking those questions.

After about ten minutes of playing the game, Janis calls the class back to attention using a familiar routine, "One, two, three, eyes on me." The class echoes back, "One, two eyes on you," as they turn to face her. "Come and sit on the mat, please. Leave your whiteboards, markers, and dice where they are," she directs before adding, "Make a thoughtful choice where you are going to sit. I don't want to have our thinking interrupted by silliness." Once students are settled in place for the plenary, Janis frames the task of the gathering: "We're going to share some of our aha moments. Some of those things that make you go 'Yes!' and some of those things that make you go 'Uhhh.'"

Grabbing a marker to record students' ideas, she directs their attention by saying, "Let's have some claims happening around this game. What do you need to know to get some points? Maybe we will come up with some new questions, and [pointing back to Angela's earlier question] maybe we will come up with an answer to this question."

"OK," Janis begins. "Tye, you put your hand up very excitedly. What do you want to share?" Pointing to the board, Tye commences with his claim. "It's something about the question. It is a draw," he states emphatically.

"So if you both roll three even digits, it is a draw?" Janis tosses back by way of clarifying. Tye nods his head and Janis pushes further: "Can you give me an example?" By way of evidence, Tye offers, "We both had 5, 8, and 2, and it was the same."

With Tye's evidence, it is clear that he may be making a different, though somewhat related claim, to Angela's question. To address this difference, Janis calls on Angela. "Angela, what do you think of Tye's evidence? He said they both had 5, 8, and 2, and it was the same number of points. Does that answer your question?" Without missing a beat, Angela offers, "Not really, because I was asking what would happen if you both rolled three even numbers, and 5 isn't an even number." Turning back to Tye, Janis asks, "Tye, can you rephrase your claim? What is it that you found out?"

"Oh," says Tye, "mine is if you both roll the exact same numbers you get the same number of points."

Over the next ten minutes, Janis record students' claims as they share them, often using conditional statements to describe what they noticed was happening in the game:

- You cannot make any numbers if your digits are odd.
- If you roll all even digits, you get a lot of points.
- If you roll a 1 and two 0s, you only make one three-digit even number.
- If you get three evens but two are the same, you don't get as many points as if you got three different even digits.
- I have 2, 4, 8 . . . I can make like twenty even numbers.
- If you get no doubles and they are all even, you get 6 points . . . and no zeros. But if you get a double, you only get 2 points.
- Each digit has only two options if you start with one digit in the hundreds place.
- If you roll two evens and one odd, you get 4 points.
- When you roll one even and two odds, you get 2 points. But we have to try it with a zero because a zero sometimes changes it.

Janis records each claim without much discussion, knowing that it is important to allow students to present their ideas, even if they are contradictory, and to get all the thinking out initially. Later the class will engage in more exploration to find evidence to support or contradict the various claims. "One of the most powerful aspects of CSQ is that anyone can make a claim," Janis says. "Once a student feels that they have made a contribution, it helps build confidence and the desire to further their understanding. There is always that moment when a child shares a claim that no one else thought of, even the teacher!"

Reflecting on my own observations of the class, I'm struck how I never once heard a student exclaim "I won!" as they were playing the game. This would not be an atypical response among a group of second graders. However, in Janis's class, students were as interested in their partner's rolls as they were in their own because all were engaged in discovering the underlying patterns and relationships while collecting evidence. The point was no longer to win but to learn. What began as a pretty basic game has turned into an opportunity to think much more deeply about mathematics. By providing a structure for their thinking, Claim-Support-Question acts as a routine that has transformed the teaching of mathematics for Janis. "CSQ has shifted the way I teach mathematics, as it has provided me with a much clearer framework when guiding my teaching and students' learning," she explains. "When students raise questions, they can take the learning in an entirely new direction. Unfortunately, we don't always have the freedom or time to explore a topic in depth, and those curriculum constraints can be a challenge, but the engagement with maths and at least articulating some of those interesting avenues is definitely worth it."

MAKING CSQ FLY IN SECONDARY MATHEMATICS

As a new teacher to Bialik, Jennifer Kain noticed a difference in her secondary mathematics students: "I could tell students were used to expressing their thinking because they themselves had grown to value their own thinking and understanding." This made her first use of the Claim-Support-Question routine smooth. "Students engaged quickly and easily with the structure of the routine because they found value in it themselves," she reflected.

When I visit Jennifer's tenth-grade mathematics class midyear, she is employing Claim-Support-Question to investigate quadratic relationships and discover the key characteristics of parabolas. The context for this exploration is looking at the relationship of the weight of a paper airplane to the distance the plane flies when thrown by hand.

To begin, Jennifer has students make claims, or predictions about what will happen. For Jennifer, these initial claims serve an important function. "CSQ has reminded me of the importance of estimating and understanding the reasonableness of a solution in maths," she explains. "I think of the claim as a prediction of what the students expect to occur. From their claims, I can do a quick assessment of the students' understanding."

Jennifer records the class's claims for the investigation on the board:

- They will fall shorter because more and more weight will pull it to the ground.

- It will travel a smaller distance.

- The paper airplane when weight is added will fly a shorter distance and fall quicker because of the added weight pushing it down.

- It would fly a shorter distance, and it would hit the floor much faster as the weight goes up.

- I expect that the paper airplane will glide for a shorter distance as more staples are added.

- It will fly lower to the ground and eventually crash.

- As you continually add weight, the plane will travel less.

- It will travel at a shorter distance. It will go up and almost straight down. The more weight you add, the shorter the distance.

Looking over the claims, it is clear that students think the relationship will be linear, with distance declining as weight increases. Many claims reflect the notion of gravity as the key variable accounting for this decline.

As students conduct the experiment in pairs, adding weight to their airplanes using staples and collecting data on each throw, it quickly becomes clear that the class's assumption of pure linearity isn't holding up. Once data are gathered, they are graphed first manually and then in a symbolic (CAS) calculator, where students also attempt to find the line of regression. This produces new evidence, and claims have to be revised as a result:

- It has a maximum.

- It increases and decreases.

- Your farthest distance would be the coordinates for your turning point.

- The x-axis is the weight of the staples, and the y-axis would be the distance flown.

- Flight distance did increase.

- After it increased, it decreased right away, making it a maximum.

The new data provide Jennifer an opportunity to discuss the parabolic shape of the data and focus on key attributes of parabolas, which is an important mathematical learning for the students. This leads to the generation of lots of questions about all the variables affecting the experiment and how best to control for them. These are largely scientific questions. However, mathematical questions emerge as well, including fundamental questions about the data and their mathematical expression, such as:

- How is there a bell curve when the numbers are unequal and unrelated?
- Why was the CAS result different?
- Why are our answers inconsistent or skewed?
- Are our data accurately reflected on the parabola?
- Why is our parabola so narrow?
- Is the graph more accurately described with a linear model?
- How does it relate to $y = a(x - h)^2 + k$?

Echoing Janis Kinda's sentiments, Jennifer notes, "I am always surprised by the variety of questions students pose. Often they are questions that I did not consider." However, it is the looking for support that she finds most powerful about CSQ: "The Support allows the students to develop their ability to reason with evidence, which often is difficult for them. It can be difficult for students to offer evidence in a math context. Instead, they often want to just explain or solve the problem. This routine allows them to slow down and give attention to the details, nuances, and complexities. Students are improving their ability to reason with evidence, but this has only come with more frequent use of the routine."

TOOLS, STRUCTURES, AND PATTERNS: ESTABLISHING ROUTINES IN THE CLASSROOM

As I mentioned at the outset of this chapter, there are many different types of routines at play in schools and classrooms. Although different researchers have classified classroom routines using various overlapping schemes (Kaser, 2007; Leinhardt et al., 1987; Yinger, 1979), I suggest four major categories for our discussion: management, instructional, interactional, and thinking. Each type is important in its own right, and all contribute substantially to the creation of the invisible infrastructure that supports the smooth running of the classroom. Furthermore, all types of routines operate on three levels simultaneously: (1) as tools for accomplishing something, (2) as structures that direct and guide actions, and (3) as familiar patterns of behavior.

Despite their similarities and the need for all four types of routines to be present in well-functioning classrooms, until now the focus of those who work with teachers has been almost exclusively on management and instructional routines (Kaser, 2007; Lemov, 2010; Linsin, 2009; Murray, 2002; Wong & Wong, 1997). This focus often proceeds from the needs of new or struggling teachers to manage classrooms and from the truism that unless the classroom is controlled and focused, then learning cannot happen. There's a danger in this one-sided focus, however. Although management and instructional routines are important, we shouldn't stop there. An exclusive emphasis on these routines places attention more on student control and teacher delivery than on the promotion of student thinking and learning.

Do an Internet search on "classroom routines," and what comes up is article after article on management routines. These are the routines teachers often set up at the beginning of the school year to ensure the smooth running of a class. They include such things as how to get attention, housekeeping chores, movement, discipline, transitioning, cleaning up, getting materials, people moving, and so on. In short, "management routines are established procedures for controlling and coordinating classroom organization and behavior" (Yinger, 1979, p. 166). Think of any task that has to be done over and over again in a classroom, and it is generally helpful to have a routine for it. Consider, for example, getting students' attention. Because this is something teachers have to do for almost every lesson, particularly if students will be working in groups, it is helpful to have a routine to facilitate this. Janis Kinda used the routine "One, two, three, eyes on me." Other teachers turn off the lights, clap a pattern, sound a chime, or raise their hand in silence waiting for students to raise their own hands and grow silent in response. Often such routines may even be agreed upon across an entire school. These routines take little time to teach and learn. However, they do require consistency of application. Without consistency, management routines quickly break down.

Management routines are established within the context of a community of practice, and they help classrooms run smoothly. It is also possible to have management routines that are more punitive and disciplinary. Such routines are generally about control and order: writing students' names on the board for speaking out, locking the class door and not allowing any latecomers in once the bell has rung, lining up perfectly quietly, and so on. Although such routines may help to impose order, they often do so at a cost. They cast students as rule breakers and teachers as wardens. Therefore, it is important to carefully examine how such routines get implemented and that they not undermine the establishment of positive relationships or undercut the learning. A good example of finding the right fit between order and learning can be seen in the videos of Tyler Hester establishing management routines during the first days of schools in his freshman English class, which can be found on YouTube (Shiksastudio, 2012).

Instructional routines capture the style, approach, tools, practices, and procedures that teachers use for carrying out instruction. To some extent, instructional routines are idiosyncratic in nature, reflecting the personality and preference of the teacher. How does the teacher run her class? How does she deliver information? What is his method of opening up discussion? How does he deal with questions? As a teacher, you might not even be aware that you have a routine way of doing such things because you do them so automatically. This means the actions have been routinized so that you scarcely need to think about them. Likewise, your students have internalized your actions as familiar "scripts" that follow predictable patterns. Coming to the mat for both an opening and closing discussion is an instructional routine in both the kindergarten class I taught and in Janis's second-grade classroom. In Caitlin Faiman's class, it was gathering around a single table with the chart paper laid out. Using the algebraic calculators was a routine in Jennifer Kain's class.

One's typical way of carrying out instruction in the classroom does constitute a routine. However, such routines may not always be the most effective way of doing things. An all too familiar example of this comes from the way teachers often end a class session. Too frequently, class ends when time runs out and the bell rings, sending students packing. That can happen on occasion, as it did to me in the kindergarten classroom, or it may be the routine for that teacher. If such a practice has become routine, it needs to be rethought, as it isn't particularly effective. Research in the United Kingdom suggests that a closing plenary session—that is, a coming together of the whole group—is a much more effective way of ending a lesson in terms of supporting students' learning (Siraj-Blatchford et al., 2011). A closing plenary enables students to share findings and raise questions as part of a summarizing discussion, as was done in Jennifer's and Janis's classes. These gatherings also allow teachers to highlight big ideas, challenge students' thinking, recap the lesson, and point a direction forward for the next lesson. Once we have allowed ineffective routines to take hold in our classrooms, usually because of lack of overt attention to alternatives, they can be hard habits to break. They require our attention and practicing a new way of doing things until it becomes a habit.

In addition to our well-worn ways of doing things, instructional routines can also be tools and structures we use to carry out certain activities that occur less frequently. For example, one of my favorite new routines is Give One, Get One, used for sharing ideas. Students begin by generating their own list of ideas related to the topic at hand. Next, students find a partner with whom to share one idea off their list, the "give one."

The partner records the shared idea, the "get one," and then shares or gives back one new idea off of his or her own list. After each student has given one and gotten one, both find a new partner to repeat the process. It basically is a version of brainstorming but with more individual accountability. The routine operates as a tool for generating ideas and a structure to facilitate the sharing process. After just a few uses, it becomes a familiar pattern that a teacher can quickly activate.

Interactional routines structure the contact between teachers and students as well as that between students and students. Although they are not limited to language and discourse, they frequently deal with these types of exchanges. Raising hands to make a contribution is a default routine we all have, but certainly not the only way to structure question-and-answer interactions. Teachers can use eye contact, a thumb held up close to the chest, or even a no-hands-up policy (Black, 2002; Buhrow & Garcia, 2006) to structure these interactions. Think-Pair-Share (Lyman, 1981), first introduced in the 1970s, is a routine for structuring interaction that is often credited with breaking the traditional question-and-response pattern of questioning. Collaborative learning structures, book clubs, Socratic seminars, and leaderless discussions (Ritchhart, 2002) all provide structures for conversation and discussion in the classroom.

Students' social and emotional learning is also supported by interactional routines by providing them structures for positive interactions rather than leaving those to chance. The Responsive Classroom approach makes extensive use of interactional routines to create an emotionally safe learning environment (Rimm-Kaufman, Fan, Chiu, & You, 2007). In chapter 5, we saw how Natalie Belli used the Ladder of Feedback to structure how both she and students gave one another feedback. Once that routine was learned, students had a vehicle that allowed them to both give and receive feedback more effectively. In chapter 8, I'll focus on interactions as a cultural force and explore some other routines that can promote positive and educationally rich interactions.

Thinking routines can be used as instructional routines as I have mentioned; however, their real power comes in their use as cognitive strategies that become patterns of behavior for students. To understand how thinking routines work in general, and the routine Claim-Support-Question in particular, it is useful to consider their triadic nature as tools, structures, and patterns. I've used these terms throughout this chapter, but a closer examination can help illuminate how thinking routines get developed in classrooms over time.

As tools, thinking routines are used to activate certain types of thinking. In this respect they are similar to cognitive strategies. Consequently, in using thinking routines, teachers need to think beyond how the routine might facilitate lesson delivery to consider how the routine provides students with a tool for thinking. Choosing the best tool for the job involves asking, What kind of thinking do my students need to do with this content? How can I best engage them in that kind of thinking? CSQ engages students in making predictions, analyzing data, looking for patterns, making generalizations, weighing evidence, and raising questions. Because these thinking moves constitute a large bulk of what it means to do mathematics, the routine is an easy fit for lots of different mathematical situations. One can see the clear link to opportunities. As we create opportunities for thinking, we must also provide our students with the tools they will need to do that thinking.

As we would with any tool, we'll find it useful to take stock of how a routine is working for us in achieving our goals. With an instructional routine, a teacher should reflect on how effective it is. With a thinking routine, it should be the students who are doing the reflecting. How did this routine help us to investigate this problem? Did it help us to dig more deeply? Did it facilitate our understanding? How might we adjust it for next time? With which parts of the routine do we need to work and develop more skill? By reflecting on the routines with our students, we help them take control of them so that they can use them independently in their own learning.

It is not uncommon for me to hear from teachers, "Thinking routines seem good for other subjects, but they just don't fit in my subject." Although it is true that any particular thinking routine might not fit with any particular content, the broader idea of thinking routines is that they facilitate, scaffold, and direct the thinking that effective learners need to do when striving to understand new content. Therefore, to develop their own or to employ an existing thinking routine effectively, teachers must ask themselves, *What kinds of thinking do I need students to do with this content, and how can I best scaffold that thinking?* When I hear that "thinking routines just don't fit with subject X," it is generally because the subject is being taught to students in a way that makes memory the only thinking students are asked to employ. Such impoverished teaching frequently leads to impoverished learning. Memory and practice may build skills and a knowledge base, but it doesn't develop understanding. In contexts such as these, using thinking routines will require some teachers to do a radical rethinking of what it means to learn for understanding.

As structures, thinking routines are designed as scaffolds for thinking. They give us as learners a framework for our thinking and often lay out a sequence in which each step builds on the next. This helps demystify the process of thinking. For many students, directions to "read this passage and understand it" are too vague and hard to put into action. However, by using a routine like Connect-Extend-Challenge (Ritchhart et al.,

2011), students have a tool for breaking down understanding by first looking for connections to what they already know, then identifying how their understanding has been extended or pushed further by the reading, and finally by raising questions and challenges that need further exploration.

Structures and scaffolds needn't be straitjackets. In the cases presented in this chapter, we saw how the teachers each thought a bit differently about claims, some as predictions and some as patterns, and about questions, sometimes as counterevidence and sometimes as issues that needed further investigation. Much of the power of thinking routines comes from their flexibility. Furthermore, it is this flexibility that is often a sign that thinking routines are becoming patterns both in the classroom and in students' minds.

As with any routine, the ultimate goal of using thinking routines is for them to become patterns of behavior. This happens as students become familiar with them and their use in different contexts. However, unlike other routines that get solidified in whole, we see more fluidity with thinking routines once they take hold. Teachers often notice that rather than being set in stone, the routine becomes more embedded and natural. For instance, students begin to recognize the important role of supporting evidence and may call for it in situations even when not using CSQ. Likewise, as students get comfortable with claims, they may begin to voice tentative interpretations and possible explanations, knowing that this doesn't represent "not knowing" but instead is a first step to understanding. We could say that it is the thinking that has become routine.

The four cases presented in this chapter demonstrate how all four types of routines affect the smooth running of a classroom. At the same time, the cases highlight the unique role of thinking routines in shaping students' learning. As we look into our own classrooms, we need to ask ourselves, What kinds of supports and structures are we providing for thinking? With what tools are we providing our students to facilitate and demystify thinking? and What kinds of thinking are becoming routine in our classroom?

MAKING THINKING
ROUTINE IN OUR CLASSROOMS

- Identify the kinds of thinking you want to make routine in your classroom. What kinds of thinking are important in your subject area? What kinds of thinking will students need to be able to do to build understanding?

- Identify thinking routines to try out. Look through *Making Thinking Visible* (Ritchhart et al., 2011) or the Visible Thinking website (http://www .visiblethinkingpz.org/) to find routines that match the kind of thinking you want to develop in your students. Identify three to five thinking routines that are potentially good fits for your goals.

- Try out and reflect on your use of a thinking routine. Make sure you introduce the routine as a tool for thinking and not as an activity. For example, "Our goal today is to deepen our understanding of the text we read yesterday. To help us accomplish that, we are going to use The 4C's to structure our discussion." Now reflect on the routine as a piece of instruction: Did it help you to engage students with the content? Did it help you structure the lesson and engage students? What felt right to you, and where did you struggle?

- Have students reflect on the thinking routines as tools. For instance, say to them, "We used The 4C's as our structure for discussion and to help deepen our understanding. How do you feel that went? Did it make discussion more productive and focused? Do you feel you are coming away with a better understanding? What was hard and what was easy about the routine? What should we try to work on improving the next time we use this routine?

- Examine students' thinking. Collect what your students produced and convene a group of colleagues to carefully examine their work for evidence of thinking. Use the Looking At Students' Thinking (LAST) protocol (appendix D) to structure your conversation.

- Create your own thinking routines. Good routines have only a few steps and make explicit the kinds of thinking effective learners would do in a situation. Are there certain learning tasks with which you regularly engage students? What thinking is necessary to accomplish those tasks well? Identifying those steps might yield a routine. Are there types of discussions you want students to be able to have independently? What are the major parts or points in that discussion? Identifying those parts might yield a routine.

- Collect new management and instructional routines. Visit other classrooms and pay attention to the routines in those classrooms. Which make transitions and instruction more efficient while also supporting students as independent learners? When and where might you use any of the new routines you observed?

- Examine your own instructional routines. Do you have routines for beginning and ending class? Do you have routines for different types of activities, such as group work, independent work, class discussion, lecture, unit review, or attention getting? How effective are these routines in helping you and your students remain focused on learning? Would it help their effectiveness if you were more consistent? Are there tweaks or adjustments to the routines you need to make?

CHAPTER 8

Interactions

Forging Relationships That Empower Learners

in•ter•ac•tion |intər'akSHən| noun: The dynamic phenom-
enon that emerges when two or more objects have an effect on
one another. • The feedback loop created between actions and
effects. As a culture shaper, interactions form the basis for
relationships among teachers and students, students and students, and teachers and teachers. Interactions knit together the
social fabric that binds individuals in community. The interactions among and across group members help to define the
emotional climate, tone, or ethos of a place. In a culture of
thinking, teachers' interactions with students show a respect
for and an interest in students' thinking while nurturing their
development as valued, competent individuals able to contribute effectively to the group.

What were some of your most significant educational experiences? Can you name a few that helped to shape you as a thinker and a learner? What experiences brought out the best in you and allowed you to reach new heights in learning? When I ask these questions of groups, I rarely get back an idea, concept, or aha moment but am instead regaled with stories of personal interaction, mentoring, connection to a group, or powerful mutual engagement with another person in the learning enterprise. To the extent that we believe that learning is largely a social endeavor as opposed to an isolated enterprise, relationships play a pivotal role. Relationships serve to motivate and engage us. They provide a supportive context for taking risks. As learners, we benefit from knowing that someone has our back and is cheering for our success even as he or she is willing to catch us should we fall. James Comer, one of America's leading advocates for school-home-community connections through his founding of the Comer School Development Program at Yale University in 1968, makes an even more emphatic declaration about the important role others play in our learning, stating, "No significant learning can occur without a significant relationship" (Comer, 1995).

Great teachers often explain their success in terms of relationships. Chemistry teacher Jeff Charbonneau, named Teacher of the Year in 2013 by the Council of Chief State School Officers in the United States, believes deeply in creating a classroom culture where learning, thinking, and joy take hold. To create such a paradise—and Jeff does in fact think of his classroom as a paradise—he believes that we must treat every day as the most important day for each student ("Jeff Charbonneau—2013 National Teacher of the Year," 2013). Doing so requires teachers to connect with individuals. "It is the relationships with students that come first," Jeff says. "If you can make a positive relationship with a student, you can teach them darn near anything. You can take them all the way to quantum mechanics and physics. Take them into the intricacies of art, visual and performing. It is the relationships that come first" ("High School Teacher to Be Honored at White House," 2013).

Award-winning high school teacher Yvonne Divans-Hutchison (Rose, 1995) echoes these same sentiments, telling prospective educators, "Do not think that because a child cannot read a text, he cannot read you. Children can tell right off those people who believe in them and those who patronize them. They can tell once they come into the room" (p. 17).

Of course, if we recognize the importance of relationships to learning, then we also must acknowledge what happens when positive relationships aren't forged. In her widely viewed TED talk, Rita Pierson (2013) recounts the story of a colleague who said to her, "They don't pay me to like the kids. They pay me to teach a lesson; the kids should learn it. I should teach it; they should learn it. Case closed." Rita's response was simple and to the point: "You know, kids don't learn from people they don't like." As Pierson so eloquently states at the end of her talk, "Every child deserves a champion, an adult who will never give up on them, who understands the power of connection, and insists that they become the best that they can possibly be." Others have called this being a "warm demander," someone who demands high standards while knowing students personally and holding them in positive regard (Bondy & Ross, 2008).

Yes, relationships do indeed matter to learning, and the nature of our relationships is revealed through our interactions. As social beings, we recognize that it is through interacting with others that we learn what a group or culture is about, how it operates, its norms and values. Interactions give us a feel for a place, help us learn how to behave in the group and to know what is expected. Through interactions, we identify who our allies and champions are.

The centrality of interactions to teaching and learning quickly becomes apparent when teachers analyze videos of teaching to uncover the qualities of classrooms that give them their unique feel. These generally emerge as the eight cultural forces. One of my favorite videos for this purpose is that of Spanish language teacher Leslie Revis, an American Teacher Awards honoree from Beaufort High School in South Carolina. Throughout the video, Leslie laughs, smiles, listens, sits beside, and touches her students. She supports them as they struggle and celebrates their success. She exudes energy and happiness. She seems a part of the group rather than distanced from it. Viewers notice these moments, as fleeting as they are. They discern Leslie's affect, her interactions with students both individually and in groups, as being especially communicative of the values and norms of her classroom. Viewers also note how the students interact with one another, their interactions often mirroring the teacher-to-student interactions. Pushing the analysis further, viewers often identify the genuineness of the teacher, her passion and use of humor, and the sense of connection being forged as important elements contributing to the feel of the classroom. Not surprisingly, viewers often comment that Leslie's classroom is a place they'd like to be in as learners.

Students, too, recognize the importance of interactions to learning. In Resnick and colleagues' review (1997) of the National Longitudinal Study of Adolescents, they found that even though students generally felt their schooling to be disconnected from their own lives and interests, virtually every student was able to identify and describe a relationship with a teacher that was meaningful to them. When Rogers and Freiberg (1994) surveyed students about the conditions under which they learned best, they mentioned such things as being trusted and respected, being part of a family, places where people care, receiving trust and respect, and viewing teachers as supportive and helpful. The teacher-student relationship lies at the heart of all these responses. In offering advice to teachers, one of the high school students interviewed by Kathleen Cushman (2005) identifies the specific types of teacher-student interactions needed to support the development of a culture of thinking: "Remind us often you expect our best, encourage our efforts even if we are having trouble, give helpful feedback and expect us to review . . . don't compare us to other students, and stick with us" (pp. 64–67).

Of course, understanding of the importance of relationship and interactions to learning is not new. Dewey (1916), Vygotsky (1978), Bruner (1996), Henry (1963), Glasser (1968), and Rogers (Rogers & Freiberg, 1994) all stressed that learning is a social endeavor in which our interactions with others not only support the learning process but are inseparable from it. At the heart of much of this theoretical work is the belief that transformative learning—that is, learning that cultivates the development of the whole person and strives for more than the simple transmission of information—is more likely to happen in community than in isolation. Such communities are largely democratic in nature, stressing mutuality, support, connection, and shared decision making. In contrast, when the simple transmission of information is viewed as the chief goal, we often see scripted programs being put in place that ignore the importance of interactions and the development of a teacher-student relationship.

More recently, research has shown that far from being a mere nicety, attention to building strong teacher-student relationships plays an important role in supporting student achievement and in particular the development of critical thinking (Cornelius-White, 2007; Pianta, Hamre, & Allen, 2012; Stupnisky, Renaud, Daniels, Haynes, & Perry, 2008). In John Hattie's review (2009) of how various educational practices, programs, decisions, curricula, and background variables influence student achievement, teacher-student relationships were identified as one of the top practices highly likely to affect learning. With an effect-size score of .72 (meaning that, all other things being equal, attention to this practice is likely to have a positive effect on student achievement 72 times out of 100), teacher-student interactions are in the rare class of variables shown to have a high impact on student achievement. More evidence of the centrality of interactions comes from the long line of research done by James Comer (2001) at the Yale Child Study Center, as well as from emerging research on social and emotional learning that is showing the value of attending to students' emotional intelligence and socialization within the group (Jensen & Snider, 2013; Tough, 2012).

The evidence overwhelmingly indicates that teachers' interactions, and the relationships that are formed as a result of those interactions, play a major role in supporting learning. However, too often teacher-student interactions are viewed as merely an artifact of teacher personality rather than an aspect of teaching amenable to change. Although the amount, quality, and context of classroom interactions seem almost endless, I attempt in this chapter to isolate some key practices and explore the following questions: What are the qualitative aspects of teacher-student interactions that teachers should strive to employ? What should coaches, facilitators, and other observers of classroom teaching look for in the behavior of teachers to identify interactions that are productive and supportive of learning and thinking? What specific instructional practices can be used to scaffold teachers' interactions with students into more productive and facilitative patterns of teaching that will enhance the culture of thinking in that classroom?

NEW ROLES FOR STUDENTS: EMPOWERING DISENFRANCHISED LEARNERS

"First of all, I want to tell you how proud I am of the work you did with the substitute while I was out," Julie Rains offers as she commences period one with her eighth-grade special education class. It is a small class of seven students, all with individualized education programs (IEPs), some with specific identified speech and language issues, and a few on the autism spectrum. The class is seated in a semicircle as Julie leans over the podium on her desk, smiling. Behind her is a largely smiling face projected on the screen as a visual cue to her emotions for students with autism. "Thank you very much for your work," Julie continues. "I wrote you a message on EdModo [the school portal], but just wanted to let you know if you haven't read it there yet." It is a short opening, establishing a link back to the class after her brief absence. It also has the effect of letting students know that Julie is in touch with the class and monitoring their progress even when she is away.

"Today we are playing Enbrighten with *Touching Spirit Bear*," Julie explains. Enbrighten, as I learned on one of my previous visits to the class, is a "game" created by Julie and her teaching colleague, speech pathologist Erika Lusky, to develop students' reading comprehension and language skills. In playing the game, students take on roles related to a specific reading comprehension strategy, such as summarizer, visualizer, vocab master, connector, questioner, clarifier, or predictor. Students then read a text together and complete their assigned role in preparation for the class discussion, which might be led or facilitated by the teacher or one of the students. Points are scored for doing one's job. The more one's response shows understanding and insight into the text, the more points are earned based on a rubric students have been given explaining what depth and insight look like for each role. However, one still gets points for attempting one's given role. In addition, double points can be earned by using evidence, connecting to others' ideas, or explaining one's thinking. As students have gained mastery of the core roles, Julie and Erika have designed additional roles, such as symbolizer, critic, identifier, defender, and judge.

An important goal for Julie and Erika in using the game is the development of students' confidence as readers. "Our goal the first term is for students to feel comfortable sharing ideas and taking risks," Erika explains. Julie elaborates, "The jobs are consistent with Literature Circle roles, but we do more scaffolding and supporting as well as modeling by being active participants ourselves." Although the points make the discussion of literature more gamelike, both Julie and Erika downplay their prominence. "In the long run, the points aren't really even important," Julie clarifies. "Initially they can serve as a motivator for some students, though. Our sixth-grade class is very competitive and very motivated by the points, but by eighth grade they don't generally need that anymore. They can just jump right into the text and learn from one another. Our goal is to get rid of the points and to have them functioning independently." These goals are clearly being met in the class of eighth graders I am observing. In setting up for today's class, Julie and Erika have already had a discussion with the class the preceding week about how they would like the game to unfold.

"We need to review what we talked about on Thursday about how we were going to do this," Julie announces. "Can you remember what we talked about?" Julie queries the class. It is not that Julie or Erika haven't taken notes on the decisions the class has made; rather, they want students to see themselves as leading and directing this class. If Julie were to read from her notes, she would be sending the message that she, rather than the students, was in control, that they could sit back and wait for her to direct them. She is stepping back to allow her students to step forward.

KATE: No leader or everyone a leader. No facilitator.

JULIE: When would a facilitator be needed? When might Ms. Lusky or I have to jump in?

GABE:	If we are arguing.
DONALD:	Or talking over each other.
JULIE:	What else did we decide?
BELLA:	Follow the roles.
BEN:	Step in if needed. And no points.
JULIE:	That's right. We voted that we would not do points today.
MADISON:	Did you assign jobs?
BELLA:	No, we did that already.
DONALD:	Kate, you agreed to be summarizer. Madison, you're visualizer . . .

As this conversation unfolds, Julie sits at her computer typing the list of decisions students have made into a word processing document that is projected on the whiteboard. This visually reminds students of the choices that have been made about how the game will be played.

It is worth noting that throughout this very brief exchange, both Julie and her students consistently use the pronoun "we" to locate themselves within the group and signal the group's responsibility to each other. While giving over some control and decision making to students, Julie doesn't remove herself or Erika from being participants in the group. They know that they have roles to play as models, participants, and colearners. Eschewing the scripted curriculum used in many special education English classes in the district, Erika and Julie align themselves with Dewey (1916) when he wrote, "The alternative to furnishing ready-made subject matter and listening to the accuracy with which it is reproduced is not quiescence, but participation, sharing, in an activity. In such a shared activity, the teacher is a learner, and the learner is, without knowing it, a teacher" (p. 166). This is the dynamic that Julie and Erika wish to create even as they maintain their role in pushing students forward, scaffolding their efforts when needed, and monitoring the progress of the group.

Once everyone is clear on his or her chosen role, Erika offers recording sheets to those who want them: "Who would like a discussion starter sheet? It is your choice at this point." Ben raises his hand and takes a sheet. "Anyone else want one? No charge today. They are free. No one else? OK, if you change your mind, just come up and get one."

"The last choice we need to make," Julie reminds the class, "is would you like me to read, listen to the audio recording, or would someone else like to read?"

"I want to read," Bella offers. With that, Julie passes out copies of chapter 19 to the class so that students may mark and notate it if they need to, and takes a seat in the circle of students. By physically moving from the front of the room into the circle, Julie helps to direct students' attention to the work of the group. Her placement also locates her as a group member.

This handover of responsibility for the Enbrighten game is an important element of its success in developing independent thinkers. Julie and Erika know that over time, they must step back to allow students to exert greater control if they want them to become independent learners. Ultimately, they are looking for their students to be active participants not only in this small group but also within the general education population. This means that students need to internalize these roles and to be able to carry them out independently and appropriately in other contexts. Engaging students in setting the parameters of the game and deciding what their roles will be, how the game will be facilitated, and who will read the text allows students to be legitimate partners in the conduct of the classroom activities (Herrenkohl & Guerra, 1998) and gives students a formative role to play in shaping classroom activity (Pianta et al., 2012). When students perceive their classes as places where their independence as learners is valued and they are given opportunities to exercise legitimate control of their learning, they are more disposed to engage in critical thinking (Mathews & Lowe, 2011; Stupnisky et al., 2008).

Bella begins to read chapter 19 of *Touching Spirit Bear*. The book is classified at the seventh-grade reading level, so I expected it to be a bit of a challenge for a special education student. However, Bella's reading is generally fluent and full of expression. She stumbles over an occasional word—"galvanized," for example—and sometimes her inflection is off, but it is solid, confident reading. In this section of the story, the main character, a juvenile delinquent named Cole, is giving attitude to his parole officer, a Native American named Garvey, and the Tlingit tribal elder, Edwin. Cole's displays of anger are causing them both to doubt whether there is any point continuing Cole's alternative sentencing to a year on an island off the coast of Alaska as part of a "circle justice" program aimed at healing rather than punishment. When Bella comes to a section break in the chapter, she pauses. As she does, Julie turns to her and says privately, "Good job." Bella beams as Julie turns to speak to the entire class. "That is a good stopping point. So take a few minutes and do your job, as you need to. Remember you can go back and look at the text."

As students begin to focus on their roles, Erika moves to sit beside a student whose role is vocab master. The student has an identified language deficiency, and Erika asks him to explain what words he has chosen—"blistered," "stammered," and "pursuit"—and what he is thinking about each word. After he explains, she asks him to write down what he just told her. Most of the class has finished, but they are waiting on Kate, the summarizer, who will start off the discussion.

"This part is mainly about," Kate begins, using the provided sentence starter to preface her comments, "Cole saw the wolf as he was building the cabin. As night falls he decided he is tired and he will hit the sack. And Garvey asks Cole if he is going to fix supper and Cole disagrees. Garvey told him he didn't have a great attitude. He is alone and gets frustrated and then decided to do the wolf dance." Kate's summary includes the major events of this section in the correct sequence but leaves out the inner struggle Cole is going through, which is a big part of this particular book.

"Connections? Comments?" Julie asks the group. When no one offers anything, Julie moves on, knowing that there will be opportunities to link back later in the conversation.

Madison moves to the front of the room and places her paper underneath the document camera. The sheet has "Visualizer" written at the top of the page, and below that she has drawn two tents, each with a person's head poking out of it and a thought bubble above their heads. Squiggly lines are written in each thought bubble.

MADISON: So I drew him sticking his head out of the tent and saying "I'm leaving tomorrow."

JULIE: Would you mind starting with the sentence starter?

MADISON: In my mind, I pictured Cole sticking his head out of the tent and saying two different things: "I'm leaving tomorrow" and "I'm staying," basically.

JULIE: What made you draw this?

MADISON: It was the first thing to come to my mind.

JULIE: How does your idea connect to Kate's?

MADISON: I don't really see it connecting too much.

Notice that Julie's press to get Madison to explain her thinking in more depth or link it back to the book didn't have much effect. Erika takes another tack by pushing for more clarity from Madison, asking her to explain once again what the squiggles mean in her drawing. This time Madison changes her explanation of her drawing.

MADISON: In this one, it is Garvey saying, "You're leaving tomorrow." In this one Cole is saying, "Why? Why do I have to leave tomorrow?"

Recognizing that Madison has captured the pivotal aspect of this section of the book, namely that Cole's time on the island may be about to end because of his attitude, Julie models the use of text-based evidence to support a point. "I have a connection with Madison's drawing," she says, directing the class's attention to page 160 of the book. Julie rises from her seat in the group, slides her copy of the page under the document camera, and highlights the passage as she reads:

"You're finished here," said Garvey, his voice hard and absolute. "There's not enough room on this island for both you and your attitude." Cole's thoughts raced. Garvey must be bluffing. But what if he wasn't? Nothing was worth that gamble. Cole stumbled from the tent. "Okay, Okay, I'll fix you some supper."

Immediately Bella responds, "He sounds like a teenager."
"What makes you say that?" asks Julie.
"Because he is sassy and teenagers can be sassy sometimes," Bella explains.

Throughout the discussion thus far, both Julie and Erika have acted as warm demanders, pushing students to contribute more and gently directing their thinking (Bondy & Ross, 2008). In doing so, they walk a fine line between supporting insecure, tentative learners used to shutting down when things become too hard and pushing students to go deeper, contribute more, and engage with one another. It is not a simple dance. In addition, they have to weigh the importance of accuracy against the goal of developing independence.

This tension comes into relief when Donald steps up to his role as vocab master and offers definitions of "blistered," "stammered," and "pursuit." Donald's definition of blistered is on target and verified by other students, but his definitions of stammered, as possibly meaning someone is upset, and pursuit, as preparing for something, are more tangential. When the class doesn't offer any elaboration or contradiction, Julie and Erika intuitively decide not to press. Donald has used what he knows and the context in which the words were used to provide a reasonable explanation of the words' meaning. On the Enbrighten scoring rubric, his actions are considered "almost there" and score a 3. For Donald, a student with identified language deficiencies, this is progress and shows a willingness to wade into unfamiliar waters. Correcting Donald's definitions might serve to undermine his confidence more than deepen his understanding. This is the call Julie and Erika have to make.

Discussion of the text really takes off when Gabe shares his connection between the wolf pack mentioned in the book and a movie he has seen, *The Boy Who Cried Werewolf*. Gabe relates how the character in the movie said she couldn't be alone or she would lose her power because wolves get their power from the pack. This prompts Kate to ask if she can check out the encyclopedia to see what it says about wolves. Once found, she places the page under the document camera and reads to the class about how wolves form their packs and the role of the alpha and the omega wolves. Mention of the omega wolf, the wolf at the bottom of the pack, prompts Julie to ask, "Who is the omega wolf in the story?" Without skipping a beat, the class answers that it is Cole.

Seth shares a portion of the text he has identified as needing more clarification, a passage in which Garvey tells Cole, "Have a good soak tomorrow," and Gabe shares his prediction that Cole will be sent back to Minneapolis. Both responses spark debate and discussion, with students throwing out many possibilities and asking each other to clarify and explain their assertions. Periodically, Erika and Julie model active listening by paraphrasing students' comments, often beginning with "What I hear you saying is . . ." And then checking, "Did I get that right?"

As the class period comes to a close, Julie steps up to share her response to her job as symbolizer. Placing her sheet under the document camera, she says, "Madison, I stole this symbol from you, I think since I've seen you use it many times." The symbol is a simple swirl. Julie reads from her page, "The swirl is my symbol for this part because Cole is confused. Being vulnerable is new to him, and he doesn't know how to control his anger even though he does want to change." She then adds extemporaneously, "I'm kind of thinking this connects to what a lot of you have said. As a whole class we aren't sure about Cole. We don't know if he is going to change." Turning to address Bella, Julie continues, "Bella, you pointed out he is acting different in different situations. I'm wondering if he is acting this way because he doesn't know how to work as a team yet. That connects to what we are talking about in class about the importance of teamwork. So that is my idea. What do you all think?"

The class claps in response. "I'm getting a clap?" Julie laughs. "Why am I getting a clap?" Kate explains, "Because you connected a lot of our ideas together, and your symbol makes sense."

Julie's participation not only locates her as a group member but also gives her a chance to model for students. By connecting to specific students and to ideas shared in the discussion, Julie is also able to communicate that she has been listening and engaged with students' contributions. This lets students know that their ideas have value.

Students in today's class each took on just one role. However, over time they have the opportunity to participate in a variety, thus developing a repertoire of useful tools. In this way, roles provide a broad intellectual framework for students to work within, in contrast to laid-out steps for completing an assignment (Herrenkohl & Guerra, 1998). In a general education class, assigning such roles and using specific participation structures can help ensure that high-status students don't dominate discussion (E. G. Cohen, 1994). With novices, it is important that teachers provide enough support and modeling, as both Erika and Julie did, so that students won't be overwhelmed. This includes modeling of both the task and the discourse patterns so that students can learn how to interact with one another.

Although the use of the Enbrighten game has goals directly related to students' development as readers, writers, and speakers, its use doesn't explain all the interactions I have witnessed in this class. The game sits within a larger context that also needs to be understood. Julie and Erika's overarching goal for their classes is the development of a culture of thinking, which for them means helping students learn from and with others, and become both active contributors who make their thinking visible and good listeners who will push and support others' thinking. "They come here, and they think we are crazy for the first few weeks. It is a different kind of environment. . . . [and] . . . class," Julie offers.

To lay the foundation for this new way of acting, the class spends their first days developing group norms. Erika explains how they build the norms the first day of class by watching an effective learning group in action. "Our mentor, Todd Bidlack, suggested that it might be effective to use the video 'Austin's Butterfly.' He thought because it featured much younger students discussing and helping each other, our students might find it nonthreatening and fun to watch." The video, produced by Expeditionary Learning (http://vimeo.com/38247060), shows Ron Berger leading various groups of students in examining how a first grader named Austin managed to produce an impressive drawing of a butterfly using feedback from his class.

Julie recounts her students' reactions. "They always comment, 'They don't sound like they are first graders.' And I ask, 'What are they doing differently?' And the class notices that it is the way they are speaking to each other. It is the way they are giving honest feedback without offending anybody." Drawing on this example, the class identifies a set of norms, now posted at the front of the room:

- Our reasoning is more important than our actual answer.
- Stumped? Call a classmate.
- We can always add on to someone else's idea.
- If we change our mind based on evidence and reasoning, we are free to say so.

On another sheet of chart paper hung beside the norms is the phrase "No hogs, no logs" written in large letters. Surrounding the phrase is a collection of sticky notes explaining individuals' interpretation of the expression. At the bottom of the sheet is written an equation "Call a Classmate + No Hogs, No Logs = No Need for Hands Up." This is a message to students that a teacher may call on them at any time to contribute, knowing that the student can defer answering by "calling a classmate" to help.

As norms rather than class rules, each focuses on a positive action learners can take to support both their own and others' learning. In this way, the norms give students a new role to play. For Julie and Erika's students, this is vital to their growth. Most of their students are accustomed to being relegated to a peripheral role in their general education classes, often concerned more with merely keeping up or flying under the radar than being active participants. Julie and Erika know that for their students to become more independent and proficient learners, they need to change the way that their students interact in class, both with the content and with each other.

BEYOND SIT AND GET: TEACHING STUDENTS TO BUILD ON ONE ANOTHER'S IDEAS

Who can tell me . . . ?

Who remembers . . . ?

What's the name for . . . ?

What do we call . . . ?

What is the main idea?

Questions such as these are pretty standard-fare "review"-type questions that call on students to recall and give back information. When teachers ask such questions, a typical pattern of discourse follows: the teacher questions, a student responds, and the teacher evaluates, QRE. This pattern, sometimes known as IRE (initiate, respond, evaluate) as well, is the default style of discourse in many classrooms (Cazden, 2001); unless we as teachers make deliberate attempts not to employ such a pattern of interaction, then the QRE form is likely to prevail.

Why might we want a different pattern of interaction? Although all teachers engage in QRE at times—for instance, at the start of a class to activate prior learning—it is important to recognize its limitations. First, the QRE form often, though not always, focuses primarily on memory as the chief cognitive function and so has limited effect in developing thinkers. Instead, classrooms dominated by QRE reinforce the notion that learning is memorizing (Bereiter & Scardamalia, 1989). Second, the discourse pattern that results can be described best as resembling a Ping-Pong match back and forth between the teacher and a single student, leaving much of the class out of the interaction. Even a skilled practitioner would have a hard time making sure everyone in the class gets to play the game. Furthermore, the teacher is the one getting most of the practice, with very little actual discourse happening, though it might feel like an engaging class . . . to the teacher at least. Even when multiple answers are collected, the pattern can feel more like a scattering of isolated responses.

For actual discussion to take hold, both students and teachers need different patterns of interaction. Instead of Ping-Pong, basketball might be a more useful metaphor for a productive discussion, one in which the ball (question) is passed around and ideas are bounced off one another, as the ball is moved down the court.

Cameron Paterson has been trying to foster just such patterns of interaction in his classroom for some time and has found the use of thinking routines and protocols to be helpful. Although his grade 12 Modern History class of high-achieving boys at a private school in Sydney, Australia, may seem a world away from Erika and Julie's special education class in Michigan, he, too, knows that students must be given new structures and roles to play in the classroom if the student-to-student interaction is to change. Cameron's students come to their senior year with their primary focus on learning what is necessary to score well on the Higher School Certificate (HSC) exam that will determine the trajectory of their university education. Consequently, there can be an underlying assumption that the teacher should merely deliver the goods and the students should sit and get. It is too often assumed, by teachers and students alike, that memorization equals preparation. Changing this passive and dependent pattern of interaction between student and teacher requires that a teacher earn the trust of the students and that new patterns of student-to-student interaction deliver in terms of learning.

When I enter Cameron's classroom, it is near the end of the school year. Course work is over, and students will soon be sitting their exams. A sample HSC question is written on the whiteboard for today's lesson: "Evaluate the impact of the Khmer Rouge on Cambodia in the period 1975–1979." As students arrive and quickly find their seats, Cameron begins: "You had an essay due today. It was a hard question. In fact, it was harder than the kind of thing you might be asked on the HSC." Pointing to the whiteboard, Cameron draws the class's attention to the HSC question. "This is the type of question you might be asked. What I would like for you to do in the next five minutes is to free-write on that question. Just write without stopping. Work through the block." With no more direction than that, students get started, most writing in their notebooks, only one on the computer. It is clear that students have done this kind of writing before, as they don't ask for clarification or further direction.

Cameron quietly moves through the classroom, and when he notices a student pausing in a contemplative manner, he tells him, "You're thinking too much. Just write." To the class as a whole he instructs, "When you think you are running out of ideas and are stuck, that is often when you come up with the best ideas. Just keep writing. No mistakes here. Just keep writing."

At the end of five minutes, Cameron calls the class back. "OK, wrap up where you are at. Now, what you have just done is prep for the activity we are about to move into. We have used the Micro Lab several times this year. I'm going to ask you to get ready for that in groups of three. Move yourself so you are in a group facing each other."

The Micro Lab protocol (Ritchhart, Church, & Morrison, 2011) is a simple structure for discussion. Working in groups of three, each member shares his thoughts on the topic or question of focus without any interruption, questions, or input from the other two members. After all three have shared, then an open discussion ensues. The structure ensures that everyone gets his ideas on the table, that participants listen to one another, and that a conversation has a strong basis on which to build.

"Decide who is going to go first, who second, and who third," Cameron directs. "Remember, you will have two minutes to speak followed by thirty seconds of silent reflective time. Just a reminder, if you run out of things to say, then your group sits there silently for the rest of your time. After the three rounds, then in the discussion is your chance to push each other's ideas. Any questions?"

"So, no arguing while they are speaking?" a student asks.

"No, not while," Cameron responds.

"So, he is arguing one side and me the other?" another student asks, thinking of another activity Cameron often uses where he writes a provocative statement on the board (for example, "Pol Pot was mad") and then pairs students up to argue both sides of the statement.

"No," Cameron explains. "We have done that before, but this is not that." Adding one last direction before setting the timer, Cameron reminds the class, "Some people found it useful to take notes last time we did this. OK, would the first speaker begin."

The class settles into a low hum as the first speaker in each group commences. Huddled in small groups, the listeners are able to make eye contact with the speaker and demonstrate attentive listening. Every once in a while, a listener writes down a comment made by the speaker. As students share their thinking about the impact of the Khmer Rouge on Cambodia, Cameron moves around the room listening in. Before moving to the next group, Cameron returns to the whiteboard and records in red marker a few of the ideas he has overheard. As the two minutes wind to a close, he has gathered a list of ideas from each of the groups: military, political, econ-4 year plan, Vietnam's impact, alliance with China.

As the timer goes off, Cameron calls for the speaker to stop and informs the class, "OK, thirty seconds of quiet." The class falls silent. A few students write brief comments in their notebooks.

The class moves through the next two rounds of the Micro Lab as Cameron acts as timekeeper, listener, and recorder. The timekeeper is a pretty straightforward and necessary role in the Micro Lab protocol and isn't too much of a departure from a teacher's traditional role in the classroom. However, the dual role of listener and recorder recasts the role of both teacher and student. By listening to what students say, pulling out their ideas, and validating them by recording them on the board, Cameron has placed students in the active role of the knowledge generators. Of course, teachers often gather ideas from the class and record them. However, those instances still tend to operate popcorn style, with individuals giving short answers and many students sitting passively. In the Micro Lab protocol, students are required to take an extended role as speaker, to lead with their ideas. Furthermore, the interaction is with their peers as colearners and discussants rather than with the teacher. Cameron's listening signals that he is attending to the conversations, that those conversations are important, and that he is interested in what students have to say. In listening in, he gets a better sense of each individual student's learning than he would in whole-class setting.

In the next round, Cameron records key ideas in blue on the whiteboard: executions—impact of death, agriculture, rural, peasants, collectivization, US role, role of terror. In the final round, he switches to green to record the ideas emerging in the discussion: bombings, religion, refugees, Sino-Soviet split, detente, importance of foreign influence, aims of K.R. The board is now full of ideas, all generated from the class, with each individual student represented.

At this point in the Micro Lab protocol, the triads would have an open conversation connecting all that was said over the previous three rounds. Cameron decides to have this conversation as a whole class, using what he has written on the board as backdrop for the conversation. "So what connections are you making now as a result of what you have just heard? What are you thinking in terms of the impact of the Khmer Rouge?"

"Probably like take economics and divide that up into categories," Elliot responds. Clearly the idea of responding to the question on the exam is foremost in his mind rather than the issue itself.

Max offers, "Probably more of a long-term impact than short-term."

Before anyone else has a chance to throw out an idea, a student in the front pipes up, "Do you want us popcorning, or are we supposed to be ice-cream-coning now?" His comment references previous discussions Cameron has had with the class about what real conversation looks and sounds like, using making popcorn as a metaphor for ideas simply being tossed out versus the metaphor of building on one another's ideas as in scoops in an ice cream cone, with each scoop resting on the foundation of the one preceding it. With the ice cream cone metaphor there is a sense of something being built, and one can look at a class discussion as constructing several ice cream cones, each of various heights, over the course of the conversation.

Cameron responds that he wants ice cream cones, and with that the conversation shifts as students begin to offer their thoughts on long-term versus short-term impacts; the rapid rise of the Khmer Rouge as a result of the bombings; the immediate suffering and torture, versus the lingering effects of eliminating the educated class. Students begin to preface their comments differently as well, using more connectors: "To go along with that . . . ," "On the other hand . . . ," "Building on that . . . ," "Adding on to what Lachie said . . ." Giving students these kinds of sentence stems, much as Erika and Julie provide their students with sentence starters for their Enbrighten roles, can be useful in supporting a new way of interacting and a different pattern of discourse.

It is clear that the discussion could now go on for some time. When a student poses the idea that the Khmer Rouge had more impact on the young than the old, Cameron lets the idea hang in the air. "That's an interesting theory. Let's hang on to that as we move into this activity." With that, Cameron directs the class into new learning roles to take their thinking deeper.

Erasing all the notes from the whiteboard, Cameron explains that they will be using the Generate-Sort-Connect-Elaborate (GSCE) routine as the structure for further exploring the HSC sample question: "Evaluate the impact of the Khmer Rouge on Cambodia in the period 1975–1979." GSCE is a routine used to create concept maps in a way that illuminates the importance and connections between ideas (Ritchhart et al., 2011). Experienced in using this routine, Cameron adapts it and uses it flexibly to scaffold the boys' learning. He divides the class into two groups and explains that the first group should "think about the keys to answering this question [the HSC prompt] based on all the ideas we have already generated. Place the things that you think are important to answering the questions close in, and those that are less important toward the outside." Turning to the other half of the class, he directs, "Watch what they are putting up and see if you agree. Your job when you go up is to draw connections between the things that they are putting up, particularly the important connections. Write big, please. Do this in silence."

In ten minutes, the whiteboard is full of ideas connected to one another and elaborations. Near the center are ideas of culture, economics, the emphasis on traditional rural life, and loss of intellectuals. The board is messy, but represents the students' thinking together, building on others' ideas, and going beyond a set of memorized bullet points of effects. To bring this home, Cameron asks the class, "What on this board is pushing your thinking beyond that initial five minutes of free writing? What are you thinking about now that you weren't then?"

MAX: It puts it more in context.

JOHN: The desire to make things last for a long time. I wasn't thinking about the molding of society and the new education of children.

CAMERON: Can I ask Jack to expand on the link between Confucian and Asian values? How does that fit in here?

JACK: It's going back to ancient values. It links to new world impact because the new world was the old world. They were holding on to Confucian values.

CAMERON: [Reading from the whiteboard] "What's rotten must be removed." Why is that an important statement?

Note that as the class responds to the latest question from Cameron, the students respond in "ice cream cone style," building on the comment that comes before by extending it, taking an element deeper, connecting ideas together. This is a mark of real discourse.

DUNCAN: All aspects of the whole society have to be cleansed. Social and racial purification.

LACHIE: Cultural.

JACK: And that purification implies change to economics as well.

ELLIOT: That's what brought them down in the end.

As the class winds to a close, Cameron asks one last thing of his students: "Would you write me a one-minute essay on how the structure of our class today contributed to your learning, please." Many teachers use one-minute papers or exit tickets as a way to close a class. By asking students to reflect on the structures Cameron has employed as a teacher to facilitate students' learning, he is setting up a feedback loop with students, letting them know that he cares about their learning and about improving as a teacher. It is a simple communication tool setting up another important teacher-student interaction (Brookfield & Preskill, 1999; Lee, 2004).

BUILDING CULTURE THROUGH AFFECT AND ACTIONS

The affective attributes researchers identify as facilitating learning, promoting academic achievement, supporting critical thinking, and creating a culture of thinking are remarkably similar and won't be surprising to anyone: empathetic, warm, caring, genuine, authentic, positive, respectful, trusting, sense of humor, and so on (Cushman, 2005; Resnick et al., 1997; C. R. Rogers & Freiberg, 1994). If you can describe your teacher in those terms, chances are you enjoyed being in his or her class. In and out of teaching, we all know people for whom such qualities seem a natural part of their personalities, but we needn't reduce these attributes to the artifacts of personality alone. Any of us as teachers can communicate these qualities through our actions: making eye contact, smiling, knowing students' names, sharing a personal side of ourselves, admitting our mistakes, showing ourselves as learners, taking an interest in students' lives, holding students in high personal regard as human beings, not making conflicts personal, following through and being dependable, listening, supporting, and so on. If being warm, caring, and genuine doesn't come automatically for you, remember that it is easier to act your way into a new way of feeling than to feel your way into a new way of acting (Pascale, Sternin, & Sternin, 2010).

The literature suggests three other fundamental actions for teachers interested in developing a culture of thinking while promoting high academic achievement, independence, and prosocial development:

- Being nondirective
- Pressing for thinking
- Supporting student autonomy

"Nondirectivity" would not be my first choice of a word to describe this teaching action, but it happens to be a term used by researchers. This alone wouldn't make it worth sticking to, but it so happens that nondirectivity comes up ahead of all other teacher interaction/relational variables as having an impact on student achievement (Cornelius-White, 2007; Hattie, 2009). That is what makes the construct worth understanding. To say that a teacher is nondirective is not to say that he or she lacks direction or fails to direct the learning of the class, but rather that the teacher is not controlling. Dominant, authoritarian figures may be good at eliciting compliance from students, but they are not as effective at promoting learning or developing thinkers.

Nondirective teachers share power with their students, allowing them to be legitimate partners in the conduct of the classroom, much the way Julie and Erika did in letting their students set the parameters for Enbrighten. Nondirective teachers also encourage student voice, meaning that students know that their contributions matter to the class and directly shape the lesson. We saw this in Cameron's classroom. His students knew that their ideas and contributions were the basis for the lesson. In contrast, if students feel that the lesson would have proceeded exactly as planned whether they were there or not, a stance some scripted programs take, then they are unlikely to feel they have a voice. Robert Pianta, who has worked extensively to both measure and develop positive classroom interactions, ties the ideas of voice and power together beautifully when he states that teachers must "provide opportunities for students to have a formative role in the classroom" (Pianta et al., 2012, p. 374).

Pressing for thinking is also one of the teacher interaction/relation variables that correlates highly with student achievement. I particularly like the phrasing of "pressing for thinking"; it captures precisely what teachers need to do. We all want our students to be thinking, and we certainly hope to encourage our students to think. We may even try to create opportunities and provide time for thinking. All good moves, but we must also *press* our students to think—meaning that we push, prod, and promote thinking. We don't let students off the hook with half answers or responses that aren't backed up with reasons and evidence.

When Madison gave a superficial explanation of her drawing as visualizer, Julie and Erika didn't let her off the hook. They pressed. Although they didn't get as much from her as they would have liked, and Julie stepped in to model what a more elaborative response might look like, the act of pressing in and of itself was important. It sent a signal to Madison and the rest of the class that Julie and Erika held expectations for a higher performance. When pressing is combined with warmth, empathy, and support—that is, when teachers are being warm demanders—students know that teachers are invested in their success.

Autonomy-supporting (Deci & Ryan, 1985) teachers are always looking for ways to step back so that students can step forward. They want their students to feel in control of their learning, to feel that they have the skills and abilities to direct and guide it and are hence competent learners (Stupnisky et al., 2008). Like good parents, they combine high demands with support (Baumrind, 1989) to encourage independence. Within this context, there is a bond of trust that develops in which students feel that it is safe to take risks as learners (Shernoff, 2013).

Julie and Erika's overarching goal is for their students to take control of their learning and to display both confidence and competence. Toward this end, they provide lots of scaffolding within a supportive atmosphere and encourage risk taking. They allow their students to step forward to act as facilitators. When a science teacher at the school reported that one of their students was able to make a claim about what was happening in a science experiment the teacher had conducted, and was also able to back up that claim with evidence, Julie and Erika knew they were making a difference. Likewise, when another student asked for a copy of the Enbrighten game to play at home and teach her parents, Julie and Erika knew that the student owned her learning.

SHAPING INTERACTIONS THROUGH ROLES

Most classrooms operate under a set of tacit norms, what Derek Edwards and Neil Mercer (2013) call "educational ground rules." If we want to break with the status quo and create new patterns of interaction both with and among our students, it is worth being explicit in defining the norms we truly want to encourage. There are many helpful resources on setting group norms (Allen & Blythe, 2004; Phipps & Phipps, 2003). One technique is to ask the group to think about what conditions they need in order to do their best learning. Another is to observe an effective learning group, as Erika and Julie did using "Austin's Butterfly," and identify what group members did that helped support learning. Cameron Patterson uses "The City of Reggio Emilia Story" (Project Zero & Reggio Children, 2001), a story of effective group work among preschoolers, to help set norms with his secondary students.

Leslie Herrenkohl and Marion Guerra (1998) suggest four important norms for groups: contribute to group work and help others contribute, support ideas by offering reasons, work to understand others' ideas, and build on one another's ideas. Such norms help build commitment to the group as well as direct the action of individuals. This commitment to the group's learning has been shown to be key to advancing the learning of all individuals (Boaler, 2008; Watanabe, 2012).

In addition, it can be useful to give students specific intellectual roles that help them acquire new thinking skills. Literature circles, book clubs, and the Enbrighten game frequently do this. When I observed Philip Cummings's sixth-grade class at Presbyterian Day School in Memphis, I noticed that he assigned roles to teams of students as they researched the problems of racial discrimination in their community. Among the roles were original thinkers, connectors, Johnny opposites, reliability cops, mind readers, and cleaning crew. The roles allowed groups to focus their attention rather than become overwhelmed with all that had to be done. Herrenkohl and Guerra (1998) taught fourth-grade science students three roles to help them build scientific explanations: predicting and theorizing, summarizing results, and relating evidence or results to the theory and prediction. They found that the biggest learning effects occurred when students took on these roles not only as they engaged in building scientific explanations but also when listening as audience members to other groups.

ASKING "GOOD" QUESTIONS

Questions are one of the prime ways teachers interact with students in classrooms. Our questioning helps to define our classrooms, to give it its feel and energy—or lack thereof. Questions are culture builders, linking students, teachers, and content together. In the cases presented in this chapter, Julie, Erika, and Cameron used questions as vehicles to direct attention, foster understanding, push beyond simplistic answers, and expose students' thinking.

As teachers, we all want to ask good questions, the kind that can drive learning and elicit deep thinking. To truly tap into the power of questions, however, we must keep in mind that our questions are rarely something we plan in advance; rather, they emerge from our goals and expectations (see chapter 2). These goals help us identify five main types of questions teachers ask:

- **Review questions** ask students to recall previous knowledge or procedures. Many teachers begin a class with review questions to reactivate prior learning. "Can you remember what we talked about yesterday?"

- **Procedural questions** direct classroom activity and behavior rather than focus on content—for example, "Does everybody have a pencil?" Procedural questions are generally less effective than stating a clear directive: "Everyone get out your pencils, please."

- **Generative questions** spark inquiry. They come in two main types: essential questions that direct long-term exploration, or authentic questions, which are content questions to which the teacher doesn't already know the answer. "How do totalitarian regimes such as the Khmer Rouge gain and sustain power?"

- **Constructive questions** advance understanding. These are questions that ask students to connect ideas, make interpretations, focus on big ideas and central concepts, extend ideas, and so on. "So what connections are you making now as a result of what you have just heard?"

- **Facilitative questions** ask students to explain or elaborate thinking, to make it visible. These are follow-up questions to a student's response that cause the student to go deeper. "What makes you say that?"

The Cultures of Thinking research team looked at teacher questioning to understand how CoT classrooms differed from more traditional classrooms and how teacher questioning changed over time as teachers worked to build a culture of thinking in their classrooms. We found that traditional classrooms are often dominated by procedural questions used by teachers to direct the work, along with review questions. Further, we observed that as classrooms increasingly become cultures of thinking, teacher questioning shifted away from asking review questions toward asking more constructive and facilitative questions. This can be understood as a shift in terms of goals. Whereas teachers asking review questions tend to do so because they want to determine what students know and remember, teachers ask constructive questions because they want to guide, direct, and push forward students' understanding of important ideas. Furthermore, facilitative questions serve the goal of making thinking visible. We saw how both of these goals played out in the classes we looked at in this chapter.

In Julie and Erika's class, the roles students assumed put them in a constructive stance of making sense of the story and building understanding rather than merely recalling information. In Cameron's class, students' intellectual work centered on a big question: How do we evaluate the impact of the Khmer Rouge? (Note: the HSC prompt was written as a directive, but I have reframed it here as an essential question.) He then used mostly constructive questions as he guided students through the exploration of that big question:

- So what connections are you making now as a result of what you have just heard?
- What are you thinking in terms of the impact of the Khmer Rouge?
- What on this board is pushing your thinking beyond that initial five minutes of free writing?
- What are you thinking about now that you weren't then?

Julie and Erika, working as warm demanders, used facilitative questions to press students to elaborate and think more. These questions signaled to students that answers without explanations aren't sufficient:

- What makes you say that?

- What made you draw this?
- How does your idea connect to Kate's?

CREATING NEW PATTERNS OF DISCOURSE

Conversation is an "unrehearsed intellectual adventure" (Oakeshott, 1959). It is a medium that brings us into contact with the thinking and perspective of others and thus fosters new insight. Through dialogue, we develop trust and respect even as we learn to care for others and to be cared for by them. However, much of the discourse that happens in the classroom isn't truly dialogic or conversational, due to the dominance of the QRE style of interaction. One way of breaking this default pattern of interaction is for us as teachers to make deliberate attempts to move from playing Ping-Pong to playing basketball. That is, we need to look for more opportunities to pass the ball/question, bring others in, and connect students in conversation. As a start, you might adopt this as a goal for a lesson. You can also share that goal with students and then ask for their feedback on how you did. This explicitness is a way of sharing power by enlisting students as allies.

The switch to "playing basketball" is largely a teacher move. However, students have a role to play as well in enabling real conversation to take place. Cameron enlisted his students by discussing with them the difference between popcorn-style comments and comments that build a conversation as in the layers of an ice cream cone. These metaphors then took hold in the classroom and allowed both Cameron and his students to monitor their efforts. Some students benefit from teachers' providing actual sentence starters they can use in prefacing their comments:

- Connecting to what _____ said . . .
- I want to agree/disagree with _____, because . . .
- Piggybacking on _____'s idea . . .
- _____'s comment is now making me think . . .
- If we follow that idea out, then . . .
- Building on _____'s comment . . .

Another teacher move that can break the QRE pattern and facilitate a different kind of interaction is use of the "reflective toss," a term coined by science teacher Jim Minstrell to describe the questioning sequence he uses to facilitate and clarify students' thinking (van Zee & Minstrell, 1997). Traditionally, researchers have characterized discourse as originating with the teacher's question. However, Jim took students' comments and ideas as the starting point for dialogue. In the reflective toss, the teacher's first goal is to try to "catch" students' meaning and understand their comments. If meaning can't be grasped immediately, then a follow-up question, such as "Can you say more about that?" or "I'm not quite following you; can you say what you were thinking in a different way?" is asked. Once the teacher grasps the meaning, then the teacher "tosses" back a question that will push the student to further elaborate and justify her thinking, both to the teacher and to herself. For instance, Jim might ask a student, "What does that tell you then?" "What do you think you were basing that on?" or even the old standby, "What makes you say that?" The idea is to push the student to think further about her response.

By creating new patterns of discourse, providing students with roles that structure learning, and asking good questions, we can do much to shape the interactions of our classrooms. These practices become even more powerful when they are situated within an atmosphere that seeks not to control students but to develop them as autonomous learners. And this goal, too, sits within a broader context. It is only attainable in an atmosphere in which students are genuinely liked and respected. We must show an interest in and a respect for students' thinking. Only then will they truly make their thinking visible to us and provide us with a window into their learning. It is within an atmosphere of mutual respect and interest that strong interactions, teacher-to-student as well as student-to-student, are built and a culture of thinking truly takes hold.

PROMOTING INTERACTIONS THAT SUPPORT THINKING AND LEARNING

- Establish norms. Although norms are typically set at the beginning of the year or when groups start, it is never too late to set them. Use the opportunity of the class embarking on a new project, activity, or group work to create norms for those efforts. Use the fishbowl technique or analyze a video of effective learning to focus students on positive actions.

- Create roles. Identify a learning situation that your students need to master (reading comprehension, building scientific explanations, doing research, analyzing data, and so on). Name the particular intellectual hats one needs to wear or stances one needs to take to effectively deal with that situation. These are the roles. Break those roles down further into a set of behaviors, actions, or questions that students can use as they assume those roles.

- Survey your students. Cushman and Rogers (2013) interviewed students, asking them such questions as: What do you wish teachers knew about you as a learner? What are the things teachers do that let you know they respect and value you? What advice would you give teachers to bring out the best in students? Create your own questionnaire, perhaps with a colleague, to find out what your students think. Be prepared to share and act on the results if you want your students to trust that you value their opinion.

- Start a connection ritual. It might be as simple as greeting each student as he or she comes into the room or finding time in class to comment on, interact with, connect back to, or notice something about every student. It might be a more elaborate morning meeting.

- Analyze your questions according to the five types (see the section "Asking 'Good' Questions"). To find out more about what kinds of questions you are asking, videotape or audio-record yourself or have a colleague observe you and record the questions you ask. Partnering or forming a triad with colleagues will give you the opportunity to be both observer and observed.

- Change the hands-up norm. Asking questions and calling on students who raise hands can force you into a QRE pattern or privilege a few students who are quick responders. Use a random-number generator or students' names written on

Popsicle sticks as an alternative. Another alternative is to call on students through eye contact only.

- Practice the reflective toss. Make sure you have caught a student's meaning. If you are unclear or think you are making assumptions, ask for more information or a restatement. After a student responds and you are confident that you have caught the meaning, pause briefly and then ask, "What makes you say that?" What are you learning about your students and their thinking and understanding as a result of this simple question?

- Solicit feedback. Create a questionnaire to give your students midyear or at the end of the term to find out how things are going for them, what is working for them as learners and what isn't, and how they view you. Don't ask any questions you aren't truly interested in or willing to act on. Be prepared to share results with your students and explain how you will make use of the information.

- Be a student of your students' culture. Connecting with students of different backgrounds, generations, ethnicities, or cultures means not assuming that they should act or respond the way you might. Find out about what gets rewarded, valued, and appreciated in the cultures of your students. What does success look like from that culture's perspective? What and who gets respect? How are conflicts dealt with?

- Practice genuineness. What part of you as a learner is appropriate to share with your students? Share a struggle as a learner, something you are excited about, or a story of how you learned from a mistake.

- Create the role of learning journalist. On a rotating basis, appoint a student to look for and record key learning moments, great examples of students building on or extending others' ideas, or good questions that were asked.

- Use protocols to structure how students interact. Simple protocols such as Micro Lab or the Final Word (www.NSRFharmony.org/content/final-word) can help students learn to listen and discuss.

- Create a culture of revision. When work, ideas, projects, drawings, or experiments move from draft form to increasingly higher levels of performance, you create a need for feedback and learning from feedback. Strategies such as the Gallery Critique can be useful in establishing this culture (Berger, Gardner, Meier, Sizer, & Lieberman, 2003).

CHAPTER 9

Environment
Using Space to Support Learning and Thinking

en•vi•ron•ment |en'vīrənmənt| noun: The surrounding conditions or influences in which a person operates. • The physical space occupied by a group or individual, consisting of its design, aesthetic, setup, displays, artifacts, and furnishings. As a culture shaper, the physical environment is the "body language" of an organization, conveying its values and key messages even in the absence of its inhabitants. The physical environment of a school or classroom will influence how individuals interact, their behaviors, and their performance. The physical space can inhibit or inspire the work of the group and the individual. Although most educators inherit a physical environment fashioned for an old paradigm of learning, there is still much that can be done in the design of that space to facilitate and promote a culture of thinking.

C lose your eyes and picture a classroom, any classroom—just not your own teaching space. A generic, made-for-television classroom will do. Take a visual walk around the room to notice what is there. Now open the door to the classroom and walk outside the room. Eyes closed. What greets you? Now, head to the library in your virtual tour and have a look around in your mind's eye. What did you notice in your virtual tour of this imagined school? What was familiar? What was inviting? What left you cold?

Chances are, the images that flashed before you were not that different from those of other readers of this book. Collectively we are bound to an image of schools, classrooms, and libraries rooted in our common experience, a kind of "nostalgic gravity" that pulls us back to the familiar (Bergsagel, 2007). We see this nostalgia being reinforced in the way classrooms are presented on television. From *Leave It to Beaver*, which premiered in 1957, to *Room 222* in 1969, to *Welcome Back, Kotter* in 1975, to *Glee* in 2009, not all that much has changed. Whiteboards have replaced blackboards and tables have replaced desks, but a forward-facing orientation of students in rows with a teacher's desk at the front enclosed in four walls with an institutional corridor just outside the door has remained a fairly constant image.

Why do schools and classrooms look the way they do? The basic design assumptions used to create school buildings are rooted in a past philosophy and understanding of what education is and what learning looks like. As discussed in chapter 2, public schools grew out of the effort to end child labor. From this beginning grew the notion of school being children's work. We also developed a factory model of schooling in which groups of students progress lockstep along a predetermined path, all learning the same thing at the same time in the same way. Factories are not about individualization; they are about standardization.

Nor are factories about happenstance, discovery, or community. Rather, they are about efficiency, conformity, and control. Hence we have classrooms of the same size, set up in largely the same way. When the bell rings, students flow out of their classroom into the corridor so as to progress to their next stop along the line. This design feature of schools has been referred to as "cells and bells," equating classrooms not only with factories but also with prisons (Nair & Fielding, 2013). Placing all the cells/classrooms along a common long corridor ensures efficiency of space and time, and makes control and supervision easier as well. There is no place for students to linger or hang out (unless you count the escape of the restroom) but in the hallway, and teachers can more efficiently monitor progress there. Once the bell rings, the hallways empty as students and teachers retreat into their assigned rooms.

The design of school buildings is a physical manifestation of ingrained and widely held assumptions about learning as well. The idea that learning is an individualized endeavor largely consisting of acquiring and storing information for later use, what is sometimes referred to as crystallized intelligence, is compatible with students sitting in rows of desks facing the front of the room, set to receive knowledge from the teacher. Distractions are kept to a minimum in these spaces so as not to detract from a focus on the teacher. In this model, students are seen as passive, as vessels to be filled. In contrast, when learning is viewed as an active, collaborative endeavor that fosters the development of fluid intelligence—the ability to problem-solve, reason, and explore new ideas with others—then the default arrangement in rows doesn't make much sense.

A maxim in the world of design is that form should follow function. However, most school buildings and the classrooms within them are stuck with a form, cells and bells, designed for an old function, full-frontal teaching. With billions of dollars projected to be spent on school infrastructure over the next decade, whether in school refurbishment or in new buildings, it is well past time to rethink the physical environment of schools and align it with our current understanding of learning (Bergsagel, 2007). We must also recognize the role that the physical environment plays in supporting teaching and learning. Although some view the physical environment as a mere nicety or even an indulgence, a recent study in the United Kingdom found a "significant impact of the built environment on pupils' learning progression" when looking at the parameters of color, choice, connection, complexity, flexibility, and light (Barrett, Zhang, Moffat, & Kobbacy, 2013).

We also need to understand the role of the physical environment in shaping culture. The constructed environment sets up and facilitates certain ways of acting and interacting. It sends messages about what is valued, important, expected, and encouraged. As a student walks into a classroom, the physical space is part of the hidden curriculum, conveying messages about how learning will happen. Nonetheless, teachers sometimes treat the physical space of the classroom as if it doesn't matter. This is frequently the case in secondary schools where teachers don't always have their own classroom. However, if the environment matters to younger children and it matters to adults—as demonstrated by the offices of firms like Yahoo, Google, and Pixar or the purposely thought-out spaces at a TED conference—why should the physical environment not matter to adolescents?

In recognizing the power of the physical environment as a culture shaper, Sir Ken Robinson states, "If you want to shift culture, it's two things: its habit and its habitats—the habits of mind, and the physical environment in which people operate" (OWP/P Architects, VS Furniture, & Bruce Mau Design, 2010, p. 58). Scott Doorley and Scott Witthoft (2011), directors of the Environments Collaborative at Stanford University's d.school, advise tinkering with physical space to see how it facilitates a different way of being: "Begin to deliberately alter your environment and you will reveal what enhances collaboration and what doesn't, what boosts creativity and what doesn't" (p. 8).

In this chapter, we visit three classrooms where teachers have not only tinkered but actively designed spaces to facilitate learning, foster new ways of interacting, and support a culture of thinking. We begin with secondary teacher Kathy Hanawalt, who teaches in a typical cinderblock classroom in a large American high school originally designed within the cells-and-bells mentality. Next we visit Nellie Gibson, a first-grade teacher in Tasmania, Australia, who teaches in a more intimate space designed for young children. We conclude by looking into Alice Maund Parker's totally redesigned and reimagined learning studio carved out of existing space at her school in Memphis.

NEW LEARNING IN AN OLD CONTAINER

"Can I have this class?" a student calls out as he sticks his head through the door of Kathy Hanawalt's classroom. Sweeping his eyes from one end of the room to the other, he smiles at Kathy, seated at her desk surrounded by a wall of personal photographs and memorabilia, and then as quickly as he appeared, he is gone, continuing his progress down the corridor.

"It's funny," Kathy says. "Students who know nothing about me or about this course just say that, 'I want this classroom.' I guess they just like the way it looks. It's comforting. The space just speaks to them." Although no different in shape or size than any of the other windowless, rectangular classrooms at Clover Park High School outside Tacoma, Washington, Kathy's room does indeed have a unique look and feel, something evident to even a passerby peeking his head through the doorway.

Most apparent from the corridor is that the florescent glare of overhead lights is missing from Kathy's classroom. Instead, floor lamps are placed throughout the space, providing a soft and homey glow. A small desk lamp illuminates Kathy's desk, which is strategically situated so that it faces looking out the door of the classroom. This allows her to see students as they enter the room, and connects her to the students passing in the corridor even when she is not teaching.

"Overhead lights are stressful," Kathy tells me. "I want the students to enter the space and feel relaxed, to have a sense of calm. Once we're all settled, I'll often turn on the overhead lights as a signal that we are ready to begin, a kind of cue. But I often like to have just the lamps on at first to create a more welcoming space." Because Kathy's room has no windows, having both floor lamps and overhead lights gives her a bit more control over the room's lighting and makes her feel more comfortable as well. "If I am going to live here, I want it to be a space I enjoy being in."

The unknown student's quick peek into the room would have also revealed the configuration of the classroom. Students' desks are arranged in the shape of a giant C, the corners of which are right angles. This formation allows everyone to see one another, view the board, and attend to Kathy. Inside the C is a table with more seating and a projector. This seating arrangement facilitates movement as well as conversation, key components in Kathy's humanities classes. When Kathy directs students into groups, the corners of the C and the center table provide places for groups to gather and work collaboratively. In one corner of the room, Kathy has established a more private space for students. Delineated by an oriental rug and framed by wooden bookshelves and a few hardy plants (recall there is no natural light), the space serves as a retreat from the group and a place for students to read or think quietly.

Kathy's arrangement of the room not only reflects her teaching style but also intuitively captures three of the four "primordial learning metaphors" identified by David Thornburg in his seminal article "Campfires in Cyberspace" (2004) and explored in his recent book *From the Campfire to the Holodeck* (2013). Thornburg names these as the campfire, the watering hole, the cave, and life. Drawing on the human proclivity for storytelling, the campfire represents those moments when we come together to listen and learn as a group from the elder of the group, who passes on his or her wisdom through storytelling. The watering hole is a place where we learn from peers in small informal groups that are more conversational and less hierarchical. The cave signifies those moments when we retreat from the group to create opportunities for individual reflection, study, and ideation. The metaphor of life captures the need to take knowledge into the world for use and application, often promoting further learning as we grapple with the contextual complexity that life offers.

Although Thornburg was interested in exploring these metaphors as they relate to learning with and from technology, his first three archetypes offer insight into the effective design of physical learning environments as well. The architectural firm Fielding Nair International has made wide use of this concept in designing new schools (Nair & Fielding, 2005). At the same time, these archetypes offer an accessible framework for individual teachers (Hewes, 2012). Kathy's large C arrangement provides the forum of the campfire with the class focused on her, the whiteboard, or the projection screen.

Although her classroom isn't big enough to provide separate watering hole spaces, Kathy is able to use the corners of the **C** and the center table for this purpose. Finally, the reading corner occupying a separate zone provides a cave space to which students can retreat. Having an environment that is flexible helps Kathy and her students transition seamlessly from one form of learning to the next.

When one moves out of the hallway and actually enters Kathy's classroom, more is revealed about how Kathy has created a space to engage learners. Along the marker tray of the whiteboard, books are perched as a kind of invitation to use. Books on sports, current popular fiction, mystery novels, and student-created books line the tray rail—a wide assortment designed to appeal to different readers.

Above the whiteboard, written on sheets of construction paper, are a set of questions representing the "throughlines" Kathy has identified to serve as an ongoing thread to focus and tie together students' learning (Blythe & Associates, 1998; Ritchhart, 2002). The questions are simple but provocative: What's the story? What's the other story? How do you know the story? Why know/tell the story? Where's the power in the story? Kathy explains the origin of the questions: "I'm teaching humanities with English, history, writing, and communication. I looked at our district curriculum, and I thought that 'story' would combine all those things. The writing of how you tell a story, the reading, historians look at what is the other story . . . So I thought those [questions] would combine all the disciplines with the major units we do on imperialism and revolution."

The question "What's the other story?" has proved particularly provocative for Kathy and her students. "That comes up all the time," Kathy shares. "We can be talking about a current event and someone will just say, 'Yeah, but what's the other story?' I live in a place students wouldn't expect me to live, and a student asked, 'Is that your other story, Mrs. Hanawalt?'" A large sheet of chart paper hung on a side wall further reflects students' engagement with this question. The poster reads "We should look at the 'other' *story* because . . . ," followed by a list:

- You don't want to be judgmental.
- You might be making assumptions.
- You'll get a better picture of the truth.
- You shouldn't assume things are as they appear.
- You might falsely accuse someone.

Beside the chart, on a sheet of blue poster board, is a photo collage made by a student showing her activities outside of class and representing her "other story." This documentation has a dynamic quality as one piece prompts other ideas and links the learning together.

Elsewhere in the room, a Chalk Talk (Ritchhart, Church, & Morrison, 2011) hangs on the wall, showing students' responses to the question "What's the relationship between reconciliation and revenge?" Scattered throughout are quotes: "The important thing is to never stop questioning" (Albert Einstein). "What are you going to do with your one wild and precious life?" (poet Mary Oliver). This latter quote is accompanied by another sheet of chart paper on which students have written their responses. These physical manifestations of class discussion, of learning, and of individuals personalize the space while connecting students to it. Their ideas hang on the wall. Their learning is visible.

There is nothing fancy, high tech, expensive, or particularly unusual about Kathy's classroom, but it is intentional and represents a departure from the standard generic box of a classroom. Kathy's desire to connect personally with students, give them a voice, engage them actively, and thread their learning together are all evident in the physical environment. Identifying and creating zones for different forms of learning give Kathy and her students greater flexibility as learners and allow them to maximize their use of the space. Even in the absence of students, the room has a lived-in look that reflects elements of not only Kathy's personality and style but also those of her students.

CURATING A CLASSROOM

"While I have always valued and sought to cocreate spaces for learning that are beautiful, I've changed how I see my role in terms of looking at space. I now see myself as a curator," Nellie Gibson explains. "You do want to create the room together with the children, but there is a special role I have as an adult to manage what comes in. I have to choose carefully. What will engage them? You never know for sure, but as a curator you prime, provide, and provoke."

Stepping into Nellie's first-grade classroom at Scotch Oakburn College in Launceston, Tasmania, you can see that her curatorial hand demonstrates both deliberate care and restraint. Missing are all the commercially made materials one might associate with a primary classroom, such as colorful carpet squares, alphabet strips, number lines, bulletin board trimmers, pocket charts, large posters of book covers sent from publishers, birthday calendars, smiling cartoon animals, and the like. Absent, too, is the explosion of primary colors typically seen in elementary classrooms. Instead, one is surrounded by evidence of students' learning. Paintings, drawings, sculptures, assemblages, and writings can be seen in careful arrangements that allow the viewer to focus, linger, and explore. Photographs of students engaged in their work accompany documented snippets of their conversation, making past events come to life. Although there is much to take in, the muted color palette makes the room not seem busy or overwhelming. Everything is displayed on white or black backgrounds, allowing the color from photographs or students' paintings to fully emerge.

On the top of one bookcase, an accordion fold of heavy white poster board, formed by taping together a series of nine-by-twelve-inch rectangles, forms a zigzag storyline of one recent episode of learning (see figure 9.1). To each rectangle a photograph of students exploring "large numbers" is carefully attached with a bulldog clip. The first panel in the display has a white sheet of paper clipped to it with the title "Counting Large Collections." Underneath are bits of conversation captured at the time of the activity:

"We have to work together"—Arabella

"Count in tens"—Archie

"To get to ten you get 5 and then get another 5"—Zac

"Oh no, we have to start again. I really think there is 100"—Rieley

"We are counting by 2's because that will be quicker"—Stephanie

The display is elegant but simple, capturing a moment of learning for later reflection. Similar documentation lines the top of several other bookcases.

The bulletin boards show a conscious restraint. Though full of student work, what is shown is a sampling of the class's learning, not every student's product. Labels are not done in large, dye-cut lettering but in simple print. It is clear that these bulletin boards aren't meant to shout to viewers across the room, but are designed to beckon them close for a detailed inspection. One bulletin board displays three sets of ideas related to reading that the class has explored: thoughtful readers, metacognition, and schema (see figure 9.2). Drawings, documentation of conversation, and photographs are found under each label. On the other side of the room is a bulletin board capturing the class's learning on three recent topics: beauty, soil, and hearts. Under the section labeled "Beauty" are a few of students' responses to the questions "What is beauty?" and "Is beauty important?"

SOPHIE: Beauty is important so that you can get good ideas from beautiful things.

STEPHANIE: Because if the place is beautiful you enjoy the time.

ARCHIE: Beauty is your family because you get company.

STEPHANIE: When I see beauty I feel excited.

XAVIER: Beauty makes me happy. Stars are beautiful because you can remember the past of their happiness. Beauty is something you enjoy.

OLIVIA: Beauty is important because it makes you love. Beauty is important because it can help us by making us feel happy.

STEPHANIE: I'm connecting onto Olivia. She is right that beauty is a time to love and help.

ARCHIE: Yes, because when you are walking around somewhere beautiful you enjoy the time.

Accompanying the bulletin boards are mobiles made from sticks wired together in an organic formation. From these mobiles hang a few more products of students' learning. I'm captivated by the mobile displaying students' paintings of hearts. These aren't Valentine's Day hearts, however. Nellie brought in an actual lamb's heart that students studied, drew, and then painted. Rather than using construction paper, students made their drawings on pages of print taken from an old novel that had been discarded, the translucency of the watercolor allowing the print to show through. The results are, well, beautiful (see figure 9.3).

Students' learning is the core business of schools and needs to be made visible. Nellie has done this in spades, making the classroom literally "thought-full." She accomplishes this not simply through a strong sense of aesthetics but through a deep understanding of the role of documentation in the learning process. Students' learning should be on display to inspire, invite, and inform—not to serve as mere decoration filling up blank space. Documentation should inspire students to reach higher and achieve more as they look at quality work that others have produced. It should invite reflection and revisiting of one's learning so as to deepen it, modify it, or take it in new directions. "One of my goals with the documentation is that I give it back to them every time," Nellie tells me. "I have them come and sit down, and show them what I have put up, and we talk about it. I am the curator of their theories and learning moments." Finally, documentation should inform the larger community of colleagues, administration, and parents about what learning looks like in this classroom and what learners are producing by way of questions and insights. In this way, it acts as a kind of institutional memory of the learning and thinking being done.

Figure 9.1   Accordion Display of Documentation on the "Large Number" Exploration

Figure 9.2   Documentation of the Class's Learning in Reading

Figure 9.3   Student's Drawing of the Heart

Documentation such as Nellie's makes learning both visible and public. Contrast this with the very private document of a student's report card that seeks to distill the mystery of learning down to a single grade, "making it almost impossible to imagine the human effort, thought, skill, creativity, or individuality that contributed to the grades a student receives" (Bergsagel, 2007, p. 54).

Not surprisingly, the parents of Nellie's students appreciate her efforts (see figure 9.4). "The walls! I love all the artwork and stories that are on display. I love that the children can see their work and feel proud of what they've created. I particularly like the black-and-white artwork," one father offers. "From the moment you walk through the door you can see an active and engaging classroom," remarks a mother, her partner adding, "We like the fact that the classroom demonstrates that the children are driving the learning from the conception of the idea through to the outcomes."

Nellie's classroom manifests visibility in other respects as well. Although it is an interior rectangular classroom no bigger than most, it appears much larger and open due to the big expanses of windows on each end. The classroom wall facing the corridor is mostly glass, and the hallway itself consists of a glass wall looking out to an eastern courtyard at the school. This permits light to filter into the room in the morning. It also allows the ongoing learning of students to be visible to others as they pass by the room, enhancing collegiality and developing a greater sense of a community of learners across the school. Activity and learning are no longer hidden from view, and both students and teachers feel more connected to one another. The opposite wall of the classroom is floor-to-ceiling glass, providing a western view over the neighboring rooftops and filling the room with afternoon sun. Also visible are the tools and resources of learning, making them available for inspiration and use.

As beautiful as the displays in Nellie's classroom are, they don't fully capture what she has come to think of as her curatorial role. Like a curator in a museum, Nellie seeks to create an environment that provokes curiosity and stimulates learning, using the environment as a third teacher (Strong-Wilson & Ellis, 2007). This might take the form of a vase of fresh hydrangeas set on a table with paper and watercolors, a stack of beautiful Tasmanian hardwood scraps arranged randomly on a table top, glass jars full of seed pods placed beside a set of magnifying glasses and drawing materials, tubs full of books, a basket full of sticks with a spool of wire for binding them together, or a tub table full of dirt for exploring (see figure 9.5). With all this on offer, Nellie is never quite sure what will capture students or where they will go with her provocations. "I have to be primed for their possibilities and follow their lead." This means that the materials put out are constantly changing, to the delight of both children and parents.

One case of following students' lead occurred when three boys began to work together to take sticks from one part of the room and place them in the tub table full of dirt. What started off as exploration turned into the creation of both a sculpture and an environment (see figure 9.6). Once the sticks were placed to their liking, the boys began to draw and cut out animals to populate their "forest." Nellie listened in on the conversation

Figure 9.4   A Parent Looks at Documentation

Figure 9.5   Science Provocation

Figure 9.6   Stick Sculpture

and noticed that the sculpture had become a vehicle for communication as well as exploration.

At one point, the boys discovered that their sculpture was actually three-dimensional. "Now they begin to communicate and move around the sculpture, making sure it looks good from every angle. At one stage, one child sends another out the door to see what the sculpture looks like as you enter the room." Nellie recounts, "Thinking they are finished, one child directs the group to sit on the couch behind the sculpture, and they discover there are holes that need to be filled with more animals." Reflecting on the result of this group's learning, Nellie explains, "Now whenever the children in our class are exploring something 3D, they always stand back and walk around what they have created, looking at it from different perspectives."

Some might explain Nellie's attention to "curating" the environment as an artifact of teaching young children, but Nellie rejects this assumption. (See "School as a Living Museum," https://www.teachingchannel.org/videos/make-student-work-public-hth, for an example of curation at the secondary level.) Informed by her experience as a long-term substitute/relief teacher in both secondary and primary classrooms, she believes that attention to the environment can be a powerful culture builder. "The killer was when I took over a year 4 class in Hobart. They had had lots of emergency teachers, and the kids were distressed," Nellie recalls. "I went in and instantly started hanging things. Putting up provocations of nature. Bringing stuff in. Asking kids about beauty. I took kids out and had them take photos. Bring stuff back."

Expounding on the impact of those actions, she reflects: "That was the first time I was aware that environment had a massive impact. It was like dominoes with one cultural force connecting to the others. The environment provides opportunities; it models, and conveys expectations. For that group of kids, they had had no continuity. There was nothing expected of them. Suddenly I had an expectation that they value the classroom space, and they had an expectation that I do the right thing by them. Altering the environment helped us begin anew as a community."

DESIGNING FOR THINKING

"This room looks completely different from the rest of the school," Alice Parker remarks, "and that is by design. My dream was that the EDGE studio would be a place for students to feel empowered as thinkers, innovators, collaborators, and risk takers." It is not often that teachers get to participate with architects, administrators, and designers in the design of teaching spaces, but Alice Maund Parker had just such an opportunity at Presbyterian Day School in Memphis, Tennessee. As part of a committee studying design thinking and exploring what it might offer to their school of elementary boys, Alice saw the connection with Visible Thinking and envisioned combining both. She then seized on the opportunity of the school's undergoing remodeling to approach the administration with her ideas to create a different kind of classroom. Working with a team of architects, she and her colleagues shared their vision of a different kind of learning space that would support thinking and innovation. Initially, Alice didn't anticipate that she would actually be the lead teacher for design thinking, but come the start of the school year, she was tapped for that role.

The name of the room, the EDGE studio, is meant to reflect the idea that this isn't a traditional classroom but a design space, a studio. The acronym EDGE reflects key steps in design thinking: **E**xplore, **D**evelop empathy, **G**row your ideas, and **E**valuate. Alice sees the acronym as a metaphor for pushing one's thought into new and creative areas as well, "going to the edge of my thinking, edgy ideas, jumping off the edge, or on the edge of my seat with ideas."

As I am guided through the labyrinth of corridors at Presbyterian Day School, it is clear when the EDGE studio comes into view, even though this is my first visit. Right away one notices that rather than a single metal door with a standard-issue sliver of a window, the door to the studio is glass with purple metal trim, purple and red being the school's colors. Not only that, but three of the four sides of the studio space consist mostly of glass as well. The room is on a corner between two hallways, and the walls facing the hallways have large windows, making the learning that happens in the studio visible to all. "I like to think of those windows as a metaphor of extending our thinking and learning beyond the room," says Alice. A third wall consists of a movable glass partition allowing the studio space to be combined with the art room next door.

This kind of openness and transparency is probably one of the biggest trends in school architecture happening around the world at the moment. Nellie Gibson's classroom had this feature, and it appears here in Memphis as well. It is worth noting that neither Nellie nor Alice teaches in new buildings, only schools that have been redesigned from the inside out. In terms of expense, modifying existing interior walls and putting in windows are a lot less expensive than erecting a new building. For dollars spent, it can make a tremendous difference to the feel of a school. Although some worry that students will be distracted, students and teachers tend to get used to the openness quickly. The windows also allow for greater supervision of students, as hallways cease to be spaces for lurking or lingering.

Peering through the glass panes as I approach the room, I notice another unique feature of the space: standing desks. They are arranged in groups of four, and there is a stool with each desk if the students want to sit. Another feature of the desks, designed by a schoolteacher in Minnesota, is the swinging footrest (see figure 9.7). This allows students to keep moving even as they sit. It's an engaging feature, and I find myself wanting to try it out. In many classrooms, teachers spend energy fighting against students' need to move—usually without much success. Dieter Breithecker (2007), an expert on ergonomic design and physical movement in schools, advises teachers to make peace with fidgeting, advising that "only a continual rhythmic change between passivity and activity, strain and relief, tension and relaxation will lead to conditions which ensure a balanced physical, emotional and mental state . . . If they [students] want to stay awake and focused, they have to be able to move even when seated" (p. 2).

Alice has clearly made her peace with fidgeting, laying out the studio space to allow for lots of movement and different configurations of students. As I enter, I see some students standing, some seated on the stools using the swinging footrest, one group lying on the floor around a sheet of chart paper, and another two groups standing in the back of the room. The fifth graders are designing a new home for Chester from *The Cricket in Times Square*. The project aims to merge fantasy and reality by creating a space that suits Chester's personality while actually being a habitat in which a live cricket could live.

As students work to explore the possible found materials that might be accessible and comfortable for Chester, a gentle buzz fills the room. Alice notes, "As a boy's school, PDS has always been intentional about allowing movement and exploration with students. The movement of the bars on the desks, permission to carve out your own space, to lay down, are all encouraged to foster learning, creativity, and new thinking."

Another thing that distinguishes the EDGE studio is that it is well lit from a variety of sources. Whereas Kathy Hanawalt brought in floor lamps to create more variable lighting into her room, creating mood, zones, and cues for activity, the newly designed EDGE studio was able to be very deliberate in attending to lighting. The windows to the hallway provide an openness to the space while allowing some light from the hallway to filter into the room. Because the art studio opens to the outside with floor-to-ceiling windows, natural light is able to make its way into the EDGE studio through the folding glass partition. Natural light affects motivation, mood, and energy, and some studies have found that getting adequate natural light improves learning (Barrett et al., 2013; Bergsagel, 2007). The EDGE studio has two sources of artificial light. New indirect lighting, the best kind of artificial light, bounces off the ceiling, providing good overall illumination without the hum of traditional fluorescents. Circular downward lights are also available to increase the lighting in the room on cloudy days (see figure 9.8).

As Alice moves around the room, listening in on groups and pushing them on their thinking, I notice that there doesn't seem to be a "front" of the classroom. Alice's desk occupies a small space in a front corner of the room next to the sink and seems purposely pushed out of the way to take up as little space as possible. There is no interactive whiteboard dictating a focus either. Instead, a large flat-screen monitor is placed high on the wall and tilted downward for easy viewing from almost any position in the room. Ample floor space allows movement and even work on the floor. Instead of a whiteboard, which might normally orient a room, the only solid wall in the studio has been painted with IdeaPaint, turning the entire wall into a giant whiteboard (see figure 9.9).

This is one idea from the EDGE studio that was easy and cheap to implement in all the classrooms at Presbyterian Day School and one that both teachers and students love. It feels as though one is breaking a taboo by "writing on the wall." With no borders except the ceiling and the floor, it also feels less constraining than a typical whiteboard. "The Idea Wall," as Alice refers to it, "has become a great space to brainstorm, draw prototypes, map out ideas, or even share a quick presentation." Because of its height, Alice uses the space above students' reach to write messages, notes, and labels. On one side there is the message "Check out Headlines from the last class." On the opposite side is the heading "A Whole Lot of Thinking about Crickets." In the center are directions for the Options

Figure 9.7   Students Work at Standing Desks with Swinging Footrests

Figure 9.8   Two Different Sources of Lighting Provide Good Illumination for Learning

Figure 9.9   Students Use the Idea Wall as They Work in Groups

Explosion thinking routine: "(1) List the Obvious, (2) Brainstorm for the Hidden, (3) Now What?" Below these headings, several students work in small groups, each with a marker in hand, adding their thoughts and ideas about what possible objects might offer a workable, yet highly original, habitat for Chester.

In reflecting on how the space works for her students' learning, particularly as it relates to design thinking, Alice highlights the adaptability of the space. "The flexibility of the EDGE studio design allows students to collaborate in many different ways," Alice says. "There are no set rules for places or spaces to work with their teams. Pretty much, anything goes. They have worked collaboratively at desks, on walls, carved out small spaces within the room, in the hallway, and in the conference room. They can even go outside as well." In this statement, it is clear that Alice sees the need more for "watering holes" than "campfires" or "caves," yet the space can be adapted for that as well. With all the places to gather, a desk or the conference room can provide a cave. Gathering around the Idea Wall or viewing the flat-screen LCD monitor is an opportunity for the group to come together in a campfire setting.

As the class comes to a close, Alice brings students together in one brief summation that captures both today's class and the power of the EDGE studio space:

This is what I heard and this is what I saw today: I saw a lot of boys writing. You were on fire. I heard wild ideas. I heard piggybacking. I heard one group beginning to evaluate one another's ideas, but then they stepped back and reminded themselves that now was not the time to judge. Great thinking today, class. Now honor your classmates, look them in the eye, and thank them. I'll meet you at the door, and give me a "Headline" for your thinking today or an "I used to think . . . Now I think . . ." as your exit ticket.

CREATING ENVIRONMENTS TO ENHANCE LEARNING AND BUILD CULTURE: FOUR FRONTS

The redesign of schools and learning spaces for the twenty-first century is an engrossing topic. A host of fetching ideas pepper the conversation of architects and designers: indoor-outdoor spaces, green buildings, community connections, learning clusters, studio spaces, learning streets, sustainability, cafes, student lounge areas, makerspaces, and so on. However, as we think about leveraging the environment to support a culture of thinking, it is important to recognize that most teachers worldwide still teach in less than ideal spaces and that the design of the majority of current school buildings originated from the thinking of the past cells-and-bells era. On top of that, those buildings are generally constructed under strict budget controls, leaving little room for bold ideas.

Even facing this stark reality of suboptimal spaces, there is no reason to despair. Nor is there reason for teachers to assume that the environment doesn't influence learning or that it can't be improved to support learning. There is much that can be done to optimize any environment. From the three case studies presented in this chapter, four fronts for consideration and action emerge: visibility, flexibility, comfort, and invitational quality.

Visibility

The notion that students' learning and thinking shouldn't be hidden but should be made visible is widely popular today (Edwards, Gandini, & Forman, 1998; Project Zero & Reggio Children, 2001; Ritchhart et al., 2011). This idea can have many manifestations. When a teacher questions and probes a student's response, he or she is making thinking visible in the sense that it becomes apparent, an entity that is now known and can be examined and discussed. Likewise, when a teacher employs a thinking routine to uncover how students are making sense of ideas, their thinking is brought to the fore. This is visibility through the act of probing and scaffolding.

Of course there can be literal visibility as well, when something can be seen with our own eyes. Perception is powerful, and being in the presence of real learning unfolding can be potent as well. However, learning moments can be fleeting; you have to be in the right place at the right time to catch them. Students working in isolation have little access to this kind of visibility unless we ask ourselves, How can I increase students' real-time visibility and access to the work other learners are doing in my classroom and at our school? This is the visibility of collaboration, both direct and indirect, achieved through the transparency of learning.

Finally, there is the visibility obtained through efforts to capture, record, or somehow document these real-time events so that they don't slip from our grasp. When it comes to supporting students' development as thinkers and learners, all three modes of visibility are important. However, it is the last two forms of visibility that have the clearest implications for shaping the environment.

If learning is a creative and imaginative endeavor done with peers, then we need to arrange our classrooms so that others can see what we are working on. We need to stop hiding learning and thinking by keeping it private. Such transparency breaks down hierarchies as students see one another learning across grade and subject areas. Students can see teachers working, planning, and thinking together. Perhaps counterintuitively, such openness can lead to more quiet and calm. In a traditional hallway, one's actions seem hidden and private, but when you can see learning going on, it is easier for students to take into account the effect of their actions on others' learning. In addition, monitoring and supervision are enhanced through such transparency.

"To collaborate effectively others need to see what is in your head," says Bill Buxton of Microsoft Research (OWP/P Architects et al., 2010, p. 65). There is a literal need to make one's thinking visible in collaborative learning situations in order to be understood and to be able to build on others' contributions. Buxton recounts passing by a conference room in which he noticed that the participants were getting bogged down and communication was stalled. He snuck into the room to place a couple of large pieces of foam-core board on the table along with some pins, sticky notes, and markers. When he returned, the room was abuzz with conversation as the ideas were now literally "on the table" for debate, examination, and modification.

Artists, actors, and all creative souls draw inspiration from those around them. This is true for students as well. How can we make our rooms more transparent so that students can see one another's efforts? This might entail arranging the desks to give students a greater view of one another. It might mean knocking out walls and adding windows to open up rooms. It might be that we create room and freedom for movement so that students can physically walk through the classroom and see what others are doing. Ask yourself, Is students' learning hidden from me? Is it hidden from others? What might I do to break through that wall of invisibility?

We owe much to the work of the teachers at the infant-toddler centers and preschools in Reggio Emilia for raising awareness about the power of documentation. With the attitude of researchers, Reggio Emilia teachers attend to the activities of their students with great interest to try to understand their learning. This is a key feature of documentation; it doesn't seek simply to capture or to record what has happened in the class but to identify key learning episodes, those moments of spark, that insightful question, or that unexpected discovery that might serve as the impetus for future learning. At its heart, documentation makes learning and thinking visible precisely because it is focused on trying to understand the learning process itself. In reflecting on the documentary aspects of your classroom, two good questions to ask are

- What can a visitor to this space tell about the learning that is happening in this classroom?
- What can that visitor tell about the individual learners, not just the teacher, who inhabit this space?

There is no single way to document thinking and learning. As Vea Vecchi, an atelierista in the Reggio schools, says, "What we are interested in is precisely an attempt to see this process [of learning] and to understand how the construction of doing, thinking, and knowing takes place, as well as what sort of influences or modifications can occur in these processes" (quoted in Krechevsky & Stork, 2000, p. 68). Observation notes, partial transcripts of conversations, audiotapes of a discussion, a list of students' responses to a prompt, photographs or videos of learning, chart-paper brainstorms, or a screen capture from an interactive whiteboard are all forms of documentation.

To those new to documenting students' thinking, it might be easy to confuse documentation with merely recording what the class has done, a sort of archive of activity amassed through the collection of various documents. However, to be useful to both teachers and students, documentation must extend beyond this. Documentation focuses on the learning process itself by trying to capture the events, questions, conversations, and acts that provoke and advance learning over time. Some of the benefits and reasons behind documentation of learning and thinking include

- Capturing individual and group learning and thinking, and making it visible
- Being able to share a story of the learning journey happening in the class
- Providing a resource for discussion, reflection, and review of learning
- Helping students connect to and build on prior learning and experiences

- Modeling and capturing processes for later reference
- Showing students the ongoing nature of learning and how their ideas change and develop over time
- Facilitating learning from and with others
- Informing our next steps as teachers
- Validating and affirming students' contributions to the class
- Providing evidence for formative assessment
- Promoting teachers' and students' self-assessment of learning
- Providing parents with a glimpse into the learning their children are doing
- Being able to identify learning "hotspots" that catapulted group or individual learning to the next level
- Seeing trends, patterns, and growth over time
- Allowing students to more easily see multiple perspectives and possibilities around a topic

One can contrast such documentation of learning to the products that are more typically on display in classrooms and schools. To be sure, such products have their place, particularly when they represent students' efforts at crafting work of high quality through dedicated revision and refinement over time. This is work that can cultivate an ethic of excellence (Berger, Gardner, Meier, Sizer, & Lieberman, 2003). Even so, such displays should aim to be dynamic and interactive rather than static. Think, too, about quality. Of course, everyone likes to see his or her work displayed, but if that work does not reflect one's best efforts and is merely put up along with everyone else's work, where is the pride? Act more as a curator, or even invite students to curate a display and decide what should go up to best represent the class's learning.

As we witnessed in Nellie Gibson's classroom, the chief goals of documentation of learning is *to inspire*, through showing quality work; *to invite*, by providing opportunities to reflect on and interact with the documentation; and *to inform*. Documentation has three audiences that it informs: teachers, students, and parents. First, it informs the teacher as to how students are thinking and communicating about complex ideas, often providing information that can be used to extend students' thinking. Second, documentation informs the student. By returning to pictures, photographs, transcripts of conversations, videos, or recordings, students have a vehicle for reflecting on their learning, seeing their strengths and weaknesses, identifying ideas worth exploring further, and consolidating ideas that they may have only touched on initially. Third, documentation informs parents. A worksheet tells a parent only what the task was and how well the student completed it, nothing of the thought, questions, conversations, or imagination that might have gone into it. Documentation can make that learning come alive and in so doing provide parents with a new model of how they might interact with their child. Finally, documentation serves the collective memory of the group, acting as a thread that pulls all learning together in a celebration and connection. It is a visibility that can help end isolation.

Flexibility

Learners and learning are dynamic. Furthermore, new modes and types of learning may require new, and perhaps not yet imagined, spaces. However, the physical space for learning is too often static. This is to the detriment of learning. Peter Barrett and colleagues' study of the impact of the physical environment on the learning of students in Blackpool, England, identified flexibility of space, the creation of zones for learning, and well-designed furniture as important contributors to academic achievement (2013).

Having flexible, easily moveable, and accommodating furniture helps make a space both more dynamic and more responsive to learning needs. Small triangular or trapezoidal tables offer multiple alternative configurations to suit learning needs. Even rectangular desks afford many options. In contrast, round tables provide a nice setting for a group but aren't easily combined to create other arrangements. Seating must also be flexible. Although chairs are often needed for long stretches of sitting, foam cubes or inflatable balls offer alternatives for shorter periods of time. The key to true flexibility, though, is to enable teachers and students to reconfigure furniture themselves quickly and without any outside help.

Even when some modicum of flexibility exists, teachers often do not take advantage of it. A common complaint I hear from secondary teachers who share a classroom space is that some teachers insist that the default setting of a classroom must be rows facing forward, placing all the burden on the teacher who wants an alternative to full-frontal teaching. This shouldn't be the case. Although direct, lecture-style presentation with the teacher at the front is sometimes the best option, it shouldn't be considered the main or default style of teaching. Furthermore, schools that wish teachers to use more varied approaches that are more responsive to students and create a dynamic learning culture shouldn't acquiesce to any single style as the default.

There are a few ways around this impasse. One is that it could be taken as a given that no teacher should have to rearrange a classroom more than once. To do so would create an undue burden on those interested in trying new things, being flexible, and taking risks in their teaching. Thus it is always the teacher who enters the class who takes responsibility for moving furniture—with, presumably, the help of his or her students—and the next teacher expects to do the same. A second option is to establish only certain rooms with a default arrangement. For example, rooms might be set up to facilitate project work (table groupings), Socratic dialogue (circle or one big table), or direct instruction (rows), and then efforts can be made to schedule people into the rooms they most prefer. Even so, one would hope that teachers vary even their dominant pattern of instruction and would have the flexibility to rearrange these spaces as needed. A third option is to employ the most flexible seating configurations, such as the **C** desk arrangement that Kathy Hanawalt used or groups of desks that simultaneously allow all to see the front of the room and to be in groups.

The number-one feature orienting a classroom has always been the chalkboard, which was replaced by the whiteboard and now its almost ubiquitous companion, a projector, turning it into an interactive whiteboard. In most cases, these ceiling-mounted devices offer no flexibility. Although a relatively new technology, these devices may be going the way of the CD. Many schools and businesses are using much better illuminated touch screens that offer greater interactivity and connectivity. Even if projectors continue to be bought, one can reasonably ask what the advantage is of a static ceiling mount over the freestanding and movable interactive whiteboard that has always been on offer. With the advent of IdeaPaint, the whiteboard itself no longer needs to be set in one place but can be on any wall, floor to ceiling, as we witnessed in Alice Parker's EDGE studio.

Beyond furniture arrangement, flexibility in space can also be achieved through the creation of zones. Zones clearly define areas of the room for different activities. These can be established simply by using a small throw rug to define a reading area, as Kathy Hanawalt did, or by setting up different provocations to establish an area's potential, as Nellie Gibson did in her first-grade classroom. In thinking about establishing fixed zones, ask yourself: What types of spaces do learners need to use both frequently and regularly? The answers are as varied as teachers and their students: play, presentation, demonstration, collaboration, wet, creative, quiet, planning, group, individual, reading, lab, dramatic, and so on. Beyond thinking about what zones you "need," you might also want to evaluate your space more broadly by asking, What does this space give permission to? What does it actively encourage?

One way of partially answering these questions about the types of zones needed for learning to thrive is through the archetypes identified by David Thornburg that were mentioned earlier: campfires, watering holes, and caves. If a classroom is large enough, it might be possible to create fixed zones for each of these. If that is not possible, then being able to quickly move furniture to create such spaces will be useful. When imagining or reimagining a whole school, one should design for and create such spaces (Nair & Fielding, 2005). That said, an important consideration in designing campfire spaces is size. What is the optimal size that would get good and regular use? How can you make this space as flexible as possible to maximize its potential?

The idea of flexibility extends beyond the space and how it will be used to the actual learners themselves. Students, of all stripes, need to be able to move within a space. Ergonomic expert Dieter Breithecker (2007) argues that fidgeting should be thought of as brain development, stating that our vestibular or balance system needs stimulation to keep us alert and focused. In short, this means some form of dynamic movement and avoidance of static sitting, which can strain muscles and cause fatigue. Some studies of the suitability of seating available to students in classrooms have found that chair and table height is inappropriate for a whopping 90 percent of students (O'Donnell, 2012). Adjustable-height desks and tables, as well as access to different furniture at different times, can be beneficial in addressing this problem.

Movement doesn't always have to be large, though for some students it might. Many chairs designed today allow for tilting back to vary one's posture without destabilizing the chair and putting it at risk of toppling over. The standing desks in Alice Parker's studio enabled students to move their legs and thus remain active. In addition, Alice allowed her students to lie on the floor to work, or to stand at the whiteboard. Tactile strips added to desks and squishable foam balls allow for simple tactile movement as well.

Comfort

The opportunity to move and vary one's posture certainly adds to one's comfort in a space. Beyond that, educators need to consider light, color, temperature, and noise. Of course, any notion of comfort with regard to space is somewhat subjective. One person may find a room too cold while another in the space finds it just right. Nonetheless, we are all affected by these environmental factors, and they have been among the most researched factors with regard to the physical environment's impact on learning (Higgins, Hall, Wall, Woolner, & McCaughey, 2005). However, this research doesn't so much point to a single optimal or best choice of light, temperature, or noise as it suggests certain parameters and minimal standards. Color is one area in which research is particularly unclear and sometimes conflicting.

In their recent study of the physical environment of schools, Barrett et al. (2013) identified light as one of the top factors that affect learning. Although optimal lighting was hard to determine, they found a preference for "naturalness," which involved "a desire for light, a dislike of glare and the importance of good artificial lighting" (p. 688). Specifically, they found that although people didn't like sitting in direct light if it caused glare, people did like to be oriented toward a light source. Architect Sean O'Donnell elaborates on the implications of this finding: "The challenge is to provide glare-free natural light supplemented by switchable and dimmable electric lighting" (2012, p. 41).

Though not classroom based, other research has shown that cortisol levels drop under poor lighting conditions or in the absence of natural light (Widrich, 2013). This can lead to inability to deal with stress and a depletion of energy. Examining the difference between adult workers in offices lit by artificial light and those in natural light, Münch and colleagues found that workers experienced greater sleepiness and decreased performance on cognitively demanding tasks in the evenings, suggesting that the effects of lighting extend beyond one's current condition (Münch, Linhart, Borisuit, Jaeggi, & Scartezzini, 2012). When direct sunlight isn't available, indirect or lensed-indirect light is preferred. Such lights bounce light off the ceiling and mimic daylight without producing glare.

Alice Parker's newly designed EDGE studio got the lighting right; the room offers views to the outdoors for natural light, with plenty of indirect light bouncing off the ceiling to fully illuminate the room on cloudy days (see Figure 9.8). Kathy Hanawalt's windowless classroom offered the most challenge in this regard. Though she couldn't very well bring natural light in or afford to replace overhead lights, she did bring in other sources of light to create a layered effect and create a homey feel (Doorley & Witthoft, 2011).

Temperature may be even less within a teacher's control than lighting. However, temperature, heating, and air quality are the most important individual elements for student achievement, claims a report by Earthman (2004). Being too hot can cause sluggishness, and being too cold causes the body to exert energy and resources in trying to keep warm, leaving less energy for concentration, inspiration, and focus (Widrich, 2013).

Some will remember the era of open classrooms, which had a very brief moment in the 1970s and 1980s. This educational experience failed largely because of issues with noise— that and the fact that teachers didn't adapt their teaching to new spaces but continued to teach in largely traditional ways. O'Donnell (2012) reports, "The ability to hear and be heard is one of the most critical elements of a successful learning environment, especially for children who have not yet learned to read or who are learning a second language. To ensure an appropriate 'signal-to-noise ratio'—meaning that the teacher, other students, and various media can be heard—both background noise and reverberation must be adequately controlled" (p. 39).

Today, openness—or, perhaps more precisely, transparency and visibility—is more readily achieved through a wall of windows between classrooms or between classrooms and corridors. Such walls provide greater acoustic privacy than complete openness. Likewise, having zones for certain activities can help reduce noise. Alternatively, having headphones available for students to screen out noise and to focus when they need to can be an option.

When the *Guardian* newspaper in the United Kingdom ran a competition for students to describe and design "The School I'd Like" in 2001, color was one of the most frequently given responses (Burke & Grosvenor, 2003). In general, students show a preference for more color and "less boring" classroom environments. However, teachers and parents tend not to share this concern (Maxwell, 2000). There is much debate over color preferences and what colors work "best" in classrooms. Claims of gender and age differences in color preference as well as motivational assertions—blue for creative tasks and red for high performance—are sometimes made. Sorting through the validity of these claims can be a challenge. However, there does seem to be much stronger support for variety and at least some use of color.

In Kathie Engelbrecht's review (2003) of the research on the effects of color, static or monotone environments were shown to produce more eyestrain and fatigue, reduced efficiency and productivity, and an increase in off-task behavior. Engelbrecht and others suggest that a focus wall, painted a contrasting, nonreflective color, helps overcome these effects. The contrast provides a visual break to the eye and allows it to more easily focus. The different color also helps attract students' attention to the front of the room. Others suggest painting walls "a chromatic range with many shades to create variety and interest without overwhelming" (OWP/P Architects et al., 2010, p. 178). This contrasting of trim colors and a focus wall was used in Alice Parker's EDGE studio. Doors and window trim were painted in a subdued red and purple, the school's colors, and a focus wall where a large LCD monitor is mounted was painted purple.

The choice of color in early childhood classrooms is often dictated by engrained "aesthetic codes" that reflect deeply rooted philosophies about children, their needs, and their development as well as the purpose and promise of schooling (Tarr, 2001). In Nellie Gibson's Reggio Emilia–inspired classroom, walls and bulletin board displays are purposely kept a neutral color to allow the color of students' artwork and photographs to dominate. To many teachers, her classroom might seem "bland."

Patricia Tarr (2001) points out the different approach often pushed by commercial companies: "In perusing both U.S. and Canadian educational catalogues, one is struck by the profusion of color; the furniture, equipment and play materials are in the primary colors: red, yellow, blue, plus green, and sometimes orange. Pastel colors are usually reserved for infant toys, or possibly girl's toys. In these catalogues you can color-coordinate your plastic drawers for storage, furniture, and fill the shelves with a wide assortment of toys, all in bright colors. These catalogues seem to be driven to saturate the environment with primary colors" (p. 5). Tarr and other advocates of a Reggio Emilia approach argue that this artificial, commercially produced environment talks down to children and denies them a chance to interact with and learn from more authentic and natural spaces. Furthermore, the use of earth tones in Reggio Emilia–inspired classrooms is meant to be more homelike and comforting, offering a welcome invitation to learners.

Invitational Quality

Classrooms are as individual as homes. Although there is no single way they must look, we want our homes to be functional, to work for the activities we conduct in them, and to be comfortable and inviting to those we welcome in. Given that students and teachers spend between six and ten hours a day at school, shouldn't classrooms be equally as inviting? This isn't to say that a classroom needs to be homey, even though an argument can be made that this creates a good transition and connection for young students. However, at the very least, schools needn't be institutional. In the *Guardian*'s "School I'd Like" design competition (Burke & Grosvenor, 2003), students often commented that a school shouldn't look or feel like a prison—no more cells and bells.

The three classrooms presented in this chapter all exuded an invitational quality that welcomed students, parents, colleagues, and visitors into the space. They were spaces adults and children alike wanted to be in. The standing desks, leg swings, and floor-to-ceiling whiteboard in Alice Parker's studio; the soft lamps, throw rugs, books, and student work in Kathy Hanawalt's room; the big windows, students' complex artwork, engagingly displayed elements from nature, and documentation of students' conversations in Nellie Gibson's room—all these classrooms sent out the vibe that the physical space was shaped by a community with great pride of ownership. Each environment offered a grand vision to learners: in this space, ideas will grab you for exploration; those in the room will support your explorations even as they challenge and push you; your learning will be celebrated.

In all three of the classrooms visited in this chapter, there was some sense of surprise, playfulness, or humor: in Nellie's room, the hanging mobiles made of sticks from the garden and suspended from the ceiling, and the stack of Tasmanian hardwood; in Alice's, a whole wall you can write on; in Kathy's, an old license plate from the time she lived in

Colorado. Doorley and Witthoft (2011) of Stanford University's d.school suggest incorporating "anything that violates the norm in a playful way" (p. 91).

Grand examples of whimsy enliven a place and show the group's penchant for fun. For instance, at Ron Clark Academy in Atlanta, there is a spiral slide in the central atrium connecting the second and first floors. At the San Francisco afterschool center 826 Valencia, founded by author Dave Eggers and Ninive Calegari, students enter the tutoring space through a "Pirate Shop," complete with trapdoors, chests, deck mops, ropes, peg legs, and glass eyes. Ninive says that for first-time students, there is "a little bit of shock and then smiles. There is an immediate sense of warmth and playfulness that is apparent" (OWP/P Architects et al., 2010, p. 198). Why shouldn't an afterschool learning space be a fun place to visit? At High Tech High in San Diego, jazz plays in the bathroom, and elaborately designed plaques hang above each urinal as a dedication to a group or individual. Math teacher John Threlkeld (Ritchhart, 2002) has a giant eight-foot-long antique slide rule suspended from one wall of his classroom.

An invitational spirit is important for schools. When visitors enter into a space, what greets them for the first time? At the Diana School in Reggio Emilia, Italy, the phrase "Nothing without Joy" is written large across the wall-sized window looking into the art studio. The core values of the school can be seen displayed in large graphic lettering throughout the public spaces. At Way Elementary in Bloomfield Hills, Michigan, quotes about thinking complement large posters of students engaged actively in exploring.

To assess this invitational quality of a classroom, we can ask ourselves some questions: What first greets me as a visitor to this space? Is this a space I would want to learn in? What draws me in and beckons me as a learner? Is there something to spark my interest here? Does my eye have a place to land, or am I bombarded with too much activity? Where is beauty in this room? How will I move within the space and create different spaces to fit my learning needs? What in this room makes me smile, takes me by surprise, or causes me to gasp in amazement? Does this space feel like a home for me and my learning, or does it seem to belong to someone else? Does the space feel static or dynamic? What will I be able to change, manipulate, or contribute to in this space to put my stamp on it? How is this space connected to nature and the world at large? Does the space feel authentic versus ordered out of a catalogue or copied from a television soundstage?

As with all the cultural forces, the physical environment sends messages to our students about what we value, how we think learning happens, and what kinds of learning and thinking are to be celebrated. Environments also send messages about how one is to move and interact in the space and with others, either connecting us as community or making that connection more of a challenge. Of course, great teaching can occur in any space, but why would we want to impede that by having an environment that doesn't fully support, embrace, and bring out the best in learners?

We live in something of a golden age when it comes to school design. Even so, money will most likely be an issue when it comes to creating learning spaces for children, and suboptimal spaces are likely to continue to be the norm in education. Nonetheless, there are lessons we can take from other, more ideal spaces; and certain design elements, such as visibility, flexibility, comfort, and invitational quality, can be employed by all teachers to support the development of a culture of thinking in their classrooms.

CREATING ENVIRONMENTS THAT BRING OUT THE BEST IN LEARNERS

- Go on a ghost walk. The Ghost Visit protocol (http://www.nsrfharmony.org /system/files/protocols/ghost_visit.pdf) is designed to focus your attention on the messages about learning and learners sent by the physical space of a school when teachers and students aren't present. What is the invitational quality or vibe of the place? What kinds of thinking and learning are valued? Taking a ghost walk through another school or classroom will help you be more sensitive to your own space. Inviting others to do a ghost walk of your school can help you understand what others see.

- Run your own "The School I'd Like" competition, though it needn't be competitive. We don't necessarily need to cater to students' whims, but it can be informative to get their perspective. Nellie Gibson interviewed both students and parents about their favorite place in the classroom to find out what aspects of the environment most attracted them and why.

- Make form follow function. Ask yourself: What am I designing my classroom for? In what kinds of activity do I want the students in my classroom to be regularly engaged? Make a list of these activities/actions and then identify how your space can most easily and effectively accommodate them.

- Think about orientation and ambience. These are two features of space that can readily be modified. Explore what you can do to quickly alter the orientation of your classroom. How can you create campfires, watering holes, and caves? What can you do to alter the ambience of your space? What lighting can be changed? How can you create a mood or setting for learning?

- Identify what is not working. Do you have any stagnant areas in your room? Places or corners that aren't being used? Clutter? These areas pull down energy and should be modified.

- Become a curator. Look at your room with a curatorial eye. Are your displays dynamic? Do they invite, inspire, and inform? Do they invite close looking, or are they dismissed after a quick glance? Is there so much ancillary color that it detracts from students' work? Do your displays highlight your creativity or that of your students?

- Rethink your desk. A teacher's desk front and center sends a clear message of authority and control. Where else might it be placed? Do you even need a desk?
- Get on your knees. Look at your room from your students' point of view. What do they see from their perspective? From their desks? When they enter the room?
- Try your hand at documentation. The book *Visible Learners* (Krechevsky, Mardell, Rivard, & Wilson, 2013) offers great tips and examples at all grade levels to help you get started.
- Create some element of surprise, playfulness, or humor. What's something you can bring into your classroom that will provoke a smile or encourage conversation? What will make your space unique? This might be something temporary or permanent.

CHAPTER 10

Moving toward Transformation

I t seems that schools and school systems are almost always in a state of flux. The never-ending stream of initiatives, programs, reform efforts, and the like ensures that schools are in a constant state of either adoption or adaptation. Some schools even incorporate "the next new thing" into their standard way of operating, announcing a different focus or theme for each school year: And now, we'll focus on technology or assessment or differentiation, or . . . thinking! Typically, change efforts of this sort are merely additive in nature, resulting in the adoption of a few new practices by the most eager and in stealth avoidance by the reluctant. Other times, change efforts are nothing more than an exercise in relabeling what teachers already do, to fit in with new frameworks, thus demonstrating compliance to an outside entity. Rarely do efforts of these types lead to serious transformation—that is, a meaningful or dramatic change in the form of the teaching and learning occurring at the school.

Because "cultures of thinking" is not a program one can merely implement, it can't be approached with a simple one-and-done mentality. Nonetheless, there are schools that focus on some of the tools for building a culture of thinking—the use of thinking routines, for example—and stop after a brief introduction and some successful implementation of those practices. However, becoming a culture of thinking is best viewed as an ongoing process, one that may well *begin* with using thinking routines, but doesn't end there. The case studies that form the core of this closing chapter provide a window on what the transformation process can look like in schools, districts, and systems. They offer inspiration rather than a recipe for what might be done. The cases show ways to begin, as well as strategies for fostering growth over the long haul.

A CLOSE LOOK AT SUBSTANTIVE CHANGE

We begin with the ongoing work to develop cultures of thinking in schools and districts across Oakland County, Michigan, just northwest of Detroit. Oakland County has a population of approximately 1.2 million and consists of twenty-eight different public school districts. The county includes small rural as well as much larger exurban districts. Oakland Schools operates as a service provider to all these diverse school districts, and since 2011 has championed and supported schools as they work toward developing cultures of thinking. To date, fourteen school districts, encompassing more than one hundred schools and collectively representing over one hundred thousand students, have been involved in the Creating Culture of Thinking project. Lauren Childs, school quality consultant for Oakland Schools, describes the last four years of work and how it has evolved to meet the needs of schools and teachers to dig deeply into what it means to become a culture of thinking. Following Lauren Childs's big-picture framing of the endeavor, we move into specific schools and districts in the county.

Rod Rock, superintendent of Clarkston Community School District in Oakland County, recounts how as a new superintendent he built the vision and laid the groundwork to support the principals in his district to take on the charge of building cultures of thinking at their schools. Principal Adam Scher of Way Elementary in Bloomfield Hills tells the story of being the first school in the county to embrace the vision of cultures of thinking. He shares the efforts of a school now in its sixth year of ongoing, dedicated transformation. Rounding out the case studies from Oakland County is the story by Ellen Cale, the visible thinking coordinator serving twelve elementary schools in the Troy School District. Ellen describes her role as a facilitator in supporting the work of teachers, helping them understand and gradually adopt the vision of a culture of thinking so that they could move forward with the ideas and practices in their classrooms.

The final two cases look at work being done at Washington International School (WIS) in Washington DC, and a special professional collaboration between Masada College and Emanuel School, two preschool through grade 12 schools in Sydney, Australia. Jim Reese, director of studies at WIS, describes the changes he has seen in the faculty's approach to these ideas over the last seven years and how the school has built capacity around cultures of thinking in a way that truly has transformed the school. My colleague Mark Church completes the case studies of change by describing how he has helped Masada College and Emanuel School push beyond their initial work with cultures of thinking ideas to take their practice to the next level through yearlong inquiry action projects.

As these case studies will make clear, there is no one single blueprint for how one begins the process of transforming a school into a robust culture of thinking. Every school is different and must begin where its teachers are in their practice and where students are in their learning. Although the exact steps and processes will be unique to each school, we have found that supporting successful transformation over time demands that leaders attend to four key areas (see figure 10.1):

1. The purpose or vision that we are striving to make a reality
2. The tools and practices that will help us achieve that vision

Figure 10.1 Four Areas of Attention in Shepherding Change

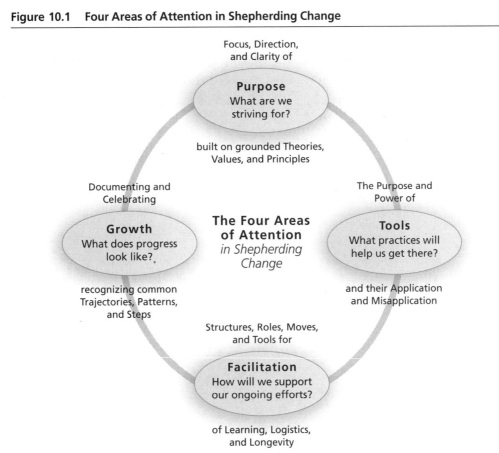

Focus, Direction,
and Clarity of

Purpose
What are we
striving for?

built on grounded Theories,
Values, and Principles

Documenting and
Celebrating

The Purpose and
Power of

Growth
What does progress
look like?

**The Four Areas
of Attention**
*in Shepherding
Change*

Tools
What practices will
help us get there?

recognizing common
Trajectories, Patterns,
and Steps

and their Application
and Misapplication

Structures, Roles, Moves,
and Tools for

Facilitation
How will we support
our ongoing efforts?

of Learning, Logistics,
and Longevity

Source: Developed by Ritchhart, Blythe, and Delforge as part of the Creative Classroom Project

3. Facilitation of the ongoing learning required to achieve the vision and implement the tools to their best effect

4. The growth we are seeing in both teachers and students that will help us recognize our progress and identify our collective next steps

As you read through the six case studies of change, pay close attention to how these four areas play out in each context. How do the leaders help build and sustain the vision of a culture of thinking? How are tools introduced, not as a program to implement, but instead as practices that support the vision? In particular, look for how the ongoing learning is supported and facilitated in each context and over time. Facilitation, rather than "training," is a major key to both growing and sustaining any complex process.

Finally, as each of the case authors recount their leadership efforts, they highlight the growth occurring along the way. Being able to recognize growth, as well as the challenges faced by teachers trying to grow, provides vital information for next steps in addition to moments for celebration. As you read, ask yourself: How do growth and development look similar and different depending on each leader's vantage point and context?

Supporting Change on a Large Scale

Lauren Childs, School Quality Consultant
Oakland Schools
Waterford, Michigan

The story began with an invitation. Jenny Rossi, a teacher leader at Way Elementary in Bloomfield Hills, invited me to join her and principal Adam Scher in thinking about growing Cultures of Thinking (CoT) beyond their school and beyond their district. Also invited to the conversation was Rod Rock, superintendent of Clarkston Schools in Clarkston, Michigan.

As we shared our respective introductions to CoT, we became excited about inviting teachers and administrators into a new collaboration that could deepen the instructional initiatives already under way in the county. Our shared understanding of CoT as an instructional approach to life in classrooms and throughout a school energized our commitment to get the conversation started. We subsequently invited interested superintendents, principals, and teachers to a one-day overview of the vision of CoT. As a large county with diverse perspectives on teaching and learning, we had to figure out how to participate collectively in this conversation. I was sure that if we could help educators join a different conversation about teaching and learning in their classrooms, we could change the conversations students were having *in* those classrooms. And so the dialogue began.

CULTIVATING THE SOIL

Jenny, Adam, Rod, and I were acutely aware that we wanted to design our way into this collaborative learning so that we built strong leadership capacity and ensured the sustainability of cultural transformation. We felt we needed to "go slow to go fast." We knew that creating cultures of thinking was unlike other educational initiatives that districts had been involved with in the past. We had to crack the mindset of "teacher training" and "'rollouts." How do we build this differently? How do we help participants engage differently? How do we sustain the communication and support of these school leaders such that they are not *doing* a new program but, rather, *living* culture change? This endeavor requires internal champions working in schools to grow the ideas in a holistic way as they build capacity and internal structures to take the learning deeper over time. We wanted something systemic, rich, and sustained. I would later understand that we were exploring a corollary of CoT Principle #6 [see appendix E, "Six Key Principles of the Cultures of Thinking Project"]: For classrooms to become cultures of thinking for students, schools must become cultures of thinking for teachers, . . . *and districts must become cultures of thinking for leaders.*

To address these issues, we designed a Cultures of Thinking Leadership Foundations seminar. Meeting once a month for the first semester of the 2011–12 school year, school teams from across the county, each consisting of a principal along with one or two teacher leaders, came together to explore the four areas they would need to attend to in order to grow a culture of thinking in their schools: vision, tools, facilitation, and growth [see fig. 10.1]. Each full-day session concluded with an assignment for the school team to go back to their building and extend their own schoolwide conversation about teaching and learning. The design of this first stage was purposefully invitational, bringing more and more people into the conversation about what it means to have a culture of thinking. In this way, the leadership teams got to know their schools better, efforts would grow organically, and leadership teams would be positioned as colearners among the staff.

At the end of the four Leadership Foundations seminars, we asked school teams to self-assess their schools' readiness to engage in schoolwide efforts [see appendices F–H]. If schools decided to continue, they increased the size of their leadership teams and committed to move forward to the next offering, four days of School Leadership seminars specifically focused on exploring the eight cultural forces in depth. These four days were organized as two days back-to-back, with a two-month interval between to allow people to try out ideas and return to share experience. In some ways, the seminars reinforced old models of "training." However, constant emphasis on our language of "learning," "leadership," and "growing the conversation" helped counter this ingrained mindset with a new vision of cultural change.

NURTURING EARLY GROWTH

At the end of the first year, a new set of questions emerged: How do we keep it growing? What might be an effective way to support the school leaders' efforts to continue the cultural shifts? At the start of the 2012–13 school year, Oakland County launched a second round of fall Leadership Foundations seminars. At the same time, we invited the original leadership teams to meet for three Leadership Development seminars designed to strengthen leaders' understanding of the research, the concepts, and the strategies for leading cultural transformation. The principals and teacher leaders helped set the agenda of these seminars by framing their own leadership priorities and bringing student and teacher artifacts with which to reflect, analyze, and determine next steps. These seminars also strengthened the networking relationships across districts, a key feature of our grand conversation.

BUILDING DEEP ROOTS

In addition to the Leadership Development seminars, we organized a calendar of half-day CoT school tours and teacher labs. For the hosting educators, the preparations, the presentations, and the opening of doors for others are a form of job-embedded professional learning that supports teachers in articulating the wisdom of their practice while raising wonderings that can spur continued learning.

CoT School Tours

The tours are a great way to introduce colleagues to the ideas and principles that shape and support a culture of thinking—what it looks like and sounds like in action—while creating professional learning on many levels. Each visit consists of the following:

- Opening session
- Learning walk through the building
- Classroom observation
- Debrief with teacher
- Continued dialogue/Q&A
- Final wrap-up and additional walk time

For the visitors, the school tours allow teachers and administrators to explore what is possible. They have the chance to look closely at the emergence of cultural transformation occurring inside familiar schools.

Some school leaders bring along the team currently in the seminar in order to deepen their understanding of what it takes to create a schoolwide culture that promotes thinking. Others bring teachers who are not attending the seminars to purposefully strengthen their collaborative efforts to tailor their own schoolwide transformation—that is, to see a model not for replication but for guidance.

For the host school, teachers and principals comment on how hosting pushes them to revisit where they are in their journey, notice shifting practices, and better understand the impact on students. As Matt Jansen, principal of Wass Elementary in Troy, shared, "The most exciting part is knowing we will grow exponentially in the next year, as this CoT tour was an affirmation for our instructional team and motivation to keep pursuing and developing a CoT in our learning community."

CoT Teacher Labs

Lab learning enables colleagues to meet in small groups over time to observe, inquire, and reflect on teaching practices as they play out in real time in classrooms, creating collaborative action/study cycles. The three key roles in a lab—host, facilitator, and observers—work together to support a deepening understanding of the principles and practices of CoT.

Host teachers not only open their classrooms for colleagues to observe and document but also open their inner practices of instructional design and pedagogical decision making. They lead dialogues about problems of practice, theories, successful impact, and evidence. The goal is not for the host to put on a "show" of perfect practice but to provide a lesson in which the aim is to provoke and support thinking from which thoughtful discussion can ensue. The **facilitating teacher** takes the lead in designing and creating the lab experience: contacting participants, establishing norms for observation, and ensuring that the debrief stays on topic. The facilitating teacher guides and shapes the postobservation conversation, often using thinking routines and protocols to make everyone's thinking visible. The facilitating teacher balances encouragement with pushing the observers to own their learning and commit to specific new actions. The **observing teachers** commit to active participation in the process and come with their own questions about developing and sustaining a culture of thinking in their individual classrooms and throughout their schools.

In preparing for a teacher lab, teachers and administrators partner to define the goals for lab learning. For example, a lab may focus on better understanding how discourse supports thinking or how documentation makes thinking visible, on learning a particular thinking routine, or on fostering student independence. In these early preparations, the facilitator and host meet to design the lab experience with attention to preobservation, observation, and postobservation activities.

The **preobservation** component of the lab sets the tone and focus for the day. Teachers spend time collectively grounding themselves in the focus of the lab, reading related research materials, setting up tools they will use during and after the observation, and understanding the context of the classroom instruction they will observe. The time together before entering into the classroom observation can result in deeper engagement, richer observation, and greater understanding for all.

In the **observation,** the host teacher focuses on the instruction of his or her students, the students engage in the tasks while ignoring the observers, and the observing teachers carefully move about at the periphery of classroom activity. However, there are possibilities for adaptation in the roles of the lab participants. Depending on the purpose of the lab, a host teacher might invite the observing teachers to interact with the students or to try out a strategy the group studied in preobservation. The facilitating teacher's role in the observation is twofold: (1) to serve as a model of observation and documentation skills and (2) to serve as a process facilitator, nurturing the commitment to silence or encouraging interaction while tending to the time and leading the group out of the classroom when appropriate.

The basic structure of a **postobservation** session generally comprises

- **Observing teachers** silently developing their notes from the observation. The host teacher joins the group after handing off classroom responsibilities.
- **The facilitating teacher** leads and documents the group's sharing out of "noticings," the thinking the observation provoked in observers, and the questions it raised. The host teacher is encouraged to remain silent, listen deeply, take notes, and receive the "gifts" of the observing teachers' noticings.

- **The host teacher** extends the group's inquiry by responding to the whole list of thoughts and questions raised by the observation, organizing thoughts and clustering ideas as is helpful to his or her own reflection.
- **The facilitating teacher** guides the group's inquiry with connections back to preobservation frameworks, research, and instructional materials. The facilitator then transitions the group to focus on individualized insights, implications, and goal setting, and to next steps.

In these conversations, the language of many thinking routines gets used. Teachers talk of seeing, wondering, connections, extensions, puzzles, challenges, and "I used to think . . . Now I think . . ."

TENDING THE GARDEN FOR A LONG LIFE

As more schools become involved, the issue of ensuring depth and sustainability becomes paramount: How do we keep it growing? What might be an effective way to support the school leaders' efforts to continue the cultural shifts? How do we create thinking spaces for teachers beyond the seminar experiences?

Answers to these questions are emerging. Principals talk about their eagerness to have more opportunities to dialogue with other principals about their role in supporting the schoolwide development of the eight cultural forces. "We just want time to talk with one another," they tell me. They also say, "As we engage with the cultural forces in the classrooms and across the school, it helps to talk with others who are also trying to support teachers and students while helping families understand the changes we are making." Two new opportunities emerged as a result of these conversations: Dialogue Circles and the Design Studio, which we began in the 2013–14 school year.

CoT Dialogue Circles

These study groups were conceived to be quite simple in structure and commitment, operating as opportunities for continuous networking, support, and new learning. Each Dialogue Circle comprises eight to twelve school leaders, across three different schools and at least two different districts. During the first session, the members got reacquainted and began articulating the interests, needs, and wonderings that might serve as a shared agenda for forming subgroups. Study groups commit to meeting face-to-face at least three times during the year. Two additional opportunities were offered: (1) facilitation of ways for them to stay connected online and (2) creation of a learning fair experience at the end of the school year for all Dialogue Circles to come together to make visible their experience during the year and reflect on the growth of the culture of thinking in their schools.

As the Dialogue Circles' outside friend and facilitator, I find myself watching the cultural forces at work in shaping a culture of thinking for adults: creating the *opportunity* for school leaders to organize into study groups, encouraging the use of thinking *routines* and *interactions* that are supporting the other CoT professional learning experiences (structured dialogues, learning walks, guided observations), and suggesting *environments* (hosting schools, classrooms, and face-to-face events). These are cultural forces I had a strong hand in planning to kick off the school leaders' hunger for more time to learn with and from each other. The more indirect impacts of *expectations, language, modeling,* and *time* seem left to the individual circles as they become active groups and create interschool visits and dialogues.

CoT Design Studio

Through my conversation with teachers, the idea of providing time to plan for and create powerful learning opportunities emerged. I wanted this to be more than just "planning time," however. It needed to be creative and imaginative. Pulling together a small team of professional learning facilitators who might offer creativity and energy, we set out to build a very different kind of "workshop" opportunity for teachers. Drawing on the best of what a traditional art studio might offer, and infused with ideas from participant-driven conferences sometimes referred to as "unconferences," we designed a new opportunity specifically to support a key driver in the growth of classroom culture: a teacher's instructional design efforts.

On four days across the school year, the CoT Design Studio is "open," 10 a.m. to 8 p.m., with the invitation to all teachers having at least an introductory grounding in CoT concepts and principles. Participants are encouraged to bring their design goals, tasks, and projects, and to plan for their own time. Depending on their release time, teachers might come for an hour or all day. The physical environment of the studio emphasizes visibility, flexibility, comfort, and inspiration with large group tables; small group tables; a circle of chairs without a table; high-toppers with laptops; two large screens, complete with back channeling, Twitter feeds, and studio announcements; and supply tables filled with paper, markers, and creativity playthings like windups, play dough, and squoosh toys. The walls are filled with reminders of the cultural forces and the six principles of CoT. Participants are encouraged to mark their table talk (for example, "Math", "Elementary ELA", "Secondary Science") as an open invitation so that teachers from other schools with similar design interests might drop in, sit down, and collaborate.

Since the CoT Design Studio idea is still quite new, we are constantly looking to create value-add opportunities that carry a strong message that studio time is about refining one's practice. We are working on the development of anchor events across the day that offer an opportunity for teachers to break from their design work for a short while and join a different conversation that might involve sharing videos, a "fishbowl" observation of teachers' designing for visible thinking, a "speed dating" session so that colleagues with similar interest can find each other, an "Ignite Talk" from a teacher on a CoT-related topic, or short panel Q&A sessions.

REFLECTIONS OF A GARDENER

The work my collaborators and I have engaged in is that of planting, cultivating, and tending to the efforts of educators in pursuit of thoughtful classrooms. The gardening metaphor serves me well as I think about the challenge of going to scale. Yes, it begins with seeds and plantings—that is, getting started with routines, reading *Making Thinking Visible*, and viewing video clips of what it looks like to engage students in thinking. However, I believe that our efforts to plant seeds have been different for having attended to the preparation of the garden itself; that is, our early, iterative conversations about preparing the leadership in schools focused us on ensuring the sprouting seeds. The garden stakes of early implementation helped us develop a strong enough roothold to actually produce schoolwide transformations.

Gardeners know that soil hardened by time and tough conditions will only allow seeds to sit on the surface and risk being blown away by winds of program rollouts and short-term training sessions. We also know that scattering lots of seeds will produce some yield, perhaps even lots of yield, but of what quality? Watching what is happening in Oakland County schools as a few seeds are carefully planted into prepared soil, and growth is nurtured, not accelerated, I see that ideas spread in their own time. We see the rich diversity of cultural transformation school by school. The pH balance of the soil may vary, but there are cultivating hands, leading hands, prepared to respond with new supports, new supplements.

This metaphor of gardening seems particularly helpful when one considers differences between organic home gardening and mass-produced engineered gardening. We are watching growth spurts that are possible when we patiently tend to some young plants with a bit more water, others on a different watering schedule, some needing pruning, others additional mulching. We are beginning to see what is possible when we move away from uniform, widespread fertilization and irrigation aimed at treating all growth as the same, and embracing the organic development of deeper understanding of teaching and learning, and thoughtful action for our students in classrooms.

Building a Vision across a School District

Rod Rock, Superintendent
Clarkston Community Schools, Michigan

Recently I received an email from a high school student in our district. His comments were straightforward and to the point, "I know that you are determined to create the education environment as a place of passion and a genuine love of learning. So I emailed you to just say the vision you have for the future of the education system is plain awesome and it is a vision that I really do agree with." Each time I receive a communication like this from a teacher, principal, parent, or student, I have a difficult time believing that it has only been four years since the Clarkston Community Schools' journey toward a culture of thinking began. I witnessed its birth and first steps, heard its first words, and saw mindsets, attitudes, and the culture of the district change.

In my experience, competitiveness, rote learning, large amounts of practice work, and multiple-choice tests are the norm in schools, while collaboration, deep thinking, and demonstrations of understanding are the exceptions. In my previous role as a director of curriculum, I had visited schools engaged with Cultures of Thinking and witnessed firsthand the depth of students' thinking, the effects on teachers' practices, and the strength of the learning environments. I sensed that this work was deeply personal and altered teachers' perceptions and beliefs. In these schools, standardized test scores were strong, yet they were not the focus of the curriculum, professional development, planning, or teaching. Instead, students were asked to think with what they know, solve problems, communicate effectively, collaborate, infer, summarize, consider multiple points of view, and make connections between ideas; thus they were well prepared for the tests. These visits convinced me that learning to think well represented the true purpose of schooling in the twenty-first century.

In fall 2010, I accepted the position of superintendent of the Clarkston Community Schools in Clarkston, Michigan. I felt that this was my chance to take learning to an entirely new level. I knew without question that the Clarkston Schools must become cultures of thinking. At my first opportunity to address the entire staff, I wore a hat, blue jeans, work boots, and a sweatshirt. I dimmed the lights in the auditorium, sat on the corner of the stage in a spotlight, and told a story of how I wanted learning to feel for the students and staff of Clarkston. In my presentation were rock-n-roll songs, video clips, and pictures of children. This was not what staff expected from a superintendent, and likewise, this was not the story of learning they had previously heard. I sent a clear message that the environment for learning was our first priority. I put on my fishing hat that morning and cast into the deep water of cultivating and fostering a culture of thinking.

Henceforth, this became our collective purpose. We sought to include everyone in this endeavor—from the district administration, to parents, to the extended community. During initial meetings with my administrative team, we established our goals and objectives for the upcoming year, and set our strategic direction. Where do we want to be? How will we get there? How do we measure our progress? These meetings were extremely important to clearly define the purpose of what we were attempting and to establish realistic goals in a defined time frame within our district's capacity for implementation. As principals were to become leaders of a culture of thinking in their schools, I sought their input in building consensus on our direction, which also enabled them to communicate expectations clearly to their staff.

At the same time, I set clear expectations for the principals. They were to lead, participate in, and model a culture of thinking. Whenever we gathered teachers together to discuss creating a culture of thinking, the building principals were present and actively engaged. At the same time, I understood that principals must lead according to their own personalities and strengths. I encouraged and allowed them to innovatively create cultures of thinking in their schools. We did not standardize implementation or follow a checklist.

Our next step into creating cultures of thinking was a systemic exploration of its concepts, led by principals and central office administrators. We identified books and materials that would allow us to develop our understanding. Teachers engaged on a monthly basis in book talks, group study sessions, and peer reflections. The ideas spread rapidly. It wasn't long before teachers began utilizing thinking routines. Touring schools, in and out of the district, became a valuable tool in understanding learning environments.

Teachers quickly came to understand the power of a culture of thinking, and we entered the next phase: consistently pressing for thinking in our classrooms. Instead of merely asking students to add details to their writing or memorize historical events, teachers challenged students' thinking to build their dispositions or habits of mind. With practice over time, students began to demonstrate good thinking. Their interactions changed from advocating points of view and being the first to give an answer to listening for understanding and building on others' ideas. Teachers noticed these changes and reinforced them by asking deeper questions, seeking evidence for conclusions, and expecting students to reason beyond the obvious.

We also sought to build an understanding of Cultures of Thinking with parents. Late in our first year, each school hosted visits, allowing parents to go into classrooms and see how differently students were experiencing education. In our second year, schools altered their traditional curriculum nights to reflect CoT values. In the process, we engaged parents directly in thinking routines, providing them tools and suggestions they could use to support our vision. In addition, I have sought to share our vision for learning beyond the schools' walls. Regularly, I attend Rotary, Optimist, and Chamber of Commerce meetings where I share videos of our students engaged in thinking. I talk with them about my philosophy and our school district's mission: *to cultivate thinkers, learners, and positive contributors to a global society.* I tell our community about the research that supports this work and how it is essential for each of our students to learn to use her or his mind well in order to thrive in the twenty-first century.

In order to build capacity for large-scale change within our school system, our teachers gather together for two hours, twice each month, as we delay the start of the school day. Eight times each year, we host daylong professional learning sessions. Herein, we assign teachers to interdisciplinary teams, and ask them to bring with them examples of students' thinking and to offer constructive feedback to one another via the use of protocols. This time is precious and powerful in creating a culture of thinking. Over the four years of our CoT transformation, whenever we get together as a staff—whether principals, teachers, bus drivers, or custodians—we engage them through thinking routines. We collectively ponder big ideas, examine the cultural forces, and monitor our thinking via the understanding map. What we as leaders model—the language we use, how we allocate time, the structures and strategies we utilize, the feedback we offer, the content of homework, and how we group our learners—is a reflection of our values.

Beyond just transforming our school system, we are strong advocates for equity of educational opportunities the world over. We believe that every child requires the best possible education, regardless of her or his abilities, social status, or zip code. Toward this end, we take groups of parents, principals, and school board members to our state capitol and to Washington DC to share our philosophy of education with legislators. We call our policymakers and send them letters. We believe that we educators are best informed as to policies that will affect our schools, children, communities, and teachers. We cannot sit idly and wait to react to punitive and ill-conceived policies and an overemphasis on standardized test scores. We must inform and advocate.

Often it is asked of me as the superintendent of schools, How do you measure a culture of thinking? How do you know it is working? To be honest, it is not difficult. As I travel around our district, I constantly encounter living evidence of its work. Beth Rogers, one of our fifth-grade teachers, is a terrific example. Early in the year, Beth engaged her students in the Sentence-Phrase-Word thinking routine. She asked them to listen to a song by Dolly Parton and to list thoughts that captured the song's meaning. Students then shared their thinking with a partner and the entire class. As I watched Beth and her students, I felt a calm confidence. They knew the routine and were able to utilize it effectively. The language of thinking was evident. What's more, those observing could not differentiate between the students who excelled and those who struggled with learning. Every child contributed.

A formerly skeptical parent told me recently of the changes she has observed in her daughter: "This Cultures of Thinking work has truly changed my child's attitude toward school. Her teachers are asking her to think much more deeply, and she is engaged like never before." One elementary school principal, Nancy Mahoney, described to me how CoT was affecting students, "When we ask our students to make their thinking visible through routines, it seems safe. Everyone in the classroom feels that their thoughts matter. Students are amazed with each other's thinking and perspectives. Thinking routines allow children to creatively and uniquely express themselves."

CoT is transformative. It alters people, minds, perceptions and beliefs, classrooms, and schools. It feels different now to be a learner or a teacher in Clarkston. Ideas spread organically. Accordingly, our environment for learning is forever altered. The change is much more powerful and deep than I could have ever imagined. We have set out to change the purpose of education—for kids to think and to use their minds well; to discover how each child is smart, where she or he fits, what she or he can contribute, and how her or his passions can become lifelong pursuits. We are telling a new story of learning. This is just the beginning of Clarkston's CoT journey. We have a lifetime to go.

Learning Together for the Long Haul

Adam Scher, Principal
Way Elementary
Bloomfield Hills, Michigan

As an educator, I've often witnessed, been an accomplice to, or served as the originator of a change process. There is an intoxicating energy to the process as well as a combined sense of hope and fear. But what is the impetus for change at a school that has been highly successful along traditional lines of schooling? What is it that we can do better? Where is it that we want to take students, and ourselves, as learners and thinkers? How do we connect our deeply held beliefs to the exploration of new practices and ideas?

Without using these exact questions, in hindsight, they were probably the questions driving our school improvement team. As we contemplated change, we began taking stock of the practices, protocols, and procedures that were already in place and deeply valued by us collectively. After identifying those things, we knew that we also had to name what was not happening in our classrooms and where our thinking might be challenged. As a school, we saw engagement as an affective quality, something visible on the outside. Collectively, we did not view engagement as a cognitive endeavor. Although we asked good questions, we didn't understand that different types of questions could be leveraged to arrive at deeper thinking and understanding. We valued student thinking—that is, as long as it was thinking that we felt comfortable with. In short, our teaching was safe. We frequently failed to create a productive struggle for our students. Our teaching didn't provoke in the manner of the word's Latin origin, *provocare*, meaning "to call forth." In our search for an instructional approach that would challenge and push us while respecting the strengths we had already developed, we came across the Visible Thinking project at Harvard Project Zero and began to learn about the Cultures of Thinking work to which it is connected.

LEARNING TOGETHER

As we began preparations to launch this new instructional approach, I tried incorporating routines into our professional development as well as during staff meetings. I like to think I would never ask teachers to do something that I wouldn't do myself, so I felt it important that I learn with them, take risks, and show that thinking routines were something we could use together as adult learners. Trying to mimic what I had seen at a workshop, I tried using the 3—2—1 Bridge thinking routine around the concept of umami, the fifth taste in food that is not sweet, sour, salty, or bitter. The routine flopped miserably. At least I thought it was the routine, until I came to understand that the flop was directly correlated to poor lesson design on my part. Using the 3—2—1 Bridge routine requires activating prior knowledge or connection making through metaphor. My use of that routine was not appropriate. There was no prior knowledge on umami among the audience, and they had no metaphors guiding their thinking. Furthermore, I never connected umami to the larger world. What role does umami play in cooking? How does it interact with the other four types of taste? What is worth knowing about umami? I had done nothing more than an activity with staff. The best I could take away from our time together was that I introduced and defined the word umami.

Something beautiful came out of the disaster, however. It was something that we witnessed over and over again the first two years. By employing a process to deconstruct our teaching when using a thinking routine, our staff learned and grew as a culture of thinking. We became students of our teaching and not just implementers of someone else's ideas. We soon found that we learned more through our flops than when the results were exactly what we expected. There were only two conditions as we moved forward: everyone must try out routines and everyone must report out his or her findings. A pact of trust formed as we learned to take risks and not be afraid of making mistakes.

The first year created great excitement as teachers shared their epiphanies and wonders. One teacher exalted that she had never heard such rich discussion before. Another noted the almost immediate impact of language change in her classroom. Students were connecting their thinking to each other and agreeing and disagreeing with each other's viewpoints in a new, respectful manner. All credit goes to the modeling in which each teacher was engaged. A third teacher was astonished at hearing and viewing the thinking of students identified as needing learning support. The routines had created new avenues, portals for students to creatively share thinking. The walls of our classrooms and hallways began to tell a story of learning and not simply the work of school. Parents came to understand through informative meetings and classroom exhibitions that we weren't just covering content; we were teaching for understanding. This was good work we were involved in. This is what authentic engagement looked like. This was learning that involved consequential change.

As part of our learning, teachers created videos showcasing thinking routines to share and discuss as a school. Each film included an introductory segment highlighting the teacher's thinking behind the lesson design, what the teacher hoped to uncover by using the routine, the focus of the lesson, and anticipated challenges. The videos concluded with the teacher's reflections. These videos were shared during professional development sessions, and the feedback was rich. Praise could be heard regarding pieces of the lesson that should be preserved. Some raised questions, suggestions, and concerns where the lesson might be improved. Some found connections between what they were watching and their own experiences. Some focused on the types of questions the teachers in the videos were asking. A celebratory current ran through the room at what was being accomplished, and a veteran staff member was literally in tears from the powerful teaching and emotion the videos evoked. My experiences tell me that teachers teaching other teachers are always the most effective form of professional development.

MOVING OUT OF OUR COMFORT ZONE

Our momentum slowed a bit during years two and three as the focus shifted from the use of thinking routines to asking ourselves, What is the role of the adult as a learner and a facilitator in a culture of thinking? How could we possibly expect our students to engage in reflection if we were not constantly modeling what good reflection looks like? We instituted monthly reflective journals as a vehicle to capture our thinking as adults. This proved to be a more challenging request than anticipated. I was shocked when asked by a teacher what she should write about as a reflection. It seemed obvious that to name the topic for her would defeat the entire purpose of the journal: to share her thinking and not mine. However, this confusion and discomfort wasn't just the concern of one teacher; it was the concern of most. Acquiescing to the use of a formalized structure, we formatted the journal to name the thinking routine tried, the context of the lesson, and the reflection on and documentation of the experience.

Initially, most teachers' responses were short and limited in terms of introspection. We were in a state of relapse, and resentment was brewing. If we had proverbially left Kansas when we moved to a new instructional approach, we had left planet Earth when we set out to reflect on our pedagogical practices. The easy thing to do would have been to eliminate the reflective writings, but then we wouldn't be creating a culture of thinking among the adults. How could we expect students to reflect on their learning if we weren't courageous enough to go there ourselves? We had to take ownership of the reflection process, both individually and collectively, so that we could understand the wonderful instruction taking place. This became a nonnegotiable. Prompts for writings were offered up, and individual meetings were held to flesh out writing ideas.

Sometimes, when the benefits of a practice can't be readily seen, it's important to take a leap of faith until they appear. I wish I could say there was a singular epiphany that inspired teachers to change their view of reflecting on their teaching. Instead, there were a series of small moments, a rebuilding of trust, and the passage of time that allowed us to reconnect with our greater purpose. The analytical reflections gradually went deeper and deeper until one teacher finally said, "Why are you forcing this structure on us? We want to be free to discuss our thinking." I couldn't agree more. When doing something over and over again, isn't it only human to want to put our own spin on things? to play with form and function? to strive for new aesthetic heights?

Last week, I was reading a batch of reflections, and a two-page response caught my interest:

> It appears that [we] teachers are comfortable designing thinking routines and working toward developing a culture of thinking for students within the walls of our classrooms. But what happens outside the classroom? Are we exhibiting the behaviors we are trying to cultivate in students during our interactions with colleagues and parents? Are we exhibiting these behaviors when we examine how we deliver our curriculum?
>
> - What is it that I hope to see in teachers?
> - What behaviors do I believe that I am demonstrating that support a culture of thinking?
> - Can teachers teach thinking if they are not thinkers themselves?
> - Do we behave as thinkers in our home environment?

The teacher concluded her reflection with a quote from John Shook [2008]:

"What my experience taught me that was so powerful was the way to change culture is not to first change how people think, but instead to start by changing how people behave—what they do . . . It's easier to act your way to a new way of thinking than to think your way to a new way of acting."

After reading this teacher's reflection, I needed to know more. What a perfect opportunity to ask, "What makes you write (say) that?" Her response was illuminating as she asked, "Are we just teachers of thinking, or do we live thoughtful lives?" I pressed her for more by asking what that might look like. "Well, I suppose," she started, "if we valued being a thinker, we would talk differently as well as changing the way we listen to one another. We would probably pause before responding and take some time to reflect on how effective our interactions are." She continued, "We would hold ourselves accountable to the same expectations we have of our students. And we would create our own productive struggles to engage in." In essence, she had defined what a culture of thinking looks like and named very specifically how the cultural forces play out in an organization. I've never met a great teacher who was satisfied, and the beauty of her dissatisfaction is a measure of what has grown at our school. This conversation could not have occurred without the learning that has taken place over these past six years.

THE RESIDUALS

Our journey—including the launch, steps, and missteps—of becoming a culture of thinking is well into its sixth year now. Like anyone who has been on a journey of change and development, I ask myself, What has held? and What can't hold? In education, there's a type of entropy that makes systems run down when energy is not there to drive them. Perhaps it's why so many "programs" come and go in our field, leaving educators dizzy if not schizophrenic in terms of vision and fit. Creating a culture of thinking is not a program. There is no thinking involved when you hear the word "program." Creating a culture of thinking is being purposeful and artful in an infinite way. It's why teachers became teachers.

The residuals, the things that have held during our change process, are many. For me as an administrator, the power in creating a culture of thinking has transformed the way I make classroom observations and conduct post-observation conversations. Now, everything revolves around the cultural forces. Conversations in the classroom and with staff are richer than in the past. In the classroom, I see students engaged with big ideas. They're making connections, reasoning, observing, identifying complexity, and empathizing, among other things, collectively. When thinking is made visible, learning is inevitable. What cannot hold in our school is passivity toward learning, dependency, and a focus on mere compliance. Those are remnants of our past. Our view of school has changed, and our thinking has never been more vibrant, vital, and yes, visible.

Creating Opportunities

Ellen Cale, Visible Thinking Coordinator
Troy School District
Troy, Michigan

My district's interest in creating cultures of thinking began in 2010. At that time, administrators across the district began to plan for implementing the Common Core Standards (CCS). Seeking best educational practice for developing the deep thinking and understanding that students would need to meet the rigorous demands of the CCS, the group studied and considered research from a variety of sources. That search eventually led to the research and development work being done at Harvard Project Zero around Visible Thinking and Cultures of Thinking (CoT).

The idea of creating a culture of thinking in our schools fit another need as well. In reaction to the economic recession of the time, the State of Michigan drastically cut educational funding. As a result, the Troy School District was forced to do some deep pruning of programs. One casualty was the Gifted and Talented program. It was hoped that Visible Thinking routines set within the broader context of creating a culture of thinking in every classroom would become the key differentiation strategy as well as bring twenty-first-century learning to classrooms. A teacher coach position was created with the intent to continue facilitation of differentiated instruction as well as coordinate the adoption of Visible Thinking routines across three elementary schools. This role became mine, and my journey began.

FIRST STEPS

Knowing the anxiety that the introduction of new strategies and curriculum adoptions can provoke among teachers, I wanted to make it easy for teachers to embrace the CoT philosophy and practices. I wanted things to go smoothly and hoped thinking routines would be the structures that would provide the "how to" that would help teachers understand the value and possibilities of building cultures of thinking in their classrooms. I eagerly incorporated routines into my first presentations to schools, modeling their integration with district curricula. However, my efforts to paint a picture of practice in broad strokes to those larger, reluctant audiences didn't have the result I intended:

- Some teachers integrated routines into their teaching practices superficially.
- Others believed they were already "doing" these strategies and changed nothing.
- Some tried a couple of routines and checked Visible Thinking off their "to do" lists.
- Still others complained, "I don't have time in my day for this" or "This is not appropriate for my students."

I realized I was giving teachers the same old rollout of a new bag of tricks, and they responded as they always had. Something new was needed, something that would allow us to go deeper, to reach all teachers and actually build understanding. Over time, a more effective approach emerged that both built the vision of a culture of thinking and facilitated the ongoing learning of teachers.

GOING DEEPER

Collectively, we came to the realization that the principal and leadership team at each school must be actively and consistently involved in setting a vision and presenting the big picture in terms of philosophy and practice to their colleagues at staff collaboration meetings. This wasn't something I could do for them as a coordinator. Although the school leadership groups might turn to me to help plan for or participate in these meetings, the school leadership team best understands staff culture and can create the most powerful presentations for their peers. These schoolwide sessions provide important opportunities for teachers to delve into the compelling reasons why thinking and understanding are crucial to learning. It also provides a great forum to launch into investigation of the eight cultural forces, explore such issues as how to make student thinking visible throughout the building, study new routines, and share successes and challenges.

To build on and deepen the work done as a whole school, principals and teacher leaders began creating opportunities for me to coach grade-level teams. This enabled me to meet teachers where they were in their practice and to tailor conversations toward common curriculum goals in the context of each grade level. Teaching teams plan together for integrating the thinking routines, questioning strategies, and supporting language into their daily plans. Team members hold each other accountable as well as support each other in their efforts.

By listening to teachers in this small-group format, I find it easier to accommodate their specific needs. For instance, when discussing the Color-Symbol-Image routine in one meeting, a teacher said in exasperation, "I just don't understand how to do this with my students." Capitalizing on that moment, I set a time to visit her classroom and model that routine for her.

I find that as I facilitate these smaller groups, I am able to shift the conversation from "how to" instruction to guiding teachers to reflect on the cumulative impact that regularly doing routines has on student thinking and the classroom culture. Thus we keep the focus on the goal, creating a culture of thinking and learning, rather than on the means, using thinking routines and other strategies. As a result, teachers become active learners, and comments have changed from "I don't have time for this" to "My students are thinking and responding in ways I never could have imagined!"

DEEPER STILL

One principal in the district began this school year by challenging teachers to commit to a personal growth goal of selecting two thinking routines and using them regularly throughout the year. The teachers were asked to document student growth in thinking and understanding by keeping work samples, looking at the thinking within the work, and building ladders of assessment to guide these reflections and subsequent teaching strategies. To support teachers, the principal carved time from mandatory staff meetings for us to meet with each grade-level team on a monthly basis.

We began with a series of meetings, not about how to do the routines, but analyzing where Visible Thinking routines fit into lesson planning. In the Harvard-Smithsonian's documentary on students' misconceptions in science, the commentator says, "We always assume that if teachers teach, students will learn, but students have minds of their own." This quote led to conversations about the need to have strategies in place to know what students are thinking in order to more effectively assess and plan for their learning.

We presented excerpts from *Making Thinking Visible* about classroom culture and used protocols and routines to frame discussions that led to discoveries as to how thinking routines enhance the learning process.

As teachers used their chosen routines regularly, the focus of our monthly meetings became the changing classroom culture. We began to note how changes that were once subtle were becoming prolific and powerful. A second-grade teacher told me in amazement that she was noticing at the beginning of new learning opportunities that students were commenting to each other, "I wonder what kind of thinking we will be doing today?" The power for her was how students were taking charge of their learning and not waiting to be told what to do. Other teachers have commented that they feel they are talking less and listening more: "I hear students automatically explaining why they said something, and then other students become engaged by respectfully agreeing or disagreeing and telling why."

To explore this shift in our own teaching more deeply, we looked to others also engaged in CoT. The Stories of Learning project in Melbourne, Australia, was one source of inspiration (www.storiesoflearning.com). Collectively we read Andrea Elliott's story, "The Journey to a Culture of Thinking." Andrea's journey of developing a culture of thinking at her school introduced teachers to the idea of developmental stages in the use of thinking routines. When teachers at my school identified that their integration of routines was moving into the "intermediate" stage of development, it generated a great deal of enthusiasm. Even more encouraging to them was the improvement in student engagement and thinking that was emerging. When teachers share class-room observations, a common thread is how students who were once reluctant to have their voices heard in class are now engaging in the conversation. "I see students who have not always been eager to have their voice heard in class now being more willing to share," one teacher said. "I think that hearing the thinking around them, seeing learning unfold by using routines, and having many opportunities to engage in conversation help them make more sense of their learning."

Concurrently, this school's leadership team created opportunities for the staff to gather and observe the LAST (Looking At Students' Thinking) protocol [see appendix D]. Monthly before school, "coffee" meetings were offered for teachers to voluntarily gather to share classroom successes and challenges and help each other find strategies for moving student thinking even deeper.

One of the teachers involved in these meetings summed up the journey thus far by noting, "This is truly a process that starts slowly and builds over time. This process creates a connected community of adult and student learners that think and share together to build deep and enduring thinking and understanding."

THE JOURNEY CONTINUES

The plan for this school is ongoing. Structured reflection by teachers on their own growth as well as growth in student thinking is constantly revisited. To accomplish this, we use grade-level meeting times to look at samples of student thinking. Protocols structure conversations around finding the thinking and identifying strategies for growing it. The leadership team has created a "Ladder of Assessment" for the thinking move Reasoning with Evidence [see appendix I] to give teachers guideposts for deepening student thinking.

Another giant step has been the implementation of job-embedded professional development through teacher labs as a way to grow cultures of thinking by giving teachers the opportunity to observe a picture of practice in a fellow teacher's classroom (for one example of how a teacher lab facilitated learning, see http://blog.oakland.k12.mi.us/jepl/2013/05/30/). This experience brings together one teacher from each elementary school in the district to engage in facilitated conversations and a classroom observation. Observing teachers have commented on the positive energy of enthusiastic teachers and engaged students. They come away with greater understanding that a culture of thinking goes way beyond the routines.

The strategies that cultivate cultures of thinking in the elementary schools in my school district share three intertwined success factors:

- Principals set the vision and create time and space for learning and growth, while maintaining an interest and presence in all aspects of teacher and student learning.
- Teacher leaders share principles and pictures of practice with their peers, and plan events that bring staff together to learn, share, and grow.
- A teacher coach facilitates grassroots conversations and anticipates and arranges for the support and learning opportunities needed for teacher growth and continuous leadership development.

These principles were validated for me recently when one of the teachers who initially had been dismissive and negative about the practices of CoT, arguing that they were time consuming and insignificant, expressed excitement to her colleagues about the changes she was experiencing in her own growth as a teacher, in her students' thinking, and in the culture of thinking in her classroom. With this type of commitment and planning, the vision of classrooms as cultures of thinking for students and of schools as cultures of thinking for teachers is becoming a reality.

Building the Capacity of Teachers to Teach One Another

Jim Reese, Director of Studies
Washington International School
Washington DC

An unfinished canvas—a work in progress, showing great potential—comes to mind when I think about the changes in our school as we build a culture of thinking. Holding on to that image has been helpful for me as I support teachers and guide this process. Over several years, we have experienced a rise in enthusiasm for, comfort with, and eventual expertise in using frameworks and tools, such as thinking routines, to strengthen teaching and deepen learning. Along the way, I have learned that each person must come to these ideas in his or her own time. As a result, this unfinished canvas has room for others to join in and make their mark.

After being part of efforts to improve teaching and learning in other schools, I have grown to understand that patience and persistence are crucial for any change initiative to achieve staying power. This is particularly true when we are talking about creating a culture of thinking. It requires much more of people than merely implementing a few new practices or tweaks to the curriculum. Past experiences have taught me important lessons about the need to let ideas take hold in an organic, grassroots way, combined with substantive, public support from key leaders in the school.

When a new head of school began at Washington International School (WIS) in 2007, he made a firm commitment to bring more rigor and cohesion to faculty professional development. Consequently, we began investing in teachers learning about a broad array of ideas around the development of thinking and understanding, especially those connected to the CoT project. This provided a variety of entry points for engagement. In other words, we invested in frameworks and tools that were complementary and that provided a common professional language for us to use across grade levels and subject areas. Thinking routines, in particular, proved to be accessible and relevant across the elementary, middle, and secondary divisions of the school.

Probably the most vital element in the success of this ongoing work has been building the capacity of teachers to teach one another and to share their enthusiasm for the ideas with colleagues and parents. It wasn't long before we had many teachers eager to lead workshops within the school and at education conferences. One high school teacher, who has presented multiple times, noted:

> Presenting has made me reflect more on my own practice. When preparing for a presentation, I have to gauge what has worked and not worked for me. During the workshop, the participants' questions and reasoning make me aware of the pedagogical choices I have made in my classroom, as well as the bridges I draw among thinking dispositions, thinking routines, and culture of thinking practices. After the workshop, evaluation forms are very enlightening, for there is always some unexpected comment. One participant once wrote, "I liked that [you] created a safe environment in which everyone could freely participate." It made me happy to read that, of course, but it also made me replay the workshop in my mind and wonder how I actually did that. In all cases, from beginning to end, it makes me more reflective.

Most recently at WIS, we have paid greater attention to the documentation of student and teacher thinking and learning. Technology has facilitated this process, of course, but more significant than the technology itself has been putting into place technology integration coordinators who understand the principles and practices around the development of a culture of thinking, who can guide teachers in thinking deeply about what they want students to understand, and who have the capacity to document, through audio and video, authentic learning experiences in and out of the classroom.

We have created an online video channel on which we post videos of teachers and students engaged in powerful learning and then reflecting on the process. One technology integration coordinator wrote about his learning:

> Documentation is not simply bringing a camera into a room and filming what's happening. It is more of a process than a product and typically works best when initiated by the teachers. It's more like storytelling when you examine all of its elements. It requires teachers to be extra thoughtful about their use of time and space and a willingness to be vulnerable and open to critique.

Another crucial element in moving toward developing a culture of thinking in the school has been the ongoing collaboration of teachers across grade levels and subject areas. For several years, we have had a number of learning groups that meet throughout the school year to explore what it means to teach and learn in a culture of thinking. Teachers self-select into these groups voluntarily and commit to meeting for an hour, at least twice a month. Each group has its own focus area, which shifts from year to year, as does the composition of each group. In the first two years, I facilitated each group, with the aim of cultivating teacher leaders who would take over the facilitation role. Now, in this our fourth year, most groups are led by teachers, with little need of guidance from me.

An early goal of each group is to build trust within the group so that everyone can be vulnerable—it's not about showing what you do well; rather, it's about delving into what you wish you could do better. Most groups begin the year by surfacing "problems of practice"—that is, issues about teaching and learning that have arisen. These questions become the driving force behind the conversations and investigations the groups pursue. This kind of conversation was not common in our school until recently. I would argue that it's not common in most schools, at least not in my experience. The use of protocols has facilitated deeper discussions, as has the modeling of thinking routines to explore the cultural forces in a classroom. The thinking routine See-Think-Wonder, for example, has proven to be quite a flexible routine in terms of its application in a variety of contexts.

One learning group this year is using an observation protocol that examines the cultural forces in classrooms. They formed themselves into small groups and are engaging in regular observations of their peers and in discussions about what they are seeing, hearing, and learning. One of the facilitators of that group reflected, "Collegiality and trust are built on validating each other's experiences and appreciating each other's challenges and achievements. An easy-to-use protocol for observation promotes openness and helps us to avoid judgment."

The group has developed some emergent understandings after several months of peer observations:

1. Awareness of thinking in the classroom is promoted when teachers think about what they are doing with other teachers who observe them.

2. It is quite useful to develop a mental collection of thinking routines to draw on when planning lessons or responding in class, but that collection shifts from context to context.

3. Documenting what we do and what we see each other do encourages reflection.

4. It is important to be rigorous in defining the specific kind of thinking we're aiming for with students.

One of our elementary school teachers, who has been facilitating a learning group and presenting workshops for several years, takes inspiration from a talk by David Perkins at a conference hosted by WIS in April 2010, in which he compared the development of a culture of thinking to a collection of elements that form a composition: "A culture of thinking evolves slowly, and it is important to recognize that time is needed to allow it to take root. While teachers might first grab onto thinking routines or protocols as activities to do in the classroom, they are things they add to their collection. Continued interaction with ideas about teaching and understanding and visible thinking brings connections. As the composition begins to form, there is a slow but definite shift in the way teachers teach and their students learn. Learning groups promote this continued interaction."

At WIS, we are excited about the successes that are readily visible through-out the school, even though certain challenges and frustrations arise each year. Teachers come and teachers go. Every time one of our solid practitioners leaves the school, I worry. Fortunately, we have been strategic about hiring new teachers open to these ideas. And we give them opportunities, early and often, to learn more. With a demanding International Baccalaureate (IB) Diploma Program, we have certain courses that are content heavy and so fast paced that teachers lament their limited ability to use these ideas as much as they'd like. Similarly, in our dual-language IB Primary Years Program in the elementary school, teachers have to collaborate carefully to ensure that these ideas are not lost among competing agendas. These challenges are ever present and aren't going to disappear. They are ongoing tensions that we must recognize and manage rather than resolve fully.

Over the years, I've noted that the best practitioners of these ideas are the teachers who embrace the challenges and see the frameworks and tools as means to bringing about better learning. Those who have shown indifference or resistance more often than not want to use the excuse of a jam-packed curriculum or an unwillingness to consider the role of complex understanding in a course to avoid taking on these ideas. The good news is that those showing resistance diminish in number every year; several years ago, we reached a critical mass of teachers who want these ideas to last. That has made a tremendous difference in the tenor of the school and our ability to focus collectively on deepening and enhancing the culture of thinking we have created. Of course, challenges and frustrations will keep the canvas unfinished. It can get messy at times. But the colors are getting deeper and richer.

Using Inquiry-Action Projects to Go Deeper

Mark Church, Cultures of Thinking Consultant
Working with Emanuel School and Masada College
Sydney, Australia

For a number of years, the leadership teams of Emanuel School and Masada College, two independent schools in the Sydney, Australia, metropolitan area, have worked to cultivate and promote rich cultures of thinking throughout their classrooms. Both schools formed teacher professional learning groups focused on making student thinking visible and experienced a reenergizing of many teachers as teacher collaboration deepened and student learning found itself as a mainstay in ongoing conversations. At the same time, both schools soon realized that simply instituting a set of practices—namely, thinking routines—was not enough to achieve the vision of schoolwide cultural change. They began to wonder: What else might we do to grow and develop our teachers' thinking about students' learning and deepen the culture of thinking being created? How might we provide rich, meaningful professional learning across both schools that would truly move the culture of thinking to the next level?

Reflecting on these questions together with the school leadership, we developed the idea of establishing a Cultures of Thinking Inquiry-Action Project Group. We knew that providing a safe, supportive, and thoughtful environment in which to pursue inquiry-action would be key to our success. To accomplish this, we needed to identify inquiry-action project study group members from volunteers from both schools. I would meet with this group three times throughout the year: first to launch the study at the beginning of the school year, next to check in collectively and refocus the projects midway, and finally to share their learning with one another at an end-of-year celebration. In between sessions, schools would provide support through ongoing study groups, each led by facilitators within the school whom I helped coach.

ESTABLISHING THE INQUIRY-ACTION PROJECT GROUPS

The following invitation was extended to all teachers at both schools to identify the nearly thirty volunteers of the first cohort:

Open to new ideas and perspectives on teaching and learning? Willing to give some actions a go in the classroom with students? Desire the opportunity to reflect on big puzzles, questions, and instructional efforts together with thoughtful colleagues from a variety of grade levels and subject areas? Eager to share your thinking and learning with a broader community of interested colleagues?

If you answered yes to these questions, then perhaps you'd like to join the Emanuel School and Masada College Cultures of Thinking Inquiry-Action Project Group this school year!

As I mentioned, we planned that the cross-school cohort would come together three times throughout the school year. The first session focused on individuals choosing and refining a question of personal relevance, related to puzzles they have regarding efforts to pay close attention to the thinking of the students they teach. For instance, David Camp, head of English at Emanuel School, felt great pressure to cover a huge amount of content in his English course and to help students prepare for high-stakes exams, and found it quite difficult to get his senior students away from a heavy reliance on him to get them through complex literature, especially Shakespeare. This overreliance on him as expert worried David, as this created an obstacle to students developing their own expertise. David's initial questions centered on how he might go about getting students to be more active and facilitate a sense of shared expertise in the classroom.

With this puzzle articulated, participants then identified a cultural force or two to closely examine in their own practice and around which to develop actions in order to provoke further reflection, be it deeper insights or further questions. A guided process for taking on this inquiry and generating possible actions set the stage for the inquiry-action projects. In David's case, he identified that he needed to create new *opportunities* and communicate different *expectations* for students to take on more of the direction of literature discussions. As a result, one action David chose to take was to have his seniors read a section of *Hamlet* outside of class and bring with them five quotes they thought captured the most critical ideas of the passage. In class, students were put into groups and asked to explain why the collection of quotes they brought were so important to the play.

THE IMPORTANCE OF ONGOING FACILITATION OF THE LEARNING

We knew at the outset of our planning that my three meetings with the cohort would not suffice to move this work to the next level they desired. Although both schools had highly capable directors of studies, it seemed necessary to create and support a cadre of dedicated facilitators at each school to shepherd small study groups of inquiry-action project participants. These facilitators would not only promote successful learning within the projects but also develop leadership capacity within each school. This group served as internal, on-the-ground champions of reflective professional learning conversations. They used protocols and processes to lead inquiry-action participants' dialogue once every two weeks based on the actions group members were undertaking in their classrooms.

I worked with facilitators on the use of protocols to help participants brainstorm through dilemmas, tune tentative plans, and reflect on classroom actions taken by participants in pursuit of their inquiry. As important as these techniques were, a crucial attribute for these internal champions was curiosity about the learning journeys of their peers. Consequently, we spent time together deepening our ability to listen to colleagues' reflections and developing our skills in asking the kinds of probing, reflective questions that might help a fellow colleague take on new actions he or she might not have even considered.

At each school, the teachers involved in the inquiry-action project were divided into smaller groups, each with its own facilitator. At the outset, we laid out an agreement that when study sessions convene, there had to be something real on the table to look at and learn from so that conversations wouldn't just circle around ideas in the absence of real classroom actions. What people tended to bring to their study group fell roughly into three categories: a dilemma, a plan in the making, or a collection of student work. Facilitators used Descriptive Consultancy, Tuning, or Looking At Students' Thinking (LAST) protocols to guide each session (see www.nsrfharmony.org for protocols). Regardless of what was "on the table," facilitators always made time for the group members to think individually about how various elements of the session's study related to their own inquiry-action project. In this way, a single teacher's "case" was explored in depth, but all teachers had a chance to use that case as a mirror to reflect on their own inquiry-action efforts.

In addition, our midyear session with participants from both schools served as an important check-in on the work. Opportunities were created for participants to reflect on their initial actions, refocus their inquiry questions, and generate possible next steps to take. At this time, it became clear that many participants seemed a bit paralyzed by all the inhibitors related to the puzzle they articulated: "Well, if the report cards don't change, then why bother?" "Well, the parents expect something different, so what's the point?" "Until the Board of Studies changes this, what can I really do?" Seeing that this was becoming a roadblock, we engaged in a Realm of Concern, Realm of Influence exercise (www.nsrfharmony.org). Participants laid out all of their concerns and then identified the concerns closest to their actual realm of influence. By bringing their awareness to what's actually in their control, participants began seeing breakthroughs in terms of actions forward, in spite of all the broader system or community challenges surrounding them.

CELEBRATING THE LEARNING

The last joint session was a celebration of learning, a sharing of insights and new questions that came up as a result of the projects undertaken by the group. Participants brought artifacts representing their inquiry-action process, documents of conversations, quotes from students, or examples of students' thinking. Exploring these artifacts created additional opportunities for peers to collaborate across schools, make connections between inquiry-action endeavors, and surface new questions for the group to consider around creating schoolwide cultures of thinking.

As we concluded our first year's efforts, I was very interested to see the way participants engaged with the cultural forces while engaging in their classroom actions. Frequently, participants would start examining one cultural force as an entry into their study, but once actions were taken and ongoing study and reflection conversations took place in collaboration with peers, they came out on the other side of their project really focused on an entirely different cultural force. One teacher, Clare Greenup of Masada College, whose central focus was on the development of agency and learning from mistakes, commented,

> What I thought was going to be all about opportunities turned out to be more about relationships/interactions and language. Before, relationships, for me,

were about getting on with the kids, being liked, respected, or kids feeling comfortable. Now I've come to realize that agency and ownership for learning isn't something I can simply bestow. Each child has to come to a personal realization that they know themselves and that they have within them the power to accomplish learning and guide their path—facilitated by the way I talked to them, the structure of my questioning, along with the openness and opportunities we created together.

Upon reflecting on the year's efforts with the facilitators, we noticed that many people seemed to initially get stuck on finding *the* right research question. However, we collectively came to realize that this kind of opportunity isn't about finding *the* right research question but about finding *a* right research question that can move actions and reflections forward. Often the first question people came up with wasn't really the question they truly cared about. The iterative nature of finding questions worth lingering with and taking action on is something we are taking into our new round of inquiry-action projects this coming year.

The inquiry-action projects allowed people to engage with the bigger purpose of creating a culture of thinking in their classroom. Until this point, the goal for many teachers seemed to be the mere implementation of routines. Identifying a puzzle around the broader notion of creating a culture of thinking in one's classroom and then using the cultural forces as entry points to explore these teaching and learning dilemmas really seemed to make the cultural forces something they learned *with* and *through* rather than something they learned about.

SAMENESS AND DIFFERENCE IN THE JOURNEY TO A CULTURE OF THINKING

As these six case studies illustrate, each school's journey to a culture of thinking is unique. There is no template, no mold to fall into. At the same time, there are common themes that emerge from which others can learn. In each of the cases, leaders were responsive to the four areas of attention laid out at the beginning of this chapter: vision, tools, facilitation, and growth. These elements worked dynamically together rather than appearing sequentially. Of particular note was how leaders constantly kept the bigger purpose of creating a culture of thinking in mind and kept reminding people of this vision.

Although almost all schools began their efforts with the implementation of thinking routines, thus giving teachers something concrete to begin doing right away, this was never an end itself. Ellen Cale recognized how her early attention to routines led some teachers to dismiss or superficially approach the development of a culture of thinking. Consequently, attention was put back on the vision rather than the tools. Mark Church, Alan Scher, and Jim Reese shared how they moved teachers' efforts beyond thinking routines to go more deeply into the cultural forces.

Four additional themes emerge from the cases that others interested in creating cultures of thinking should keep in mind: leadership, time, documentation, and ownership.

Individual teachers can certainly create powerful cultures of thinking in their classrooms; however, for schools to become cultures of thinking, leadership is important. This leadership is often distributed across a school, which promotes ownership, but the head of a district or a school has a special role to play. These individuals keep teachers focused on the vision, often amid competing demands and pressures that might divert attention. Leaders steer the grand conversation, to use Lauren Childs's term, to a culture of thinking and make room for teachers to dwell in this space. Leaders also bring in parents and community to broaden the vision and increase support for change.

All the cases reflect multiyear efforts and show the importance of time. Creating a culture of thinking is not the "thing we will do this year" but an ongoing goal for the long haul. Consequently, attention has to be paid not only to "How will we begin?" but also to "How will we push ourselves to the next level?" Simultaneously, there is the need to provide time for teachers' learning and in-depth study. Sometimes time can be carved out from existing meetings. Sometimes voluntary options are provided. In other instances, ongoing release time is needed so that teachers can really immerse themselves in study, reflection, and learning.

Documentation efforts relate to capturing and celebrating growth. At the same time, these efforts often provide a vehicle for learning. Rod Rock, Adam Scher, and Jim Reese shared how they produced videos to capture what teachers were doing and share with the larger community. These videos help to tell the story of learning happening in the school. Written reflections were also used to help teachers personally capture and become aware of the changes happening in their classrooms. Although the teachers at Way Elementary initially resisted this, they came to find it a valuable tool.

Finally, all six cases demonstrate the importance of allowing teachers to own the process of creating a culture of thinking. This means listening to teachers, engaging teachers in teaching one another, and providing avenues for teacher leadership. Doing so gives the efforts an organic, bottom-up spirit, which enables teachers to feel empowered. Teachers should never get the sense that "cultures of thinking" is something that is done to them. Creating a culture of thinking must always be a goal that individuals embrace to improve their teaching and advance the learning of their students. From this place, teachers can then support, push, and nurture the efforts of their colleagues as the school collectively grows into a culture of thinking, and the lives and learning of all are truly transformed.

APPENDIXES

APPENDIX A. MY REFLECTIONS ON THE LEARNING ACTIVITIES IN THIS CLASS

Date _____ Class Period: _____ Subject: _____

Rank your choices 1, 2, and 3.

#1 is what the class spent the most time doing, #2 for the next most, and then #3. In this class period, we spent ***MOST*** of our time . . .

	Looking closely at things, describing them, noticing details, or detecting patterns.
	Building our own explanations, theories, hypotheses, or interpretations.
	Reasoning with evidence and supporting our ideas with facts and reasons.
	Wondering, raising issues, and showing curiosity about what we are studying.
	Making connections between different things, to the world, or to our own lives.
	Looking at things from different perspectives and points of view to see things in a new way.
	Identifying the central or core ideas, forming conclusions, or capturing the essence of things.
	Digging deeply into a topic to uncover mysteries, complexities, and challenges.
	Organizing and pulling together ideas, information, notes, and experiences to make sense of them.
	Reflecting on where we are at in our learning and understanding to determine where to go next.
	Using and applying what we have been learning to solve new problems or create something original.
	Reviewing and going over information from the readings or previous class work.
	Reading, listening, or getting new information about the topic we are studying.
	Practicing the skills and procedures the class has already learned.

In this class, I was really pushed to think *(Circle one)*

NOT AT ALL   A LITTLE   SOME   A LOT

As a learner, it would have helped me if **I** had . . .

As a learner, it would have helped me if the **teacher** had . . .

APPENDIX B. LADDER OF FEEDBACK

4. Suggest
Make suggestions for improving the work. This step is sometimes blended with step 3: people state concerns and then offer suggestions for addressing them.

3. Question
Share your questions and concerns. Avoid absolutes: "What's wrong is . . ." Use qualified terms: "I wonder if . . ." "It seems to me. . ." Focus on ideas, products, or particular aspects of the work and not the person.

2. Value
Comment on the strengths of the work. Express what you like about the ideas or matters at hand in specific terms. Do not offer a perfunctory "Good, but . . . ," and hurry on to the negatives.

1. Clarify
Ask clarifying questions to be sure you understand the ideas or matters on the table. Avoid clarifying questions that are thinly disguised criticism or suggestions: "Have you thought of . . ."

APPENDIX C. SUCCESS ANALYSIS PROTOCOL

Powerful Learning Opportunities

This protocol is designed for small groups of three or four in which everyone takes a turn as a presenter while the rest of the group acts as questioners. There is no need for a facilitator, as groups can self-facilitate using the protocol prompts and times. Each round ends with the group documenting their learning, so someone should be assigned this role, or it may be rotated.

1. **Identify a success** (1 minute)
   Do a mental review of the lessons you have taught over the last year. Identify an example of a powerful learning opportunity from your own teaching. This should be an instance where you felt that students were highly engaged, actively involved in thinking, and building a robust understanding of the topic at hand. Most likely, this was a teaching occasion when you walked away wishing every class could be just like that.

2. **Reflect in writing** (5 minutes)
   Describe in writing the powerful learning opportunity you identified. Be as specific as you can about what was planned, what happened, how you and students responded, and so on. How was this experience different from other episodes of teaching you have had? Name those qualities, actions, or elements.

   Steps 3–6 are repeated until all members of the group have had a turn.

3. **Share the success** (4 minutes)
   Each person shares the story of the powerful learning opportunity he or she identified.

4. **Ask clarifying questions** (1–2 minutes)
   The listeners ask clarifying questions about the event. Clarifying questions are short, focused questions designed to elicit missing details and background information about the event. Generally, they can be answered in a sentence or a few words.

5. **Ask probing questions** (3–5 minutes)
   The listeners ask probing questions about the event. Probing questions are designed to get the presenter to reflect on, elaborate on, and build a greater understanding of the event. Good probing questions require introspection and lead to insights.

6. **Record criteria** (2–3 minutes)
   Extrapolating from the story and questioning, the group identifies and records the criteria or qualities of the event that seemed most important to its success. As each group member shares, new criteria are added to the list.

   The group holds a final reflection after all group members have shared.

7. **Reflect on application** (5 minutes)
   The group reflects on all the criteria of powerful learning opportunities that the group identified and discusses how each might be applied to their teaching. Groups might want to identify their top best-bets-for-success criteria and/or share their findings with other groups who have also been engaged with the protocol.

APPENDIX D. LOOKING AT STUDENTS' THINKING (LAST) PROTOCOL

Roles

Presenting teacher: Brings work to share, listens to the discussion, responds at the end
Facilitator: Keeps track of time, asks the lead questions for each phase, redirects as needed
Documenter: Records the group's discussion

1. Presenting the work (5 minutes)	Presenting teacher provides the context, goals, and requirements of the task.
	Ask clarifying questions that will help you understand and read the work.
2. Reading the work (5–10 minutes)	Read the work silently.
	Take notes for later comment.
	Categorize your notes to fit in with the stages of the protocol.
3. Describing the work (5 minutes)	What do you see?
	Raise one another's awareness of all the features of the work.
	Avoid interpretation and just point out what things can be seen.
4. Speculating about students' thinking (10 minutes)	Where in the work do you see thinking? What aspects of the work provide insights into students' thinking?
	Interpret the features of the work.
	Make connections to different types and ways of thinking.
5. Asking questions about the work (10 minutes)	What questions does this work raise for you?
	Frame questions to get at broad issues as well as specifics.
	Ask the question behind the question. Rather than "How long did this take?" ask, "This raises questions for me about the time needed to do this kind of work."
	NOTE: Presenting teacher does not respond to the questions at this point.
6. Discussing implications for teaching and learning (10 minutes)	Where might this work go next to further extend and build on students' thinking?
	Suggest practical possibilities and alternatives for the presenting teacher.
	Raise general implications that the work suggests for promoting students' thinking.
7. Responding to the discussion (presenting teacher) (5 minutes)	What have you as presenting teacher gained from listening to the discussion?
	Highlight for the group what you found interesting in the discussion.
	Respond to those questions that you feel need addressing by you.
	Explain briefly where you think you might now go with the work.
8. Reflecting on the protocol (5 minutes)	How did the process go and feel?
	Reflect on general observations.
	Notice improvements and changes since the last time the group used the protocol.
	Make suggestions for next time.
9. Thanking the presenting teacher, the documenter, and the facilitator	The group acknowledges everyone's contribution.
	Decide how the documentation will be shared, used, and archived for the group.
	Establish roles for the next meeting.

APPENDIX E. SIX KEY PRINCIPLES OF THE CULTURES OF THINKING PROJECT

1. **Skills are not sufficient; we must also have the disposition to use them.** Possessing thinking skills and abilities alone is insufficient for good thinking. One must also have the disposition to use those abilities. This means that schools must develop students' inclination to think and awareness of occasions for thinking as well as their thinking skills and abilities. Having a disposition toward thinking enhances the likelihood that one can effectively use one's abilities in new situations.

2. **The development of thinking and understanding is fundamentally a social endeavor,** taking place in a cultural context and occurring within the constant interplay between the group and the individual. Social situations that provide experience in communicating one's own thinking as well as opportunities to understand others' thinking enhance individual thinking.

3. **The culture of the classroom teaches.** It not only sets a tone for learning but also determines what gets learned. The messages sent through the culture of the classroom communicate to students what it means to think and learn well. These messages are a curriculum in themselves, teaching students how to learn and ways of thinking.

4. **As educators, we must strive to make students' thinking visible.** It is only by making thinking visible that we can begin to understand both what and how our students are learning. Under normal conditions, a student's thinking is invisible to other students, the teacher, and even to himself or herself, because people often think with little awareness of how they think. By using structures, routines, probing questions, and documentation, we can make students' thinking more visible, fostering better thinking and learning.

5. **Good thinking utilizes a variety of resources and is facilitated by the use of external tools to "download" or "distribute" one's thinking.** Papers, logs, computers, conversation, and various means of recording and keeping track of ideas and thoughts free up the mind to engage in new and deeper thinking and help ensure that our thinking doesn't get lost.

6. **For classrooms to be cultures of thinking for students, schools must be cultures of thinking for teachers.** The development of a professional community in which deep and rich discussions of teaching, learning, and thinking are a fundamental part of teachers' ongoing experience provides the foundation for nurturing students' thinking and learning.

APPENDIX F. LAYING THE FOUNDATION FOR A CULTURE OF THINKING

The following checklist can be a useful guide for discussion by each school's leadership team in determining readiness to advance the work developing a culture of thinking. However, we recognize that other factors may also play into decisions of timing and commitment. Some schools may want to delay until next school year or later to continue to grow internal interest and lay the foundation, which is fine.

In Place/ Completed	In Process/ Developing	Needs More Time/Attention	
			We as a leadership team are discussing CoT ideas beyond the sessions and are excited and interested in learning along with our teachers about what this can look like at our school.
			We are visiting classrooms and having (nonevaluative) conversations with teachers about the culture of the classroom in order to deepen our own understanding of classroom and school culture.
			We are beginning to try out some of the routines and protocols in staff meetings and classrooms.
			As a staff, we are having conversations about our students as thinkers and learners and the messages we are sending our students.
			We have thought about how CoT fits within the other programs and initiatives at our school and our overall vision of the kind of school we want to create so that CoT won't be viewed as just one more thing to try/do.
			We have devised a plan for how to facilitate and support the ongoing learning about these ideas at our schools. This includes setting aside time for teachers to meet to analyze student work, share ideas, and read and discuss relevant articles and texts.

(continued)

			We have identified interested teachers at our school who are willing to try out new things, take risks, share openly with others, and question their teaching practice. These are individuals who are also likely to share ideas openly with others in a spirit of professional inquiry.
			We're committed to the idea of developing a culture of thinking at our school and are willing to keep going even though some teachers, parents, or students might not "get it" to begin with. We see this as an ongoing, evolving process of improvement, not a quick fix.
			We've done some additional background work to get a better sense of how others are building cultures of thinking. This might be reading books such as *Making Thinking Visible* or teacher articles from www.StoriesofLearning.com, watching and discussing videos, or visiting schools.
			We have identified a few specific goals and potential outcomes for our students that we hope our involvement with CoT will help us meet. For example: increasing student participation in class discussion, helping students be more independent as learners, developing students' curiosity and self-direction, developing students' reflection and metacognition, or other such goals.
			We have had some whole-school discussions about our future involvement with CoT and allowed for people to raise questions, issues, and concerns early on about what this might mean and why we should commit to it collectively.
			We've identified a sister school that we can visit, share ideas with, and communicate about this process as we both are going through it.

APPENDIX G. LEADING A CULTURE OF THINKING AT MY SCHOOL

Self-Assessment

Imagine that someone were to shadow you in your role on a random day. How likely would this visitor be to notice each of the following actions described here? For each statement, assign a rating between 5 and 1 using the following scale:

5 = Hard to miss it

4 = Highly likely to notice

3 = Hit or miss depending on the circumstances

2 = Not very likely to notice

1 = I doubt anyone would notice

EXPECTATIONS	Rating
1. I make a conscious effort to communicate to the people I interact with (parents, teachers, students) that our school is a place in which thinking is valued not as an extra or aside but as a foundation of learning.	
2. I establish a set of expectations for ongoing professional learning and risk taking with the people I supervise in order to communicate that their job entails more than just getting the work done and getting good test results.	
3. In making decisions in my role, whether individually or in a group setting, I consistently frame the issue in terms of how any particular decision, outcome, or practice will have an impact on student learning. When decisions and issues don't have a direct impact on the core mission of the school to enhance students' learning and development, I do my best to minimize my own and others' time spent on such issues.	
4. I reward, praise, and comment on the development of our students as thinkers and learners rather than as effective test takers. I recognize teachers' efforts that support this development, and I let it be known that although scores matter, tests are not the chief measure of our effectiveness as educators.	

(continued)

LANGUAGE	Rating
1. I seldom use generic praise comments ("good job," "great," "brilliant," "well done") with others and instead give specific, targeted, action-oriented feedback that focuses on guiding future efforts and actions.	
2. I invite others into the conversation by using "conditional" phrases, such as "could be," "might be," "one possibility is," "some people think," or "usually it is that way, but not always."	
3. When discussing or commenting on classroom observations, I try to notice and name the thinking, not just the activity, occurring in the classroom, saying things like "I noticed the students really supporting their ideas with evidence" or "I noticed you got students to evaluate the effectiveness of their strategies."	
4. I use inclusive, community-building language, talking about what "we" are learning or "our" inquiry.	

TIME	Rating
1. In the meetings and conversations I lead, I make time for people to think through ideas, ensuring that both others and I come prepared to do so.	
2. I respect that everyone's time is valuable, and consequently plan meetings to have a clear focus and purpose and to ensure that they start and end on time.	
3. I avoid disseminating an abundance of ideas without providing the time to process them.	
4. I monitor the amount of time I talk so as not to dominate the conversation.	

MODELING	Rating
1. Although I may not be able to attend everything that is going on at the school, I know that my presence (even briefly) can send a message to people that I value and care about what they are doing. Consequently, I make sure I am present at and participate in events, meetings, and groups in order to show others that I value their efforts and learning.	
2. I demonstrate my own curiosity, passion, and willingness to consider alternative perspectives. I show that I am interested in the core mission of the school to develop students as learners and thinkers, and demonstrate to others that I look beyond just my specific responsibilities.	

(continued)

Developed by R. Ritchhart 2013. Reproduced from *Creating Cultures of Thinking* by Ron Ritchhart. Copyright © 2015 by Ron Ritchhart. Reproduced by permission.

APPENDIX G   *(Continued)*

3. I know that teachers at the school are watching my every move to understand what I value, deem worthwhile, and consider important. Consequently, I model the behaviors and interactions I want to reinforce in others.	
4. I make sure that I am present and available so that people don't associate me only with being in my office.	

OPPORTUNITIES	Rating
1. In meetings, I focus people's attention on big issues, important ideas, and meaningful connections between the task at hand and our core mission as a school.	
2. I try to create opportunities for the individuals with whom I work to direct their own learning and become independent rather than being dependent on me.	
3. I create avenues for us to collect data and evidence that will inform our work and help us to better understand how our collective efforts are contributing to the fulfillment of the school's mission.	
4. I provide opportunities to reflect on our progress and how our efforts are affecting the learning that is happening at the school.	

ROUTINES	Rating
1. I use protocols, thinking routines, or other specific structures to help organize the thinking of the people and groups with which I work and to help us discuss, reflect, and problem-solve.	
2. I've looked at my own working patterns and the way I lead groups to see if I have developed patterns of work or structures that are *not* effective. I actively work to change these ineffective patterns or structures.	
3. I am good at matching a routine, structure, systems, or protocol with appropriate issues so that my group and the people I work with are collectively able to achieve a deeper level of understanding and to process information more effectively.	
4. In my area, I am constantly looking at the systems and processes we use so that I can help streamline some of the things we need to do. This means having efficient systems to accomplish some needed tasks so that teachers aren't overly burdened with "work" and can keep their energies on student learning.	

(continued)

INTERACTIONS	Rating
1. I ensure that all individuals show respect for each other's thinking in groups I lead. Ideas may be critiqued or challenged, but people are not.	
2. I strive to be a collaborator and problem solver, not a blocker, when people come to me with their concerns, needs, or issues. They see me as someone working with them to ensure the best education for students at the school.	
3. Individuals are pushed to elaborate their responses, to reason, and to think beyond a simple answer or statement—for example, by using the "What makes you say that?" routine.	
4. I listen to others and show a genuine curiosity and interest in their thinking. It is clear that I value their thinking.	

ENVIRONMENT	Rating
1. Displays in my work space communicate positive messages about learning and thinking to people who come into my space. A visitor would be able to discern what the school cares about and values with respect to learning.	
2. I arrange my work space and the various spaces I make use of to facilitate thoughtful interactions, collaborations, and discussion. I make sure that the spaces work for people and don't stand in the way of good thinking and learning, whether for adults or students.	
3. My wall displays have an ongoing, inchoate, and/or dialogic nature to them; they are not merely static displays.	
4. I use a variety of ways, including technology, to document and capture the thinking and decision-making processes of the groups with whom I work.	

APPENDIX H. THE DEVELOPMENT OF A CULTURE OF THINKING IN MY CLASSROOM

Self-Assessment

Imagine that someone were to stop into your classroom on any random day or at any time. How likely would this visitor be to notice each of the following actions described here? For each statement, assign a rating between 5 and 1 using the following scale:

5 = Hard to miss it

4 = Highly likely to notice

3 = Hit or miss depending on the circumstances

2 = Not very likely to notice

1 = I doubt anyone would notice

EXPECTATIONS	Rating
1. I make a conscious effort to communicate to students that my classroom is a place in which thinking is valued.	
2. I establish a set of expectations for learning and thinking with my students in a similar way that I establish behavioral expectations.	
3. I stress that thinking and learning, as opposed to "completion of work," are the outcomes of our class activity.	
4. "Developing understanding," as opposed to knowledge acquisition only, is the goal of classroom activity and lessons.	
5. Student independence is being actively cultivated so that students are not dependent on me to answer all questions and direct all activity.	

LANGUAGE	Rating
1. I make a conscious effort to use the language of thinking in my teaching, discussing with students the sort of thinking moves required by such verbs as "elaborate," "evaluate," "justify," "contrast," "explain," and so on.	
2. I seldom use generic praise comments ("good job," "great," "brilliant," "well done") and instead give specific, targeted, action-oriented feedback that focuses on guiding future efforts and actions.	

(continued)

3. I use "conditional" phrases such as "could be," "might be," "one possibility is," "some people think," or "usually it is that way, but not always."	
4. I try to notice and name the thinking occurring in my classroom, saying things like "Sean is supporting his ideas with evidence here" or "Jen is evaluating the effectiveness of that strategy."	
5. I use inclusive, community-building language, talking about what "we" are learning or "our" inquiry.	

TIME	Rating
1. I make time for students' questions and contributions.	
2. I provide the "space" for students to extend, elaborate, or develop the ideas of others.	
3. I avoid disseminating an abundance of ideas without providing the time to process them.	
4. I give students time to think and develop ideas before asking for contributions.	
5. I monitor the amount of time I talk so as not to dominate the classroom conversation.	

MODELING	Rating
1. Thinking (my own as well as students') is regularly on display in the classroom.	
2. I demonstrate my own curiosity, passion, and interest to students.	
3. I display open-mindedness and a willingness to consider alternative perspectives.	
4. It is clear that I am learning too, taking risks, and reflecting on my learning.	
5. Students model their thought process by spontaneously justifying and providing evidence for their thinking.	

OPPORTUNITIES	Rating
1. I ensure that rich thinking opportunities are woven into the fabric of my teaching and that students aren't just engaged in work or activity.	
2. I focus students' attention on big subject matter issues, important ideas in the world, and meaningful connections within my discipline and beyond.	

(continued)

APPENDIX H *(Continued)*

3. I provide students with opportunities to direct their own learning and become independent learners.	
4. I take pains to select content and stimuli for class consideration in order to provoke thinking.	
5. I provide opportunities to reflect on how one's thinking about a topic has changed and developed over time.	

ROUTINES	Rating
1. I use thinking routines and structures to help students organize their thinking.	
2. I use thinking routines flexibly, spontaneously, and effectively to deepen students' understanding.	
3. I am good at matching a routine with appropriate content so that students are able to achieve a deeper level of understanding.	
4. Thinking routines have become patterns of behavior in my classroom; that is, students know particular routines so well that they no longer seek clarification about the mechanics of the routine.	
5. Students use routines and structures to further their understanding and as a platform for discussion, rather than as work to be done.	

INTERACTIONS	Rating
1. I ensure that all students respect each other's thinking in my classroom. Ideas may be critiqued or challenged, but people are not.	
2. I make it clear that mistakes are acceptable and encouraged within my classroom.	
3. Students are pushed to elaborate their responses, to reason, and to think beyond a simple answer or statement—for example, by using the "What makes you say that?" routine.	
4. I listen to students and show a genuine curiosity and interest in students' thinking. It is clear that I value their thinking.	
5. I listen in on groups and allow them to act independently, rather than always inserting myself into the process.	

(continued)

ENVIRONMENT	Rating
1. Displays in the room communicate positive messages about learning and thinking, to inspire learning in the subject area and connect students to the larger world of ideas.	
2. I arrange the space of my classroom to facilitate thoughtful interactions, collaborations, and discussion.	
3. My wall displays have an ongoing, inchoate, and/or dialogic nature to them; they are not merely static displays of finished work.	
4. I use a variety of ways, including technology, to document and capture thinking.	
5. A visitor would be able to discern what I care about and value with respect to learning.	

APPENDIX I. ASSESSMENT LADDER

Reasoning with Evidence

Levels of Development		What Teacher Needs to Do to Move Students Up the Ladder	
Fully Independent	Consistently uses a broad range of text and other resources. Questions and uses valid resources. Applies evidence appropriately. Writes a coherent support statement. Prompts others to support claims.	**Self-Coaching**	Encourages sharing of thinking through speaking and writing with adults and peers. Suggests a broad range of resources for finding evidence.
Self-Aware	Understands the importance of using evidence to support claims. May need direction in finding strong and appropriate evidence. May question validity of evidence. Responds to models for finding evidence and writing strong support statements.	**Coaching**	Encourages self-motivation for continuing to expand thinking, resources, and responses so that reasoning with evidence becomes a habit.
Developing	Can say "why" when prompted. Offers simplistic responses that may show some higher-level thinking. Uses own experience as evidence. Relies on models for responding. Needs prompting and reassurance from teacher.	**Supporting**	Supports student with models and suggestions that promote expansion of sources and written work. Provides opportunities for practice.
Only with Teacher Direction	Has difficulty making a claim. Does not understand the need to support with evidence. Prompts may provoke a limited response. Needs much teacher support.	**Directing**	Provides consistent and direct models. Prompts consistently with "What makes you say that?"

REFERENCES

Akyol, Z., & Garrison, D. R. (2011). Understanding cognitive presence in an online and blended community of inquiry: Assessing outcomes and processes for deep approaches to learning. *British Journal of Educational Technology, 42*, 233–250.

Allen, D., & Blythe, T. (2004). *The facilitator's book of questions: Tools for looking together at student and teacher work.* New York, NY: Teachers College Press.

Amabile, T., Hadley, C. N., & Kramer, S. J. (2002). Creativity under the gun. *Harvard Business Review, 80*(8), 52–61.

Anderson, R. (2011, July). Staggered block scheduling: Efficient timing in American high schools. *10 Ideas for Education,* pp. 10–11. Retrieved from http://www .rooseveltcampusnetwork.org/blog/2011-10-ideas-education

Armstrong, N. (2012). Could you explain what you mean by that? Individual feedback sessions (IFS). *Stories of learning.* Retrieved from http://storiesoflearning.com/

Arnstine, D. (1995). *Democracy and the arts of schooling.* Albany: State University of New York Press.

Askell-Williams, H., Lawson, M. J., & Skrzypiec, G. (2012). Scaffolding cognitive and metacognitive strategy instruction in regular class lessons. *Instructional Science, 40*, 413–443.

Attia, M. *Race to nowhere.* Reel Link Films, 2011.

Baker, J. E. (2007). *Teacher talk, teaching philosophy, and effective literacy instruction in primary-grade classrooms.* Cookeville: Tennessee Technological University.

Bandura, A. (1986). *Social foundations of thought and action: A social cognitive theory.* Englewood Cliffs, NJ: Prentice Hall.

Barell, J. (1991). *Teaching for thoughtfulness: Classroom strategies to enhance intellectual development.* New York, NY: Longman.

Barrett, P., Zhang, Y., Moffat, J., & Kobbacy, K. (2013). A holistic, multi-level analysis identifying the impact of classroom design on pupils' learning. *Building and Environment, 59*, 678–689.

Baumrind, D. (1989). Rearing competent children. In W. Damon (Ed.), *Child development today and tomorrow* (pp. 349–378). San Francisco, CA: Jossey-Bass.

Bereiter, C., & Scardamalia, M. (1989). Intentional learning as a goal of instruction. In L. B. Resnick (Ed.), *Knowing, learning, and instruction: Essays in honor of Robert Glaser* (pp. 361–392). Hillsdale, NJ: Erlbaum.

Berger, R., Gardner, H., Meier, D., Sizer, T. R., & Lieberman, A. (2003). *An ethic of excellence: Building a culture of craftsmanship with students*: Portsmouth, NH: Heinemann.

Bergsagel, V. (2007). *Architecture for achievement: Building patterns for small school learning.* Mercer Island, WA: Eagle Chatter Press.

Beyer, B. (1998). Improving student thinking. *Clearing House, 71*, 262–267. doi: 10.1080/00098659809602720

Biggs, J. B. (1987). *Student approaches to learning and studying.* Research monograph. Hawthorn, Victoria: Australian Council for Educational Research.

Black, P. (2004). *Working inside the black box: Assessment for learning in the classroom.* London, England: Granada Learning.

Black, P., & Wiliam, D. (2002). *Inside the black box: Raising standards through classroom assessment.* London, England: Department of Education & Professional Studies, King's College London.

Bloom, B. (1974). Time and learning. *American Psychologist, 29*, 682–688.

Blythe, T., & Associates. (1998). *The teaching for understanding guide.* San Francisco, CA: Jossey-Bass.

Boaler, J. (2008). Promoting "relational equity" and high mathematics achievement through an innovative mixed-ability approach. *British Educational Research Journal, 34*, 167–194.

Boaler, J., & Brodie, K. (2004, October). The importance, nature and impact of teacher questions. In D. E. McDougall & J. A. Ross (Eds.), *Proceedings of the 26th annual meeting of the North American chapter of the International Group for the Psychology of Mathematics Education* (Vol. 2, pp. 773–781). Retrieved from http://www.pmena .org/html/proceedings.html

Boix-Mansilla, V., & Jackson, A. (2011). *Educating for global competency: Preparing our youth to engage the world.* New York, NY: Asia Society.

Bondy, E., & Ross, D. D. (2008). The teacher as warm demander. *Educational Leadership, 66*(1), 54–58.

Borja, R. R. (2004, May 6). Singapore's digital path. *Education Week's Technology Counts, 23*(35), 30–36. Retrieved from www.edweek.org/media/ew/tc/archives /TC04full.pdf

Bradt, S. (2006, February 23). High school AP courses do not predict college success in science. *Harvard University Gazette.* Retrieved from http://news.harvard.edu/gazette /2006/02.23/05-ap.html

Breithecker, D. (2007). Beware of the sitting trap in learning and schooling. Retrieved from http://www.designshare.com/index.php/articles/sitting-trap/

Bronson, P., & Merryman, A. (2010). The creativity crisis. *Daily Beast.* Retrieved from http://www.thedailybeast.com/newsweek/2010/07/10/the-creativity-crisis.print.html

Brookfield, S. D., & Preskill, S. (1999). *Discussion as a way of teaching.* San Francisco, CA: Jossey-Bass.

Brown, D. (2010). An open letter to educators. YouTube. Retrieved from http://www .youtube.com/watch?v=-P2PGGeTOA4

Brown, J. S., & Burton, R. R. (1978). Diagnostic models for procedural bugs in basic mathematical skills. *Cognitive Science, 2*, 155–192.

Brown, J. S., Collins, A., & Duguid, P. (1989). Situated cognition and the culture of learning. *Educational Researcher, 18*(1), 32–41.

Brundrett, C. (2010, October 11). Year 12 students face many different pressures. *Herald Sun.* Retrieved from http://www.heraldsun.com.au/news/opinion/year-12-students -face-many-different-pressures/story-e6frfhqf-1225936859020?nk=6c68db09a29d 01d141dece9a3add6841

Bruner, J. (1996). *The culture of education.* Cambridge, MA: Harvard University Press.

Buhrow, B., & Garcia, A. U. (2006). *Ladybugs, tornadoes, and swirling galaxies: English language learners discover their world through inquiry.* Portland, ME: Stenhouse.

Burke, C., & Grosvenor, I. (2003). *The school I'd like: Children and young people's reflections on an education for the 21st century.* New York, NY: Routledge.

Buzzelli, C., & Johnston, B. (2002). *The moral dimensions of teaching: Language, power, and culture in classroom interaction.* Chicago, IL: University of Chicago Press.

Camp, B. W., Blom, G. E., Heber, F., & Doorninck, W. J. (1977). "Think aloud": A program for developing self-control in young aggressive boys. *Journal of Abnormal Child Psychology, 5*(2), 157–169.

Carpenter, T. P., Corbitt, M. K., Kepner, H., Lindquist, M., & Reys, R. (1980). Problem solving in mathematics: National assessment results. *Educational Leadership, 37,* 562–563.

Carroll, J. B. (1963). A model of school learning. *Teachers College Record, 64,* 723–733.

Cazden, C. B. (2001). *Classroom discourse: The language of teaching and learning.* Portsmouth, NH: Heinemann.

Cheprecha, T., Gardner, M., & Sapianchai, X. (1980). Comparison of training methods in modifying questioning and wait-time behaviors of Thai high school chemistry teachers. *Journal of Research in Science Teaching, 17,* 191–200.

Chilcoat, G. W., & Stahl, R. J. (1986). A framework for giving clear directions: Effective teacher verbal behavior. *Clearing House, 60*(3), 107–109.

Chua, A. (2011). *Battle hymn of the tiger mother.* London, England: Bloomsbury.

City, E. A., Elmore, R. F., Fiarman, S. E., & Teitel, L. (2009). *Instructional rounds in education: A network approach to improving teaching and learning.* Cambridge, MA: Harvard Educational Publishing Group.

Claxton, G., Chambers, M., Powell, G., & Lucas, B. (2011). *The learning powered school: Pioneering 21st century education.* Bristol, England: TLO Limited.

Cobb, P., Wood, T., Yackel, E., Nicholls, E. J., Wheatly, G., Trigatti, B., & Perlwitz, M. (1991). Assessment of a problem-centered second-grade mathematics project. *Journal for Research in Mathematics Education, 22*(1), 3–29.

Cohen, D. K. (1990). A revolution in one classroom: The case of Mrs. Oublier. *Educational Evaluation and Policy Analysis, 12,* 311–329.

Cohen, E. G. (1994) *Designing groupwork: Strategies for the heterogeneous classroom.* New York, NY: Teachers College Press.

Collins, A., Brown, J. S., & Holum, A. (1991, Winter). Cognitive apprenticeship: Making thinking visible. *American Educator, 15*(3), 6–11.

Collins, A., Brown, J. S., & Newman, S. F. (1989). Cognitive apprenticeship: Teaching the craft of reading, writing, and mathematics. In L. B. Resnick (Ed.), *Knowing, learning, and instruction: Essays in honor of Robert Glaser* (pp. 453–494). Hillsdale, NJ: Erlbaum.

Comer, J. P. (1995). Untitled lecture given at Region 4 Education Service Center, Houston, TX.

Comer, J. P. (2001). Schools that develop children. *American Prospect, 12*(7), 30–35.

Comer, J. P., & Gates, H. L. (2004). *Leave no child behind: Preparing today's youth for tomorrow's world.* New Haven, CT: Yale University Press.

Conference Board, Partnership for 21st Century Skills, Corporate Voices for Working Families, & Society for Human Resource Management. (2006). *Are they really ready to work? Employers' perspectives on the basic knowledge and applied skills of new entrants to the 21st century U.S. workforce.* Retrieved from www.p21.org/storage /documents/FINAL_REPORT_PDF09-29-06.pdf

Cornelius-White, J. (2007). Learner-centered teacher-student relationships are effective: A meta-analysis. *Review of Educational Research, 77*(1), 113–143. doi: 10.3102/0034 65430298563

Costa, A. L. (1991). Do you speak cogitare? In A. L. Costa, *The school as a home for the mind* (pp. 109–119). Palatine, IL: Skylight Publishing.

Covey, S. (1994). *First things first.* New York, NY: Free Press.

Craik, F.I.M., & Lockhart, R. S. (1972). Levels of processing: A framework for memory research. *Journal of Verbal Learning and Verbal Behavior, 11*, 671–684.

Cruess, S. R., Cruess, R. L., & Steinert, Y. (2008). Role modelling—Making the most of a powerful teaching strategy. *BMJ, 336*, 718.

Cushman, K. (2005). *Fires in the bathroom: Advice for teachers from high school students.* New York, NY: New Press.

Cushman, K., & Rogers, L. (2013). *Fires in the middle school bathroom: Advice for teachers from middle schoolers.* New York, NY: New Press.

Dangel, J. R., & Durden, T. R. (2010, January). The nature of teacher talk during small group activities. *Young Children*, 74–81.

Davey, B. (1983). Think aloud—Modeling the cognitive process of reading comprehension. *Journal of Reading, 27*(1), 44–47.

Deci, E. L., & Ryan, R. M. (1985). *Intrinsic motivation and self-determination in human behavior.* New York, NY: Plenum.

Denton, P. (2007). *The power of our words: Teacher language that helps children learn.* Turners Falls, MA: Northeast Foundation for Children.

Dewey, J. (1916). *Democracy and education: An introduction to the philosophy of education.* New York, NY: Macmillan.

Doorley, S., and Witthoft, S. (2011). *Make space: How to set the stage for creative collaboration.* Hoboken, NJ: Wiley.

Doyle, W. (1983). Academic work. *Review of Educational Research, 53,* 159–199.

Dweck, C. S. (2006). *Mindset: The new psychology of success.* New York, NY: Ballantine Books.

Dweck, C. S. (2007, October). The perils and promise of praise. *Educational Leadership, 65*(2), 34–39.

Dweck, C. S., & Leggett, E. L. (1988). A social-cognitive approach to motivation and personality. *Psychological Review, 95,* 256–273.

Earthman, G. I. (2004). *Prioritization of 31 criteria for school building adequacy.* Baltimore: American Civil Liberties Union Foundation of Maryland.

Edwards, C. P., Gandini, L., & Forman, G. E. (1998). *The hundred languages of children: The Reggio Emilia approach—Advanced reflections.* Greenwich, CT: Ablex.

Edwards, D., & Mercer, N. (2013). *Common knowledge: The development of understanding in the classroom* (Routledge Revivals). New York, NY: Routledge.

Eisner, E. (2003). Preparing for today and tomorrow. *Educational Leadership, 61*(4), 6–10.

Engelbrecht, K. (2003, June 18). *The impact of color on learning.* Paper presented at NeoCON. Retrieved from http://sdpl.coe.uga.edu/HTML/W305.pdf

Ferlazzo, L. (2011). *Helping students motivate themselves: Practical answers to classroom challenges.* Larchmont, NY: Eye On Education.

Fernandes, M. A., & Moscovitch, M. (2000). Divided attention and memory: Evidence of substantial interference effects at retrieval and encoding. *Journal of Experimental Psychology, 129*, 155–176.

Filstad, C. (2004). How newcomers use role models in organizational socialization. *Journal of Workplace Learning, 16*, 396–409.

Fiori, N. (2007, May). Four practices that math classrooms could do without. *Phi Delta Kappan*, pp. 695–696.

Fisher, D., & Frey, N. (2008). Releasing responsibility. *Educational Leadership, 66*(3), 32–37.

Fisher, D., & Frey, N. (2011, June). The first 20 days: Establishing productive group work in the classroom. *Engaging the Adolescent Learner* (series). Newark, DE: International Reading Association. Retrieved from http://fisherandfrey.com /_admin/_filemanager/File/First_20_Days.pdf

Flink, C., Boggiano, A. K., & Barrett, M. (1990). Controlling teaching strategies: Undermining children's self-determination and performance. *Journal of Personality & Social Psychology, 59*, 916–924.

Ford, M. P., & Opitz, M. F. (2002). Using centers to engage children during guided reading time: Intensifying learning experiences away from the teacher. *Reading Teacher, 55*, 710–717.

Fried, R. L. (1995). *The passionate teacher.* Boston, MA: Beacon Press.

Friedman, T. (2013, March 6). The professor's big stage. *New York Times*, p. A23.

Gambrell, L. B. (1980). Think-time: Implications for reading instruction. *Reading Teacher, 34*, 143–146.

Gardner, H. (1991). *The unschooled mind.* New York, NY: Basic Books.

Gardner, H. (2013, February 22). Health, happiness, and time well spent. *Cognoscenti.* Retrieved from http://cognoscenti.wbur.org/2013/02/22/time-well-spent-howard -gardner

Gettinger, M., & Walter, M. J. (2012). Classroom strategies to enhance academic engaged time. In S. L. Christenson, A. L. Reschly, & C. Wylie (Eds.), *Handbook of research on student engagement* (pp. 653–673). New York, NY: Springer Verlag.

Glasser, W. (1968). *Schools without failure.* New York, NY: Harper & Row.

Gorski, R. (2011, January 18). 45% of students don't learn much in college. *Huff Post College*. Retrieved from http://www.huffingtonpost.com/2011/01/18/45-of-students -dont-learn_n_810224.html

Goyal, N. (2011, October 27). It's time for a learning revolution. *Huff Post Teen*. Retrieved from http://www.huffingtonpost.com/nikhil-goyal/post_2586_b_1034887 .html

Hari, R., & Kujala, M. V. (2009). Brain basis of human social interactions: From concepts to brain imaging. *Physiological Reviews, 89*, 453–479. doi: 10.1152 /physrev.00041.2007

Harris, M. J., & Rosenthal, R. (1985). Mediation of interpersonal expectancy effects: 31 meta-analyses. *Psychological Bulletin, 97*, 363–386.

Harvard-Smithsonian Center for Astrophysics. (Producer). (1987). A private universe. [DVD series]. Annenberg Learner, http://www.learner.org/resources/series28.html

Harvard-Smithsonian Center for Astrophysics. (Producer). (1997). Minds of our own. [DVD series]. Annenberg Learner, http://www.learner.org/resources/series26.html

Harvey, S., & Goudvis, A. (2000). *Strategies that work: Teaching comprehension to enhance understanding*. Portland, ME: Stenhouse.

Haston, W. (2007). Teacher modeling as an effective teaching strategy. *Music Educators Journal, 93*(4), 26–30.

Hattie, J. (2009). *Visible learning: A synthesis of over 800 meta-analyses relating to achievement*. New York, NY: Routledge.

Hattie, J., & Timperley, H. (2007). The power of feedback. *Review of Educational Research, 77*, 81–112.

Heath, S. B. (1999). Dimensions of language development: Lessons from older children. In A. S. Masten (Ed.), *Cultural processes in child development: The Minnesota symposia on child psychology* (Vol. 29, 59–75). Mahwah, NJ: Erlbaum.

Henry, J. (1963). *Culture against man*. New York, NY: Random House.

Herrenkohl, L. R., & Guerra, M. R. (1998). Participant structures, scientific discourse, and student engagement in fourth grade. *Cognition and Instruction, 16*, 431–473.

Hewes, B. (2012, April 12). Using archetypes to match learning spaces with physical and digital spaces. *Bianca Hewes*. Retrieved from http://biancahewes.wordpress.com

/2012/04/22/using-archetypes-to-match-learning-spaces-with-physical-and-digital
-spaces/

Hiebert, J., Stigler, J., Jacobs, J., Givvin, K., Garnier, H., & Smith, M. (2005).
Mathematics teaching in the United States today (and tomorrow): Results from the
TIMSS 1999 video study. *Educational Evaluation and Policy Analysis, 27*, 111–132.

Higgins, S., Hall, E., Wall, K., Woolner, P., & McCaughey, C. (2005). *The impact of
school environments: A literature review.* London, England: Design Council.
Retrieved from Research Centre for Learning and Teaching, School of Education,
Communication and Language Sciences, Newcastle University, ncl.ac.uk/cflat/about
/documents/designcouncilreport.pdf

High school teacher to be honored at White House. (2013, April 22). *CBS This Morning.*
Retrieved from http://www.cbsnews.com/videos/high-school-teacher-to-be
-honored-at-white-house/

How to remake education. (2009, September 27). *New York Times Magazine.* Retrieved
from http://www.nytimes.com/2009/09/27/magazine/27toolssidebar2-t.html?_r=0

Hunter, M. C. (1982). *Mastery teaching.* Thousand Oaks, CA: Corwin Press.

Immordino-Yang, M. H. (2008). The smoke around mirror neurons: Goals as
sociocultural and emotional organizers of perception and action in learning. *Mind,
Brain, and Education, 2*, 67–73.

Ironside, P. M. (2006). Using narrative pedagogy: Learning and practising interpretive
thinking. *Journal of Advanced Nursing, 55*, 478–486.

Jakes, D. (2012). What if the story changed? (K12 online conference). *David Jakes
Presentation Resources.* Retrieved from http://jakes.editme.com/changethestory

Jeff Charbonneau—2013 National Teacher of the Year. (2013). *Responsibility: Children's
Education.* Retrieved from http://ing.us/about-ing/responsibility/childrens-education
(This web page is no longer active.)

Jensen, E., & Snider, C. (2013). *Turnaround tools for the teenage brain: Helping
underperforming students become lifelong learners.* Hoboken, NJ: Wiley.

Johnston, P. H. (2004). *Choice words: How our language affects children's learning.*
Portland, ME: Stenhouse.

Johnston, P. H., Ivey, G., & Faulkner, A. (2011). Talking in class. *Reading Teacher, 65*,
232–237.

Kaplan, C., & Chan, R. (2012). *Time well spent: Eight powerful practices of successful, expanded-time schools*. Boston, MA: National Center on Time and Learning.

Karweit, N., & Slavin, R. E. (1981). Measurement and modeling choices in studies of time and learning. *American Educational Research Journal, 18*, 157–171.

Kaser, C. H. (2007). *Series on highly effective practices: Classroom routines—4. Use of classroom routines to support the learning process*. Department of Communication Disorders and Special Education, Darden College of Education. Retrieved from http://education.odu.edu/esse/research/series/routines.shtml

Kegan, R., & Lahey, L. L. (2001). *How the way we talk can change the way we work*. San Francisco, CA: Jossey-Bass.

Killingsworth, M. (2012). *Happiness from the bottom up*. Unpublished doctoral dissertation. Harvard University Graduate School of Arts and Sciences, Cambridge, MA.

Knapp, M. S., Shields, P. M., & Turnbull, B. J. (1992). *Academic challenge for the children of poverty: Summary report*. Washington, DC: Office of Policy and Planning, US Department of Education.

Koestner, R., Ryan, R. M., Bernieri, F., & Holt, K. (1984). Setting limits on children's behavior: The differential effects of controlling versus informational styles on intrinsic motivation and creativity. *Journal of Personality, 52*, 233–248.

Kostelnik, M. J., Whiren, A. P., Soderman, A. K., Stein, L. C., & Gregory, K. (2002). *Guiding children's social development: Theory to practice*. Stamford, CT: Delmar (Cengage Learning).

Krechevsky, M., Mardell, B., Rivard, M., & Wilson, D. (2013). *Visible learners: Promoting Reggio-inspired approaches in all schools*: Hoboken, NJ: Wiley.

Krechevsky, M., & Stork, J. (2000). Challenging educational assumptions: Lessons from an Italian-American collaboration. *Cambridge Journal of Education, 30*(1), 57–74.

Lakoff, G., & Johnson, M. (1980). *Metaphors we live by*. Chicago, IL: University of Chicago Press.

Lampi, A. R., Fenty, N. S., & Beaunae, C. (2005). Making the three Ps easier: Praise, proximity, and precorrection. *Beyond Behavior, 15*(1), 8–12.

Langer, E. (1989). *Mindfulness*. Reading, MA: Addison-Wesley.

Langer, E., & Piper, A. (1987). The prevention of mindlessness. *Journal of Personality and Social Psychology, 53,* 280–287.

Lapp, D., & Fisher, D. (2007, November). *Improving high school student achievement through teacher practices.* Paper presented at the 41st annual California Reading Association Conference, Ontario, CA.

Lapp, D., Fisher, D., & Grant, M. (2008). "You can read this text—I'll show you how": Interactive comprehension instruction. *Journal of Adolescent and Adult Literacy, 51,* 372–383.

Larrivee, B. (2002). The potential perils of praise in a democratic interactive classroom. *Action in Teacher Education, 23,* 77–88.

Larson, R. W. (2000). Toward a psychology of positive youth development. *American Psychologist, 55,* 170–183.

Lave, J., & Wenger, E. (1991). *Situated learning: Legitimate peripheral participation.* Cambridge, England: Cambridge University Press.

Lee, V. S. (2004). Idea item #1: Displayed a personal interest in students and their learning. *POD-IDEA Center Notes.* Youngston, OH: Youngston State University.

Leinhardt, G., Weidman, C., & Hammond, K. M. (1987). Introduction and integration of classroom routines by expert teachers. *Curriculum Inquiry, 17,* 135–175.

Lemov, D. (2010). *Teach like a champion.* San Francisco, CA: Jossey-Bass.

Linsin, M. (2009, November 7). Why routines make classroom management easier. *Smart Classroom Management.* Retrieved from http://www.smartclassroom management.com/2009/11/07/why-routines-make-classroom-management-easier -plus-one-great-idea/

Lipsett, A. (2008, June 11). National curriculum constrains teachers and pupils. *Guardian.* Retrieved from http://www.theguardian.com/education/2008/jun/11 /schools.uk4

Liu, E., & Noppe-Brandon, S. (2009). *Imagination first: Unlocking the power of possibility.* San Francisco, CA: Jossey-Bass.

Loehr, J., & Schwartz, T. (2003). *The power of full engagement: Managing energy, not time, is the key to high performance and personal renewal.* New York, NY: Free Press.

Lundgren, U. P. (1977). *Model analysis of pedagogical processes.* Stockholm, Sweden: Department of Educational Research, Stockholm Institute of Education.

Lyman, F. T. (1981). The responsive classroom discussion: The inclusion of all students. In A. S. Anderson (Ed.), *Mainstreaming Digest* (pp. 109–113). College Park: University of Maryland Press.

Lyons, L. (2004, June 8). Most teens associate school with boredom, fatigue. Gallup. Retrieved from http://www.gallup.com/poll/11893/most-teens-associate-school-boredom-fatigue.aspx

Maisuria, A. (2005). The turbulent times of creativity in the national curriculum. *Policy Futures in Education, 3,* 141–152.

Maleuvre, D. (2005). Art and the teaching of love. *Journal of Aesthetic Education, 39*(1), 77–92.

Marshall, H. H. (1987). Building a learning orientation. *Theory into Practice, 26,* 8–14.

Marshall, H. H. (1988). Work or learning: Implication of classroom metaphors. *Educational Researcher, 17*(9), 9–16.

Marshall, H. H. (1990). Beyond the workplace metaphor: The classroom as a learning setting. *Theory into Practice, 29,* 94–101.

Marton, F., & Saljo, R. (1976). On qualitative differences in learning: I. Outcome and process. *British Journal of Educational Psychology, 46,* 4–11.

Maslansky, M., West, S., DeMoss, G., & Saylor, D. (2010). *The language of trust: Selling ideas in a world of skeptics.* New York, NY: Prentice Hall Press.

Mathews, S. R., & Lowe, K. (2011). Classroom environments that foster a disposition for critical thinking. *Learning Environments Research, 14,* 59–73.

Maxwell, L. E. (2000, Winter). A safe and welcoming school: What students, teachers, and parents think. *Journal of Architectural and Planning Research, 17,* 271–282.

McCloskey, M. (1983). Naive theories of motion. In D. Gentner & A. L. Stevens (Eds.), *Mental models* (pp. 299–324). New York, NY: Erlbaum.

McIntosh, E. (2012). Stop ping pong questioning. *edu.blogs.com.* Retrieved from http://edu.blogs.com/edublogs/2012/02/stop-ping-pong-questioning-try-basketball-instead.html

McLaughlin, M. W., Irby, M. A., & Langman, J. (1994). *Urban sanctuaries: Neighborhood organizations in the lives and futures of inner-city youth.* San Francisco, CA: Jossey-Bass.

McMurrer, J. (2007). *NCLB Year 5: Choices, changes, and challenges: Curriculum and instruction in the NCLB era*. Washington DC: Center on Education Policy.

McNeil, L. (1983). Defensive teaching and classroom control. In M. W. Apple & L. Weis (Eds.), *Ideology and practice in schooling* (pp. 114–142). Philadelphia, PA: Temple University Press.

Mednick, S. A. (1962). The associative basis for the creative process. *Psychological Bulletin, 69*, 220–232.

Meier, D. (2003). *In schools we trust: Creating communities of learning in an era of testing and standardization*. New York, NY: Beacon Press.

Meyer, D. (2012, April 17). Ten design principles for engaging math tasks. *dy/dan*. Retrieved from http://blog.mrmeyer.com/?p=12141

Miller, R. L., & Benz, J. J. (2008). Techniques for encouraging peer collaboration: Online threaded discussion or fishbowl interaction. *Journal of Instructional Psychology, 35* (1), 87–93.

Minstrell, J. (1984). Teaching for the development of understanding of ideas: Forces on moving objects. In C. W. Anderson (Ed.), *Observing Science Classrooms: Perspectives from Research and Practice. 1984 AETS Yearbook* (pp. 55–73). Columbus, OH: ERIC Clearinghouse for Science, Mathematics and Environmental Education.

Morehead, J. (2012, June 19). Stanford University's Carol Dweck on the Growth Mindset in Education. *OneDublin.org*. Retrieved from http://onedublin.org/2012/06/19/stanford-universitys-carol-dweck-on-the-growth-mindset-and-education/

Münch, M., Linhart, F., Borisuit, A., Jaeggi, S. M., & Scartezzini, J.-L. (2012). Effects of prior light exposure on early evening performance, subjective sleepiness, and hormonal secretion. *Behavioral Neuroscience, 126*(1), 196–203.

Murray, B. P. (2002). *The new teacher's complete sourcebook: Grades K–4*. New York, NY: Scholastic.

Nair, P., & Fielding, R. (2005). *The language of school design: Design patterns for 21st century schools*. Minneapolis, MN: DesignShare.

National Education Association. (2003, August). *Status of the American public school teacher 2000–2001*. Washington DC: Author.

Newmann, F. M., Bryk, A. S., & Nagaoka, J. K. (2001). *Authentic intellectual work and standardized tests: Conflict or coexistence?* Chicago, IL: Consortium on Chicago School Research.

Newmann, F. M., Wehlage, G. G., & Lamborn, S. D. (1992). The significance and sources of student engagement. In F. M. Newmann (Ed.), *Student engagement and achievement in American secondary schools* (pp. 11–39). New York, NY: Teachers College Press.

Nickerson, R. J. (1985). Understanding understanding. *American Journal of Education, 93*, 201–239.

Nystrand, M., & Graff, N. (2001). Report in argument's clothing: An ecological perspective on writing instruction in a seventh-grade classroom. *Elementary School Journal, 101*, 479–493.

O'Donnell, S. (2012). The design of elementary schools. In J. Duarte (Ed.), *Learning in twenty-first century schools: Toward school buildings that promote learning, ensure safety, and protect the environment. Report of a Meeting of the IDB Education Network* (pp. 35–48). Washington DC: Inter-American Development Bank. Retrieved from http://idbdocs.iadb.org/wsdocs/getDocument.aspx?DOCNUM =36894958

Oakeshott, M. (1959). *The voice of poetry in the conversation of mankind: An essay.* London, England: Bowes & Bowes.

OWP/P Architects, VS Furniture, & Bruce Mau Design. (2010). *The third teacher: 79 Ways You Can Use Design to Transform Teaching & Learning.* New York, NY: Abrams.

Palinscar, A. S., & Brown, A. L. (1984). Reciprocal teaching of comprehension-fostering and comprehension-monitoring activities. *Cognition and Instruction, 1*, 117–125.

Palmer, P. J. (1998). *The courage to teach: Exploring the inner landscape of a teacher's life.* Hoboken, NJ: Wiley.

Papert, S. (1980). *Mindstorms: Children, computers, and powerful ideas.* New York, NY: Basic Books.

Pascale, R. T., Sternin, J., & Sternin, M. (2010). *The power of positive deviance: How unlikely innovators solve the world's toughest problems* (Vol. 1). Boston, MA: Harvard Business Press.

Paul, A. M. (2013, May 3). The new marshmallow test: Students can't resist multitasking. *Slate*. Retrieved from http://www.slate.com/articles/health_and _science/science/2013/05/multitasking_while_studying_divided_attention_and _technological_gadgets.3.html

Pearson, P. D., & Gallagher, M. C. (1983). The instruction of reading comprehension. *Contemporary Educational Psychology, 8*, 317–344.

Pennebaker, J. W. (2011a). *The secret life of pronouns.* New York, NY: Bloomsbury Press.

Pennebaker, J. W. (2011b). The secret life of pronouns. *New Scientist, 211*(2828), 42–45.

Perkins, D. N. (1992). *Smart schools: From training memories to educating minds.* New York, NY: Free Press.

Perkins, D. N. (1999). From idea to action. In L. Hetland & S. Veenema (Eds.), *The Project Zero classroom: Views on understanding* (pp. 17–25). Cambridge, MA: Project Zero.

Perkins, D. N. (2003). *King Arthur's round table: How collaborative conversations create smart organizations.* Hoboken, NJ: Wiley.

Perkins, D. N. (2009). *Making learning whole: How seven principles of teaching can transform education.* San Francisco, CA: Jossey-Bass.

Perkins, D. N., & Grotzer, T. A. (2005). Dimensions of causal understanding: The role of complex causal models in students' understanding of science. *Studies in Science Education, 41*(1), 17–165.

Phipps, M. L., & Phipps, C. A. (2003). Group norm setting: A critical skill for effective classroom groups. *MountainRise, 1*(1). Retrieved from http://coral.s3servers.com /other/norm.pdf

Pianta, R. C., Belsky, J., Houts, R., Morrison, F., & National Institute of Child Health and Human Development (NICHD) Early Child Care Research Network. (2007). Opportunities to learn in America's elementary classrooms: Supporting online material. Available from http://www.sciencemag.org/cgi/content/full/315/5820 /1795/DC1

Pianta, R. C., Hamre, B. K., & Allen, J. P. (2012). Teacher-student relationships and engagement: Conceptualizing, measuring, and improving the capacity of classroom interactions. In S. L. Christenson, A. L. Reschly, & C. Wylie (Eds.), *Handbook of research on student engagement* (pp. 365–386). New York, NY: Springer Verlag.

Pierson, R. F. (2013). Every kid needs a champion. *TED.* Retrieved from http://www.ted .com/talks/rita_pierson_every_kid_needs_a_champion

Pink, D. H. (2009). *Drive: The surprising truth about what motivates us.* New York, NY: Riverhead Books.

Pink, D. H. (2010, September 12). Think tank: Flip-thinking—the new buzz word sweeping the US. *Telegraph.* Retrieved from http://www.telegraph.co.uk/finance /businessclub/7996379/Daniel-Pinks-Think-Tank-Flip-thinking-the-new-buzz-word -sweeping-the-US.html

Project Zero & Reggio Children. (2001). *Making learning visible: Children as individual and group learners.* Cambridge, MA: Project Zero.

Queensland Studies Authority. (2009). *Student assessment regimes: Getting the balance right for Australia.* Brisbane, Australia: Author.

Quinn, C. (2006, October 4). Slow learning. *Learnlets.* Retrieved from http://blog .learnlets.com/?m=200610

Rao, M. S. (2010). *Soft skills: Enhancing employability: Connecting campus with corporate.* New Delhi, India: IK International.

Ravitch, D. (2011). *The death and life of the great American school system: How testing and choice are undermining education.* New York, NY: Basic Books.

Resnick, M. D., Bearman, P. S., Blum, R. W., Bauman, K., Harris, K. M., Jones, J., & Taylor, T. (1997). Protecting adolescents from harm: Findings from the National Longitudinal Study of Adolescent Health. *Journal of the American Medical Association, 278,* 823–832.

Rimm-Kaufman, S. E., Fan, X., Chiu, Y.-J., & You, W. (2007). The contribution of the Responsive Classroom approach on children's academic achievement: Results from a three year longitudinal study. *Journal of School Psychology, 45,* 401–421.

Ritchhart, R. (2000). *Developing intellectual character: A dispositional perspective on teaching and learning.* Skokie, IL: UMI Dissertation Services.

Ritchhart, R. (2002). *Intellectual character: What it is, why it matters, and how to get it.* San Francisco, CA: Jossey-Bass.

Ritchhart, R. (2004). Creative teaching in the shadow of the standards. *Independent School, 63*(2), 32–41.

Ritchhart, R. (2012). The real power of questions. *Creative Teaching and Learning, 2*(4), 8–12.

Ritchhart, R., Church, M., & Morrison, K. (2011). *Making thinking visible: How to promote engagement, understanding, and independence for all learners.* San Francisco, CA: Jossey-Bass.

Ritchhart, R., Hadar, L., & Turner, T. (2009). Uncovering students' thinking about thinking using concept maps. *Metacognition and Learning, 4,* 145–159.

Ritchhart, R., & Langer, E. (1997). Teaching mathematical procedures mindfully: Exploring the conditional presentation of information in mathematics. In J. A. Dossey, J. O. Swafford, M. Parmantie, & A. E. Dossey (Eds.), *Proceedings of the nineteenth annual meeting of the North American chapter of the International Group for the Psychology of Mathematics Education* (pp. 299–305). Columbus, OH: ERIC Clearinghouse for Science, Mathematics, and Environmental Education.

Ritchhart, R., Palmer, P., Church, M., & Tishman, S. (2006, April 7–11). *Thinking routines: Establishing patterns of thinking in the classroom.* Paper presented at the annual meeting of the American Educational Research Association, San Francisco, CA.

Ritchhart, R., Palmer, P., Perkins, D. N., & Tishman, S. (2004). *Visible thinking: Pictures of practice* [DVD]. Cambridge, MA: Project Zero, Harvard Graduate School of Education.

Ritchhart, R., & Perkins, D. N. (2008). Making thinking visible. *Educational Leadership, 65*(5), 57–61.

Robinson, K. (1999). *All our futures: Creativity, culture and education.* London, England: National Advisory Committee on Creative and Cultural Education.

Robinson, K. (2010). Bring on the learning revolution! TED. Retrieved from http://www.ted.com/talks/sir_ken_robinson_bring_on_the_revolution.html

Rogers, C. R., & Freiberg, H. G. (1994). *Freedom to learn* (3rd ed.). New York, NY: Merrill.

Rogers, R. D., & Monsell, S. (1995). Depth of processing and the retention of words in episodic memory. *Journal of Experimental Psychology, 124,* 207–231.

Rogoff, B. (1990). *Apprenticeship in thinking.* New York, NY: Oxford University Press.

Rose, M. (1995). *Possible lives: The promise of public education in America.* Boston, MA: Houghton Mifflin.

Rose, M. (2009). *Why school?* New York, NY: New Press.

Rose-Duckworth, R., & Ramer, K. (2008). *Fostering learner independence: An essential guide for K-6 educators.* Thousand Oaks, CA: Corwin Press.

Rosenshine, B. (1997, March 24–28). *The case for explicit, teacher-led, cognitive strategy instruction.* Paper presented at the annual meeting of the American Educational Research Association, Chicago, IL. Retrieved from http://www.formapex.com /telechargementpublic/rosenshine1997a.pdf

Rowe, M. B. (1986). Wait-time: Slowing down may be a way of speeding up. *Journal of Teacher Education, 37*(43), 43–50.

Saphier, J., Haley-Speca, M. A., & Gower, R. (2008). *The skillful teacher: Building your teaching skills.* Acton, MA: Research for Better Teaching.

Schmoker, M. (2009). What money can't buy: Powerful, overlooked opportunities for learning. *Phi Delta Kappan, 90,* 524–527.

Schoenfeld, A. H. (2010). *How we think: A theory of goal-oriented decision making and its educational applications.* New York, NY: Routledge.

Shepard, L. A. (2000). The role of assessment in a learning culture. *Educational Researcher, 29*(7), 4–14.

Shernoff, D. J., Csikszentmihalyi, M., Schneider, B., & Shernoff, E. S. (2003). Student engagement in high school classrooms from the perspective of flow theory. *School Psychology Quarterly, 18,* 158–176.

Shernoff, D. J. (2013). *Optimal learning environments to promote student engagement.* New York, NY: Springer Science + Business Media.

Shiksastudio. (2012). *Classroom management—Week 1, day 1.* Richmond, CA: Leadership Public Schools.

Shook, J. (2008). *Managing to learn: Using the A3 management process to solve problems, gain agreement, mentor and lead.* Cambridge, MA: Lean Enterprise Institute.

Shulman, L. (2008). It's all about time. *Carnegie Perspectives.* Retrieved from http:// www.carnegiefoundation.org/perspectives/its-all-about-time

Sikes, P., Measor, L., & Woods, P. (1985). *Teacher careers: Crises and continuities.* Lewes, England: Falmer Press.

Silva, E. (2007). *On the clock: Rethinking the way schools use time.* Washington DC: Education Sector Reports.

Silver, E. A., Kilpatrick, J., & Schlesinger, B. (1995). *Thinking through mathematics: Fostering inquiry and communication in mathematics classrooms*: New York, NY: College Entrance Examination Board.

Silver, E. A., Mesa, V. M., Morris, K. A., Star, J. R., & Benken, B. M. (2009). Teaching mathematics for understanding: An analysis of lessons submitted by teachers seeking NBPTS certification. *American Educational Research Journal, 46*, 501–531.

Siraj-Blatchford, I., Shepherd, D. L., Melhuish, E., Taggart, B., Sammons, P., & Sylva, K. (2011, June 30). Effective primary pedagogical strategies in English and mathematics in key stage 2: A study of year 5 classroom practice drawn from the EPPSE 3–16 longitudinal study. [UK] Department for Education. Retrieved from https://www .gov.uk/government/publications/effective-primary-pedagogical-strategies-in -english-and-mathematics-in-key-stage-2-a-study-of-year-5-classroom-practice -drawn-from-the-eppse-3-16-lon

Sizer, T. (1984). *Horace's compromise: The dilemma of the American high school.* Boston, MA: Houghton Mifflin.

Sizer, T., & Sizer, N. F. (2000). *The students are watching: Schools and the moral contract.* Boston, MA: Beacon Press.

Sophia W. (2011, December 3). AP classes: Absolutely preposterous weapons of mass instruction. *Huff Post Teen.* Retrieved from http://www.huffingtonpost.com/2011/12 /03/ap-absolutely-preposterou_n_1127539.html

Stahl, R. J. (1994, May). Using "think-time" and "wait-time" skillfully in the classroom. *ERIC Digests.* Retrieved from http://eric.ed.gov/?id=ED370885

Starr, J. (2012, January 31). Superintendent's book club: "Drive" by Daniel Pink. Montgomery County Public Schools. Retrieved from http://www.montgomery schoolsmd.org/departments/superintendent/bookclub.aspx

Strong-Wilson, T., & Ellis, J. (2007). Children and place: Reggio Emilia's environment as third teacher. *Theory into Practice, 46*, 40–47.

Stupnisky, R. H., Renaud, R. D., Daniels, L. M., Haynes, T. L., & Perry, R. P. (2008). The interrelation of first-year college students' critical thinking disposition, perceived academic control, and academic achievement. *Research in Higher Education, 49,* 513–530. doi: 10.1007/s11162-008-9093-8

Tarr, P. (2001, October). Aesthetic codes in early childhood classrooms: What art educators can learn from Reggio Emilia. *ERIC Digests.* Retrieved from http://eric.ed .gov/?id=ED459590

Taylor, C. (2005). *Walking the talk.* London, England: Random House Business.

Thompson, D. R., Senk, S. L., & Johnson, G. J. (2012). Opportunities to learn reasoning and proof in high school mathematics textbooks. *Journal for Research in Mathematics Education, 43,* 253–295.

Thornburg, D. D. (2004). Campfires in cyberspace. *International Journal of Instructional Technology and Distance Learning, 1*(10), 3–10.

Thornburg, D. D. (2013). *From the campfire to the holodeck: Creating engaging and powerful 21st century learning environments.* Hoboken, NJ: Wiley.

timetoast. (2011). The history of child labor. Retrieved from http://www.timetoast.com /timelines/157322

Tishman, S., & Perkins, D. N. (1997). The language of thinking. *Phi Delta Kappan, 78,* 368–374.

Tosteson, D. C. (1979). Learning in medicine. *New England Journal of Medicine, 301,* 690–694.

Tough, P. (2012). *How children succeed: Grit, curiosity, and the hidden power of character.* Boston, MA: Houghton Mifflin Harcourt.

Trilling, B., & Fadel, C. (2009). *21st century skills: Learning for life in our times.* San Francisco, CA: Jossey-Bass.

Trowbridge, D. E., & McDermott, L. C. (1981). Investigation of student understanding of the concept of acceleration in one dimension. *American journal of Physics, 49,* 242–253.

Tucker, M. S. (2011, May 24). *Standing on the shoulders of giants.* Washington DC: National Center on Education and the Economy. Retrieved from http://www.ncee .org/wp-content/uploads/2011/05/Standing-on-the-Shoulders-of-Giants-An -American-Agenda-for-Education-Reform.pdf

20-Time in Education. (2013). Home. Retrieved from http://www.20timeineducation .com/

US Department of Education. (1998). *Trying to beat the clock: Uses of teacher professional time in 3 countries*. Washington DC: Author.

Van Rossum, E. J., & Schenk, S. M. (1984). The relationship between learning conceptions, study strategy and learning outcome. *British Educational Research Journal, 54*, 73–83. doi: 10.1111/j.2044-8279.1984.tb00846.x

van Zee, E., & Minstrell, J. (1997). Using questioning to guide student thinking. *Journal of the Learning Sciences, 6*, 227–269.

Vygotsky, L. S. (1978). *Mind in society*. Cambridge, MA: Harvard University Press.

Wagner, T. (2008). *The global achievement gap: Why even our best schools don't teach the new survival skills our children need—and what we can do about it*. New York, NY: Basic Books.

Watanabe, M. (2012). *"Heterogenius" classrooms: Detracking math and science, a look at groupwork in action*. New York, NY: Teachers College Press.

Weber, B. (2009, June 3). Daniel C. Tosteson, longtime dean who revolutionized Harvard Medical School, dies at 84. *New York Times*, p. A25.

Wertsch, J. V. (1995). The need for action in sociocultural research. In J. V. Wertsch, P. D. Rio & A. Alvarez (Eds.), *Sociocultural studies of mind* (pp. 56–74). Cambridge, England: Cambridge University Press.

Wesch, M. (2007). A vision of students today. YouTube. Retrieved from http://www .youtube.com/watch?v=dGCJ46vyR9o

Wesch, M. (2008). Anti-teaching: Confronting the crisis of significance. *Education Canada, 48*(2), 4–7.

Whimbey, A., & Lochhead, J. (1999). *Problem solving and comprehension*. Mahwah, NJ: Erlbaum.

Widrich, L. (2013, February 14). The science of how temperature and lighting impact our productivity. *buffer*. Retrieved from http://blog.bufferapp.com/the-science-of -how-room-temperature-and-lighting-affects-our-productivity

Willis, J. (2011, October 5). Three brain-based teaching strategies to build executive function in students. *edutopia*. Retrieved from http://www.edutopia.org/blog/brain -based-teaching-strategies-judy-willis

Wilson, D. G. (2007). *Team learning in action: An analysis of the sensemaking behaviors in adventure racing teams as they perform in fatiguing and uncertain contexts.* Unpublished doctoral dissertation. Harvard University, Cambridge, MA.

Wilson, M. B. (2012). *Interactive modeling: A powerful technique for teaching children.* Turners Falls, MA: Northeast Foundation for Children.

Winerman, L. (2005). The mind's mirror. *Monitor on Psychology, 36*(9), 48–52.

Wiske, M. S. (Ed.). (1997). *Teaching for understanding.* San Francisco, CA: Jossey-Bass.

Wong, H. K., & Wong, R. T. (1997). *The first days of school: How to be an effective teacher.* Mountain View, CA: Harry K. Wong.

Woods, P. (1993). Critical events in education. *British Journal of Sociology of Education, 14,* 355–371.

Woods, P. (1995). *Creative teachers in primary schools.* Buckingham, England: Open University Press.

Yinger, R. (1979). Routines in teacher planning. *Theory into Practice, 18*(3), 163–169. doi: 10.1080/00405847909542827

Yng, N. J., & Spreedharan, S. (2012, August 24). Teach less, learn more—Have we achieved it? *Today.* Retrieved from http://guanyinmiao.files.wordpress.com/2012/08/teach-less-learn-more-have-we-achieved-it.pdf

Young, R. M., & O'Shea, T. (1981). Errors in children's subtraction. *Cognitive Science, 5,* 153–177.

Zhao, Y. (2006, May 9). A pause before plunging through the China looking glass. *Education Week.* Retrieved from http://www.edweek.org/ew/articles/2006/05/10/36zhao.h25.html

Zhao, Y. (2009). *Catching up or leading the way: American education in the age of globalization.* Alexandria, VA: Association for Supervision and Curriculum Development.

Zohar, A., & David, A. B. (2008). Explicit teaching of meta-strategic knowledge in authentic classroom situations. *Metacognition and Learning, 3,* 59–82.

SUBJECT INDEX

Classroom: languages of, 85–86; routines, 190–195; and teaching style, 30; uncovering the story of, 35

Coaching, as level of development, 327

Cognitive apprenticeship, 125, 129–132

Comfort zone, moving out of, 283–285

Communication, effective, 164, 164–165

Conceptualization of an event, 161

Conditional language, 85

Conference Board, 17

Connect-Extend-Challenge, 194–195

Connections, 31, 31–32, 43, 44, 47–48, 66, 70–73

Consolidation stage of an event, 161

Constructive questions, 221–222

Convergence stage of an event, 161

Corporate Voices for Working Families, 17

Cosi fan tutti, 90, 92

CoT Design Studio, 272–274; defined, 273; metaphor of gardening, 274–275

CoT Dialogue Circles, 272–273

CoT School Tours, 269–270

CoT Teacher labs: facilitating teacher, 270, 271, 272; host teacher, 270, 272; observation, 271–272; observing teachers, 270, 271; postobservation session, 271–272; preobservation, 271

Courage to Teach, The (Palmer), 128

Cultural forces, 6–10; environment, 9–10; expectations, 7, 37–60; interactions, 9; language, 7;

modeling, 7–8; opportunities, 8–9; time, 7–8

Culture: crafting a different story for schools, 29–34; current story, 24–29; as the enactment of a story, 20–34; uncovering the old story, 22–24

Culture of thinking: development in classroom, 323–326; directives, and inhibition of creation of, 41–42; leading at school, 319–322; as ongoing goal for the long haul, 303

Culture transformation, 11

Cultures of Thinking initiative, 24

Cultures of Thinking Leadership Foundations seminar, 268

Curiosity, as driver of new learning, 138

Curiosity moments, 138

D

Deep vs. surface learning: looking for, 60; strategies, encouraging, 42

Descriptive Consultancy, Tuning, or Looking At Students' Thinking (LAST) protocols, 300

Design Thinking Schools, 111

Developing, as level of development, 327

Diana School, Reggio Emilia, Italy, 257

Directing, as level of development, 327

Directives, and inhibition of creation of culture of thinking, 41–42

Discourse, new patterns of, creating, 223–224

Disenfranchised learners, empowering, 204–212

Dispositional apprenticeship, 125

G

Gallery Critique strategy, 226

General time audit, conducting, 111

Generate-Sort-Connect-Elaborate (GSCE) routine, 216

Generative questions, 221

Generative topics, Teaching for Understanding (TfU) framework, 48

Genius Hour or 20% Time, 111

Ghost Visit protocol, 259

Give One, Get One routine, 192–193

Global Achievement Gap, The (Wagner), 27

Goal of education, 15–16

"Good questions," asking, 221–223

Gradual release of responsibility, 125; modeling for independence, 132–135; planning for, 138

Grants Managers Network, 132

Group culture, 1–11; creation of, 11

Growth mindsets, developing, 60

Growth vs. fixed mindset, developing, 42–43, 55–58

H

Harvard Project Zero, 281–286

Horace's Compromise (Sizer), 167

Host teachers, CoT Teacher labs, 270, 272

I

Identifying, gathering, and reasoning with evidence, 32

Identity, language of, 74–75

Imagination First (Liu/Noppe-Brandon), 26

Independence: defining, 60; modeling for, 132, 132–135

Independence vs. dependence, encouraging, 54; promoting, 42–43

Initiative, language of, 75–76

Inquiry-action project groups: establishing, 298–299; using to go deeper, 298–304

Instruction formats, 161–162

Instructional Rounds, 143

Instructional routines, 192, 197

Intellectual Character (Ritchhart), 18

Interactional routines, 193

Interactions, 199–226; building culture through affect and actions, 218–220; as cultural force, 9; as culture shaper, 199; defined, 199; disenfranchised learners, empowering, 204–212; "good questions," 221–223; new patterns of discourse, creating, 223; promoting, 225–226; questions, 221–222; shaping through roles, 220–221

Interactive modeling, 125, 135–136

Invitational quality of a classroom, 257

Ishmael (Quinn), 21

K

Knowledge, teaching for understanding vs., 47–50

L

Ladder of Feedback, 121, 124, 134, 136, 193, 308

National Educational Association, 26
National Institute of Child Health and Human Development Early Child Care Research Network, 25
National Institute of Child Health and Human Development (NICHD), 219
New England Association of Farmers, Mechanics and Other Workingmen, 43
No Child Left Behind reform, 26
Nondirective teachers, and power, 219
Noticing, giving students practice in, 139

O

Oakland Schools, Waterford, MI, 267–275; building deep roots, 269–272; CoT Design Studio, 273–274; CoT Dialogue Circles, 272–273; cultivating the soil, 267–268; gardener metaphor, 274–275; nurturing early growth, 268–269
Observation and analysis, 138
Observing teachers, CoT Teacher labs, 270, 271
Ongoing facilitation of the learning, importance of, 301
Ongoing feedback, Teaching for Understanding (TfU) framework, 49
Only with Teacher Direction, as level of development, 327
Opportunities, 141–170; categorizing, 159–163; as cultural force, 8–9; as culture shaper, 141; defined, 141; duration and scope of, 160; realizing, 165–168; recognizing, 163–165; use of term, 141
"Opportunities to learn," use of term, 143

Outcomes, thinking differently about, 16–19
OWP/P Architects et al., 231, 248, 255, 257

P

Paired Problem Solving technique, 132
Partnership for 21st Century Skills, 17
Perceiving details, nuances, and hidden aspects, 32
Performances of understanding, Teaching for Understanding (TfU) framework, 49
Perspectives, 32
Postobservation session, CoT Teacher labs, 271–272
Power of Full Engagement, The (Loehr/Schwartz), 108
Practice, learning from, 135–136
Praise and feedback, language of, 81–82
Preobservation, CoT Teacher labs, 271
Preparation stage of an event, 161
Prioritizing, learning from, 98–102
Private Universe (1987), Harvard-Smithsonian Center for Astrophysics series of videos, 50
Procedural questions, 221
Project Zero & Reggio Children, 220, 247

Q

Quadrant of quality, 108
Quality education, 19
Queensland Studies Authority, 27
Questions, 31–32; constructive questions, 221–222; facilitative questions, 222; generative

NAME INDEX

Teitel, L., 143, 166

Thoele, S. P., 82–83

Thornburg, D., 232, 252

Threlkeld, J., 257

Timperley, H., 81, 82

Tishman, S., 179

Tosteson, D. C., 125–126

Tough, P., 204

Trigatti, B., 166

Trilling, B., 19

Trowbridge, D. E., 50

Tucker, M., 18

Turnbull, B. J., 166

Turner, T., 70

V

Van Rossum, E. J., 52

van Zee, E., 223

Vecchi, V., 249

Verkerk, L., 62, 76

Vygotsky, L. S., 20, 129–132, 203

W

Wagner, T., 17, 26, 27, 53–54

Wall, K., 253

Watanabe, M., 220

Weber, B., 125

Wehlage, G. G., 163

Weidman, C., 173

Wenger, E., 129–132

Wertsch, J. V., 129–132

Wesch, M., 24, 26

West, S., 84

Wheatly, G., 166

Whimbey, A., 132

Whiren, A. P., 55

White, K., 39–43

Widrich, L., 254

William, D., 81

Willis, J., 132

Wilson, D., 79–80, 259

Wilson, M. B., 136

Winerman, L., 127

Witthoft, S., 231, 254, 257

Wong, H. K., 191

Wong, R. T., 191

Wood, T., 166

Woolner, P., 253

Y

Yackel, E., 166

Yinger, R., 173, 191

Yng, N. J., 154

You, W., 193

Young, R. M., 49

Z

Zhang, Y., 230

Zhao, Y., 18, 26

Zohar, A., 70